The Australian Independent Companies and the Commandos into which they evolved were unique sub-units of the Australian Army during the Second World War. The very concept of such units was a radical one for the deeply conservative Australian Army and came about because of the personal intervention from the Chief of the General Staff, who alone advocated their establishment. The Independent Companies were unlike any other unit in the Australian Army. They were raised to fight in an autonomous, unconventional manner and while supporting them, were independent of higher formations.

During 1942 and 1943 the Independent Companies conducted a multitude of tasks that tested their attributes and skills to the full, be it trekking across and surveying virgin tropical wilderness, long range patrols, raiding and harassing, stalking the enemy and amazingly skilled stealthy close range reconnaissance. As the war progressed, the Army, which had never approved of allowing too much independence to its sub-units, reassessed its requirement for such troops and in a sweeping change transformed the Independent Companies into Commando Squadrons. These were to be much more tightly controlled than the Independent Companies had been, essentially designed to operate as light infantry rather than a radically unconventional model.

Throughout 1944 and 1945 Australian Commandos participated in every campaign fought by the Australian Army. The Second World War Australian Commando experience was very much one of an army unready for the challenge that was initially imposed on it, but an Army that rose to the trial and eventually, despite missteps, ultimately successful mastered the manner in which it chose to employ its commandos.

Gregory Blake was born in Melbourne in 1955. Since a very early age, he has had a keen interest in military history and has written numerous articles on the subject, for publications in Australian, the UK and the US. He has an MA and PhD in Military History from the Australian Defence Force Academy and is a secondary school History teacher. Greg served with the Australian Army Reserve during the 1970s and 1980s. He is an accomplished artist.

Jungle Cavalry

The Australian Independent Companies and Commandos 1941–45

Gregory Blake

Helion & Company

Helion & Company Limited
Unit 8 Amherst Business Centre
Budbrooke Road
Warwick
CV34 5WE
England
Tel. 01926 499 619
Fax 0121 711 4075
Email: info@helion.co.uk
Website: www.helion.co.uk
Twitter: @helionbooks
Visit our blog http://blog.helion.co.uk/

Published by Helion & Company 2019
Designed and typeset by Mach 3 Solutions (www.mach3solutions.co.uk)
Cover designed by Paul Hewitt, Battlefield Design (www.battlefield-design.co.uk)
Printed by Hobbs the Printers, Totton, Hampshire

Text © Gregory Blake 2019
Photographs © as individually credited
Maps drawn by George Anderson © Helion & Company 2019

Every reasonable effort has been made to trace copyright holders and to obtain their permission for the use of copyright material. The author and publisher apologize for any errors or omissions in this work, and would be grateful if notified of any corrections that should be incorporated in future reprints or editions of this book.

ISBN 978-1-911628-82-8

British Library Cataloguing-in-Publication Data.
A catalogue record for this book is available from the British Library.

All rights reserved. No part of this publication may be reproduced, stored in a retrieval system, or transmitted, in any form, or by any means, electronic, mechanical, photocopying, recording or otherwise, without the express written consent of Helion & Company Limited.

For details of other military history titles published by Helion & Company Limited contact the above address, or visit our website: http://www.helion.co.uk.

We always welcome receiving book proposals from prospective authors.

Contents

List of Photographs		vi
List of Maps		viii
Introduction		ix
1	An Army Unready – The Formation of the Independent Companies	17
2	"All Rounders" – Recruiting and Training the Independent Companies	31
3	"Dumped and Written Off" – New Ireland and New Caledonia	47
4	"Surrender Be Fucked" – Timor 1942	62
5	Kanga Force – The 'Ragged Arsed Fifth'	85
6	Kokoda-Buna	109
7	Jungle Cavalry – 1943	127
8	Bena Force and Kaiapit	158
9	"The Doldrums of War" – Atherton 1944–1945	175
10	"The Little Bastards were Dug in to Stay" – Aitape-Wewak Campaign 1944–1945	204
11	"Spreading our Gospel" – The Commandos on Bougainville	224
12	"We Blew the Hell out of the Place" – Borneo 1945	251
13	Australian Commandos in the International Context	270
Conclusion		293
Bibliography		296
Index		308

List of Photographs

In Text

Patrol report Harcourt to McNider, 23 November 42.   121

In Plate Section

No.7 Infantry Training Centre, Tidal River, Wilson's Promontory 1941. (Courtesy Keith Reynolds)   i

Men of the 2/5th Independent Company during training at No.7 Infantry Training Centre, Tidal River 1941. (Australian War Memorial)   i

2/3rd Independent Company men on New Caledonia 1942. It is apparent that their time on New Caledonia was far more comfortable than that of their comrades of 2/1st Independent Company in the islands north of Australia or 2/2nd Independent Company on Timor. (Arden family photograph collection. National Library of Australia)   ii

2/2nd Independent Company allied with local Timorese people burn down huts belonging to pro-Japanese Timorese, Timor 1942. A great deal of the fighting that took part in Timor from November 1942 until January 1943 was against pro-Japanese Timorese. (Australian War Memorial)   ii

Two men of 2/6th Independent Company patrolling through the jungle on their advance towards Buna, November 1942. The style of dress and automatic weapons accurately reflect the appearance of Independent Company soldiers at this period of the war. (Australian War Memorial)   iii

Major Harry Harcourt 2/6th Independent Company, wearing the beret, in conference with Brigadier General Hanford McNider of the U.S. 32nd Infantry Division, centre wearing helmet, and staff during the move towards Buna November 1942. Harcourt frequently met with McNider and other senior U.S. officers during 2/6th Independent Companies deployment with U.S. 32nd Infantry Division. (Australian War Memorial)   iii

Vickers guns were employed by 2/3rd Independent Company to harass the Japanese along the Komiatum track during the Salamaua campaign. In this image Private 'Stumpy' May fires his Vickers gun at a Japanese mountain gun some 1900 metres distant, in an effort to distract the gun from firing on Australian positions. (Arden family photograph collection. National Library of Australia)   iv

List of Photographs vii

A portrait by war artist Ivor Hele of Signaller Peter Pinney 2/3rd Independent Company, during the Salamaua campaign. Pinney would later say that this image accurately captured both his combat worn dishevelled appearance and state of mind at the time, and was a far more realistic portrayal than any photograph. (Australian War Memorial) iv

'A' platoon of 2/3rd Independent Company wait to attack Timbered Knoll as the knoll is pounded by artillery and mortars and raked by Vickers machineguns, 29 July 1943. This photo depicts the men wearing the mixture of gear they would normally take with them into combat. The string of grenades attached to the belt of the man on the right of the photo and the bandolier of ammunition he also wears is typical of this. (Arden family photograph collection. National Library of Australia) v

Early in the attack on Timbered Knoll, by 'A' Platoon of 2/3rd Independent Company, Private Bill Robins has been seriously wounded, shot through both lungs. Corporal Roly Good, the Company medic prepares a field dressing for Robins and reaches out to him. This photo, which is a still from a film taken by combat cameraman Damian Parer, was taken ten seconds after Robins had been hit. (Arden family photograph collection. National Library of Australia) v

Private Leonard Mahon of 2/3rd Independent Company during the assault on Timbered Knoll. The style of dress of the Independent Companies has evolved with jungle green uniforms, and gaiters. Automatic weapons remain predominant. (Australian War Memorial) vi

On the summit of Timbered Knoll following the battle. From left to right Major George Warfe, Lieutenants John Barry, John Lewin and Syd Read. (Arden family photograph collection. National Library of Australia) vi

Men of Bena Force, 2/2 Independent Company, July 1943. Bena Force conducted a campaign of patrolling and harassment which denied the Japanese access to the strategically important Bena Bena Plateau from May until September 1943. (Australian War Memorial) vii

Shooting Japanese wounded following the battle of Timbered Knoll. War artist Ivor Hele captured this moment as photography of such action was forbidden. As Ron Garland an officer with 2/3rd Independent Company admitted there was no option but to methodically destroy the Japanese as even their wounded would attempt to kill Australian soldiers. Such was the brutal nature of the Jungle War. (Australian War Memorial) vii

Members of 2/4th Commando Squadron stand to one side as a Matilda tank rolls past them on Tarakan, May 1945. Matildas provided invaluable support for the Squadron in its assault on Tarakan Hill. (Australian War Memorial) viii

Major Norman Winning of 2/8th Commando Squadron, standing to the right, liaises with indigenous guides, Bougainville, June 1945. In their relentless unconventional campaign against the Japanese on Bougainville 2/8th Commando Squadron worked closely with indigenous people. (Australian War Memorial) viii

List of Maps

1	Independent Company deployments June 1941–December 1941. 2/1st Independent Company was deployed across a vast arc from Kavieng New Ireland to Vila New Hebrides, 2/2nd Independent Company was deployed to Timor and 2/3rd Independent Company was deployed to New Caledonia.	61
2	Timor 1942. This map indicates the area in which the Australian Commandos operated. This area fluctuated over time with the ebb and flow of operations both by the Commandos and the Japanese.	73
3	The Salamaua Raid 28 June 1942. 2/5th Independent Company and the New Guinea Volunteer Rifles raided Salamaua on the night of 28 June in a highly successful operation against an enemy force many times greater than their own.	94
4	The Buna Campaign November 1942–January 1943. This map shows the position taken by 2/6th Independent Company between two battalions of the US 126 and 128 Infantry Regiments during the campaign November to December 1942.	123
5	The Salamaua Campaign January–September 1943. 2/3rd Independent Company ranged over a wide arc of territory out on the left flank of 3rd Division.	151
6	Independent Company deployments 1942–1943. 2/5th Independent Company was deployed to Wau later joined by 2/7th Independent Company, 2/6th Independent Company to the Kokoda Track and Buna, 2/4th Independent Company joined 2/2nd Independent Company on Timor and 2/3rd Independent Company took part in the Salamaua campaign.	157
7	The Central Highlands indicating the region protected by Bena Force and the approximate front line of Bena Force patrols from May until September 1943. Bogadjim the objective of Bena force patrols is also marked.	161
8	The Battle of Kaiapit 19–20 September 1943.	173
9	The Aitape – Wewak Campaign November 1944–August 1945.	219
10	The southern Bougainville Campaign November 1944–August 1945. 2/8 Commando Squadron operated as an autonomous force out on the flank of 3rd Division.	249
11	Tarakan May–August 1945, showing the areas where 2/4th Commando Squadron operated.	262
12	The Balikpapan campaign in Borneo July–August 1945 showing Commando movements in support of 7th Division.	268

Introduction

Captain David Dexter crouched in the cover of the thick scrub. The tangled chaos of tropical trees, vines, bushes and matted leaves closed in all about him. Somewhere just ahead down a track which cut through the confusion three men were moving rapidly along the track and coming towards him. He was not worried about those three men; they were his boys after all. What interested him though was what was following them.

It was 29 September 1943. The night before Dexter had swum his 17 man patrol of the 2/2nd Independent Company across the swollen Ramu River, using a wire strung up by the stronger swimmers to help their comrades across. They had been given very specific orders to 'unsettle' the enemy so as to distract them and make them think that they were under attack from a much stronger force, and Dexter intended to do just that. The Japanese were lurking in a fortified location known as Kesawai on the other side of the river. It was necessary to hit those Japanese and hurt them hard. There was a trick to this though. It was necessary not to take too many risks and not give the enemy the slightest clue they were approaching them. The best plan would be to give the Japanese a big surprise and Dexter planned it to be a bloody one. The biggest problem was how to find the enemy. They knew generally where they were but the country was thickly timbered, visibility was minimal and it was just as likely if you went about stumbling around searching the only way you would ever find them was by accidentally stumbling upon them. That would be no good. The answer was to be cunning and get the Japanese to come to you, and by doing so be suckered into an ambush. All that needed to be done was to dangle some bait and lure them in. So, the bait, three blokes, was dangled. They were sent off down a track towards Kesawai, the idea being that they make themselves known to the enemy. When that happened and the Japanese had been hooked, they were to run back down the track towards the patrol. Hopefully the Japanese would follow. At 7.40 a.m. Lance Corporal Poynton, Private Birch and Indigenous Policeman Tokua, the three decoys, were sent on their way. The trio set off at a trot down the track intending to get as close as they could to the Japanese at Kesawai. It was vital that they should be noticed, and the best way to do that was to announce their arrival. This they did by throwing several hand grenades into Japanese machinegun posts, and each emptying three magazines of the Owen sub-machinegun they carried into the Japanese lines. They then departed making sure to leave obvious footprints as they fled. The ruse worked like a charm and no sooner had the three began to beat a retreat down the track than the Japanese led by some indigenous guides followed them. The bait had been taken. Poynton got back to Dexter and told him he was being followed. The Australians had arranged themselves in a U shape around a clearing, Owen guns on the flanks and Bren guns and a grenade launcher at the base. They were ready to spring their trap. Just before 10.00 a.m. two indigenous men armed with bows and arrows came down the track, behind then sauntered Japanese troops talking and gesticulating, obviously completely unaware of what was awaiting them. The patrol braced on the edge of the clearing, crouching low, their grease blackened faces blending into the shadows. Soon some 60 Japanese came into the clearing, still utterly oblivious to what awaited them. Suddenly a broadside of massed automatic weapons fire from the Owen Guns and Bren Guns erupted. The fire slashed into the Japanese like, what one of the commandos later recalled, a reapers scythe. One Bren gun, fired by Lieutenant Doug Fullerton, firing straight down the track took a particularly fearsome toll. Private Peter Campbell, another Bren Gunner, fired off four magazines. The firing lasted for about six minutes. When it was over some 45 Japanese lay dead, some, the lucky ones, managed to run back around the bend in the track while others scrambled down a slight slope to get away. Their cover blown, and no longer secret, the patrol now had to watch out for a counterattack by fresh troops the Japanese would bring up, which was what they normally did in such circumstances. Sure enough the counter attack came, killing one commando, Private Cyril Doyle, and wounding Dexter five times. With absolutely no intention or reason for outstaying their welcome, the patrol silently and expertly vanished back into the jungle.[1]

Dexter's ambush was a classic example of guile, expertise and cunning. It was typical of an innumerable number of skilful and bloody clashes staged by Australian Army commandos in their long and arduous war against the Japanese during the Second World War.

This is the story of those Commandos, sub units of the Second Australian Imperial Force (AIF). The daring and ability of those Commandos in the jungle was second to none. It is a story of a force that began its existence as Independent Companies whose concept of war was as radical as it was unconventional. The history of these companies within the Australian Army was at the beginning a troubled one. At the time of their inception they were seen as a very much unwanted imposition onto an Army that was utterly unready for them. Initially dismissed and within less than a year of their formation disbanded by the Army, the companies seemed destined for un-mourned oblivion until December 1941. In that month Australia's war changed from one where combat was against distant foes in lands far away, to one where the enemy posed an

---

[1] David Dexter, 'The New Guinea Offensives, Australia in the War of 1939–1945', Series One Army, Volume VI, *Australian War Memorial*, Canberra, 1961, p. 435; Cyril Ayris, *All the Bull's Men – No.2 Australian Independent Company (2/2 Commando Squadron)* (2/2 Commando Association, 2006), pp. 415–417.

existential threat to Australia itself. Australia, with the majority of its trained troops abroad in North African and the Middle East, an effectively non-existent air force and a navy, which like the army, had its most effective units far away from the homeland, desperately sought some way of addressing the challenge. It was in such circumstances that the Independent Companies were hastily resurrected. With a new lease of life the Independent Companies would eventually evolve into a force that operating autonomously achieved outstanding success. Eventually though, the companies were drawn back into the fold of an army that had at an institutional level never trusted their independent concept of warfare. They were re-designated Commandos, retrained and compelled to operate in a much more conventional manner. The Australian Army Commandos as a collective group have certainly never received the attention they deserve. It is a story which has until now only been at best partially told. This book it is hoped will help to redress this oversight.

This history focuses on the experience of those specialist unconventional forces which formed part of the Australian Army. Australia's specialist unconventional forces came from two distinct pedigrees, the first being the Independent Companies and Commandos raised by the Australian Army and the second being the covert commando groups Z and M Force raised by Special Operations Australia (the Australian manifestation of the British Special Operations Executive). The task of Z Force was clandestine operations, special reconnaissance, sabotage and intelligence gathering behind enemy lines. M Force was a specialized unit whose task was gathering intelligence on Japanese shipping and troop movements. Neither Z nor M Force formed part of Australian Army's order of battle. Because of this neither Z nor M force will be considered in this history.[2]

The concept for the Independent Companies originated in 1940 with the British suggesting that Australia set up small units as Commandos ostensibly to operate in the Middle East and Mediterranean theatres. To this end, a team of British specialists arrived in Australia to establish such units, and they remained until the formation of a cadre of Australians capable of managing their training. The men who made up the subsequent Independent Companies were at first all volunteers. As the war progressed Independent Companies began to evolve methods of operations suited to their autonomous character; scouting, flank protection, close reconnaissance of enemy formations, terrain surveying and raiding characterized their service. The Companies saw themselves as 'jungle cavalry' filling the role of the 'eyes, ears and claws' of their parent Divisions.[3] The understanding by the Army of how to employ Independent

---

2   For a comprehensive survey of Z Force operations see: C.A. Brown, *The Official History of Special Operations – Australia* (SOA Books: Lexington, Kentucky, 2011). For reference to the work of M. Force see: David Horner, *SAS: Phantoms of the jungle: A History of the Australian Special Air Service* (Allen and Unwin: Sydney, 1991), pp. 25–27.

3   Arthur Bottrell, *Cameos of Commandos* (Specialty Printers: Adelaide, 1973), p. 41; the term Jungle cavalry was adopted by 2/6 Independent Company in 1943 see: Australian War Memorial, AWM52 2/2/582/6, Commando Squadron War Diary November

Companies effectively evolved in a patchwork and idiosyncratic manner. With the Army espousing no set 'Commando' doctrine, the influence of local commanders and their individual appreciation of how to employ Independent Companies became paramount. Such was the management of the Independent Companies until late 1943 when the concept of the Independent Company was discontinued and replaced by Commando Squadrons. In a reflection of the changing nature of the war from late 1943 to 1945 the role of the Commandos Squadrons within the Army would be fundamentally transformed and redefined.

The published literature of the Independent Companies and Commando Squadrons is diverse in character. What material there is tends to fall into two distinct yet complementary categories. The first of these are Unit histories written by both members of the Companies and Squadrons and secondary authors. These offer collections of personal and collective memories by members of the Companies and Squadrons and overviews of the unit service histories. The second category is works that deal generally with the histories of Australia's Pacific War campaigns.[4] These works deal with broad subjects involving multitudes of units and actions. These can be sub divided into works that are scholarly or populist in nature. In the scholarly works the role played by Independent Companies and Commandos is dealt with in an uneven manner. The official Australian Histories of the War in the Pacific offer a good amount of information about the role played by individual Commando units, although at no time delving into the Army's management of them. Other works offer an uneven coverage which ranges from quite good to sketchy. There is, however, within the existing collection of works on the Australian Army's Commandos no single account that offers a comprehensive history of the Commandos, as this history does.

In this history we will be asking a number of questions. These questions include, from where the original inspiration to form the Australian Independent Companies came and what was the nature of the response from the Army? How did the Army's management of its Commandos evolve during the war, and how fundamental was the change from Independent Companies to Commandos when it occurred in late

---

    to December 1943; General Stanley Savige inferred the term 'Jungle Cavalry' in his 'Tactical and Administrative doctrine for jungle warfare applicable to all formations under command 2 Aust. Corps (AIF)' see: *Australian War Memorial*, AWM52 2/2/58, HQ 2 Aust. Corps (AIF) (New Guinea): N,G. Press Unit, 1945; see also *Australian War Memorial*, AWM52 2/2/58, 2/6 Commando Squadron War Diary November to December 1943.

4   For the official histories see: Lionel Wigmore, 'Australia in the War of 1939–1945, Vol. IV, The Japanese Thrust', *Australian War Memorial*, Canberra, 1957; Dexter, 'The New Guinea Offensives'; Dudley McCarthy, 'Australia in the War of 1939–1945 First Year Vol. V: Kokoda to Wau', *Australian War Memorial*, Canberra, 1959; and Gavin Long's 'The Final Campaigns, Australia in the War of 1939–1945 Vol, VII', *Australian War Memorial*, Canberra, 1963. For a good account of the role played by Independent Companies in the Salamaua Campaign see: Phillip Bradley, *To Salamaua* (Cambridge University Press: Melbourne, 2010).

1943? What was the contribution of the Independent Companies – Commandos to the Australian Army's war effort and in what way did the Australian Commando experience share and differ to that of its Allies?

It would be remiss of me not to acknowledge the individuals and institutions that assisted me researching this history. Archival material relevant to the operations of the Independent Companies/Commando Squadrons is to be found at the Australian War Memorial in a wide range of series, these being specifically Second World War unit War Diaries, Second World War Unit and Headquarters files, Personal Papers, recorded interviews and unpublished manuscripts.[5] The National Archives of Australia Canberra, Melbourne and Sydney offer a great deal of material related to the formative and later operational period of the Independent Companies.[6] The papers of Peter Pinney a member of both 2/3rd Independent Company and 2/8th Commando Squadron are held at the Freyer Library of the University of Queensland and provided a comprehensive collection of personal observations and reminiscences.[7] The State Library of New South Wales is custodian of the diary of Damian Parer, who spent considerable time with the Independent Companies in 1942 and 1943 and whose insights on his experience are most valuable.[8] Sources outside Australia were also of value; particularly due to the paucity of material within Australia related to the original agency responsible for the formation of the training mission for the Australian Independent Companies. The National Archives of the United Kingdom fulfilled this role admirably. The National Archives offered a great deal of material related to the Military Intelligence – Research (MI(R)) sub unit which was the agency responsible for establishing the Companies in Australia.[9] The resources of the Liddell Hart Centre for Military Archives at King's College London offered the personal papers of Field Marshal Sir John Dill, and the personal papers of Major General Robert Laycock Commando commander and later head of Combined Operations.[10] The Imperial War Museum provided the taped recording of an interview with Michael Calvert who was one of the three primary members of the British 104 Military Mission who trained Independent Companies in Australia.[11] The British Library allowed access to

---

5   The Australian War Memorial (AWM) series consulted were AWM52, 54, 55, 63, 67, 93, 113, 124, 172, 193, 243, 315, 361, DRL, 3 DRL, MH1, PR87, PR91, SO4, SP4.
6   The National Archives of Australia (NAA) series consulted were A571, A1241, A12383, A1608, A2670, A2680, A2684, A5954, A6390, A7665, B883, B3476, B6390, MP385, MP508, MP729, MP742, MP917/2 and SP300.
7   University of Queensland, (UQ) UQFL288, Papers of Peter Pinney.
8   State Library of New South Wales, (SLNSW) MLMSS 1097, The Diary of Damien Parer.
9   The UK National Archives (TNA) series consulted were WO208, HS8/256, 257, 258, 260, 261, 263, 294
10 The Liddell Hart Military Archive (LHMA) series consulted were Dill 3/2/1-6, Laycock 1/3, 2/3, 2/5, 2/8, 4/1, 4/11, 4/21, 5/7, 5/27, 6/3, 6/13 and 6/16.
11 Imperial War Museum, (IWM) IWM9942, Michael 'Mad Mike' Calvert.

books specifically related to the subject of MI(R) and Commando training.[12] United States sources were equally valuable especially for the activities of 2/6th Independent Company during the time when it was attached to the U.S. 32nd Infantry Division at Buna. The archives consulted in this case were The Dwight D. Eisenhower Archives in Abilene Kansas with special thanks to Dave Holbrook from the Archives whose friendly welcome and assistance were greatly appreciated. The Eisenhower archives offered the Journal of the 1st Battalion 128th Infantry Regiment which referred frequently to 2/6th Independent Company.[13] The National Archives and Records Administration in Washington D.C. offered material related to the service of 2/6th Independent Company with US Forces. Of particular value was the collection of material related to the official U.S. Army history of the campaign in Papua.[14] The MacArthur Memorial Archives in Norfolk Virginia has a comprehensive collection of Historical Index Cards which provided a wealth of information concerning the activities of 2/5th Independent Company during 1942.[15] The advice and assistance of James Zobel at the Memorial was invaluable. Annette Amerman at the United States Marine Corps History Division is to be thanked for directing me to material as well as her insights related to the Marine Corps Raiders.[16] In the same way the United States Marine Corps Archives Branch Division made available their extensive collection of transcribed oral histories and personal correspondence.[17] Complementary to these sources was the Marine Raiders Museum, which while not a repository of archival material, is surprisingly well endowed with artefacts related to the Marine Raiders. The recorded interviews of Historian Neil MacDonald with officers and men of the 2/3rd independent Company held by the Australian War Memorial are of immeasurable value.[18] In these interviews the recollections of John Lewin, Ron Garland, John Winterflood and other prominent members of the 2/3rd Independent Company offer unmatched first hand material. Online interviews with David Dexter, former officer with 2/2nd Independent Company and former Commando Stephen Murray Smith

---

12   Joan Bright Astley, *The Inner Circle – A View of War at the Top* (The Memoir Club: Stanhope, 2007); D. Gilchrist, *Castle Commando* (Oliver and Boyd: Edinburgh, 1960).
13   Dwight D. Eisenhower Archives (DDEA) Journal of 1st Bn 128th Infantry, September – November 1942 (incomplete), SERIES II LIBRARY, DDEA.
14   The National Archives and Records Administration (NARA) series consulted were: RG 319, RG407, RG496, WWII Operations Reports, 1940–48, Records of the Army Staff, Center of Military History, Victory in Papua.
15   MacArthur Memorial Archives (MMA) Historical Index Cards (Actual) Record Group 3.
16   United States Marine Corps History Division, (USMCHD) Series PC56.
17   United States Marine Corps Archives, (USMCA) Transcribed interviews: Major General Thomas Halcomb, Major General Omar T. Pfeiffer, Lieutenant Colonel Evans Carlson, Lieutenant Colonel James Roosevelt and Sergeant Charles Land.
18   Australian War Memorial, AWM S04152-64 and AWMS04173, Interviews by Neil MacDonald with members of 2/3 Independent Company.

held at the National Library of Australia are of equal value and importance.[19] In the same light interviews with Japanese veterans conducted by Dr. Peter Williams during visits to Japan provide a window onto an alternative view of the war.[20] Frequent discussions and encouragement from Professor Craig Stockings and Doctor David Stahel were a constant source of inspiration, as was the constant support of the staff from the School of Humanities and Social Sciences of the Australian Defence Force Academy. My heartfelt thanks for the encouragement to proceed with writing this book and securing a publisher goes to Professor Peter Stanley of the Australian Defence Force Academy. To all of these stalwart individuals I am deeply grateful.

Embark with me now on an exploration of the history of the Australian Army's Commandos during the Second World War. This is a story of a truly extraordinary group of individuals who fought a war unlike any other in the most inhospitable of natural environments against a determined and ruthless enemy. It is my hope that you enjoy the experience as much as I have had in presenting it to you.

---

19 David Dexter interviewed by Mel Pratt for the Mel Pratt collection, 1976 <http://nla.gov.au/nla.oh-vn719109> (consulted 10 August 2015); Stephen Murray-Smith interviewed by Hazel de Berg in the Hazel de Berg collection, 1961 <http://nla.gov.au/nla.oh-vn237365> (consulted 9 August 2015).
20 Dr Peter D. Williams and Naoko Nakagawa interviews 2006: Major Masao Horie, Major Takahisa Okamoto, Lt. Colonel Masuo Shinoda, Captain Kokichi Nakamura.

1

An Army Unready – The Formation of the Independent Companies

The inspiration for the formation of the Australian Independent Companies took place a world away from Australia.

It was July 1940 and the British Army having been trounced by the Germans had hastily retreated to the coasts of France and evacuated whatever it could back to Britain. In three Operations; Dynamo from Dunkirk; Cycle from Le Havre and Ariel from other Atlantic ports Britain had at the cost of abandoning a significant proportion of its war fighting materiel rescued its army from catastrophe. Gathering then what it could Britain awaited what everyone assumed would be the inevitable invasion by the victorious Germans. It was at this desperate time that British Field Marshal Sir John Dill the Chief of the Imperial General Staff and Lieutenant General Sir Cyril Brudenell-White the Chief of the Australian Army General Staff began a private and very personal conversation. At some stage during this conversation the topic of the establishment in Australia of Independent Companies came up. Independent Companies were a novel innovation. First raised in Britain in late 1939, they were units of reinforced Company size, some 260 soldiers. The companies were technically designed to operate independently to harass and discomfit the enemy. The British army was encouraged to raise such companies by Lieutenant Colonel Colin Gubbins the future head of the Special Operations Executive. Several Independent Companies were sent to Norway to engage in the campaign being fought there in the early months of 1940. Unfortunately for the companies few British commanders understood just what to do with such unusual units and they achieved very little. Thus under something of a cloud they were returned to Britain and remained in official limbo until they were disbanded. Many of the now redundant members of the companies, not being the sort of fellows to be dissuaded, transferred into the newly formed Commandos. Nevertheless the concept of Independent Companies had been firmly established and would be soon adopted by Australia.

In July 1940 the British Prime Minister Winston Churchill, ever the pragmatist had determined that if Britain should go under and be occupied by the enemy the war would be continued by the Empire. To ensure that this occurred, the formation of irregular forces designed to strike back at the enemy would be encouraged throughout the Empire. Thus the idea came about to establish British Military Missions in various places throughout the world, Each of these Missions would foster an element of unconventional warfare which could be used to continue the war. It was the establishment of such irregular formations in Australia which motivated the conversation between Dill and White. For Dill and White to have such a private conversation was in the context of the time and the personalities involved perfectly reasonable. Dill knew several prominent members of the Australian military establishment being reminded in a letter of his Australian 'friends' Morsehead, Wynter and Bridgeford on 21 July 1940.[1] There is every reason Dill would have also known White from the time he served as General Staff Officer of the Australian 1st Division during 1917. This as at the time White had been a Brigadier General on the Staff of the ANZAC Corps. White had also been the first Australian Officer to attend the Imperial Staff College at Camberley in 1906 of which Dill would have been aware.[2] Thus approaching White would not have been an entirely unexpected initiative. That this was conducted in very much the form of a gentleman's agreement, without recourse to any formal structure, is also not surprising, given the multitude of interpersonal relationships that existed within the Imperial military hierarchy of the day. In their conversation White agreed for a British team to come to Australia and train Independent Companies. So confidential was this conversation that no primary record of it exists. A search of Dill's and White's papers including White's personal diary make no mention of it.[3] White himself did not help matters by telling no one about the agreement he made with Dill, even to the point of not informing his deputy Chief of the General Staff Major General John Northcott. Thus the Australian Army knew nothing of this arrangement. Whether or not White did intend to inform the army that he had arranged for Independent Companies to be established and trained in Australia will never be known. As it happened White was to die in an airplane disaster on the outskirts of Canberra on 13 August 1940. White along with the Minister for the Army and Repatriation, the Minister for Air and Civil Aviation and the Minister in charge of Scientific and Industrial Research all died in the crash of the Lockheed Hudson on its approach to land. Along with White died any firsthand knowledge of the arrangement to train Independent Companies in Australia.

1   LHMA, Dill 3/3/2, Captain Beeman to Dill 21 July 1940. These Australian friends were Brigadier Leslie Morsehead, Major General Henry Wynter and Brigadier William Bridgeford.
2   Robert.C Stevenson, 'The Anatomy of a Division: The 1st Australian Division in the Great War, 1914–1919', Thesis submitted for Degree of Doctor of Philosophy, University of New South Wales, 2010, p. 310; John Bentley, 'Champion of ANZAC: General Sir Brudenell White, the First Australian Imperial Force and the emergence of the Australian Military Culture 1914–1918', Doctor of Philosophy thesis, School of History and Politics, University of Wollongong, 2003, p. 6.
3   Dill's papers are at the Liddell Hart Centre for Military Archives at King's College London. White's papers can be found at the Australian War Memorial, the National Archives of Australia and his personal Diary at the National Library of Australia.

An Army Unready – The Formation of the Independent Companies   19

Meanwhile in Britain the process of organising the Australian training mission had been put into motion. The organisation given the job was a small sub unit of Military Intelligence known as Military Intelligence – Research (MI(R)). MI(R) was an interesting if not slightly eccentric group of officers whose task was to think and plan for unconventional ways to harm the enemy. It had begun as the General Research office with a staff of only one officer in 1938 but by the beginning of 1940 had changed its name to MI(R) and blossomed to nine officers, one military typist and three female civilian stenographers. This small group was commanded by Colonel Jo Holland a chain smoking, gruff, sharply intelligent personality who possessed a temper which intimidated all around him. Holland and MI(R)'s role was to find imaginative and unconventional ways to bring harm to the enemy. They excelled at ideas of how to do so including inventing devices such as the limpet mine, advocating for the use of helicopters, fostering clandestine missions to various countries, and supporting the idea of forming Independent Companies. For the Australian mission MI(R) created 104 Military Mission. Lieutenant Colonel John Mawhood was to command the Mission. Typical of MI(R)'s operational culture the rank of Lieutenant Colonel for Mawhood was in reality a ruse. Mawhood had served with the British and Australian armies during the First World War but had left the army in 1923 and from then until the beginning of hostilities in 1939 worked for the British internal security service MI5. His rank of Lieutenant Colonel had been granted to him for forms sake, so that he would have some military status and capacity to impose authority when required. This subterfuge would later cause serious repercussions for Mawhood in his relations with the Australian army. Two officers were chosen as chief instructors for the Mission. Unlike Mawhood both these were established members of the army but in keeping with MI(R)'s penchant for selecting the atypical these instructors, like Mawhood, were far from what could be described as regular soldiers.

One of the tasks MI(R) had set itself was to compose a list of individuals who possessed specific skills not matter how esoteric those skills were. When a Mission came up that required specific skill sets that list would be consulted and individuals with the required skills called upon. The First of those called for 104 Military Mission was Captain Freddy Spencer Chapman. Spencer Chapman's resume read like something out of a Boys Own adventure annual. A Territorial Army officer Spencer Chapman belonged to the 5th Battalion of the Seaforth Highlanders and had spent a great deal of his time prior to the war engaged in adventures which were anything but military. He had surveyed the Greenland coast from an open boat; taken part in the British Arctic Air Route Expedition; conducted a further private expedition to Greenland; trekked with Reindeer across Lapland; climbed mountains in Sikkim and Tibet; and visited Lhasa. He was a noted expert on birds, had been awarded the Arctic medal in 1931 and the Gill Memorial Medal (Royal Geographical Society) in 1941. In addition he had written several books including *Northern Lights*, *Watkins Last Expedition*, and *Lhasa: The Holy City*.[4] Spencer

---

4   Frederick Spencer Chapman and H.G. Watkins, *Northern Lights; the official account of the British Arctic air-route expedition, 1930–1931* (Chatto and Windus: London, 1932);

Chapman was a supreme individualist and very much, in the opinion of those who knew him a lone wolf type of adventurer.[5] His greatest skill was in field-craft, in which he had a phenomenal ability to move through and live off the land for extended periods of time. It was for this skill that he was recruited by MI(R) to go to Australia. The second officer was Captain Michael Calvert. Calvert, whose nickname was 'Mad Mike', was a Royal Engineer and his skill and passion was for demolitions. He had before the war boxed and swum for Cambridge University and the Army, which had left him with a battered nose and a good natured rubbery face. His style was that of a rebel and a maverick and he was full of original ideas especially on irregular warfare. In his area of demolitions he was described as a 'definite destruction fanatic' and able to blow up anything from battleships to brigadiers.[6] Both Spencer Chapman and Calvert were experts in the skills needed for the Mission to Australia and New Zealand and were snapped up by MI(R). Accompanying Spencer Chapman and Calvert were two senior Non Commissioned Officers; Staff Sergeant. P. Stafford, from the Duke of Wellington's Regiment to teach demolitions and Sergeant F.A. Misselbrook, from the Royal Corps of Signals to teach Signals.[7]

On 6 October 1940, 104 Military Mission embarked from Britain aboard the SS *Rimutaka*.[8] They went well prepared having aboard half a ton of plastic explosive, 36 Tommy guns, 50,000 maps of South Pacific islands and 'Hurricane' radio sets for ground to air communication.[9] Sailing via the Panama Canal and New Zealand the Mission arrived in Australia in November. They may have switched ships prior to this as the *Rimutaka* normally finished its run to the antipodes in Wellington New Zealand. On arrival in Australia the consequences of the failure by White to inform the army that any such mission was enroute hit home. Michael Calvert recalled that when the team stepped ashore they were confronted with accusations they were foreign agents, even Nazi saboteurs, which was an easy presumption to make by port authorities when confronted with a totally unexpected ship full of weapons, explosives radios and maps. This distrust did not abate with officers attempting to trick the team members into revealing their Nazi affiliations. Other aspects of the Mission caused the Australian military to regard Mawhood's team with suspicion. Mawhood's less than conventional military background caused immediate suspicion.

Frederick Spencer Chapman, *Watkin's Last Expedition* (Penguin: Middlesex, 1938);,
Frederick Spencer Chapman, *Lhasa: the Holy City* (Chatto & Windus: London, 1938).
5   AWM, AWM52 2/2/54 2/2, Commando Squadron War Diary May 1945 to February 1946.
6   Frederick Spencer Chapman, *The Jungle is Neutral* (Chatto & Windus: London, 1950), pp. 8–9; AWM, AWM52 2/2/54, 2/2 Commando Squadron War Diary May 1945 to February 1946; 'Cdo New Britain' Vol 1:1, 11 July '45, p. 6.
7   E. Walker, 'History of No.7 Infantry Training Centre and the formation of the Independent Companies 1941–1942', *Despatch Monthly Journal of the New South Wales Military Historical Society*, Vol. XII No.12, June 1977, p. 335.
8   Ralph Barker, *One Man's Jungle A Biography of F. Spencer Chapman* (Chatto and Windus: London, 1975), p. 179.
9   IWM, IWN 9942 Reels 3–5, Michael 'Mad Mike' Interview.

Spencer Chapman insisted on wearing his regimental kilt, but as he was from the 5th Battalion of the Seaforth Highlanders and that battalion wore a different tartan to the remainder of the regiment he was suspected of being an imposter. For his part Calvert was suspected as his attitude towards common soldiers was relaxed and somewhat informal which was, according to those Australian officers who were watching him, not at all how a British officer would be expected to behave. The suspicion of the Mission as an enemy inspired operation eventually dissipated thanks to the intervention from Major General Vernon Sturdee the new Australian Chief of the General Staff, who himself had been an advocate of raising special groups of what he called 'assault troops' and was, unlike his peers, at least aware that a team of British trainers had been planned to be sent to Australia.[10]

The arrival of the training team to Australia had been badly mismanaged. In a communiqué of 26 March 1941 the British War Office admitted that not informing Australia of the imminent arrival of the mission was something of a blunder. It is not entirely accurate, however, to find the British War Office solely at fault for the unheralded arrival of the mission and the confusion that it caused. On 28 August 1940 Australian authorities were indeed informed by the War Office that Lieutenant Colonel Mawhood and his party would be departing for Australia in September indicating that there was some awareness in Australia of the arrival of 104 Military Mission, even if the nature and purpose of the mission was unknown.[11] On 9 October 1940 the Australian Military Board Chief of the General Staff issued a directive for the establishment of a special secret School of Demolitions and made reference to a training team arriving from Britain to run the school.[12] This directive was issued while the *Rimutaka* was at sea to New Zealand indicating that at least some elements of the Army were aware of the arrival of a training team from Britain, even if the purpose of the mission had been confused. There had, however, been no 'formal approach' from Britain to Australia regarding despatching a training Mission to Australia. In this case the fault lies with Britain, but at the same time it does appear there was a degree of foreknowledge in Australia that a mission was imminent but this knowledge was muddled and misunderstood and one assumes because it was 'secret' the information was not distributed. As such fault for the failure to inform the Australian Government of the arrival, or more accurately failure to pay heed to the imminent arrival of the Mission, was not entirely due to British inefficiency.

The mission was finally accepted for what it was, as opposed to what it had been imagined to be. This did not, however, result in an enthusiastic response from the

---

10   IWM, IWM 9942 reels 3–5, Michael 'Mad Mike' Calvert Interview; On 30 September 1940 Sturdee advocated the formation of special service 'assault troops' for the Australian army see: NAA, A1608 G39/2/1, War 1939 – Special Operations Executive (Mawhood Mission), Sturdee to the Minister 30 September 1940.
11   NAA, MP729/6/0 38/401/172, Extracts from files dealing with the Object and Control of 104 Military Mission.
12   AWM, AWM193, 3, Special School of Demolitions Mission 104.

Army. Indeed progress towards establishing a training program for Independent Companies moved at a snail's pace. One factor influencing this tardiness may have been the continuing ambiguity of just what the purpose of the Mission was. On 21 January 1941 a cablegram from the Australian Prime Minister's department identified the three objects of the Mission as countering enemy fifth column activity in Australia, training Independent Companies, and organising native guerrilla operations in enemy held territory.[13] The very next day a similar cablegram reinforced the anti-fifth column purpose of the mission.[14] In fact there were no definite written instructions received from Britain as to just what the object of the Mission was. The lack of any specific directives frustrated the Australian Army's ability to form a special training centre appropriate to the purposes of the mission.[15] A further reason for the Army's reticence in accepting the Independent Company training program was the conservative nature of those who made the decisions within the army. During 1940–1941 the Army was institutionally antithetical to challenges to its entrenched doctrine, presumptions and authority. Illustrative of this mind set was the experience of Major Dudley McCarthy.[16] He left a critical appraisal of the ability of those in command within the Australian Army to accept ideas from those outside their own circle. McCarthy was required to attend a conference in 1942 to discuss the modification of Australian Divisions for tropical warfare. The main topic of discussion was which bits of equipment were required as well as the need to change clothes on a regular basis. None of the senior officers present had any experience in Tropical conditions apart from postings to Australia's Northern Territory. McCarthy had experienced active service in New Guinea, Java, Timor and Malaya and brought up the issue of actually being able to supply a change of clothes to troops in the forward areas and the practicality of doing so considering the total absence of motor transport. He was as he says 'driven into the ground like a tack', for his impertinence in speaking and told forthwith 'thank you, McCarthy, we will discuss that no further'.[17] It was with this institutional reluctance to allow any contest to the authority of the established order, which the Independent Companies certainly represented, with which 104 Military Mission had to contend.

13 NAA, A1608 G39/2/1, War 1939 – Special Operations Executive (Mawhood Mission) Prime Minister's Department Cablegram to Secretary of State for Dominion Affairs 21 January 1941.
14 Ibid.
15 Ibid.
16 Dudley McCarthy would also become one of the historians who wrote the official history of Australia's involvement in the Second World War see: Dudley McCarthy, 'First Year: Kokoda to Wau, Australia in the War of 1939–1945', Series One Army, Volume V, South West Pacific Area, *Australian War Memorial*, Canberra, 1959.
17 AWM, AWM67 2/40, Gavin Long Notebook 40, Maj. D. McCarthy Aust L.O. to US VI Army – Humbolt Bay July 1944.

An Army Unready – The Formation of the Independent Companies 23

Even so, planning for the training program did progress. A site for the Independent Company Training centre needed to be found. Mawhood delegated the task of selecting the site to Calvert. Calvert scouted around keeping in mind that he had been told by Army Headquarters in Melbourne that the site had to be near Melbourne. Various sites in Victoria and New South Wales were inspected, but one site attracted repeated attention. This was Wilson's Promontory in southern Victoria.[18] Wilson's Promontory offered a range of varied terrain from forests, to scrub, mountains and swamps. One attraction was that it was similar to the Scottish training grounds for British Commandos. Wilson's Promontory's weather was harsh. Cold grim winters, a feature of the Promontory, would toughen the men for war in a European environment.[19] For all these reasons Calvert chose Wilson's promontory. Once again, however, even though the site for the training centre had been chosen the Army dragged its feet and during December and January no steps were taken to further the establishment of the Independent Company training program. It was not until February 1941, that infrastructure had been erected at Wilson's Promontory to house the trainees and training staff. The cost of establishing and maintaining the training centre was not insignificant, which was no doubt a further reason for some within the Army to be unenthusiastic about the project.[20]

A significant reason for the continual delays may have been due to the continuing confusion caused by the Australian Army's presumption of the role Mawhood was to play and the role Mawhood had chosen to play. It is understandable that Australian military authorities assumed that Mawhood as mission commander would take charge of the establishment of the Independent Company training centre. This was not the case. Mawhood's interest was firmly fixed on his internal security role; he chose not to be involved in the day to day management of the training centre. This perplexed the Australian military who refusing to acknowledge Mawhood's actual priorities, repeatedly accused Mawhood of shirking his duty. The consequent delays in establishing the training program were blamed, at least by the Australian military, on the reluctance of Mawhood to manage the program as they believed he should have.[21] Mawhood

---

18 Bottrell, *Cameos of Commandos*, pp. 289–90.
19 David Rooney, *Mad Mike – A Life of Michael Calvert* (Leo Cooper: London, 1997), p. 25; Don Astill, *Commando white diamond: memoir of service of the 2/8 Australian Commando Squadron, Australia and the South-West Pacific 1942–1945* (Loftus: NSW), p. 5.
20 In June 1941 the estimate of the total cost for the training centre projected forward to 30 June 1942 was for capital items £284,000 and for maintenance £296,000 a total of £580,000. Capital items included buildings £60,000, Stores and camp equipment £24,500 and ammunition, clothing, weapons, equipment, transport vehicles, and medical equipment £199,500. Maintenance items included pay and allowances, camp expenses, general expenses, and special intelligence funds, see: NAA, A1608 G39/2/1, War 1939 – Special Operations Executive (Mawhood Mission) Spender to the Prime Minister 6 June 1941.
21 NAA, A1608 G39/2/1, War 1939 – Special Operations Executive (Mawhood Mission) Blamey to the Minister for the Army 10 July 1942.

told a different story relating how the training of the Independent Companies had been obstructed by the refusal of the Australian Army to supply resources. He cited the absence of required stores and the lack of interest in the training program at Army Headquarters with only one visit from an officer from Army Headquarters occurring.[22] Another reason for tardy response to establishing the training program was that in Britain the interest in fostering Independent Company training in remote regions such as Australia was waning and this was reciprocated by important elements within the Australian Army. The reasons for the British lack of interest were that when MI(R) was closed down in October 1940 and the Special Operations Executive (SOE) inherited its missions SOE had little interest in missions outside Europe.[23] As such SOE was keen to divest itself of what for it would have been the distraction of 104 Military Mission. The official Australian attitude towards the Mission was equally unenthusiastic with the Chief of the General Staff telling the British Secretary of State for Dominion Affairs that the Australian Army did not wish to assume control of 104 Military Mission as it was not in the Army's best interests. This was justified for three reasons. The first of these was the relationship between the Para-military and civil security intelligence aspects of the Mission remained uncertain. The second was that there were confidential considerations regarding one of the officers of the Mission – no name was mentioned but this was undoubtedly Mawhood. The third reason was that the Mission was not working in the interests of Australia, but was in fact appearing to favour the interests of New Zealand. This was because Mawhood, whose responsibilities for establishing a security service related to both Australia and New Zealand spent a great deal of time in New Zealand and that he had been accused of using his lectures to Independent Company trainees there to belittle the Australian General Staff and ingratiate himself with the New Zealanders.[24] This opinion was echoed by the Deputy Chief of the General Staff.[25] Quite obviously there was an unfortunate divergence of priorities, expectations and understanding between the Australian and British military authorities in regard to the Independent Companies.

Even so, the Australian Army did, for a time and to its credit, manage to motivate itself to administer the formation of the Independent Companies, albeit in a most hesitant manner. In February 1941 a commanding officer was appointed, in lieu of Mawhood, to command the Independent Company training centre. This was Major William John Scott. Scott was a rather idiosyncratic choice for the post. A decorated veteran of the Great War he had become during the 1920s a prominent spokesman for various conservative political organisations and in the 1931 the chief of staff for the

22 NAA, MP508 251/758/395, Mawhood to AHQ, 16 July 41.
23 Astley, *The Inner Circle*, p.42; TNA, HS 8/260, MI[R] Progress Reports, Report of the Organisation within the War Office for the conduct of Para-Military Activities, 25 Aug 40.
24 NAA, MP742/1/0 M/7/168, Sturdee to Army Minister 14 March 1941; MP508 251/758/395, NAA; Deputy CGS Northcott 9 July 1941.
25 NAA, MP742/1/0 M/7/168, Deputy C.G.S to Minister 23 July 41.

clandestine politically conservative militia known as the 'Old Guard'. Scott's enthusiastic advocacy for all things Japanese during the 1930s attracted critical attention. By 1940 Scott was appointed to the General Staff where his arrogance and high handedness caused tensions. He was then appointed to command the Independent Company Training Centre.[26] At first glance it appears that Scott's appointment may have been symptomatic of the Army's disinterest in the Independent Company project; what better way to employ a problematic underling than to side-track them with a task considered of little real importance. Perhaps at the time this was so, but as events turned out Scott's appointment was to be brief and he departed in May 1940. His replacement, Major Stuart Love, was an entirely different personality and as it turned out one eminently suitable for the task. Love was a highly decorated veteran of the Great War. He had mined in Arnhem Land in 1910, served in West Africa before the First World War and had a great understanding of how to develop effective relationships with indigenous people, a significant skill considering the environments in which the Independent Companies would find themselves operating.[27] Love would prove to be an inspiration to the men under him. Michael Calvert referred to him as, 'my great friend and hero'.[28] Post war Commando associations commended Love for his old soldier practicability and inspired imagination.[29] Love also provided a guiding and restraining influence on the unbridled impetuosity of 104 Military Mission trainers such as Spencer Chapman.[30]

Even with the Army now paying some attention to the Independent Companies just what role the Companies were to play remained a vexed question. Even those whose task it was to train the Companies had no firm idea what they were training for. Spencer Chapman expressed this uncertainty stating that as the idea of the ANZAC independent Companies was so new and shrouded in so much secrecy that no one had

---

26 William John Scott (1888–1956) Australian Dictionary of Biography <http://adb.anu.edu.au/biography/scott-william-john-8373> (consulted 12 October 2016). Scott went on to command the Australian troops on Ambon after their original commander was relieved of command for pointing out the futility of the situation the troops were facing there. Scott surrendered to the Japanese invaders on 3 February 1942. His handing over of fellow Australian prisoners of war to the Japanese was the cause of controversy and he was despised by most of his fellow prisoners.
27 *2/2 Commando Courier*, Vol.20. No. 188, November 1965, p. 12 <https://doublereds.org.au/couriers/1965-11%20-%20Courier%20November%201965.pdf> (consulted 12 October 2016). Love's military awards were DSO and bar, MC, Croix de Guerre avec palme, five times MID. Love was also a widely read and cultured man, being a published author of poetry, an authority on Geoffrey Chaucer, and an expert of Renaissance Art.
28 Michael Calvert, *Prisoners of Hope*, Cooper, London, 1971, p.11.
29 See: *2/2 Commando Courier*, Vol.6 No.68, December 1952, p. 5. <https://doublereds.org.au/couriers/1952-12%20-%20Courier%20December%201952.pdf>; *2/2 Commando Courier*, Vol.20 No.188, November 1965, p. 12, <https://doublereds.org.au/couriers/1965-11%20-%20Courier%20November%201965.pdf> (consulted 16 October 2016).
30 Barker, *One Man's Jungle*, p. 180.

any real idea what their purpose was or how they should operate.[31] Michael Calvert also admitted that the Army had no real idea of what to do with the Companies when they were trained. Calvert, however, had thought about the issue and had come up with some basic understandings of what the companies were to do. His answer as simple, they were to act as guerrillas and use their skills to kill the enemy who in Calvert's opinion would be the Japanese.[32] There was also at the time a notion doing the rounds that the companies served British and not Australian interests, and that they had been raised so they could 'go and save Britain'.[33] Another fanciful idea was that the companies were to be sent to China.[34] Such was the confusion of the purpose and role of the companies at their inception.

On 21 May 1941 there was at last some clarification of the role to be played by the training mission. Mawhood wrote to the C.G.S stating that in line with Imperial War Cabinet directives Para-military activities would be divided into two clearly distinct branches – Civil and Military. Following on from this Independent Companies would be the military component and be composed of specially selected men, highly trained and well-armed. They would be used as assault troops to raid enemy lines of communications and carry out sabotage missions. Most importantly it was to be clearly understood that Independent Companies were not to engage in fifth column or counter fifth column activities.[35] This definition of the missions function came some six months after the arrival of mission in Australia and indicates just how muddled and misunderstood the purpose and management of the mission had been by all parties up until that time.

The activities of 104 Military Mission was wound up on 25 September 1941.[36] Personnel were transferred out of Australia and the Mission ended. Australian cadres of officers and Non Commissioned Officers to act as Independent Company trainers had been formed and trained and were prepared to take over that training. As such there was no further need for British trainers. It was not as if this eventuated without some forward planning with a note of 22 May 1941 stating that the training of additional Australian companies would be carried out by Australians having been

---

31 Spencer Chapman, *The Jungle is Neutral*, pp. 7–8.
32 IWM, IWM 9942 reels 3–5, Michael 'Mad Mike' interview. Calvert's presumption that he was training troops to fight the Japanese was in line with the common perception of the time, in 'David Dexter interviewed by Mel Pratt for the Mel Pratt collection [sound recording] 1976' <http://nla.gov.au/nla.obj-221579220> (consulted 26 November 2015). David Dexter mentions that when he joined the army in 1940 he was definitely being trained to fight a 'Yellow Enemy' which he was under no illusions would be the Japanese.
33 IWM, IWM 9942 reels 3–5, Michael 'Mad Mike' Calvert interview.
34 AWM, AWM 52/2/52 Box 44, 2/7 Commando Regiment Outline History, June 1943, 2/4 Aust Independent Company Summary of Unit History.
35 NAA, MP742/1/0 m/7/168, Mawhood to CGS 21 May 1941.
36 NAA, A1608 G39/2/1, War 1939 – Special Operations Executive (Mawhood Mission), Department of the Army to the Sec Dept of Def Co-Ord 30 Sept 41, Military Mission 104.

forwarded from the Australian Prime Minister's office to the Acting Prime Minister of New Zealand.[37]

Although they accepted such a development both Spencer Chapman and Calvert were disappointed. Both had had hoped that they would get an Independent Company to Command but on consideration recognised that they were not Australians and this would be politically unacceptable. Calvert said that this resulted in the members of 104 Military Mission departing Australia somewhat 'under a cloud'.[38] Spencer Chapman was sent to 101 Training School in Singapore. Calvert's situation was somewhat more complicated. Frustrated by being kept out of action during his time with the training mission he had considered deserting and joining the Australian army under an assumed name. He shelved such notions when he found he had been posted to the Jungle Warfare School in Burma.[39] Sergeant Stafford wished to remain in Australia, having married an Australia woman, and serve with an Independent company as an officer. Granting Stafford a commission was, however, not deemed appropriate and he was posted to Rangoon on 11 September.[40] Spencer Chapman departed on 15 September and Calvert to Rangoon on the same day. Misslebrook was sent by sea to Singapore on 25 September.[41]

Once 104 Military Mission had been wound up the Australian Army revealed its true feelings and dropped the axe on the Independent Company program cancelling it altogether. The reason given was that no use could be envisaged for such companies.[42] In truth the reasons for the cancellation of the Independent Company training program went far deeper. From the very beginning the Independent Companies had not been an Australian idea. It had been an innovation foisted on them by the British with no prior consultation and nebulous direction once in place. The dual civil and military priorities for the mission had resulted in uncertainty and pronounced hostility from the Army's hierarchy directed towards the mission commander whose task was to implement the security aspects of the mission. Compounding this was the very nature of the companies. There was no tradition of the unconventional warfare the companies represented within the Australian Army. When the Army came to understand the nature of the Companies it could not as an institution accommodate such a radical conception. Viewed through this prism the Independent Companies offered nothing

---

37 Ibid.
38 IWM, IWM 9942 reels 3–5, Michael 'Mad Mike' Calvert interview.
39 Calvert, *Fighting Mad*, p. 55.
40 NAA, A1608 G39/2/1, War 1939 – Special Operations Executive (Mawhood Mission), Col. Mackenzie Director of Mil Operations 13 Aug 41 to Sigs Cipher Office; NAA, A1608 G39/2/1, Secretary Prime Minister's department from Secretary Dept. of Defence Coordination and Sec of State for Dominion Affairs London 19 August 1941.
41 NAA, A1608 G39/2/1, War 1939 – Special Operations Executive (Mawhood Mission), Department of the Army to the Sec Dept. of Def Co-Ord 30 Sept 41, Military Mission 104.
42 NAA, A1608 G39/2/1, Copy of Attorney General's file 1955/4428: Lieutenant Colonel Mawhood – Report on Security in Australia.

to the Army and only diverted resources away from those forces that were fighting what they considered the real war. It is most likely that the only reason the companies survived as long as they did was that they had derived from Britain, with the blessing of the former Chief of the General Staff and the Imperial connection was still at that time sufficiently strong to ensure that they were not summarily disposed of while the British contingent remained on hand. When that was no longer the case the entire program was disposed of quickly and with no remorse. Running concurrently with the institutional bias against the companies was the rampant hostility expressed by the Army against Lieutenant Colonel Mawhood. Mawhood's case generated masses of paper work in which he was accused of shirking his duties and malingering and calls were made for his dismissal and forcible return to Britain. So intense and farcical did the animosity become that senior officers were spreading the rumour that the Mawhood in Australia was not the real Mawhood, who according to them had been murdered and thrown overboard on the way to Australia. This nonsense continued until it was stopped by the personal intervention of a very angry Federal Attorney General William Morris Hughes.[43] Such a poisonous relationship did not help the cause of the Independent Companies.

Even so, three Australian companies had been trained to varying degrees of competency. Two New Zealand companies had also been trained but these were disbanded when they returned home from Wilson's Promontory.[44] One of the Australian companies companies, the 2/1st Independent Company had been despatched in July 1941, before it had completed its guerrilla warfare training, to garrison various Royal Australian Air Force (RAAF) stations scattered across the islands to the north of Australia. The other two companies the 2/2nd and 2/3rd were left in limbo, neither being disbanded not given any tasks. Those Australian personnel still involved in the training program, the officer and Non Commissioned Officer cadre of the 2/4th Company, were given the choice to return to their former units or transfer as a group to a light armoured squadron, which most elected to do.[45]

Such was the fate of the Australian Independent Companies.

---

43 NAA, A12383 A/2/1, attachment 1 Copy of Attorney General's file 1955/4428: Lieutenant Colonel Mawhood. Mawhood would eventually be transferred to the Australian Attorney General's Department to work on internal security. In this way he would be protected from the hostility of the Army.
44 E. Walker, 'History of No.7 Infantry Training Centre and the formation of the Independent Companies 1941–1942', pp. 334–39; in regard to the lack of acceptance of the Independent Companies in New Zealand a pencil note signed by 'Goss' (perhaps Brigadier Leonard Goss) dated 27 June 1941 makes note that, 'I have had a short talk with Lt-general Sir Guy Williams about para Military Activities and he is of the opinion that there is really no necessity for troops of this nature in New Zealand.' See: NAA, MP508 251/758/395.
45 AWM, AWM 52/2/52 Box 44, *2/7 Commando Regiment Outline History*, Jun 1943, 2/4 Aust Independent Company Summary of Unit History.

All of this was to change on 7 December 1941, however, with the Japanese attack on Pearl Harbor and the invasion of Malaya, Hong Kong and the Philippines the next day. The existential threat posed to Australia by these events provided the catalyst for the companies' resurrection. Faced with a paucity of organised military resources within Australia to confront the Japanese threat the Army scrambled to meet to the challenge. Australia was critically short of every kind of military asset. In December 1941 the Australian Army had available within Australia 132,000 full time A.I.F. troops. It also had two cavalry divisions and four infantry divisions less one brigade of Militia who were poorly equipped and sketchily trained. The situation for war fighting materiel was less than satisfactory. Compared to war establishment there was available 74% of rifle and light machinegun ammunition, 17% of mortar ammunition, 25% of artillery ammunition, and 1.1% of 2pdr anti-tank gun ammunition. In addition, only 73% of rifles, 21% of pistols and 49% of light machineguns were on hand. Ironically the number of medium machine guns and 3" mortars on hand exceeded war establishment but without ammunition they would have been of little use.[46] The bulk of Australia's regular army was overseas on the North Africa and the Middle East. Its air force was tiny and possessing many aircraft not at all suitable for modern warfare. The navy as with the Army was abroad serving Imperial interests. It was in these parlous circumstances that the Australian Army turned to the Independent Companies, a military resource which could be easily tapped. There were still on hand the remnants of an Independent Company training program, one with an organised and existing infrastructure. This could be easily be revitalised. It was an existing military asset where there were very few, any thought of what could be done with the companies when they were raised again was not considered. No doubt it was thought that a trained soldier was a trained soldier and in such circumstances beggars could not be choosers. The Independent Company training centre was reopened on 25 December 1941 under the command of Major Mac Walker.[47] With uncharacteristic enthusiasm, driven no doubt by the exigencies of the moment, the Army decided to form a further five Independent Companies bringing the number of companies up to eight.

It is tempting to view the sudden resurrection of the Independent Company program as something of an epiphany for the Australian Army, the beginning of a process by the Army was prepared to sponsor the integration of unconventional special force sub units. Such was, however, not the case. There is no evidence of a sudden manifestation of any special understanding or appreciation for the Independent Company concept within the Australian military establishment. There had been during the establishment of the Independent Companies no attempt to devise an official doctrine for the

---

46 See: AWM, AWM 124 4/105, Defence of Australia and Adjacent Areas – Chiefs of Staff Appreciation, December 1941.
47 E. Walker, 'History of No.7 Infantry Training Centre and the formation of the Independent Companies 1941–1942', p. 337; George Lambert, *Commando – From Tidal River to Tarakan, the story of No.4 Independent Company AIF later known as 2/4th Australian Commando Squadron AIF* (self-published, no location, no date), p. 14.

use of such companies, nor any thought of how they would be deployed. Nor was there any clear concept of just how the companies were to be employed once deployed, nor any attempt to develop any such concept. What occurred was in fact a simple reflex action born of desperation. Even so, the reappearance of the companies did mark a watershed moment in the history of the Australian Independent Companies. They became ipso facto a fixture within the Australian Army; recognised sub units on the order of battle, no longer an unwelcome imposition. Most significantly with this the companies began an evolutionary process which would see them gradually transform themselves from awkward appendages into regular sub-units of an Army that would eventually develop an operational understanding of how to employ such troops for any number of complex and demanding tasks.

The reactivated companies would require personnel and training. Just how this was achieved, from the commencement of the Independent Company mission in 1941 and on into 1942 is a story which reveals the uniquely independent nature and character of those who volunteered to join the Companies and the radically unorthodox methods employed to prepare the Companies for war.

2

"All Rounders" – Recruiting and Training the Independent Companies

The training and recruitment regimes experienced by the Independent Companies and Commandos during the years 1941 to 1945 occurred in two very distinct phases. The phases relate to the early and later period of the Independent Company-Commando history. The first phase 1941–1943, the Independent Phase, was characterised by the qualities of voluntarism, self-reliance and operational independence. The second phase, the Commando Phase, did not permit voluntarism or encourage operational independence. The training programs experienced during each of these phases reflected those aspects applicable to the recruitment and training ethos of each phase. This Chapter will examine the recruitment and training which occurred during the Independent Phase of the Australia Commando story.

A fundamental element of the recruitment for the Independent Companies during 1941–1943 was the voluntary nature of that recruitment. The voluntary recruitment ideal was in keeping with the independent ethos of the companies and reflected the divergence of the companies from the mainstream processes of the Army. The Army did not practice voluntary recruitment for specific formations in general; rather recruits joined the army and were sent to units and formations chosen for them. The qualities sought from volunteers were specific. When recalling the types of men who were sought Jack Boxall of the 2/5th Independent Company observed that the men who were selected were strong, tough types who looked as if they would have a go at anything and most importantly had to be 'all rounders'.[1] Volunteers were expected to exhibit self-reliance, intelligence and independence. They were expected to be able to operate without direct supervision if necessary. Volunteers for the Independent Companies were to be men who had volunteered for Australian Imperial Force (AIF) service, and who were prepared to undergo very hard training under trying conditions, as well as be prepared to be returned to their original units if they could

---

1 Andy Pirie, 'Commando – Double Black. An historical narrative of the 2/5th Austral an Independent Company later the 2/5th Cavalry Commando Squadron', *2/5th Commando Trust*, Harbord N.S.W, p. 10.

not cope with the training.² These qualities were no different to those the British Commandos, which was hardly surprising considering the British Commando pedigree of the Australian Independent Companies.³

Each man who presented for service in an Independent Company was, at least in theory, required to appear before a selection board. When they did operate selection boards were established with one member of each board being an officer from Land Headquarters.⁴ There was no set means by which candidates for Independent Companies were enticed to apply to join the companies. The Army promulgated a system of official notices both spoken and written. Notices were posted on unit notice boards. Such notices could be as simple as 'Wanted – volunteers for a 'hush hush' squad to report to the Orderly Room'.⁵ Others could be in the form of a questionnaire asking for men to volunteer for an unspecified task and posing questions such as 'can you swim, surf or sail a boat, can you climb mountains, are you one hundred percent fit'.⁶ Army units were actively scouted for personnel considered suitable for the Independent Companies.⁷ From time to time recruitment officers visited camps and asked for anyone who would be interested in a special 'hush hush' unit that would carry out very dangerous missions.⁸ Volunteers were called for when on parade with the officers doing the calling knowing very little about what they were asking their men to volunteer for. Recruitment could be by these formal means or by less formal methods. The less formal approach was often the case with the recruitment of officers. Social connections, patronage and 'the old boy network' played its part of the process. It was observed that the British system of recruiting officers for special service units had a great deal to do with 'The familiar school tie or membership of the right gentleman's club'.⁹ It was no surprise that the Australian experience at times imitated the British model although with an Australian flavour. David Dexter, who served with 2/2nd Independent Company during the war described how he was recruited. On leave in Melbourne, he was at the Scots Hotel and happened to encounter an officer wearing a kilt. He got talking to the officer and was told that the officer was 'looking for some rugged types'

2   Lambert, *Commando – From Tidal River to Tarakan*, p. 14.
3   LHMA, Laycock 1/3, Papers of Major General Sir Robert Laycock.
4   NAA, MP385 106/7/789, Guerrilla Warfare Foster Raising and Training of Personnal [sic] Organization of Coys and RTFs, Movement of Coys and RTFs, Selection of Personnel for Independent Companies – LHQ 29 June 42.
5   AWM – MSS1960, Geoffrey Thomas Fraser, *Highly Irregular* (Self-Published: Sunshine Coast, 2003), p. 21.
6   Ayris, *All the Bull's Men*, pp. 26–7.
7   NAA, MP508 251/758/395, N-7 Infantry Training Centre, Military Forces Northern Command Victoria Barracks Brisbane, 23 Aug 41.
8   Pirie, 'Commando – Double Black', p. 3.
9   Andrew L. Hargreaves, *Special Operations in World War II – British and American Irregular Warfare* (University of Oklahoma Press, 2013), pp. 184–6.

and if they were interested in 'something secret'.[10] Dexter and his friends gave the officer their names. The officer in the kilt happened to be Captain Freddy Spencer Chapman. Dexter mentioned that Captain Mike Calvert also frequented the same pub and recruited in the same manner.[11] Dan O'Connor became an officer in 2/4th Independent Company. His recruitment experience was very much illustrative of the importance of social connection and patronage. O'Connor had just graduated from the Royal Military College Duntroon when he saw a line of officers waiting to be interviewed for 'special service'.[12] Without knowing anymore, he joined the line. The major conducting the interview recognised O'Connor from his Officer Cadet days and with that he was accepted into the Independent Companies as a Lieutenant and ordered to report to the training camp at Wilson's Promontory.[13] The experiences of other officers without the social connections were characterised primarily by the desire to engage in some form of activity which offered purpose and the allure of the challenge of the unknown. Lieutenant John Winterflood of 2/3rd Independent Company had joined the militia out of University where he had secured a Degree in Science. He attempted to join the Air Force but was compelled by the Manpower Directorate to return to University. Not happy he transferred into the AIF joining an Engineer unit. Stationed at Tamworth New South Wales with no equipment and little to occupy his time he despaired of the boredom and asked his Commanding Officer if there was anything else he might be able to do. The reply was, did he want to do something that 'sounds dangerous'. Winterflood did not hesitate and answered with, 'That'll do!'[14] With that he made his way to Wilson's Promontory and began training. Alan Thompson was a Lieutenant with the 5th Battalion Australian Military Forces (AMF) – the Militia. He had been told that AMF officers could join the AIF but found this to not be a certain thing. He was told by a friend to 'apply for anything that comes along, particularly if it sounds hush-hush'. In July 1941 he did so applying for the Independent Companies. He was accepted.[15]

A common thread with the ordinary soldiers who volunteered was the desire to engage in something out of the ordinary, anything to break the monotony of their army life. This fact was important as it attracted a certain type of soldier to the companies. These were individuals with a sense of audacity, the yearning to try something out of the ordinary regardless of what others were doing. They exuded 'independence' the cardinal attribute fostered by the Independent Companies. Geoffrey Fraser who was a member of 2/4th Independent Company recalled how he found himself

---

10 David Dexter interviewed by Mel Pratt for the Mel Pratt collection [sound recording] 1976 <http://nla.gov.au/nla.obj-221579220> (consulted 13 June 2016).
11 Ibid.
12 Lambert, *Commando – From Tidal River to Tarakan*, p. 6.
13 Ibid.
14 AWM, AWM SO4156, Lieutenant John Winterflood interviewed by Neil MacDonald.
15 Lambert, *Commando – From Tidal River to Tarakan*, p. 7.

applying for Independent Company service. He had checked the camp notices daily and one day saw a notice asking for volunteers for a hush-hush squad. He thought it would be interesting and attended an interview during which he was asked if he would place explosive charges against a ship or if he would parachute into any area. He laconically replied, 'yeah right' and a few days later he was taken into an Independent Company.[16] Even though it was an adventure which he had been told offered little chance of survival, Fraser's reaction was 'oh well, I thought. I might be mad but at least here were 249 mad men with me.'[17] Norm Odium, a veteran of Greece and Crete, exhibited a keenness for special operations from an early time practicing to be a 'commando' during his spare time when he was stationed in Palestine. On his return to Australia he volunteered to join the Independent Companies and was accepted into the 8th Independent Company.[18] A sense of patriotic duty also motivated Independent Company volunteers. The desire to play a positive role in the defence of the nation while at the same time being allowed to exercise individuality and initiative was a key motivator.[19] Ralph Coyne who served as a signaller with 2/2nd Independent Company gave his reason for volunteering as 'this wonderful country of ours was under threat. Whatever was asked of us, it was up to me to do my very best.'[20] Jack Boxall, who would join 2/5th Independent Company was more pragmatic recalling the reason he volunteered as 'I considered that if my country was to be disrupted, it would be better to do it in someone else's backyard'.[21] Others volunteered simply to break the monotony of regular service. Alan Oakley, Jack Oddy, Stuart Muir, Alan Sutherland, and Bill Gibbs were training with a heavy machinegun when they saw a note in their orderly room advertising for volunteers for 'secret and hazardous' duties. Thinking that anything was better than lumping heavy machine guns all over the place they volunteered and were accepted into 'No.4 Cadre of the Guerrilla School'.[22] Some motivations appeared to have been influenced by the promise of extra remuneration, promotion and leave. Jack Jones reasons for volunteering were entirely motivated by personal gain. He was attending a lecture at the Engineer training depot at Tamworth when he was sent for by the commanding officer (CO) who asked him if 'He would feel like volunteering for some special hush-hush unit which he seemed to know absolutely nothing about'. He was not interested until the CO offered him 10 days leave at which he jumped at the chance to volunteer.[23] Extra pay was also an enticement. There was a proposal that Independent Company Privates be paid

16 AWM, MSS1960, Geoffrey Thomas, p. 21.
17 Ibid, pp. 18–19.
18 Astill, *Commando White Diamond*, p. 4.
19 Lambert, *Commando – From Tidal River to Tarakan*, p. 13.
20 Ralph Coyne, *The First Commandos – Ralph Coyne's wartime experiences 1942–1945* (Petraus Books, Belconnen, 2009), p. 6.
21 Pirie, 'Commando – Double Black', p. 4.
22 Lambert, *Commando – From Tidal River to Tarakan*, p. 7.
23 Ibid.

10/- per day, when pay for a regular unit Private was 5/- per day.[24] This encouraged some Sergeants to drop their stripes and volunteer to become 'Commando' Privates.[25] The lure of extra pay was, however, illusionary and never did eventuate with stories of extra pay for Independent Companies being officially repudiated in late 1943.[26] Offering material incentives was another tactic used to encourage troops to volunteer for Independent Company Service. Volunteers from Western Australia were provided with first class accommodation aboard the train on their long journey from Perth to the Eastern states and were allowed to eat in the dining car. In contrast, ordinary troops had to contend themselves with the cattle car with minimal comfort and be fed at sidings.[27] One other element unique to the Independent Companies that may or may not have been an incentive to join was that when they had successfully completed their training course Independent Company soldiers were issued with British Battle dress, to which was attached their double diamond unit flashes. They wore this as their walking out uniform. This was in contrast to the much less dapper regular Australian Ordinary Ranks service dress. When asked why they were wearing British battledress Independent Company soldiers would invariably quip they were a 'mobile laundry' unit.[28]

Despite the enthusiasm of those who did succeed in joining the Independent Companies the recruitment process for the companies was fraught with challenges. Resistance to recruiting came from within army units and from individual officers. When deciding on the allocation of personnel to units the Army did not favour the Independent Companies. One example of this was when 2/3rd Independent Company was seeking signallers, engineers, service and ordnance corps members it was told that they were not available due to competition for the same personnel from the lone Australian Armoured Division.[29] The same occurred with 4th Infantry Division which drew attention to the fact that the withdrawal of specialist personnel to join the Independent Companies would seriously affect the fighting efficiency of the Division.[30] A call for volunteers from the 33rd Training Battalion resulted in

24   Army History WW2 <http://www.diggerhistory.info/pages-conflicts-periods/ww2/pages-2aif-cmf/00-2nd_aif-index.htm> (consulted 10 January 2017).
25   AWM, AWM67 2/67, Gavin Long Notebook 67, interview with K. Stephens, *2/3 Independent Company*, Torokina, 22 Feb 1945.
26   Smailes, Jim, *The Independents* (Kewdale Printing Co, Perth, 1994), pp. 6–7; AWM, AWM52 2/2/53 Box 45, 2/9 Cavalry Commando Regiment November to December 1943, 2/9 Aust Cav Regt Administrative Instruction No.16. 3 Dec 43.
27   Pirie, 'Commando – Double Black', p. 4.
28   Coyne, *The First Commandos*, p. 7. British battledress was still being worn when on leave by Independent Company members in June 1943. It was, however, withdrawn in December 1944 see: AWM, AWM 52/2/52 Box 452/7 Commando Regiment War Diary October to December 1944, Aust Cav (Commando) Regt Routine Orders 2 December 1944,.
29   NAA, MP508 251/758/395, N-7 Infantry Training Centre, Military Forces Northern Command Victoria Barracks Brisbane, 23 Aug 41.
30   NAA, MP729/7 37/423/96, 16 June 42 – LHQ Melbourne – Independent Coys AIF.

no one stepping forward. Whether this as because the battalion did not encourage its soldiers to do so, or that the men genuinely did not want to volunteer was never explained. The battalion resorted to the time honoured method of detailing men without giving them an option to join the Independent Companies. This method of ensuring recruits went directly against the instruction put forward by the Army for the recruitment to the Independent Companies, yet it was done nonetheless.[31] A number of men subsequently complained of being 'shanghaied' into the Independent Companies. One such was an international footballer who wanted out of the unit. He was returned to his unit within a week of letting it be known how he felt.[32] The Army was concerned that all who joined the companies should do so of their own free will. The official attitude on recruitment for the Independent Companies was that all must be volunteers and that the process of detailing soldiers against their will must cease.[33] Consequently instructions were issued that any personnel who had been 'detailed' to Independent Companies against their will were to be returned to the Training Depot and from there back to their unit.[34] In fact the High Command 'demanded' unit commanders be 'unselfish' in releasing personnel.[35] Unit commanders were encouraged to not hold back from sending even their best personnel.[36] Such a response was indeed unexpected from an institution which did not have any particular interest in the Independent Companies per se. It did, however, reveal the cross currents within the Army bureaucracy in relation to the management of the Independent Companies, with some positive and some obstructionist. This was very much characteristic of the general muddled appreciation for the companies that existed at that time.

The quality of the men who were finding their way to the Independent Companies was a further challenge. Only one in five of the Independent Company recruits were found to be suitable for one reason or the other, be it health, lack of physical staying power or psychological unsuitability[37] Others who could not master the requisite skills, such as Morse code were removed.[38] The wastage of personnel during the

---

31 NAA, MP385 106/7/789, Guerrilla Warfare Foster Raising and Training of Personnal (sic) Organization of Coys and RTFs Movement of Coys and RTFs, Selection of Personnal (sic), 21 July 42.
32 AWM, AWM MSS1960, Fraser, *Highly Irregular*, p. 21; NAA, MP385 106/7/789, Guerrilla Warfare Foster Raising and Training of Personnal (sic) Organization of Coys and RTFs Movement of Coys and RTFs, Selection of Personnal (sic), 21 Jul 42.
33 NAA, MP385 106/7/789, Guerrilla Warfare Foster Raising and Training of Personnal (sic) Organization of Coys and RTFs Movement of Coys and RTFs, Selection of Personnal (sic), 21 Jul 42.
34 Ibid.
35 NAA, MP729/7 37/423/96, NAA, 9 Jun 42 – LHQ – Allied Land Forces in S.W. Pacific Area.
36 AWM, AWM52 1/5/10/3, June 1942 5th Division General Staff Branch, Independent Companies – AIF Promulgation of Information in Unit Part 1 Orders, 27 Jun 42.
37 Astill, *Commando White Diamond*, p. 5.
38 AWM, AWM MSS1960, Fraser, *Highly Irregular*, p. 22.

training period for Independent companies was considered severe.[39] Following Japan's entry into the war the assessment of those who were sent the way of the Independent Companies may not have been as rigorous as it could have been. It was thought that some who had been rejected in the past on medical grounds were now being allowed to volunteer.[40] After recruitment when soldiers discovered the nature of the work they would be expected to do it sometimes caused further problems. On at least one occasion a number of men who had volunteered decided to opt out of training and return to their units. They did this after being told by an officer what the role of the Companies would be and that in guerrilla warfare circumstances may arise that would result in the taking prisoners not being possible. Disturbed by the thought of killing prisoners the men declined to serve in the Independent Companies.[41] Concerned over its ability to find adequate numbers for the Independent Companies on 12 May 1942 the Army cast a wider net decreeing that volunteers could now be taken from Militia units, although preference would be given to AIF volunteers.[42]

Having volunteered, or found their way into the Independent Companies by other means the trainees were despatched to No.7 Infantry Training Centre at Daly River Wilson's Promontory. There their training began in earnest. The demands placed on the trainees were intense with lectures, exercises with weapons, demolition, signals and field-craft. Volunteers were taught the skills of scouting, concealment, ambush and infiltration as well as unarmed combat.[43] Indeed considerable thought at the local level, had been put into just what type of training programme Independent Companies should receive. The preamble to the No.7 Infantry Training Centre Introductory Lecture on guerrilla warfare clearly identified the purpose of the training as guerrilla warfare.[44] The training instructions for the programme emphasised that there was an, 'unlimited scope for a vivid imagination'.[45] Such an expectation certainly challenged the conventional military mindset.

Defining the role of the guerrilla received special attention with three types being identified. These were semi-independent raids and co-ordinated raids, and what was identified as 'True' guerrilla warfare which consisted of guerrillas using their intimate

---

39 NAA, MP385 106/7/789, Guerrilla Warfare Foster Raising and Training of Personnal (sic) Organization of Coys and RTFs Movement of Coys and RTFs, Selection of Personnal (sic), 21 Jul 42.
40 Lambert, *Commando – From Tidal River to Tarakan*, p. 3.
41 Ibid, p. 13.
42 NAA, MP385 106/7/789, Guerrilla Warfare Foster Raising and Training of Personnal (sic) Organization of Coys and RTFs Movement of Coys and RTFs, Selection of Personnal (sic), 21 Jul 42.
43 Lambert, *Commando – From Tidal River to Tarakan*, p. 8.
44 AWM, AWM54 380/6/2, No.7 Infantry Training Centre Field Craft Lecture 1 – introductory – Lecture Guerrilla Warfare.
45 NAA, MP729/7/0 – 37/323/4, Training Instructions Independent Companies late ca.1940.

knowledge of the terrain to remain hidden except when they struck at the enemy.[46] Not surprisingly, Lawrence of Arabia was often used as an exemplar for this latter type of operation.[47]

Subsequently the training programme that was developed was focussed solely on producing guerrilla fighters. It was understood from the beginning that the training was to be extremely practical and not unduly tied down by conventional military procedures.[48] A certain skill set needed to be developed to produce an effective 'guerrilla'. The ideal volunteer should be an all-rounder; a crack shot, a strong swimmer, a good cook, a capable medic, a skilled bushman, ride a horse, a competent mechanic, able to hunt, live off the land and find their way in the dark as well as handle all sorts of weapons, explosives and booby traps.[49] Quite obviously finding such a resume of skills in one person would be next to impossible, but it did highlight what type of individuals the Independent Company training cadre was seeking.

Of all the skills taught it was field-craft that received the most attention. Field-craft emphasised the ability of the individual to survive independently in challenging environments and circumstances. The Independent Company soldier was expected to arrive at the right place in a fit state of mind, body and equipment so that he could destroy the enemy.[50] Field-craft was the perfect vehicle for inculcating self-confidence, self-reliance and the independent ethos within the volunteers. The dominance of field-craft training was reflected by the fact that it received 87.5 hours of time within the training cycle, as opposed to Weapons Training 73.5 hours and Demolitions 49 hours.[51] The range of the skills covered in the field-craft course was extensive and diverse and included map reading, observation and reconnaissance, cross country navigation and stalking, concealment, camouflage and raiding.[52]

Captain Freddy Spencer Chapman was responsible for field-craft training and he went about the task with enthusiastic zeal. Although he was somewhat eccentric and could be talking about Snow Buntings in the Arctic one moment and how to strangle an enemy in unarmed combat the next, Spencer Chapman was recognised as absolutely the best teacher for all forms of field-craft.[53] Spencer Chapman's attitude

---

46 AWM, AWM54 380/6/2, No.7 Infantry Training Centre Field Craft Lecture 1 – introductory – Lecture Guerrilla Warfare.
47 Ibid.
48 Ibid.
49 AWM, AWM 3DRL/6766, Arden, John PH 'Jack', pp. 7–8.
50 AWM, AWM54 380/6/2, No.7 Infantry Training Centre Field Craft Lecture 1 – introductory – Lecture Guerilla Warfare.
51 AWM, AWM54 34/6/1, L.HQ. Guerilla Warfare School May-June 1942, Guerilla Warfare School Syllabus.
52 AWM, AWM54 34/6/1, L.HQ. Guerilla Warfare School May-June 1942, Guerilla Warfare School Syllabus, Nos 6 & 7 Aust Ind. Coy Cadres, Weds 22 Apr – Tuesday 28 Apr 42.
53 Moynahan, Brian, *Jungle Soldier – The True Story of Freddy Spencer Chapman* (Quercus, London, 2009), p. 94; Barker, Ralph, *One Man's Jungle a Biography of F. Spencer Chapman*

to training was uncompromising. He was adamant that it was the state of mind of the soldier that was the crucial element in training.[54] He had no time for what he called 'regular soldiers' as he considered that such individuals could not be trained as Commandos. Spencer Chapman was not reluctant to back up his words with deeds and during his time at Wilson Promontory made a point to out-run, out-climb and out-shoot the trainees. He could not abide being beaten by anyone.[55] Proving this point Spencer Chapman once climbed the 754 metre Mount Latrobe on Wilson's Promontory in a two and three quarter hour record and when this was beaten by a trainee by half an hour, he climbed the mountain again this time in one and three quarter hours, a record that was not beaten.[56] Spencer Chapman identified his priorities for training as getting a party from A to B in any sort of country at day or night and arriving fit and ready to carry out their task. He emphasised gaining knowledge of the night sky, choosing clothing carefully, what to take and how to carry it, tracking the enemy, living off the country, remembering routes and escaping the enemy if caught.[57] Spencer Chapman, being very much the individualist taught his trainees personal skills of survival in the wilderness. It was not surprising that these skills were of a particular unconventional nature. One skill taught by Spencer Chapman was what he called 'train the eye'.[58] Trainees were taught how to read the ground, to see and assess each fold and nuance in the terrain and spot as second nature good ambush positions. They were taught to 'listen'; to hear the sounds of the wilderness around them including the noise of birds and animals, and most importantly the importance of the lack of the noise of birds and animals, recognising that when these fell silent, danger threatened.[59] Spencer Chapman's technique was to tell stories no doubt gleaned from his remarkable experiences and then turn the stories into lessons from which the men learned new skills.[60] At first Spencer Chapman's eccentricity worked against him. His clipped mode of speech, continual wearing of the kilt, aesthetic good looks and frequent stories about Greenland and the Himalayas made a poor impression on the troops who made fun of him behind his back. When Spencer Chapman instituted the call of the British Tawny Owl be used as the rallying call for the Company, the reaction was 'what the bloody hell does he think we are?'[61] Nevertheless as the men got to know Spencer Chapman and as they saw for themselves his uncanny ability to

(Chatto & Windus, London, 1975), pp. 179–180.
54 Ibid, p. 34.
55 David Dexter and Mel Pratt. David Dexter interviewed by Mel Pratt for the Mel Pratt collection [sound recording] 1976 <http://nla.gov.au/nla.obj-221579220> (consulted 12 July 2016).
56 Moynahan, *Jungle Soldier*, p. 94.
57 Wigmore, *The Japanese Thrust*, p. 84.
58 Walker, 'History of No.7 Infantry Training Centre and the formation of the Independent Companies 1941–1942', p. 336.
59 Ibid.
60 Barker, *One Man's Jungle*, p. 181.
61 Ibid.

live and operate in the wild their respect grew and he became an invaluable source of knowledge and inspiration for morale among the volunteers.[62]

Practical field-craft exercises were often conducted at night during the hours of 2.00 a.m. and 7.00 a.m. One common night exercise was where two Sections were separated and the men were scattered through the scrub. A lantern was lit at the end of each section. The object was to sneak through, and put the other sections light out.[63] During these exercises trainees would be shown how to tactically stalk through country, forage and live off the land and survive in environments without recourse to the normal military line of communication. One exercise in particular bore the distinctly idiosyncratic character those managing the training. This was called 'The Akbar' a name attributed to Spencer Chapman because of the time he had spent in north India and the Himalayas and had thus enjoyed an imagined association with the legendary 'Akbar the Great'. The 'Akbar' was a three-day exercise that involved humping heavy packs over mountains, through rivers and swamps, living on iron rations and moving constantly, no matter what. Participants were allowed only 10 minute rest each hour.[64]

Another essential skill taught was that of demolitions. While it was given less time that either field-craft or Weapons training it was considered essential that each man be able to confidently handle explosives.[65] As befitting a subject in which a mistake could result in dramatic if not fatal consequences the attention to detail was exacting. Subjects covered in the demolitions course included identifying various explosives, detonating explosives, placing charges, calculating charges, booby traps and reconnaissance of targets.[66] Independent Company trainees worked with various explosives.[67] Training included using limpet mines, time pencils, Molotov cocktails and sticky bombs.[68] Captain Michael Calvert was in charge of demolition training and he did so with 'infectious enthusiasm'.[69] Calvert's methods were forthright. In an effort

---

62 Ibid.
63 Pirie, 'Commando – Double Black', p. 7.
64 Lambert, *Commando – From Tidal River to Tarakan*, p. 9.
65 AWM, AWM54 380/6/2, No.7 Infantry Training Centre Field Craft Lecture 1 – introductory – Lecture Guerrilla Warfare,
66 AWM, AWM54 34/6/1, L.HQ. Guerrilla Warfare School May–June 1942, Guerrilla Warfare School Syllabus, Nos 6 & 7 Aust Ind. Coy Cadres, Weds 22 Apr–Tuesday 28 Apr 42.
67 The explosives employed were including Gelignite, Monobel (TBR), TNT slabs, Ammonal CTG TBR, PHE TBR, GC slabs, gunpowder, and ST grenades. Trainees were taught the use of different forms of detonators, fuses, flares, plasticine explosives, switches, trip mechanisms, and igniters, see: AWM, AWM54 34/6/1, L.HQ. Guerrilla Warfare School May-June 1942, Guerrilla Warfare School Syllabus, Nos 6 & 7 Aust Ind. Coy Cadres, Weds 22 Apr – Tuesday 28 Apr 42, AWM54 34/6/1.
68 Pirie, 'Commando – Double Black', p. 8.
69 Spencer Chapman, *The Jungle is Neutral*, pp. 8–9; David Dexter interviewed by Mel Pratt for the Mel Pratt collection [sound recording] 1976 <http://nla.gov.au/nla.obj-221579220> (consulted 15 July 2016).

to get the men to recognise that 'noise doesn't hurt' Calvert would without warning explode a stick of gelignite in the sand nearby during a lecture to show the men that the noise of an explosion could not hurt. He would later detonate the same amount of explosive packed with metal to show how explosives when properly prepared could indeed hurt.[70] Trainees were taught to light a 'plug' of Gelignite which had a short fuse, place it in a hole in the ground and then walk away resisting the temptation to run. They normally managed to walk twenty paces before the 'plug' exploded.[71] Trainees responded enthusiastically to this regime. They were excited at being able to blow up anything that they could, and being able to throw explosives about as if they were fire crackers.[72] Training with explosives was nevertheless dangerous. In one incident, instantaneous fuses were mistakenly used in a night exercise, killing the soldier who set the charge.[73] Complementing Calvert's own skills were those of some of his trainees. Calvert acknowledged that he learned a lot about explosives from the Australian trainees at Wilson's Promontory, this was because many of them were gold miners who knew how to use explosives.[74]

The deliberately inculcated spirit of independence fostered amongst the trainees would have unanticipated consequences once they became accustomed to handling explosives. In a decidedly anarchic act the trainees' booby trapped the unit's Warrant Officer Latrine. They put cortex in a ring around the bottom of the latrine seat. It exploded and put the target (who no one liked) into the hospital for six months. They also blew up the Officer's wet mess. Officers had access to unlimited alcohol while the troops could only get lemonade. Six cases of explosive were used, one on each corner and two in the middle of the room. The Officer's Mess was wrecked. The perpetrators were charged £15 each for damage, but they thereafter got their own wet mess.[75] This clearly illustrated the temperament of the type of men who had elected to become members of Independent Companies. As for why the trainees thought they were being instructed in demolitions remained purely speculative. Lieutenant John Winterflood of 2/3rd Independent Company assuming that his company would be sent to Europe once they had completed their training was convinced that they would be tasked with blowing up a heavy water plant in Norway.[76]

70   IWM, 9942 reels 3–5, Michael 'Mad Mike' Calvert interview.
71   Henry F. Treichel, *Commando Army Service 1941–1946* (Wahpunga, 1994), p. 19.
72   AWM, AWM S04159, Roy Burbury interviewed by Neil MacDonald; AWM, AWM SO41173, Michael 'Mick' Sheehan 2/5 Independent Company interviewed by Neil MacDonald,.
73   Coyne, *The First Commandos*, p. 8. The dangers of training in the manner, was ever-present. Robert Hancock of 2/3rd Independent Company in a letter to his parents: AWM, AWM PR91/052, Hancock. R letter to his parents 6 Jan 1942, relates how two soldiers drowned during a river crossing exercise when they tangled in their equipment.
74   IWM, 9942 reels 3–5, Michael 'Mad Mike' Calvert interview.
75   AWM, AWM 3DRL/6766, Arden, John PH 'Jack', p. 12.
76   AWM, AWM S04156, Lieutenant John Winterflood interviewed by Neil MacDonald.

42   Jungle Cavalry

Interestingly considering the significance of the information gathering and dissemination role Independent Companies would contribute to AIF operations in coming years individual training did not overly focus on signals. Each days training began with a session devoted to signals, but this was only one half hour at 8.00 a.m. to 8.30 a.m. There were also seven three and a half hour sessions including Morse code tests, which were conducted on Sundays, for a total of 29.5 hours.[77] Each man was required to operate Wireless radio sets and Signals lamps and have a working knowledge of Morse code.[78] Failing to grasp the intricacies of Morse in particular was responsible for some trainees abandoning the course and returning to their units.[79] Overall signalling was certainly not given as much time as the field-craft, weapons or demolitions in the individual training program. This was perhaps because each Independent Company had its own dedicated Signals Section and non-signals members while expected to have a working knowledge would not be required to have an expert knowledge.

Cross training, or at least a capacity to adopt a modicum of diverse skills was another aspect of Independent Company training. This was one area of Independent Company training which differed markedly to the training received by regular standard infantry. Because of the concentration on guerrilla warfare and the special tactics that such work would require the focus of the weapons training for the Independent Companies was different than that given to the regular infantryman. The training of a standard regular army rifle section 1940–1941 consisted of a 112-hour course. Included in the course were training for anti-tank, bayonet, gas, field works and protective works.[80] Furthermore 32 hours of the total of 112 hours of training for the standard infantry recruit was spent operating as part of larger formations involving Squad drill, Platoon drill, Company drill, Battalion drill. All of this was based on the Infantry Training Manual 1937.[81] Independent company trainees received no training above company level and very little of that. They did not train in gas warfare, digging fieldworks, or anti-tank tactics. As guerrillas they were meant to operate by stealth there was no use for bayonet charges and bayonet training did not feature on the Independent Company training syllabus.[82] The Infantry Training Manual of 1937 was certainly not used as a guide for Independent Company training.[83] There was a heavy emphasis in

77 AWM, AWM54 34/6/1, L.HQ Guerrilla Warfare School May-June 1942, Guerrilla Warfare School Syllabus,
78 Pirie, 'Commando – Double Black', p. 10.
79 AWM, AWM MSS1960, Fraser, *Highly Irregular*, p. 22.
80 AWM, AWM 193 364 PART 9, 2 District Base Defence Scheme, Annexure 3 Training Appendix XI, XII.
81 Ibid.
82 Pirie, 'Commando – Double Black', pp. 8 and 10.
83 Interestingly work with bayonets was mentioned by at least one Independent Company trainee, indicating that it does appear to have been taught on an informal basis, see: Pirie, 'Commando – Double Black', p. 9; AWM, AWM54 34/6/1, L.HQ Guerrilla Warfare School May-June 1942, Guerrilla Warfare School Syllabus, Nos 6 & 7 Aust Ind. Coy Cadres, Weds 22 Apr – Tuesday 28 Apr 42.

Independent Company training on handling automatic weapons. Trainees mentioned being able to fire Thompson Sub Machineguns and Bren guns during training whenever they chose, and Officers and Non Commissioned Officers experienced an intensive course in firing and maintaining automatic weapons.[84] No such exposure to automatic weapons occurred during the training of a standard infantry section with light machine gunners being trained separately to riflemen. There was no cross over between the two in skill sets.[85] In contrast to this Independent Company soldiers cross-trained on all weapons with all Independent Company soldiers becoming proficient in all weapons including the Bren Light Machinegun.[86]

Across the board the practical and physical nature of training was paramount, physical fitness was essential.[87] Trainees could spend up to 18 hours per day in the field. This was accepted by the men who considered that it toughened them up and sorted out those who could not maintain the pace.[88] The training was uncompromising and designed to harden the men to the realities of war. Geoffrey Fraser's account of his experiences illustrates just how, when he described an early morning training session. After having swum in the icy waters off the promontory Fraser's Section was paraded before their unarmed combat instructor. The instructor was named Bonnie Muir, a former world class wrestler. Muir selected a man from the squad, told him to hit him, the man protested saying that Muir would hit him back. Muir said he would not. The man hit Muir who then smashed the man in the face. When the man complained Muir said 'You have all learned something – never to trust anyone in such a position.'[89] Fraser thought that the point was well learned.

Through their period of instruction assessment of Independent Company trainees was unrelenting. The officers watched the trainees continually. Their task was to pick those they considered were suitable for Independent Company work. They were looking for men who were good shots, but more importantly whose personalities would allow them to live and work cooperatively with a small group in extreme conditions. High on their priority was looking for those who did not grouch, were easy to get on with, could tell a joke when things get grim, and maintain their drive and determination under any conditions.[90] It was understood that trainees would be returned to their units if they were found to be unsuitable for Independent Company

---

84　AWM, AWM 504159, Roy Burbury Interviewed by Neil MacDonald; Astill, 'Commando White Diamond', p. 5.
85　AWM, AWM 193 364 Part 9, 2 District Base Defence Scheme, Annexure 3 Training Appendix XI, XII.
86　AWM, AWM54 34/6/1, L.HQ Guerrilla Warfare School May-June 1942, Guerrilla Warfare School Syllabus, Nos 6 & 7 Aust Ind. Coy Cadres, Weds 22 Apr – Tuesday 28 Apr 42.
87　Pirie, 'Commando – Double Black', p. 7.
88　Ibid, p. 17.
89　AWM, AWM MSS1960, Fraser, 'Highly Irregular', p. 21.
90　AWM, AWM 3DRL/6766, Arden, John PH 'Jack', p. 7.

training.[91] The task of identifying those who could not cope with physical strain and duress involved tests such as the trek to Sealer's Cove. This involved a full day trek across rough country with no food, no water, no smoking and no talking. At the end of the day the party would be met by trucks. The men were told that the trucks were there to give a ride to any man with sore feet that thought he could not make it back to camp. Anyone who took the offer and boarded the trucks was immediately sent back to his unit.[92] It was also understood that trainees could elect to return to their units within the first month of training with no loss of face.[93] In fact one in five trainees was returned to units. The reasons for this were health, lack of physical staying power or psychological unsuitability.[94]

A significant issue concerning the training of the companies during the independent phase was the relationship, or more accurately lack of a relationship, that existed between the Australian Army and the Independent Companies during the first year of Independent Company training programme. Despite the fact that one element of the Army was actively supporting the efficient recruitment of Independent Company volunteers the Army as an institution in 1941 had no real interest in the long term welfare, or even existence of the Companies. The failure of the Army to establish a reinforcement stream for the original three Independent Companies from November 1940 until December 1941, demonstrated that there was no intention to support the longevity or long term maintenance of the Companies. This was reflected in the abbreviated training the Independent Companies received during this time. This had nothing to do with the standard or quality of the input from the individual trainers who were acknowledged to have performed well, but everything to do with the overall attitude of the army to the training of the companies in general.[95] Lieutenant Colonel Mawhood on two occasions advised that the first companies had not completed their guerrilla warfare training.[96] He warned that such Commando units would end up fighting as ordinary line units and in consequence be cut to pieces, thus achieving nothing and rendering no service to their own side.[97] While one could accuse Mawhood of being overly critical of a military establishment which despised him, his concerns were not without foundation as in the case of 2/1st Independent Company which was deployed outside of Australia in July 1941 before

---

91 Lambert, *Commando – From Tidal River to Tarakan*, p. 14.
92 Astill, *Commando White Diamond*, p. 3.
93 Coyne, *The First Commandos*, p. 7.
94 Astill, *Commando White Diamond*, pp. 4–5.
95 NAA, A1608 G39/2/1, War 1939 – Special Operations Executive (Mawhood Mission), From Blamey CinC Army Land Forces HQ 10 July 42 – to Minister for Defence on Lt. Col Mawhood.
96 NAA, A12383 A/2/1 Attachment 1, Copy of Attorney General's file 1955/4428: Lieutenant Colonel Mawhood – Report on Security in Australia. Mawhood to Evatt 18 Sept 41.
97 Ibid.

it had completed its guerrilla warfare training. Mawhood's complaints went further with him accusing the Army of issuing inadequate rations, not granting proper leave after the six-week training course was completed, not providing specialist instruction and guidance, failing to deliver special equipment or restock supplies of explosives. He also pointed out that the Army had not established a dedicated command sub-unit to manage and facilitate the training of Commandos. Mawhood pointed out that those men who were training felt that because of the faulty organisation that they have been abandoned in an isolated area and neglected by all higher than their own company officers.[98] Unsurprisingly considering Mawhood's poisoned relationship with Army High Command his criticisms fell on deaf ears.

By mid-1941, two Independent Companies had been trained or more accurately partially trained, and the training of the third company was well under way. With the termination of the Independent Company training program in November 1941 the whole concept of Independent Companies as part of the Australian Army entered a period of enforced hiatus. With the hasty revitalisation of the program in December 1941 the training regimen the Australian trainers instituted followed on directly from the Independent character which had been established by their British forerunners. This continued until November 1942, when No.7 Infantry Training Centre was closed down and training for the Independent Companies was transferred to the new Guerrilla Warfare School in Canungra Queensland. The intention of the Guerrilla Warfare School at Canungra was to provide a tough and realistic training in a physical environment close to what the troops would experience in New Guinea. There was an eight week training course for Independent Companies, double what was scheduled for other troops.[99] The Guerrilla Warfare School soon gave way to the Jungle Warfare Centre, which was to train troops from every branch of the army, except Signals, in the skills required for Jungle Warfare. The School comprised three sections, a reinforcement-training centre, an Independent Company training centre, and a tactical school.[100] Things did not always go well for the Independent Company Troops at Canungra. When the veteran 2/6th and 2/7th Independent Companies arrived at Canungra in February 1943 for what would be 'refresher' training, they were treated as 'rookies' by the camp commander Lieutenant Colonel Alex 'Bandy' MacDonald, who did not like Independent Companies.[101] While the course syllabi at No.7 Infantry Training Centre had remained firmly aligned with the Independent ethos this was not so at Canungra. Elements of standard infantry training crept into

---

98   NAA, MP508 251/758/395, Mawhood to AHQ 16 Jul 41; NAA, MP508 251/758/395, War 1939 – Special Operations Executive (Mawhood Mission) Mawhood to Evatt 18 September 1942.
99   Dexter, *The New Guinea Offensives*, p. 229.
100 L.H.Q. Training Centre (Jungle Warfare) Canungra, Qld During WW2 <http://www.ozatwar.com/locations/canungracamp.htm> (consulted 13 January 2017).
101 David Dexter interviewed by Mel Pratt for the Mel Pratt collection [sound recording] 1976 <http://nla.gov.au/nla.obj-221579220> (consulted July 2016).

the Independent Company syllabi for example, drill and bayonet fighting, illustrating the continuing resistance by elements of the Army to the very notion of unconventional independent units.[102]

The recruitment and training methods of the Independent Companies during 1941 and 1942 were very much the product of an independent unconventional military ethos. It was the product of a military culture that refused to be restrained by conventional military expectations. This unconventional independent ethos embodied every aspect of the selection of personnel and individual and collective training of soldiers. The training goals set, curriculum established, syllabi followed and practical exercises engaged in represented a conscious and deliberate shift away from orthodox infantry training. Understandably the Army, which quite simply did not understand what the Independent Companies were, or appreciate such a radical ethos, chose to distance itself from them during 1941. When the Independent Companies were resuscitated in December 1942, this rejection was not so pronounced. There was at the time a need for trained troops and the resuscitation of the companies was very much a case of practical necessity.

The skills and independent ethos fostered by its unique training programme would provide the Independent Companies with a resume of unconventional military skills that would serve them well in the most trying circumstances during 1942 and 1943.

102 Ibid.

3

"Dumped and Written Off" – New Ireland and New Caledonia

In mid-1941 the Army quite literally had no idea what to do with the three Independent Companies which at that time been trained. There was no plan for the employment of the companies.[1] This indecision was symptomatic of the uncertainty which characterised the Army's attitude to Independent Companies at that time. A combination of factors influenced this uncertainty. There was at that time a very limited capacity within the Australian military to think beyond immediate tactical considerations, and such tactical considerations were overwhelmingly influenced by the demands of conventional warfare. Strategic decision making, which might have involved committing Commandos to operations outside of the mainstream, was invariably deferred to Britain.[2] The Independent Companies as they were constituted and trained, in the opinion of the Army, offered nothing to support ongoing operations. As such there was simply no place such formations could be employed. There were, however, three companies in existence and something had to be found for them to do.

Despite its commitment to and focus on the war in North Africa and the Middle East Australia was not entirely oblivious to the strategic situation in the Far East, in particular Japan's role in the region. Throughout its history Australia had cast a wary eye on the Asian regions to it north. Australia had watched the rise of Japan as a potential threat to Australia since before 1901.[3] Lulled, however, by the promise of security provided by what was presumed to be British dominance in the Far East, Australia did very little in practical terms to address such concerns. Even so by January 1940 the potential military threat from Japan had been recognised by the Australian General Staff.[4] By 1941 that concern had evolved into the presumption that a war between the

---

1 NAA, MP729/7 37/421/359, Employment of Independent Companies A.I.F.
2 David Horner, *High Command Australia and Allied Strategy 1939–1945* (Allen and Unwin: Sydney, 1982), p. 136.
3 Ibid, p. 25.
4 AWM, AWM54 243/6/158, Draft Appreciation on the employment of the A.M.F in the defence of Australia by General Staff – 16 January 1940.

British Empire and Japan was now probable.⁵ Despite this no decisive steps were taken in Australia to prepare for such an eventuality. Troops were deployed to Singapore and to locations on islands to the north of Australia, but this was merely a token and no other preparations on a national level were made. On 10 June 1941 The Australian Naval Board reported that an unmarked twin engine monoplane flew over Kavieng in New Ireland. It was also reported that three large ships and two small ships had been seen off Sali in New Ireland and that a flying boat had landed at North Cape on New Ireland. The Aircraft at least were considered to be Japanese. In addition an unidentified vessel had passed by Lorengau on Manus Island to the north of New Guinea.⁶ On 20 June 1941 the Chiefs of the General Staff determined that as possible foreign reconnaissance of Rabaul and Australia's advanced bases had occurred it was therefore necessary to take precautionary measures to protect R.A.A.F airbases and seaplane sites in New Guinea, the New Hebrides and the Solomon Islands.

As for the Independent Companies the 2/2nd Independent Company was sent to 7 Military District in the Northern Territory of Australia. There was no specific reason given for this deployment, but it can be assumed that it was to bolster the number of troops in the far northern region of Australia due to concerns about Japan.⁷ In June 1941, as part of a general deployment of a limited number of troops to what was called the island barrier chain to the north of Australia, it was decided to despatch 2/1st Independent Company to New Ireland an island adjacent to New Britain to the north of New Guinea.

The 2/1st Independent Company was identified as being available to move by sea to Rabaul on 8 July 1941 and that a reconnaissance party from the Company would proceed to Rabaul on 18 June.⁸ On 11 July 1941 the Company was transferred from Rabaul to Kavieng New Ireland.⁹ Sections of the Company, each of 25 men, were then deployed to the islands of Manus, Buka and Tulagai and to Vila in the New Hebrides. The balance of the Company, some 150 men remained at Kavieng. This deployment stretched over an arc of more than 1000 kilometres across the northern approaches to Australia. This made it impossible for the component parts of the Company to have any hope of supporting each other and having being deployed in such small numbers having no realistic hope of resisting any move by an aggressor. Further comprising the integrity of the Company the tasks allocated to each of the widely dispersed Sections were extraordinarily contradictory. The mission given to the Sections was to protect and deny to the enemy the local airfields, R.A.A.F equipment and stores on

---

5   AWM, AWM 243.6/5, Operational Planning Directive No.1, possibly written Nov 41, Rowell.
6   TNA, 208/4556, Japan Moves in South Asia.
7   NAA, MP729/7 37/421/359, Employment of Independent Companies A.I.F.
8   AWM, AWM MH 1/149, No 1 Independent Coy Operations 1941–1943, Department of the Army Military Board (Chief of the General Staff) Army Headquarters Victoria Barracks MELBOURNE, S.C.1, 20 Jun. 41, A.H.Q. Operation Instruction No.16.
9   NAA, MP729/7 37/421/319, Northcott from Sturdee – From Lark, 11 Jul 41.

the islands they were deployed to. In a masterpiece of doublespeak the Sections were instructed to destroy the airfields if threatened by the enemy 'under certain circumstances', these circumstances were never defined. Then in the same document the Sections were instructed not to destroy the airfields, the reasoning being that if they did friendly aircraft could not use them and if the enemy occupied them they would repair them quickly anyway.[10] Just what the men of 2/1st Independent Company made of this contradiction is not recorded. In addition to guarding, destroying or not destroying the airfields the Sections were meant to train local indigenous recruits to assist defend R.A.A.F facilities.[11] It was obvious that the Army had no firm idea what its Commandos were to achieve on the islands, other than simply be there. It appeared that they were in effect simply a trip wire force sent to garrison a string of remote military assets in the anticipation that if those assets were attacked some word of that would make its way back to Australia.

There was amongst the confusion a glimmer of pragmatic reasoning behind the deployment of the Company, even if narrowly conceived. It had been especially noted when selecting the Company for the mission that the Company had been trained in demolitions and were fully equipped for that role.[12] Demolition was, at least in theory, the primary reason for occupying the island airfields and as such it was logical that a unit with the knowhow and equipment to carry out such a task should be chosen. Deploying an Independent Company, that was modest in size and unattached to any higher formation, would also not put any undue strain on the resources of the Army. Demolition was only one of the skills of an Independent Company, but for the Army, uninterested in exploiting the full range of unconventional characteristics of the Company, this was of little concern.

On 22 July 1941 Major James Edmonds-Wilson, the commanding officer of the Company, wrote an appreciation in which he emphasised the importance of the Company's mission. His appreciation deferred entirely to the official line stressing the financial cost of the airbases and their strategic importance to Australia's outer defences.[13] That Edmond-Wilson should respond in the way that he did at that time is understandable. There was little real concern for any 'enemy' action apart from wariness about the possible intrusion of German naval raiders in the waters around the islands. Two German auxiliary raiders the *Orion* and *Komet* had stopped at Emirau

---

10 AWM, AWM MH 1/149, No 1 Independent Coy Operations 1941–1943, Department of the Army Military Board (Chief of the General Staff) Army Headquarters Victoria Barracks MELBOURNE, S.C.1, 20 Jun. 41, A.H.Q. Operation Instruction No.16.
11 Ibid.
12 AWM, AWM MH 1/149, No 1 Independent Coy Operations 1941–1943, Chief of the General Staff, no date.
13 AWM, AWM113 MH 1/149 Part 4. Defence of the New Hebrides and role of No.1 Independent Coy and other AIF units in it, Operation Order No.1 – by J. Edmonds-Wilson Major, 1st Oct 41.

Island, to the north west of Kavieng on 19 December 1940 and landed 514 prisoners.[14] There was certainly no stated concern by Edmonds-Wilson for any danger from Japan.[15]

The appointment of Edmond-Wilson as commander of 2/1st Independent Company which was, at least in theory, a front line combat unit was a curious one. He was described by those under him as 'not a field officer', and he himself freely admitted that his aptitude was for administration and that he knew little of weaponry or field-craft. He subsequently delegated tactical matters to his officers.[16] There is no way of knowing but given the less than forthright direction given to the Company Edmunds-Wilson's appointment may well have been merely as a caretaker for a unit which was not expected to engage in serious combat. Nevertheless Edmunds-Wilson was not oblivious to his overall situation and he oversaw plans to withdraw if an enemy landing made defence impracticable.[17] As it was however, in the last few months of 1941, with no sense of any imminent danger, the Company settled into a comfortable routine. The component of the Company at Kavieng spent its time working on preparations to defend the airfield and town against possible enemy invasion.[18] The Sections on Manus, Buka and Tulagai set about preparing defensive positions, and organising their stores and provisions. The section stationed in Vila New Hebrides had a somewhat different environment to manage. Vila was a British-French condominium and as such was subject to issues not present elsewhere. Chief amongst these was the maintenance of a rapprochement between the French and British communities. Captain Allen Goode, the officer in command at Vila, had the task of managing the civilian defence of Vila. In this role he had been appointed Commanding Officer New Hebrides Defence Force and had command of the local French Home Guard. He reported that maintaining a working relationship with the French population on the island was most difficult, and that he could not trust many of the French civilians whose loyalties, due to the influence of Vichy France, were uncertain.[19]

---

14   Mary Murray, *Escape a Thousand Miles to Freedom* (Rigby Limited: Adelaide, 1965), pp. 28–9.
15   AWM, AWM113 MH 1/149 PART 4, Defence of the New Hebrides and role of No.1 Independent Coy and other AIF units in it, Operation Order No.1 – by J. Edmonds-Wilson Major, 1st Oct 41.
16   Andy Mc Nab, *We were the first: The unit history of No.1 Independent Company* (Military History Publications: Loftus, 1996), p. vii.
17   AWM, AWM MH 1/149, No 1 Independent Coy Operations 1941–1943, Detailed Instructions for the Employment of No.1 Independent Company for the protection of Aerodromes at Lorengau, Kavieng, Namatanai, Bukka and Keita (when ordered).
18   AWM, AWM113 MH 1/149 PART 4, Defence of the New Hebrides and role of No.1 Independent Coy and other AIF units in it, Operation Order No.1 – by J. Edmonds-Wilson Major, 1st Oct 41.
19   AWM, AWM113 MH 1/149 Part 4, Defence of the New Hebrides and role of No.1 Independent Coy and other AIF units in it.

Throughout this time Japanese reconnaissance of New Ireland and Kavieng took the form of visits by small ships carrying groups of 'students' who would take photographs and notes of Kavieng's airfield, buildings and infrastructure. These visits were met with suspicion by local residents but Edmunds-Wilson, lacking any instructions from Australia on what to do about them ordered that they should not be interfered with.[20]

The issue of just how little attention the Army was paying to the Company manifested itself in August 1941. The Director of Personal Services, the Army agency responsible for supplying troops, discovered that while it had been supplying the 1500 personnel on Rabaul it had no knowledge of the 234 personnel of 2/1st Independent Company at Kavieng, New Ireland.[21] That the Directorate was unaware of the Company's presence on New Ireland indicates that the Army, for whatever reason, had not informed it of the Company being there. This oversight may have been due to the strain under which the Army's bureaucracy was working at the time. It is, however, equally possible that it was symptomatic of an endemic disinterest by the Army of its Independent Companies, especially once they had left Australia. Luckily for the Company their discovery by the Director of Personal Services, secured them maintenance.[22]

When Japan entered the war Australia was caught unprepared. Serving the needs of Imperial defence the majority of Australia's regular Army was outside the country in North Africa and the Middle East or the Malay Peninsula. The Air Force in Australia was effectively non-existent and little had been done to prepare Australia's air defences. Those naval assets that were available were returning from the Mediterranean and Far East and were under the command of the Royal Navy not Australia. The vast majority of the land forces that were available were Militia formations many of who were of questionable quality.[23] So parlous was Australia's situation that the decisions made at that time by government and the military tended to exhibit a degree of panic and not clear thinking.[24] One such decision was what to do with the isolated garrisons, one of

---

20   Murray, *Escape a Thousand Miles to Freedom*, pp. 28–9.
21   AWM, AWM123 521, Movement of Troops from 28th May, 1941 to 6th January 1942.
22   AWM, AWM113 MH 1/149 PART 4, Defence of the New Hebrides and role of No.1 Independent Coy and other AIF units in it; and Consideration and Recommendations for Vila and Tulagi Major J. Edmonds Wilson, 22 July 41.
23   The equipment on hand for AMF Militia units on 30 Nov 1941 fell far below war establishment. For example there was available at that time 74% of the requirement for .303 ammunition, 23% .45 ammunition, 17% 3" mortar ammunition, 25% 25pdr 18-pdr and 4.7-inch artillery ammunition, in the case of actual weapons available 73% rifles, 49% light machine guns, and 77% web equipment and so on. Ironically the number of medium machine guns and 3" mortars on hand exceeded war establishment but without ammunition they would have been of little use. See: AWM, AWM 124 4/105, Defence of Australia and Adjacent Areas, Chiefs of Staff Appreciation, December 1941, Percentage of Materiel on Hand for AMF Units, 30 Nov 41.
24   Horner, *High Command Australia and Allied Strategy 1939–1945*, p. 143.

which was 2/1st Independent Company, which had been placed in the so called Island Barrier to the north of Australia. It was recognised that the garrisons were unsupportable and could not resist any Japanese move against them. Despite this it was decided to leave them in place. This effectively sentenced all of those forces to annihilation. To reasons such a decision was made reflected to desperate circumstances of the time. In a most secret cablegram of 13 December 1941 Herbert Evatt the Minister for External Affairs discounted the question of withdrawal from what he deemed to be Australia's advanced observation line. Evatt's concerns were motivated by international political considerations as he was concerned that if Australia did not show some form of assertiveness in the region it would weaken the resolve of the Dutch in the Netherlands East Indies.[25] The official military appreciation from the Chiefs of Staff echoed Evatt's line.[26] Subsequently the Chiefs of Staff concluded that despite there being no hope to reinforce the observation line and that it could not possibly hold out against the weight of attack expected that the enemy must be made to fight for it.[27] This fatalistic decision sentenced those troops who were part of the observation line to destruction. It was to such a fate that 2/1st Independent Company was consigned.

The Company was not unaware of its circumstances and that it had been left to its own resources.[28] Under Edmund-Wilson's direction a survey of the approaches to Kavieng was undertaken. The survey concluded that a frontal attack on Kavieng would be too dangerous for an invader to attempt, and that any Japanese attack would have to come from the south of Kavieng. Therefore priority would be given to defensive measure from that direction.[29] Nevertheless Edmund-Wilson oversaw plans to withdraw if the enemy landing did succeed.[30] On 19 December 1941 an order was received to evacuate all European women and children to Rabaul within 24 hours. This was not possible to conduct in the time given due to many of the evacuees living some distance from Kavieng. Concerns were raised by the local Chinese community that because of a lack of available shipping they were to be left behind, which in fact

25   John Robertson and John McCarthy, *Australian War Strategy 1939–1945* (University of Queensland Press: St. Lucia, 1985), p. 217.
26   AWM, AWM54 243/6/15, Appreciation on the Defence of Australia and Adjacent Areas – by Australian Chief of Staff December 1941.
27   AWM, AWM54 243/6/15, Appreciation on the Defence of Australia and Adjacent Areas – by Australian Chief of Staff December 1941.
28   AWM, AWM MH 1/149, No 1 Independent Coy Operations 1941–1943, Detailed Instructions for the Employment of No.1 Independent Company for the Protection of Aerodromes at Lorengau, Kavieng, Namatani, Bukka and Keita (when ordered).
29   AWM, AWM MH 1/149, No 1 Independent Coy Operations 1941–1943, Reports Kavieng No1. Indep Coy – Reasons why frontal attack on Kavieng is too dangerous. Ironically it was just such a frontal assault that occurred when the Japanese did invade, the assault meeting no resistance.
30   AWM, AWM MH 1/149, No 1 Independent Coy Operations 1941–1943, Detailed Instructions for the Employment of No.1 Independent Company for the Protection of Aerodromes at Lorengau, Kavieng, Namatani, Bukka and Keita (when ordered).

is what occurred.³¹ The evacuation of European women and children did eventually occur with the men singing to their departing women and children as they sailed from the harbour.³²

At 6.00 a.m. on 21 January 1941 the war came to Kavieng. Two Japanese air raids hit the town, the first raid lasting for about 45 minutes and the second raid lasting for 20 minutes.³³ A ship, the *Induna Star*, was strafed and five 2/1st Independent Company men who were aboard were wounded, two severely. Japanese bombs hit the wharf and the area near the airfield which included an engineering shop.³⁴ One Japanese aircraft was shot down and three others damaged.³⁵ Kavieng was evacuated at 7.00 p.m. on the same day. By midnight only Edmunds-Wilson and six civilians remained in the town, while some soldiers remained at the airfield. For reasons best known to themselves Edmunds-Wilson and his compatriots indulged in an alcohol fuelled feast that evening and retired to bed despite having heard engine noises out in the harbour late that night.³⁶ The Japanese landed at 3.00 a.m. on 22 January bringing a steamer right up to the wharf and disembarking some 1500 troops, so much for the conclusion that the Japanese would not dare a frontal assault. They met no resistance. Edmunds-Wilson tumbled out of bed, awakened by Peter Levi the owner of the house he was in. He and Levi leaped into a car and drove through the gathering and somewhat bewildered Japanese soldiers to make their escape, picking up local resident Harold Murray who wearing his pyjamas and without his false teeth leaped onto the car's running board.³⁷ Reaching the airfield Edmunds-Wilson cried out 'Blow her! Blow her! The Japs are here!'³⁸ Some demolitions were carried out, the extent of which is problematic as the Japanese landed aircraft on the runway the same day.³⁹ While the evacuees gathered at the airfield arguing about what to do next Japanese troops appeared at the end of the runway and began firing at them. When this happened Edmunds-Wilson shouted for everyone to go into the bush, keep together and keep moving.⁴⁰ Those on the airfield must have done so as Japanese troops who took part in the landings reported seeing no enemy at the airfield and make no mention of meeting any serious resistance or suffering notable numbers of casualties.⁴¹

31 Murray, *Escape a Thousand Miles to Freedom*, pp. 39–40.
32 Ibid, p. 42.
33 Ibid, pp. 54–6.
34 Ibid, p. 60.
35 Ibid, p. 59.
36 Ibid, p. 74.
37 Ibid, p. 76.
38 Ibid.
39 AWM, AWM54 616/8/11, New Ireland – Notes on Interview with Evacuees at the time of the Japanese landing 21/1/42.
40 Murray, *Escape a Thousand Miles to Freedom*, p. 77.
41 AWM, AWM54 253/5/7, Allied Translator and Interpreter Section. Captured Documents Nos 58 + 74. Diaries of members of Kure No 3 Special Landing Party – March 1942,

When the Japanese landed three men from the Company were in Kavieng. They had been sent there the night of the 21–22 January to carry out demolitions on the waterfront, but for whatever reason this was not achieved. It may have been that the three men decided to loot a local shop instead. The Manager of the Burns Philip store caught three soldiers looting his shop during that night.[42] He identified these as Commandos. The soldiers had blown the lock of the door which the Manager says was the 'only thing they blew up from start to finish'.[43] There is no mention of the men again and it is presumed they escaped the town.

Having hastily evacuated the airfield and trekking for two days the evacuees both military and civilian gathered at Kaut several miles into the bush from Kavieng. There they made contact with Port Moresby informing them of what had occurred, using civilian radios as all the military radios were unserviceable. The orders they received in reply were forthright if not unrealistic. 2/1st Independent Company was to continue to resist the Japanese by fighting a 'Stay Behind' guerrilla war.[44] Such an order does indicate that someone in authority had some notion of the potential uses of an Independent Company but in the circumstances the order was impractical, more reflective of a panicked response rather than a considered one. The tactical, logistical and health circumstances the company was confronted with made it impossible to embark on a protracted guerrilla campaign. The lack of food was major factor in determining what options were open. Indigenous gardens in the hills were very rare and any party trying to survive on foraging indigenous food would starve.[45] Edmunds-Wilson, now forced into the unfamiliar role of commanding in a war situation, had a conference with his Medical Officer in which he discussed the health of the men. It transpired that many were suffering from fatigue, malaria, dysentery and skin diseases. It was consequently decided that the company's only hope was to leave the island at once and the order to stay and fight on was ignored.[46] The only means of escaping from the island was to make use of the *Iuduna Star* which was hidden nearby. It was imperative that the vessel be secured and put to sea before the Japanese discovered it. Subsequently the Company departed the island aboard the *Induna Star* on 29 January. The evacuation was conducted in a hasty manner with food, clothing, blankets, arms, ammunition, and general equipment being abandoned. The civilians who had retreated to Kaut with the Company were not taken with the Company. Confronted in later years with accusations of abandoning the civilians the Company claimed that the civilian District Commissioner when told of the plan to escape aboard the *Induna Star* refused

Note book of Hideo Inetsugu – Yano Unit, Kure No.3, S.L.P – captured at Milne Bay Sept 42.
42   Burns Philip was a major Australian shipping line and merchant that operated in the South Pacific.
43   AWM, AWM67 3/413, Personal Records Gavin Long – Waters Planter New Ireland.
44   Murray, *Escape a Thousand Miles to Freedom*, pp. 83–92.
45   McNab, *We were the first*, p. 33.
46   Ibid. According to McNab the officers concerned were not aware of the food situation.

to join the exodus saying if the civilians were caught with the military they would be treated as spies and shot.[47] Civilian sources deny this and blame Edmunds-Wilson directly calling him a 'bloody fool'.[48] The anticipated flight to freedom was short lived. The *Induna Star* was intercepted by the Japanese and the Company became Prisoners of war. Sadly many of them were to die on 1 July 1942 when the ship they were being transported on was sunk by an American submarine.[49]

The Sections of 2/1st Independent Company which had been deployed to Manus, Buka, Tulagai and Vila fared better than their comrades on New Ireland. In the case of Manus, Buka and Tulagai the Japanese did not descend on them until February – March 1942. When that occurred, the tiny garrisons sensibly withdrew after demolishing what they could. Those on Manus Island did booby trap the wharf and wounded a Japanese soldier.[50] On Buka and Tulagai the Sections withdrew to Bougainville where several of them did valuable work as coast watchers.[51] When the Japanese landed on Buka Island they knew exactly how many members of 2/1st Company were on the island. It is not known if this information came from indigenous agents of the Japanese, or from documents that may have been abandoned by the Company in its hasty retreat from Kavieng.[52] For the section on Vila the Japanese were never a threat. The Vila Sections greatest challenge was to reconcile the French colonists there to being under the authority of 'les Anglais'. Vila was eventually occupied by an American Garrison.

For those of 2/1st Company who had confronted the Japanese the final tally for those that managed to escape and make their way back to Australia was 64 being four officers and 60 Other Ranks from the original 330 who had been deployed.[53] The Company was never reconstituted. It was a tragic end for the first of Australia's Independent Companies.

47   Ibid, pp. 83–92.
48   Murray, *Escape a Thousand Miles to Freedom*, p. 77.
49   1st Independent Company <https://www.awm.gov.au/unit/U56146/> (consulted 14 March 2016).
50   AWM, AWM54 253/5/7, Allied Translator and Interpreter Section. Captured Documents Nos 58 + 74. Diaries of members of Kure No 3 Special Landing Party – March 1942, Note book of Hideo Inetsugu – Yano Unit, Kure No.3, S.L.P. – captured at Milne Bay Sept 42.
51   Four members of 1st Independent Company John Mackie, Edward Otton, David Sly and Henry Wigley were to be awarded US Silver Stars for their work a Coast Watchers see: NARA, 200.6, BOX 1731, RG496, Records of General Headquarters, South West Pacific Area and United States Army Forces, Pacific, Adjutant General – General Correspondence 1942–45.
52   A.B. 'Bud' Feuer (ed.), *Coast Watching in the Solomon Islands* (Paeger: New York, 1992), p. 24.
53   AWM, AWM MH 1/149, No 1 Independent Coy Operations 1941–194, Major A.L. Rose C.T. School Brisbane to 'Lionel'.

The history of the 2/1st Independent Company reveals a great deal about the failure of the Army at that time to fully embrace the Independent Companies. The Company was deployed for reasons of expediency with no regard for its ability as an unconventional force. The overall deployment of the Company, with Sections scattered across a vast arc of islands demonstrates that the Army had little regard for maintaining the integrity of the Company. It is also to be remembered that the Company had been deployed before it had completed its guerrilla warfare training. The appointment of an officer such as Edmunds-Wilson, who had limited capacity for front line command, was ill-considered. The reaction of the Company when the Japanese invaded, indicted that it was not prepared physically and psychologically to resist the enemy. Its retreat from Kavieng was little more than a race to the safety of the bush. Its evacuation during which stores, weapons and equipment were abandoned illustrates its incapacity to manage in anything like an efficient manner in circumstances of intense pressure and duress itself. This was no reflection on the men themselves. Some members of the Sections on the islands managed to survive and rendered valuable service as coast watchers. It however casts a dim light on the leadership of the Company at the time.

The 2/1st Independent Company had been deployed piecemeal across a vast remote and unsustainable area. The Company was employed in a cynical and deliberate manner and there had never been any intention to support, reinforce or withdraw it. When war came it could do nothing to resist the Japanese onslaught and was annihilated as a unit. Such was the manner in which the Army chose to employ its first Independent Company.

The 2/3rd Independent Companies despatched from Australia in 1941 was to have a very different experience to that of 2/1st Independent Company. It was the good fortune of the 2/3rd Independent Company to be deployed, as 'Robin Force', to the French Colony of New Caledonia were it arrived on 23 December 1941. While occupying New Caledonia itself had no interest for Australia the Australian Government was very much concerned about who controlled New Caledonia. New Caledonia's strategic position, sitting astride the sea communications to the United States and within air range of the Australian East coast and New Zealand posed a serious dilemma if an unfriendly power should gain control of the island. That New Caledonia could fall under unfriendly influence became of particular concern following the fall of France in June 1940. Many French colonies had openly sided with the Vichy government in France and while New Caledonia had not yet done so there was a significant Vichy presence on the island.[54] Machinations began almost immediately in Australia to ensure that New Caledonia would not fall under Vichy control. The light cruiser HMAS *Adelaide* was detailed to proceed to Vila and take on board a

---

54 'Petainist' or Vichy sympathisers numbered some 15% of the population in Noumea and 5% in rural areas. They were mostly from the wealthy classes with some military officers, see: AWM, AWM 113 MH1/108, New Caledonia Report Captain T. Kneen – 4 Independent Company 4 June, 1941–23 October 1941.

Monsieur Sautot a confirmed de Gaullist and deliver him to Noumea as a replacement for the current Governor who expressed Vichy sympathies.[55] This was achieved on 19 September 1940 amidst general acclamation and direct action by the public to thwart an attempted counter move by pro-Vichy elements.[56] Following this success concerns for New Caledonia did not abate, especially so as apprehensions of Japan's intentions increased during 1941. In February- March 1941 Australia sent a Military Mission consisting of one Army, Navy and Air Force representative to New Caledonia. It reported back on 9 April 1941 giving a general summary of the defence situation, the requirements of Free French forces in the area, negotiations for an Australian expeditionary force, and the internment of local Japanese.[57]

The first use of the Independent Companies in relation to New Caledonia was an indirect one. In early June 1941 Captain Paul Kneen of the 2/4th Independent Company was sent to the New Caledonia under the assumed identity of Gunner Keen. His mission was a clandestine one, very much akin to the original internal security role of 104 Military Mission. Kneen was to report on the local population, in regard to French activities, Japanese activities and Local indigenous feeling. He was also to report on the possibility of local trainees for Independent Company work and the potential scope for Independent Company activities in New Caledonia. On 4 June Kneen reported to Australian artillery Captain Charles Carty-Salmon, who was aware of the subterfuge. Kneen acted as Orderly Clerk to Carty-Salmon until 24 July 41. Under that cover Kneen set to work and eventually produced a report that ran to 36 pages and was both comprehensive and insightful. He assessed the European French and indigenous population as friendly to the Allied cause. He cautioned that the French did not want a permanent Australian presence but welcomed the material support Australia offered. He warned of Japanese activity on the island, which at the time consisted of Japanese military officers pretending to be employees of firms. These officers watched Australian military equipment being unloaded at the wharf and corrupted at least one local Gendarme. He assessed New Caledonia as being ideally suited for Independent Company work.[58]

When war with Japan came on 7 December 1941 concerns for New Caledonia's fate became much more focussed. In December 1941 the Chiefs of Staff determined that the probable Japanese course of action would be to capture New Caledonia as well as other outlying islands and use these to mount attacks on mainland Australia.[59] At

---

55 AWM, AWM 3DRL 8052 419/45/13, Sir Paul Hasluck Official Historian – Research on New Caledonia.
56 Ibid.
57 AWM, AWM 3 DRL 8052 419/45/13, War Cabinet Agenda – New Caledonia – Importance of Taking Immediate Action to Prevent it Falling into Japanese Hands.
58 AWM, AWM 113 MH1/108, New Caledonia Report Captain T. Kneen – 4 Independent Company 4 June, 1941–23 October 1941.
59 AWM, AWM 124 4/105, Defence of Australian and Adjacent Areas – Chief of Staff Appreciation, December 1941.

the same time the War Cabinet expressed its concerns noting that New Caledonia was important because of its value in the production of nickel and chromium and that Japanese control of New Caledonia would interfere with American naval forces in the region and provide an ideal jumping off place for the invasion of Australia. The Cabinet was also aware that the domestic political situation on New Caledonia could result in a faction on the Island requesting the Japanese to land and restore Vichy control.[60] Recommendations were made to assist New Caledonia economically by providing loans and financial backing. Visits by Australian warships and flying boats were also scheduled, and a plan formulated to cooperate with the Free French military forces on the island. It was considered that if these steps were not taken New Caledonia would fall to the Japanese within three months.[61]

It was in such circumstances that on 15 December 1941 it was recommended that an independent company be sent to New Caledonia as a demonstration of Australian support and to enhance the morale of the French. A secondary motive was to place a demolition trained force on the island tasked with destroying the nickel and chromium mines in case the Japanese landed there.[62] At the time there were two Independent Companies in Australia 2/2nd and 2/3rd Independent Companies. The 2/2nd Independent Company had been deployed to the Northern Territory and thus committed. The only Independent Company that was available was 2/3rd Independent Company, which like its compatriot Company had been posted to the Northern Territory. It had not yet arrived, however, and was aboard a train on its way to Darwin, when the order went out for it to deploy to New Caledonia. The train was halted, turned around and headed back to Sydney.

Despatched aboard the passenger liner *Ormiston* complete with jacketed waiters and served grapefruit for breakfast the Company arrived in Noumea on 23 December 1941.[63] On arrival the Company negotiated with the Free French military and assumed responsibility for the northern portion of the island. The Company dispersed in Sections with each Section occupying one of 13 areas. Within each of their areas the Sections were to conduct reconnaissance and establish dumps for ammunition, explosives and food. Each of the Section's camps was hidden from view. Preparations for the destruction of roads, mines, and any installations useful to an invader were made and each section undertook the responsibility for training the French militia in their area.[64] The soldiers of the 2/3rd Independent Company enjoyed a relatively

60 AWM, AWM 3 DRL 8052 419/45/13, War Cabinet Agenda – New Caledonia – Importance of Taking Immediate Action to Prevent it Falling into Japanese Hands.
61 Ibid.
62 Horner, *High Command Australia and Allied Strategy 1939–1945*, p. 143.
63 AWM, AWM SO4158, John Lewin interviewed by Neil MacDonald; AWM, AWM 54 565/4/1, Report on Operations by No.3 Indep. Coy in New Caledonia, 23 Dec 41 to 31 Jul 42.
64 AWM, AWM 54 565/4/1, Report on Operations By No.3 Indep. Coy in New Caledonia, 23 Dec 41 to 31 Jul 42.

relaxed life. Six months tinned rations had come with the company but these had been cached. No further rations were received from Australia. Food, however, was not in short supply although because pay from Australia for the soldiers was non-existent it resulted in making it difficult to purchase local produce. The matter was eventually resolved when French authorities began paying the men the equivalent of 2/10p each per day in French Francs.[65] With this money local supplies could be purchased. Even with the availability of local food it was only when the Americans arrived on the island in March 1942 that the Company was assured of a steady supply of rations. Replacement of clothing became a serious issue as no replacement clothing had been received from Australia. The Company eventually began wearing US military clothing once US Forces arrived, but kept their Australian boots and continued to wear their slouch hats.[66] From the point of view of the Australian military which had after its initial landing not supplied the Company at all 2/3rd Independent Company's sojourn in New Caledonia was got at a bargain basement price.

The Company did not squander its time. A small hospital was built, reconnaissance was conducted and preparations made to demolish the nickel mines and construct road blocks. Roads were built, motor vehicles repaired and water transport put to use. A communication network using radios powered by locally purchased car batteries was established which allowed communication with Australia. Despite this it was a rare event to receive any communication from Australia.[67]

To not pay soldiers, to not send rations or clothing, to hardly ever communicate with them indicates a serious abandonment of fundamental responsibilities by the Australian Army. The company had been sent away from Australia and then forgotten. This was not lost on the members of the company. Lieutenant John Winterflood stated that on departure from Sydney the Company had been left with the very clear message that they had been 'written off' and were not coming back.[68] Reinforcing this conclusion are the recollections of Lieutenant Ron Garland another officer of the Company who was of the opinion that the Company had been, 'dumped in a foreign colony without any administrative back up'.[69]

The Americans who arrived on New Caledonia were raw inexperienced troops.[70] It became apparent that they would require some tutelage in how to operate in a tropical environment. To this end Independent Company Sections were attached to a number of US companies as instructors. The experience proved a positive one with training

---

65 Ibid.
66 Ronald Garland, *Nothing is Forever: the history of 2/3rd Commandos* (Malabar Heights, NSW: self-published, 1997), pp. 32–6.
67 AWM, AWM 54 565/4/1, Report on Operations By No.3 Indep. Coy in New Caledonia, 23 Dec 41 to 31 July 42; AWM, AWM S04158, John Lewin interviewed by Neil MacDonald, no date.
68 AWM, AWM S04156, John Winterflood interview by Neil MacDonald, no date.
69 Garland, *Nothing is Forever*, p. 35.
70 AWM, AWM S04158, John Lewin interviewed by Neil MacDonald, no date.

being carried out in an amiable and enthusiastic manner. At the request of the US Headquarters a course on guerrilla warfare was conducted by the company for US Officers and NCOs. Some 2/3rd Independent Company Non Commissioned Officers attended a US mortar school.[71]

The men of the Company were constantly on alert and not without reason. During 1–4 July 1942 a four engine Japanese flying boat had appeared over the island. Japanese submarines had been spotted close to the island and there were reports of a 'fairly strong' Japanese naval force in the southern Solomon Islands. An attack was expected at any time. In May the Company was once again split into independent Sections and sent to the north of the island.[72] It was fully understood by the Company at this time that other than demolition of vital assets its primary role after a Japanese invasion they were to conduct a guerrilla war against the invader and to harass them as long as possible.[73] This was in marked contrast to the lack of any timely positive direction to the 2/1st Independent Company. This was at least some indication that the Army was coming around to appreciating how an Independent Company could be employed, even if at the same time it provided no support to enable the company to comply with its instructions. The New Caledonia experience came to an end for 2/3rd Independent Company in August 1942 when it was returned to Australia. It arrived in Brisbane wearing American uniforms and carrying American carbines.[74] Unit discipline had disintegrated. Lieutenant John Winterflood recalled, 'We were rabble of 240 men spoiled by NC French and wine'.[75] Not all of the company returned to Australia. Its Commanding Officer Major George Matherson remained and was seconded as a temporary Lieutenant Colonel and jungle warfare and commando instructor to the US Forces on the island. He went on to serve with US Forces on Guadalcanal being awarded the US Distinguished Service Cross for his service. He stayed with US Forces and went to Bougainville where he was killed in action on 30 January 1944.

The manner in which the 2/1st and 2/3rd Independent Companies were sent to war is a clear example of the very poor understanding of unconventional operations within the AIF in 1941. One Company had been deployed before the war with Japan had commenced and the other shortly after. Both companies had been sent out for opportunistic reasons. One was to garrison an indefensible remote forward defence line. In the second case the Company was deployed to bolster the morale of an ally and provide some hope of denying the enemy valuable natural resources if an invasion occurred, yet given no administrative backup to enable it to effectively do so. It is difficult given the context of these deployments not to reach the conclusion that the AIF Independent Companies

---

71 AWM, AWM 54 565/4/1Report on Operations By No.3 Indep. Coy in New Caledonia, 23 Dec 41 to 31 July 42.
72 Ibid.
73 AWM, AWM S04156, John Winterflood interview by Neil MacDonald, no date; Garland, *Nothing is Forever*, p.13 and pp. 17–18.
74 AWM, AWM SO4158, John Lewin interviewed by Neil MacDonald.
75 AWM, AWM S04156, Lieutenant John Winterflood interviewed by Neil MacDonald (no date).

were seen as expendable. Indeed this was the case for 2/1st Independent Company. There was certainly during 1941 and into the first months of 1942 no serious intention by the Army to effectively employ the full range of skills and attributes the Independent Companies had to offer. As a milestone in the evolutionary development of how the Army managed the companies during the Second World War this period ranks as the lowest point.

The second Independent Company raised in 1941, the 2/2nd Independent Company, would have a vastly different experience to the other two. Despatched to Timor it would ultimately find itself engaged in a campaign in which it was compelled to exercise every element of self-reliance, initiative and cunning to fight a guerrilla war for 11 months against the Japanese invader.

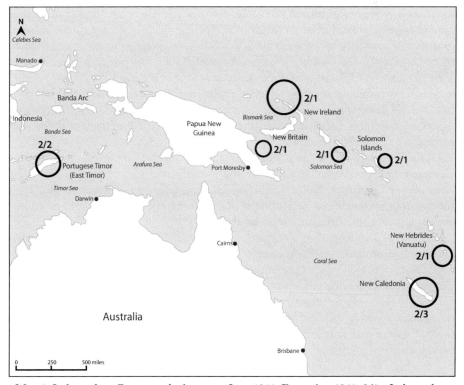

Map 1 Independent Company deployments June 1941–December 1941. 2/1st Independent Company was deployed across a vast arc from Kavieng New Ireland to Vila New Hebrides, 2/2nd Independent Company was deployed to Timor and 2/3rd Independent Company was deployed to New Caledonia.

4

"Surrender Be Fucked" – Timor 1942

The employment of the 2/1st and 2/3rd Independent Companies was done with little consideration for how to make use of the Companies in the most efficient and effective manner. In the case of the 2/1st Independent Company the results were tragic with the Company being annihilated. The 2/3rd Independent Company did not suffer that fate but instead it wiled-away its time on New Caledonia forgotten by the Army and contributing very little to the war effort. The 2/2nd Independent Company, the last of the three original Independent Companies, would find itself posted to the island of Timor and there, in contrast to the experiences of the other two Companies, become involved in an ongoing unconventional guerrilla campaign where it was able to inflict considerable discomfit on the enemy. The story of how the Company did that demonstrates a remarkable example of the fortitude, resilience and courage of Australia's Second World War Commandos.

During its training at No.7 Infantry Training Centre the 2/2nd Independent Company had been managed in very much the same manner as had the 2/1st independent Company. It did, however, have the advantage, denied to the 2/1st Independent Company, of being able to complete its full training cycle and subsequently operate for several months as a fully constituted company. In December 1941 the 2/2nd Independent Company was in the Northern Territory of Australia, a vast region of coastal tropical swamp and forest and inland arid desolate wilderness. Characteristically reflective of the Army's general management of Independent Companies at that time any serious planning or detailed instructions for what the Company was to do in that location were absent. This would change in December when the Company received orders to depart for Timor and join 'Sparrow Force', the AIF garrison already at Koepang; part of what would become the ill-fated Island Barrier chain of garrisons.[1] Typically, other than the Army informing the Company that it was going to be deployed, the purpose of the deployment was not initially made

---

1   This was Sparrow Force, consisting of 1197 personnel from 2/40 battalion, field artillery, anti-aircraft artillery, anti-tank, engineers, signals, medical and service troops, Defence of

apparent. Captain David Dexter was serving with the Company at the time recalled the confusion that characterised the move with an early briefing the officers received not mentioning Timor at all. The consequence of this was the consensus amongst the officers that they were being sent to Zanzibar.[2] It was not until a follow up briefing that Timor was mentioned. During this briefing some maps of Timor were produced and the officers given information on local climatic conditions on Timor.[3] It was at least now known that the Company would be expected to 'hold' Timor as part of the 'outer arc' to defend Australia, with no firm idea of just what this meant.[4]

The Company set sail from Darwin on 10 December and arrived in Timor two days later. Not surprisingly there was no specific function detailed for the company on Timor. The most they were aware of was a 'probable' role for them to defend the Atamboea airfield in the middle of the island, but as it transpired nothing eventuated from this.[5] It was not until 16 December 1941 that a specific task for the Company was found. It was decided to send 155 men of the Company and some 260 Dutch infantry to Dili in Portuguese East Timor. The balance of the Company, some 55 men, would follow on 22 December.[6] The object of the exercise was to 'protect' the Portuguese colony from the Japanese and prepare the airfield at Dili for demolition. Such protection was to be offered with or without the consent of the neutral Portuguese Government.[7] As an unattached sub-unit whose departure would not weaken any of the other components of Sparrow Force, despatching 2/2nd Independent Company on such a task was logical. It was also a bonus that the Company had been trained and equipped for demolition work. On the morning of 16 December the Company, went aboard the Dutch warship *Soerabaja*. The *Soerabaja* was coastal class defence ship, launched in 1909, and by 1941 it had certainly passed its prime. So decrepit was the ship that it was described by those boarding her on the night of 16 December as a 'rust bucket'.[8] Further to that the men of 2/2nd Independent Company were bemused by the main armament of the ship, twin 28cm guns, which being soldiers they misidentified as a single 10 inch gun. They were concerned that should those guns fire, their recoil could well sink the ship. During the night's voyage the men attempted to sleep on the deck to escape the crowded airless squalor and heat from the engines on the lower decks, only to be driven below by a sudden rain squall.[9] As it turned

    Australia and Adjacent Areas – Chiefs of Staff Appreciation, December 1941, see: AWM, AWM 124 4/105.
2   David Dexter interviewed by Mel Pratt for the Mel Pratt collection [sound recording] 1976 <http://nla.gov.au/nla.obj-221579220> (consulted 13 June 2016).
3   Ayris, *All the Bull's Men*, p. 51.
4   David Dexter interviewed by Mel Pratt for the Mel Pratt collection [sound recording] 1976 <http://nla.gov.au/nla.obj-221579220> (consulted 13 June 2016).
5   Ayris, *All the Bull's Men*, p. 51.
6   Wigmore, *The Japanese Thrust*, pp. 470–80.
7   Ibid.
8   Ayris, *All the Bull's Men*, p. 59.
9   Ibid.

out the Portuguese did not resist the arrival of the Australian and Dutch troops and 2/2nd Independent Company quickly set about preparing Dili airfield for demolition and reconnoitring the surrounding countryside. Unlike of 2/1st Independent Company the commander of 2/2nd Independent Company, Major Alan Spence, was an officer who firmly understood the practical realities of tactics and combat. Under Spence's guidance the Company set about preparing food and ammunition caches in the hinterland, and mapping the terrain to locate every point which could be used for ambush, observation or concealment, a fortuitous exercise considering future events.

As this was being done, malaria, the bane of all military operations in the tropics struck. There was no quinine available from Australian stores and what could be procured was got from the Dutch. Soldiers rolled it into cigarette paper in an attempt to mask the taste. It was, however, very much trying to shut the gate after the horse had bolted. Ultimately 95% of the company would succumb to the disease. Following this many men suffered from diarrhoea which was brought on by the unrelieved diet of Bully beef and biscuits compounded by the tropical heat and humidity.[10] Late December and early January were a challenging time for the company. During January things improved with a new camping ground being set up for one of the platoons of the company at a site called Three Spurs, after three prominent spurs in the area. Three Spurs was 10 kilometres out of Dili on the main road leading to Dutch Timor and provided fresh water and cool sea breezes. The men's health began to recover.

On the night of 19–20 February 1942 the anticipated Japanese invasion of Timor occurred. In the following days Sparrow force at Koepang was overwhelmed by Japanese infantry, parachutists and tanks and after a dogged but doomed defence was forced to surrender. The Japanese assault on Dili came on the night of 19 February. Dili was shelled and troops landed. Searchlights from Japanese ships illuminated the town. The timing of the assault was unexpected although it had been anticipated. The men of 2/2nd Independent Company were scattered in and around Dili as well as out at Three Spurs. At first it was hard for those in Dili to appreciate what was happening. The assumption made by some was that it must be Portuguese troops landing; the imminent arrival of a force sent from Mozambique to reinforce the Portuguese garrison had been rumoured. The explosions of shells from the naval bombardment soon dissuaded them of that misconception. Chaos and confusion reigned as scattered groups of 2/2nd Independent Company soldiers scrambled into what cover they could find. Telephone communication in Dili failed and it was impossible to know what was happening outside of the immediate range of the observer. As this was happening Japanese troops moved on Dili airfield. Awaiting them was Lieutenant Gerry McKenzie and No.2 Section who had been posted to the airfield prior to the invasion. Incongruously the Japanese seemed unconcerned as to what awaited them

---

10 Ayris, *All the Bull's Men*, pp. 75–76; David Dexter interviewed by Mel Pratt for the Mel Pratt collection [sound recording] 1976 <http://nla.gov.au/nla.obj-221579220> (consulted13 June 2016).

laughing and talking as they went; it can only be assumed that they had been told not to expect any serious opposition. McKenzie's Section attacked with Bren gun fire and bayonets killing a number of Japanese and forcing the rest to retreat, and as Japanese numbers increased continued to hold their positions and fight throughout the night. When morning came the Japanese under the cover of heavy mortar fire made a determined move against the airfield. Japanese aircraft circled overhead waiting to attack targets on the ground. Running out of ammunition and facing overwhelming odds McKenzie's defenders detonated the demolition charges that had been prepared on the airfield. The hangar exploded and large craters erupted on the airstrip. Left with little recourse the defenders withdrew ducking and weaving from Japanese fire as they did so. McKenzie and several of his men found a truck and drove off towards Three Spurs to raise the alarm about the Japanese invasion, only to be ambushed as they rounded a bend in the road. Fighting their way out of the ambush they remained hidden for the remainder of the day.

Other troops did not fare so well. One truck with 16 men on board had headed into Dili at 6.00 a.m. Those on board were anticipating spending the day on leave in town unaware of the Japanese landings. The truck got to within a few kilometres of Dili when it was ambushed. At first the men thought that they had been attacked by the Portuguese but this was soon dispelled when the Japanese began to bind their wrists with signal wire. Four men were separated from the group, and the truck driven off with the remaining 12 captured men in the back. The four who had been left behind were bound and made to walk towards Dili. As they were walking the party was ambushed by Dutch troops who fired machineguns. The four Australians jumped into a ditch by the roadside seeking shelter. When the firing stopped the Japanese recovered the 2/2nd Independent Company men from the ditch, stood them up and turned them around so that they were facing away from them. They then shot and bayoneted the four men. One, Private Keith Hayes, miraculously survived despite having been shot in the neck. He staggered off into a rice field and lay there until discovered by two Timorese boys who carried him to their village where his wounds were treated by their mother. All but one of the men who remained on the truck were killed. The lone survivor, Private Peter Alexander, recalled that the group had been ambushed by a machinegun, most likely Dutch. Several Japanese were hit and this put them in a very bad mood. The captured men were lined up and a signal wire passed through the binding on each man's wrists which bound them all together. One Japanese soldier brandishing a light machinegun walked up and down the line pointing at the tethered men and then at his weapon. Another Japanese soldier placed a cigarette in the mouth of each man. It was plainly apparent what was planned for the captured party. It was at that point that Alexander was cut loose from the line and led away to be interrogated by a Japanese officer. The officer was sitting under a palm tree a couple of hundred metres away eating from a can of baked beans. Alexander never saw his mates again and their bodies were never found. It was thought that their bodies had been incinerated.

Timor is a long narrow island some 466 kilometres long and 99 kilometres wide running on an east west axis. The country in the Eastern Portuguese section of the island into which the 2/2nd Independent Company retreated was mountainous with irregular roughly parallel ranges which followed the islands main axis. Mount Remelau (now Foho Tatamailau) the highest peak rose some 2,963m in the centre of a high plateau. In the north the mountains came close to the sea while they descended more gently in the south. The countryside varied between sandstone, slate and porous limestone formations, which was entirely infertile and along the coasts patches of flat fertile ground and mangrove flats. The eastern portion of the island was generally fertile. The vegetation varied from scrub with scattered Eucalyptus trees, very similar to that in northern Australia although there were more palm trees. There were a number of ridges covered only in stunted grass and some tropical growth in the wet stream gullies. The broad stony bottomed rivers ran relatively short courses and had steep banks. During the dry season from April to November these only held pools of water but in the wet season from December to March could transform into raging torrents. Access to this country from the lowlands, especially in the rainy season, was particularly difficult. Tracks were narrow and steep and not easily used. All movement in the mountains was only by foot. Roads suitable for motor transport could only be relied on in the dry season and were unusable during the wet season.[11] Such conditions would assist the company greatly in its guerrilla campaign. The indigenous population at the time spoke around 15 different languages with up to 40 dialects. The Company would associate with two main groups of indigenous people during its campaign. These were the Mambae, a rebellious, proud and resilient people who lived in the central mountain area, and the Noga Noga who were friendly but unreliable when it came to adhering to timetables. Up until August 1942 the indigenous people invariably provided invaluable intelligence assistance to the Company informing them of Japanese movements. They also acted as porters and provided ponies to carry stores, two vital contributions to the commandos. From August this support became much more problematic with many Timorese bowing to the inevitability of Japanese dominance and subsequently withdrawing their support from the Australians.

The Japanese launched two battalions against what presumably they assumed were the battered and desperate remnants of the Allied force in Dili. One battalion moved in from the right and one from the left. Rather than meeting disorganised and defeated enemies this move was met with aggression. Two platoons countered the Japanese move, one against the right battalion and the other against the left. The left platoon lost three killed and two wounded but killed approximately 40 Japanese before the Japanese got behind them and forced its withdrawal. The platoon that moved against the right arm of the Japanese pincer included men from McKenzie's Section which

---

11 AWM, AWM54 571/1/9, Report by Captain N.B. Trebeck GSOIII (O) Northern Territory Force on visit to Lancer Force, 20 Oct – 9 Nov 42.

had fought at the airfield. They encountered the Japanese force led by an officer riding a horse. He was shot and in the ensuing fire-fight thirty seven Japanese were killed.[12]

Meanwhile Escaping as best they could from the Japanese in Dili Captain Bernard Callinan and Private Cyril 'Budd' Doyle joined with four Dutch Javanese soldiers as well as two Timorese guides. They eventually found a small Chinese run shop and stopped there for a meal. While there they noticed a Buick sedan pulled up. The sedan belonged to the Portuguese Governor and was waiting there to take the Governor's wife, children and female friends on an excursion. Wanting something to carry them the 38 kilometres to Company Headquarters at Railaco, Callinan approached the ladies in the car. Despite his best efforts he could not persuade them to loan him the car. During this a Portuguese man arrived who said he could get a truck to carry Callinan. Before there was any sign of this truck, however, the driver of the Buick started the engine at which Callian, who had no intention of being left without transport, drew his pistol and persuaded the driver to turn off the engine. The truck then arrived but was of no use because it only had three working wheels. Luckily a 1925 Chevrolet Tourer was found as a substitute, and while this was being fuelled Callinan apologised to the ladies for the pistol incident. Callinan and Doyle then took the Chevrolet, driven by the same driver who Callinan had levelled his pistol at, on a precarious ride along a treacherous road to Railaco. It was a ride made even more daunting by the driver's habit of approaching every corner at top speed and only dropping down in gear rather than using brakes to reduce speed.

When Callinan arrived at the Headquarters he met with the five senior officers of the company. They realised that they had no communication with the outside world, no transport other than ponies provided by the Timorese, and no chance of receiving any supplies. They were also aware that they were vastly outnumbered by the enemy who were advancing out from Dili as well as up from Dutch Timor. There was also a story that the Dutch troops in Dili had been captured and massacred by the Japanese. Having no knowledge of what had occurred down south in Dutch Timor, and consequently presuming that Allied forces were still resisting there, the decision was made to preserve the fighting capacity of the company. This was to be done to distract the Japanese from using their forces in Dili to support their campaign in Dutch Timor. That such a decision was made, when the situation the company faced was unknown but undoubtedly precarious demonstrated the remarkable self-confidence and resilience of the Independent Company.

It was decided to move the Company across the Glano River into the mountainous country of the Timorese hinterland and then blow the bridge across the river. This would involve moving the Company's essential stores and ammunition which given the amount of material would be a major undertaking. With this Company Headquarters was withdrawn to Vila Maria which was 35 kilometres from Dili, 'A'

12 Bernard Callinan, *Independent company: The Australian Army in Portuguese Timor 1941–43* (Heinemann: Richmond, Vic, 1984), pp. 65–66.

platoon fell back from its position on Three Spurs. The plan was that to create the time necessary for such redeployment that harassment to distract the Japanese would begin immediately.

The move across the river did not come easy. Because of a chronic lack of transport, and fear that the Japanese, who in Dili were only half an hour away, would seize the stores, a great deal of heavy material including gelignite, limpet mines, booby traps, grenades and incendiary devices had to be destroyed. The smoke from the destruction of these stores at Three Spurs sent a great a mushroom cloud curling up into the air. The effort to move the stores was immense. Because there were no trucks everything had to be physically carried which included 100,000 rifle and machine gun rounds and 60,000 submachine gun rounds.[13] Porters and ponies, some of who were press ganged, were provided by the Timorese, which lessened the burden. The Glano River Bridge was a five-span structure made from steel and masonry. It was demolished after 'C' Platoon crossed. The explosion was obviously heard by the Japanese in Dili and they sent aircraft over to check out what had happened.

Communication with the outside world was impossible as the transmitters they possessed did not have the range to reach northern Australia. They did make contact with a Dutchman who spoke good English and on 9 March he reluctantly told them that the entire Dutch East Indies had surrendered to the Japanese and that fighting must stop. This news was met with desolation by both the men of the company and indigenous Timorese who were with them. Despite this it soon became apparent that plans needed to be made. There were three priorities which needed to be addressed. The first of these was countering the mass of rumours which threatened to undermine morale and resilience. The second was to ensure that everyone was kept working, and the third to maintain an offensive spirit.[14] Vigorous patrolling was instituted to deal with the first two challenges. Whenever there was a rumour a patrol would go out to check it, relying on the axiom that one could only believe what one saw for themselves. So frequent were the patrols the Timorese began calling it the war of 'Pigi Pigi', an allusion to the Australian's explanation to the Timorese of their incessant movement from place to place as 'pigi pigi Maria' or going to Vila Maria.[15]

In line with the intention to maintain the offensive spirit the first contact with the enemy came when a convoy of Japanese trucks returning from depositing Japanese troops was ambushed. The ambush was initiated by Lieutenant Tom Nisbet stepping out onto the road in front of the first truck and attempting to fire his Tommy gun at the driver. The gun jammed at which the rest of the ambush party attacked. As it turned out only one truck was stopped, which ran into a tree, its driver fleeing into the surrounding bush. The next day the Japanese responded by occupying and interrogating the inhabitants of a nearby village and from that discovering the location of the

---

13   Callinan, *Independent Company*, pp. 139–40.
14   Ibid, p. 66.
15   Ibid, p. 51.

ambushers. A fire-fight ensued in which several Japanese and two 2/2nd Independent Company men were killed.

Patrols went out to hunt isolated Japanese patrols and operated in very much a hide and seek manner, killing Japanese they encountered and then vanishing. In response the Japanese conducted heavy conventional attacks against villages suspected of harbouring Australians, they also fired randomly into valleys in which they thought Australians may be lurking. Added to this the Japanese carried out repeated sweeps to trap the Australians, none were successful, but what it did was to provide opportunities to harass the Japanese. This was aided by what was described as the 'almost unbelievable ineffectiveness' of the Japanese patrolling in the Timorese countryside.[16] Clashes with the enemy were subsequently frequent. In one incident 15 Japanese were killed when their truck was ambushed. In another incident two commandos stripped off down to their shorts, boots and socks and blackened their bodies with the grease and soot from dirty cooking pots. At night, in the Company of two Timorese, they crept into a village in which some of the huts were being used by the Japanese. They fired their Tommy guns and threw hand grenades into the huts killing the Japanese in them.[17]

The Japanese meanwhile made the first of what would be two demands that the commandos surrender. They did this by formal letter carried to them by Ross Smith the Australian consul and local representative of QANTAS airlines. In this demand the Japanese stressed that every other Allied soldier in the Netherlands East Indies had surrendered and that Japan had occupied New Caledonia, which was not true. The Japanese pointed out that further resistance was pointless and that if the Independent Company failed to surrender they would be considered as brigands. Drawing upon a rather liberal interpretation of its status the company informed the Japanese that it not surrender because it was a special unit of the Australian Army and took its orders directly from Army headquarters in Melbourne, and until orders were issued from Melbourne to do so it would not surrender. It was also not inclined to do so to an enemy which had shot unarmed prisoners as had occurred in Dili. The response given has been described in different ways depending on the source. These range from firm but polite rebuttals to a much more earthy 'surrender be fucked', sentiments which were not relayed in the official response.[18]

On 22 April Australia was contacted by radio. The construction of the transmitter which facilitated this communication was the product of the extraordinary initiative, knowhow and persistence of Signaller Max Loveless. The device was constructed literally from bits and pieces collected over a period of time from a variety of sources,

---

16 Ibid, p. 88.
17 Ibid, pp. 90–103.
18 Ayris, *All The Bulls Men*, p.196. The account which related this colourful response was second hand and claimed to be what had been said at a meeting of officers to discuss the Japanese surrender demand. The account came from a member of the Company who was nearby and is consistent with the character of the members of the Independent Company.

including thefts from Japanese occupied Dili. The device would become known as 'Winnie the War Winner'. Winnie occupied a room about 3.4 metres square. The room was cluttered with wires and bits and pieces. A generator which powered the batteries for the transmitter had been taken from an old car was connected by a rope and series of wheels to large wheel with handles that was turned by Timorese. This provided enough power for the transmitter to reach northern Australia. The first message sent on 19 April was by Morse and was simply 'YFC…YFC…YFC'. This had been the radio pre-fix for Sparrow Force. The message was received in Australia but only faintly because Winnie's batteries had gone flat. There was no follow up message, and because of this the message was treated sceptically in Australia. Nevertheless a response was sent from Australia and received in Timor. The following night communication was made again. Suspicious that the Japanese might be sending the message operators in Australia asked the name and address of the wife of one of the soldiers in 2/2nd Independent Company that an operator in Australia knew. The answer came back and with it confirmation that contact had been made with the troops on Timor. This radio communication with Australia was perhaps the most significant achievement of the Independent Company during its campaign in Timor. It not only informed Australia of the company's existence, but meant that the company was no longer isolated and a much needed lifeline with the outside world had been established. This would provide administrative and limited logistical support as well as the capacity to transfer staff to and from Australia and coordinate airstrikes against enemy targets.

Two systems of supply from Australia were established using Winnie. The first of these was from the air using Hudson bombers. The Hudsons dropped essential supplies as well as comforts such as cigarettes, newspapers, soap, playing cards and magazines. This was greatly appreciated by the men of the company. Supply from the sea was delivered by using small vessels such as the *Kuru* a small ship, which to onlookers looked like a toy boat.[19] Generally the supply service delivered appropriate material even though at times it failed. One such incident was when the company received new radio sets. The acid for the radios batteries turned out to be distilled water. Frantic messages were sent back to Australia to supply the acid. In the next shipment a bottle arrived which contained more distilled water. One more attempt was made and the acid was finally delivered.[20] Contact with Australia also provided the means to establish a mail system and it was permitted to write one letter a week. These letters were generally rather brief and voluntarily censored by the writers.

Contact with Australia also allowed the first evacuations to occur. Amongst these were Brigadier Veale and Colonel van Stratten who were to brief the army on the situation and the possibility of retaking Timor. Wounded men were evacuated as well, plus a written nominal roll of those present. When news was received that the evacuees had returned to Australia it was a great psychological boost for the Company

19 Callinan, *Independent Company*, p. 140.
20 Ibid, p. 141.

which felt that it had now re-joined the Australian Army after having been cut off from it. It was also felt that their relatives in Australia, who having no other news of Timor other than Japanese reports which had announced that all Allied troops on the island had been killed or captured, would now be given some hope. The departure of Veale required a reorganisation of the force and Major Spence who had commanded the company was promoted to Lieutenant Colonel and given command of the whole of Sparrow Force. Bernard Callinan was promoted to Major and given command of the Company.[21]

Maintaining efficient communication between the disparate elements of the company was vital. In the early stages of the campaign this was done using the Portuguese telephone system. This was a single wire party-line system listened to by more than the caller and recipient, which included the Japanese. Messages were sent by cipher and when plain speech was used sentences were constructed as batches of rhyming slang to confuse Japanese listeners. One such ruse was to refer to boots as 'daisy roots'. This was effective as the Japanese never did make use of any information passed on the telephone.[22] When new radio sets arrived after communication with Australia had been re-established it allowed the company to communicate with all its sub units along the entire 100 kilometres front of operations. At the peak Sparrow Force has 25 radio sets in operation.[23] Even so radio communication was kept to a minimum to prevent the Japanese triangulating the location of the company's headquarters. Consequently, the bulk of communications was still carried on the Portuguese telephone system.[24]

Fundamental to this campaign was the relationship between the Commandos and the indigenous population. Ensuring the maintenance of a good working relationship was essential for the Commandos if they wished to continue operating in the Timorese wilderness. Fortunately the Commandos were able to establish good relations with most of the Timorese they encountered, at least until August when a fundamental change in circumstances, which had been engineered by the Japanese, resulted in turning many Timorese against the Australians. While relations were good the indigenous people provided assistance by scouting ahead for any sign of the Japanese, supplying food and shelter, carry loads and providing pack animals whenever they were needed. Perhaps the most evident example of the close relationship which developed between the Commandos and the indigenous people was that of the *Creados*. *Creado* was the Portuguese term for the indigenous Timorese people, but in the context of the Commandos it was reserved for the young Timorese boys who attached themselves to individual Commandos.[25] The *Creados* proved to be unques-

---

21 Ibid, p. 112.
22 Ibid, p. 113.
23 Ibid, p. 171.
24 Ibid, p. 141.
25 'Creado' is the Portuguese term for the indigenous Timorese.

tionably loyal and would carry the Commandos extra kit, find food and shelter for the Commando, scout for him, and often at the risk of their lives assist him in any way they could. Without their *Creados* the Commandos would have found it immeasurably more difficult to operate effectively in the Timorese wilderness. The bond of loyalty and mutual trust that developed between the Commandos and their *Creados* became very strong. The *Creados* remained with the Commandos until the Commandos withdrew from Timor, that parting causing a great deal of sorrow for both *Creado* and their Commando companion. Ensuring supplies from the Timorese required money. This was provided in haversacks sent in the normal supply chain from Australia. Each haversack held £100 of silver coins. Originally pennies had been provided but the Timorese favoured the silver coins.[26]

The nature of the guerrilla campaign dictated that there could be no personnel who were not capable of fending for themselves. This necessitated organising some way of dealing with those who, for a variety of reasons, had been deemed to be 'ineffective'. Some 179 Australian refugees from Dutch Timor, including Brigadier Veale, the commander of Sparrow Force, had made their way into Portuguese Timor. These were mostly unarmed, many being from non-combatant arms such as dentists, butchers, bakers, postal, and even refrigerator specialists. Such personnel had no infantry training and needed to be brought up to a level of proficiency as combat soldiers to enable them to both defend themselves as well as contribute to the ongoing campaign. Those who required it were treated by the company doctor in the hospital which had been established at the town of Ainaro. They were then given basic infantry and Independent Company training and once their trainers were satisfied were fed into the company's platoons as replacements. It was important that everyone was able to operate as a rifleman in true Independent Company fashion. The company did not operate as a collective body but as independent Platoons and those Platoons further sub divided into independently operating Sections. This method of deployment allowed the company to strike at the enemy over a wide stretch of territory. This had a dual benefit in keeping the enemy off balance not knowing from where the next attack would come from as well as helping to create an illusion of greater numbers of Australians than there actually were.

To imagine the guerrilla force in Timor as a gang of freebooters would be entirely incorrect. A fundamental attribute of the force was its internal organisation and careful consideration of every move it made. Headquarters was established at a fixed location from which all administrative and operational instructions came. The Headquarters was not some shambolic collection of ragged fugitives but an organisation composed of numerous officers each with their own task. These officers undertook the roles of Brigade Major, staff Captain, signals officer, transport officer, supply officer, and pay officer. They liaised with Australia, organising resupply and distributing those supplies.[27]

---

26 Callinan, *Independent Company*, pp. 188–89.
27 Ibid, pp. 104–8.

"Surrender Be Fucked" – Timor 1942   73

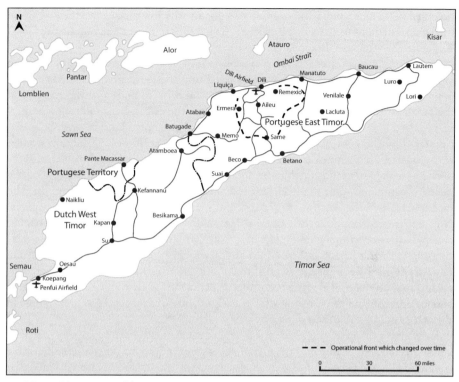

Map 2 Timor 1942. This map indicates the area in which the Australian Commandos operated. This area fluctuated over time with the ebb and flow of operations both by the Commandos and the Japanese.

The Japanese in an effort to curtail the guerrilla attacks established base camps in the hinterland. The necessity for the Japanese to maintain communications and supply with these camps provided the opportunity to harass the Japanese line of communication. Attacks on Japanese convoys mounted the tally of Japanese killed and they responded by establishing strong points along the roads from which patrols would venture out. These patrols, which invariably operated in a noisy manner, had little luck in contacting the guerrillas. The Commandos would shadow these patrols, paying attention to where they were camped. They would observe the camps and once the camps routine was understood mount raids on the camps.[28] Two or three raids a week

---

28 The Japanese use of noise was not entirely as inept as it may appear. Japanese troops often used inordinate noise to attract attention while an outflanking party was moving stealthily. They also used noise to improve their morale which was frequently challenged in the jungle environment. Japanese troops could, and did, mount silent attacks, but it was more frequent that they would be noisy.

occurred. Characteristic of these raids was one in which a camp was attacked while the Japanese troops were having breakfast. A short sharp burst of automatic fire killed 12 before the attackers disappeared into the bush.[29]

Never seeing the raiders and suffering constant casualties had a deleterious effect on Japanese morale. Japanese soldiers complained that the Australians seemed to jump out of the ground kill them and then vanish.[30] In an effort to find some way to hit back the Japanese encouraged the Timorese to turn on the Australians offering a bounty on the head of any Australian who was killed. This attempted largesse was, however, countered by the poor behaviour of Japanese troops in relation to Timorese women and property. In a sign of frustration the Japanese eventually began to blame every mishap on the Australians, which in its own way was a mark of the success of the guerrilla campaign. One night 11 Japanese soldiers had their throats cut in Dili. The Japanese blamed the Australians for this and searched the town for the guilty party. No culprits were found for this crime, although it was thought by the Australians that it may have been committed by Japanese Naval Infantry who had a very poor relationship with the Japanese Army.[31] In another incident two anti-aircraft guns were removed from their mountings and thrown into the sea while their crews were sheltering from the rain. This had been done by two Portuguese, but Australians were blamed and three of the miscreant Japanese gun crew were executed as an example to the others not to shirk their duties.[32]

Patience was an attribute which the independent elements of the company practiced and perfected. An example of the virtue of persistence was the destruction of a small concrete bridge which spanned a creek. The Japanese had for some reason decided that the bridge was important and place a permanent guard of forty men on it. Aware of this the guerrillas watched it for some weeks. Eventually the Japanese decided that the bridge did not deserve such attention and withdrew their guards. The bridge was blown up the very next day.

Being proactive was another fundamental attribute of the guerrilla campaign. When it became obvious that Japanese movement in certain directions would adversely affect the dispositions of the company, roads and bridges, which facilitated any moves in those directions, were damaged to retard any Japanese movement on them. Attracting the enemy's attention away from areas which could adversely affect the Company was also a ploy employed. One such effort was a raid into Dili itself. Twenty men under the command of Captain 'Bull' Laidlaw blacked themselves up and crept into Dili after dark. They passed silently down the streets taking note of houses in which Japanese soldiers could be seen. They remained undetected until a Japanese soldier appeared three metres from Laidlaw who promptly shot him. With this everyone

29 Callinan, *Independent Company*, p. 104.
30 Ibid, p. 104.
31 Ibid, p. 105.
32 Ibid.

opened fire shooting Japanese soldiers as they stumbled out of their beds or rooms. A covering party which had positioned itself on the beach joined in. As Japanese reinforcements rushed in the raiders withdrew. The following day the Japanese searched every house in Dili, collected and burned their dead and displayed a pile of Australian boots and clothing saying it had come from the raiders all of who had been caught and killed. There was no way of knowing how many Japanese were killed in the raid, but it was nonetheless a severe blow to Japanese prestige. Soon after the raid the Japanese, lashing out impotently, attacked and occupied the town of Remexio, but finding no Australians in it withdrew back to Dili. They did, however, increase their security of Dili adding barbed wire and posting permanent sentries on all important points.

It would be a misinterpretation of the nature of the Guerrilla campaign on Timor to presume that the Commandos were under constant pressure from the Japanese. Throughout May, June and July the Japanese made no attempt to challenge the guerrillas in the mountains. They seldom ventured beyond 20 kilometres from Dili with the town of Emera being their furthest forward garrison. They would eventually withdraw even from this, which allowed the guerrillas to occupy it and begin to harass the coastal road which ran out of Dili. Even when this road was damaged and blocked the Japanese made no attempt to clear it. It seemed that the Japanese were satisfied to hold and control the port of Dili and unconcerned what was occurring beyond it. The Commandos were frequently killing small numbers of Japanese in ambushes but this was not obviously of any great concern to them. Eventually Japanese reluctance to make contact with the guerrillas became a major frustration and the Commandos found that they had to deliberately harass the Japanese to get any reaction out of them. Just why the Japanese behaved in this manner can perhaps be explained by a comment made by the Japanese commander to David Ross the Australian Consul in Dili when he stated that his understanding of guerrilla warfare was that he needed ten to one odds in his favour to successfully conduct a counter guerrilla campaign. He did not have this number of troops, although he hoped to have them eventually.[33] Until he did it seemed he was content to remain relatively inactive.

The situation of Timor was very much a sideshow to what was happening elsewhere in the South West Pacific, but nonetheless, it was not ignored by high command in Australia. In June 1942 there was some discussion regarding Timor between the Australian Commander in Chief General Thomas Blamey and The Supreme Commander of Allied Forces in the South West Pacific General Douglas MacArthur. Blamey and MacArthur talked about whether or not to mount an operation to seize Timor or conversely to abandon it and withdraw 2/2nd Independent Company. It was decided to maintain the company on Timor to assist in any future operations that may be conducted against the island.[34]

33   Ibid, p. 135.
34   MMA, Historical Record Index Card GHQ SWPA G-3 Journal 3 June 42.

In June the Japanese made the Australians another offer to surrender. This was delivered by Ross. The Japanese considered the Australians to be in bad way because they had seen an Australian without a shirt which to their way of thinking indicated the privation of the Australians. The Japanese aware of the Australians reluctance to surrender following the killing of the surrendered Australians captured during the invasion of Dili assured the Company that those who surrendered would be treated as prisoners of war according to international law. When their appeals were rejected Japanese frustration was evidenced by the Japanese commander insisting that if the Australians were real soldiers they should come into Dili and fight it out man for man.[35]

In August the Japanese reluctance to engage the Commandos suddenly ceased. This coincided with the arrival of Japanese reinforcements. Now, perhaps because they possessed the required number of troops to counter the guerrillas, they finally moved against the Commandos. The Japanese concentrated some 2,000 troops and 1,000 pro-Japanese Timorese.[36] Four columns were organised with one pushing from the Manututo in the North, one from the South to capture Atsabe an important supply and command point for the Commandos, and two columns from the area of Dili and Remexio which lay just to the east of Dili. In responding to this offensive it was important for the company not to withdraw too quickly eastward to the far corner of the island. By doing so this would surrender too much territory and confine the guerrillas into a small area in which the Japanese could use their numerical superiority to grind down and annihilate the company. Consequently the company resolved to defend every ridge and spur until forced from them. Constant patrolling and skirmishing with the Japanese was instituted, but this combined with the lack of food and difficulty of transporting ammunition began to wear down the company. Some relief was received when supplies were dropped from aircraft from Australia while other aircraft bombed the Japanese. There was however, no hope to resist the Japanese in the long term. When the Company had been forced to retreat some thirty kilometres it soon became apparent that despite their best efforts not to allow it, they were being pushed into the extreme corner of the island. Faced with the choice between either gradual annihilation or surrender it was decided that the Company as a whole would counter attack one of the Japanese columns. This would be an all-out effort, a final battle in which the company would go down fighting.[37] The day set for the counter attack was 20 August. On that day the men of the company set out to assault the enemy. To their stunned surprise the Japanese could not be found, they had vanished.

A consistent feature of Australian accounts of the Japanese August offensive is that it was designed to destroy the Commandos.[38] It is not certain that this was so. The

---

35 Ibid.
36 AWM, AWM 571/4/55, Timor – Report on Operations.
37 Callinan, *Independent Company*, p. 152.
38 McCarthty, *Kokoda to Wau*, p. 608; Callinan, *Independent Company*, p. 143; Ayris, *All the Bull's Men*, p. 311.

abrupt cessation of the offensive certainly mystified the Australians. They sort for an explanation thinking that it may have been because the Japanese were running out of supplies or had tired of suffering casualties.[39] These reasons may have played a part in explaining what occurred, but there is another explanation which is equally compelling. The Japanese intention may have been to neutralise the guerrillas not necessarily to destroy them. Their offensive had succeeded in pushing back the Commandos some 30 kilometres into the undeveloped hinterland. Thus the Commandos no longer posed an immediate threat to Dili and its environs. By doing so the Japanese August offensive had achieved its purpose and its unexpected termination was explainable. Another feature which has eluded Australian appreciation of the August offensive is seeing it as linked to other events occurring at that time. At the same time as the August offensive the Japanese used aircraft to bomb almost all the towns in Portuguese Timor in an effort to disrupt the headquarters infrastructure of Sparrow Force; damage the morale of the Portuguese and Timorese and begin the gradual elimination of Portuguese administration in Timor. The Japanese at this time also pushed hard to dominate the indigenous population and turn them against the Commandos. They did so by employing propaganda telling the Timorese that Japan had bombed Portugal and destroyed it and that Australia had been invaded and occupied by Japan. They emphasised that the war in Timor was over and that Japan was now in control of the island. That Japan was master of the sea and thus had finished England and Australia. That Japan was not at war with the Timorese and that it was the white man who was the enemy of the Timorese.[40] The Japanese also employed the age old tactic of the carrot and the stick. They demonstrated unambiguously which side, Japan or Australia, was the most profitable to support. They did this by a combination of bribes and brutal reprisal. Timorese in general were not particularly interested in the war between Japan and Australia, but they could be motivated by payment if they cooperated with the Japanese and reprisals if they did not cooperate. These reprisals usually involved the public hanging of individuals as well as the burning of homes. Presented with a situation in which there was no protection from either the Portuguese or Australians the Timorese were left with the devil's choice; cooperate for material gain or do not and suffer material loss and death. Faced with such an option many Timorese acquiesced to Japanese demands. If the August offensive is viewed as only one component of an overall Japanese plan to link its counter insurgency operations to its intention to establish their dominance in Portuguese Timor the termination of the offensive when it occurred makes sense.

The consequence of this Japanese pressure was that armed bands of Timorese began to be sent out against the Australians. Such bands would normally number around 50 or 60 and be accompanied by a handful of Japanese armed with light machineguns.

---

39 Callinan, *Independent Company*, p. 152.
40 AWM, AWM54 571/1/9, Report by Maj. Bernard Callinan on the Situation in the Western Part of East Timor.

Clashes with Timorese became frequent while fights with Japanese, who were no longer venturing forth in large numbers, became less so. Throughout November and December most of the armed clashes the Commandos were engaged in were with these pro Japanese Timorese. With the numbers of indigenous supporters becoming less and less the Commandos found their operational range becoming more and more restricted. This aspect of the Japanese counter insurgency policy proved to be highly successful and would ultimately have a decisive impact on the ability of the Australians to maintain their guerrilla campaign.

At the same time a new war broke out, but this one did not involve Australians and only indirectly involved the Japanese. Incited by Japanese propaganda against the white man the Timorese of one region gruesomely murdered the local Portuguese administrator. The Portuguese colonial authorities responded harshly. Even with the Japanese occupation of Timor the Portuguese as a neutral nation had been permitted to maintain a military force on Timor. This consisted of two companies of infantry with a couple of machineguns. These troops, who were Timorese, moved against those who had murdered the administrator and burned every village and crop. They killed indiscriminately, carried off women and children, drove off any livestock and looted what was left behind. The Australians found themselves in a dilemma. They understood the Portuguese intention to restore the rule of law, but at the same time viewed with concern the disruption of Timorese civilian society which was not at all in the interests of Sparrow Force. Nevertheless such a war had come and was being fought with brutal relish by rival groups. Realising that it would be entirely counterproductive to declare for one side or the other the Australians remained strictly neutral; although they did make it known that any unfriendly act against them would be punished in a manner which would make the Portuguese actions look like child play. Ironically Portuguese successes against the rebel Timorese incited concern among the Japanese who realised that the Portuguese military campaign was restoring Portuguese dominance and control over Timor. Subsequently the Japanese imposed their authority on the Portuguese Governor who was their prisoner in Dili and the Portuguese military campaign ceased. To eliminate the last vestiges of Portuguese influence the Japanese created a 'neutral zone' into which all Portuguese were to move by 15 November. Any Portuguese found outside this zone after that date would be considered to be aiding the Australians and killed. The Japanese also began a program of removing recalcitrant Timorese from Portuguese Timor and deporting them to Dutch Timor and replacing them with more cooperative Timorese from Dutch Timor. The reaction from many Portuguese was to seek protection from the Australians and it was suggested by them that if their women and children could be evacuated to Australia they would fight alongside the Australians. Weapons were needed for this and a request was made to Australia for these, but no reply was received.[41]

---

41   Callinan, *Independent Company*, p. 178.

In September Australian reinforcements arrived on Timor. An advanced party consisting of Major 'Mac' Walker the Commanding Officer of 2/4th Independent Company and the Company Platoon commanders arrived on 16 September and the remainder of the company aboard the destroyer HMAS *Voyager* on 23 September. The landing did not go entirely according to plan. During the embarkation *Voyager* went aground due to the nature of the coast and tides in the area. Nevertheless by sun rise the company and all its stores had been landed, but *Voyager* remained firmly embedded. A Japanese reconnaissance aircraft flew over and was soon after followed by bombers. Despite dropping over 100 bombs only one hit the *Voyager*. Japanese aircraft also strafed the beach head area as well, but caused no casualties. Left with no alternative the captain of the *Voyager* ordered the ship to be demolished and it was blown up. Japanese aircraft harassed the parties of Independent Company soldiers and Timorese, which included many pack horses, as they moved away from the beachhead. One bonus for the Independent Companies was that weapons salvaged from the Voyager included some Vickers machineguns, although they declined the offer of an anti-aircraft gun as it weighed two tonnes and could not be packed onto horses to move.

The Japanese response to the wreck of the *Voyager* was to mass approximately 900 troops and move against the beachhead on 27 September. During this move the Japanese advance guard of 250 troops was ambushed several times killing an estimated 70 or more of them including their commanding officer and his second in command. Dissuaded by this experience the advance guard eventually turned south and went into Dutch Timor. This left the main body of 600 to 700 Japanese still to be dealt with. The Australians had some 200 troops to oppose them. The plan was to throw a force in front of the Japanese to delay them, and while this occurred send in parties to raid their flanks and rear. The plan, however, failed because the flanking parties lost contact with the Japanese who changed the direction of their advance. This mishap, however, had an unexpected benefit for the Australians as the lack of contact convinced the Japanese that there were no Commandos in the area and they departed. A further positive development for the Australians was that because the Japanese had brutally murdered two Portuguese priests and a Portuguese civilian they had encountered and burnt buildings in the town of Ainaro the local Timorese communities declared war on the Japanese. Even so the Japanese movements did compress the Australians into an increasingly limited area and restricted their capacity to manoeuvre freely. It also placed Japanese troops in positions from which they could move to surround the Australians.

Japanese numbers on Timor continued to increase through November and they began to press in from the north against the Commandos. It was at this time that orders were received by Sparrow Force giving it a new role. It was no longer to engage the enemy in anything more than platoon strength. It was instead to observe and report on enemy movements and dispositions. Consequently Japanese activity around Dili was carefully watched by hidden observation parties and messages sent back to Australia whenever a likely target presented itself. It now rained incessantly for hours each day, generally in the afternoon, and this restricted the ability of Allied aircraft to respond to calls. The inclement weather also upset radio communications with most messages having to be transmitted before noon. Even though boots were in short supply and this resulted in some Commandos not being able to join patrols opportunities to inflict harm on the Japanese still occurred. On 22 November a party of Commandos operating further east than they had done up until that time ambushed a vehicle containing five Japanese officers and they were killed. The Japanese, however, remained aggressive and maintained constant pressure on the Commandos. In the early hours of the morning of 24 November they attacked the village of Alsai in which Commandos were camped. Firing from higher ground they completely surprised the Commandos forcing them to conduct a hasty retreat. Despite their surprise the Commandos rallied and manoeuvred themselves into a position from which they could hit back at the Japanese. Moving from cover to cover they engaged the Japanese in a fire fight which eventually ceased and it was assumed that the Japanese had withdrawn. As with all fights at this time the Japanese had employed Timorese to assist them, and these had clashed with Timorese loyal to the Australians. It was claimed that in the fight two Japanese and 30 of the Japanese allied Timorese were killed with four of them being beheaded by Timorese loyal to the Australians. There was no record of any Australian allied Timorese casualties, although one old man was later reported as wounded implying that there were casualties. There were no Australian casualties. The same day a party of 12 Japanese were ambushed and seven or eight of them were killed.[42]

It was at this time that the Japanese began shifting their interest to the eastern end of the Island. They built air strips, began to build up stores of war materials and supplies and developed the port of Baucau in preference to Dili to unload and load ships. Significantly for Sparrow Force this new Japanese presence posed a fresh threat to the Australian controlled areas. As this occurred, the Japanese were becoming progressively wary and much more difficult to catch out with ambushes. When they did advance it was always slowly and carefully. In the meantime the Japanese continued to organise Timorese to attack the Australians. Because of these tactics it became progressively more difficult to isolate and kill Japanese and the spreading conflict and reduction in Timorese support progressively reduced the areas over which the Commandos could range. This began to have a serious impact on the areas, from which food could be collected, a vital consideration for the guerrillas. It was only along the north coast road that effective ambushes of Japanese could occur, but these could only be conducted with the greatest care as a constant watch had to be maintained to warn of roving Timorese-Japanese groups.

Incongruously, the military establishment in Australia continued to issue advice to Sparrow Force on how they should conduct their campaign. No doubt well-meaning such advice was based on ideas gleaned from combat experience in the deserts of North

---

42   Lambert, *From Tidal River to Tarakan*, pp. 159–61.

Africa and open country of the Middle East and included artillery support. Such advice was of no use whatsoever to Sparrow Force in the tropical scrub and forests of Timor. Subsequently, the advice was dutifully ignored.[43] Equally incongruously, in November word was received three journalists would visit Sparrow Force. Somewhat bemused it soon became obvious to the men of Sparrow Force that the powers to be in Australia wished to make something of a 'glamorous business' of the Timor Campaign. Despite their disapproval they knew that they had no option but to tolerate the imposition.[44] As it turned out Damien Parer, an accomplished combat photographer, who was one of the visitors, demonstrated by his obvious sincerity, commitment to his profession and cheerful good nature that his intentions were to present the Timor campaign in a professional manner. So impressed were the Commandos with Parer that any scepticism regarding the visit by the journalists quickly dissipated. The correspondents left for Australia on 17 November and with them went Lieutenant Colonel Spence who handed over command to Bernard Callinan.

It was also at this time that for security reasons the name of the Force was changed from Sparrow Force to Lancer Force.

Ultimately however, no matter how well organised or effective the guerrilla operations were the physical strain of the ongoing effort began to have its effect on the men. The primary concern was for health and wellbeing. The 2/2nd Independent Company had been in constant action in a tropical environment for nine months. On Timor there was no place that the troops could fully relax, no place to escape the constant strain and tension of watching for Japanese. Consequently many men were beginning to show symptoms of nervous distress. There had been a noticeable increase in the incidence of illnesses such as skin complaints, tropical ulcers and recurrent malaria. This was having a serious effect on the number of men able to conduct operations. From a grand total of 330 men only 200 could be considered fit for service. Boots and clothing were in also in poor condition. Suffering from a lack of balanced diet chronic dysentery affected all and with only 20 of the original company not suffering with recurring malaria, the health of the troops was precarious at best. So poor was the condition of the Company that Major General Jack Stevens the commander of Northern Territory Force described them in the best Australian vernacular as 'rooted' and insisted that they required rest and medical treatment.[45] As early as 7 September command in Australia considered withdrawing 2/2nd Independent Company and replacing it with 2/4th Independent Company.[46] This was argued against by other elements of the command who claimed that removing 2/2nd Independent Company would give a bad impression to the Timorese of Australian weakness, strengthen the

---

43 Callinan, *Independent Company*, p. 168.
44 Ibid, p. 182.
45 AWM, AWM54 571/1/9, Northern Territory Force to Land Force Melbourne, 12 Nov 42.
46 G. Lambert, *From Tidal River to Tarakan*, p. 82.

Japanese hold on Timor, and subsequently the Timorese would not support 2/4th Independent Company.[47] Even Major General Stevens, who by November most definitely had changed his mind, argued in October that to withdraw 2/2nd Independent Company would weaken Australia's position in Timor.[48] It was, however, given the parlous physical state the Company was in, inevitable that something had to be done to relieve it. Subsequently the evacuation from Timor of 2/2nd Independent Company was arranged and this occurred in stages between 10 and 16 December.

With 2/4th Independent Company now alone the Campaign on the ground became increasingly precarious. When the Commandos were forced to evacuate a region, Japanese allied Timorese war-bands burned out and looted those areas. This forced the Timorese population who had lived there to flee into the hills taking their livestock with them. At a stroke this removed indigenous support and food supplies from the Commandos and it became increasingly difficult to prevent the Japanese moving wherever they wished to. Daily clashes were occurring with pro-Japanese Timorese and consequently the situation for the Commandos became more and more difficult. By 31 December it became apparent that the Japanese, now moving at will, were poised to capture a vital food producing area which the Commandos relied upon. This would force Lancer Force into a smaller much more contained area against which Japanese forces could concentrate and ultimately annihilate the Australians. Faced with this it was decided to evacuate Lancer force and withdraw from Timor. This was achieved on 10 January 1943 using the destroyer HMAS *Arunta*. A small party of 2/4th Independent Company remained behind to spy on the Japanese, but this proved to be a forlorn hope and they were withdrawn by submarine on 10 February.

The Timor guerrilla campaign had continued for some 11 months during which for at least nine months the guerrillas maintained continual harassment against the occupiers and inflicted numerous casualties. This was in itself an extraordinary effort especially so as from its very beginning the campaign rested on a two factors over which the Commandos had little or no influence. The first of these was the nature of the Japanese response, which until August was not robust at all, thus providing the Commandos with the opportunity to take the war to the Japanese. The second and ultimately most important was the maintenance of the support for the Commandos from the indigenous population. This was often very supportive but it was never assured and would over time become increasingly tenuous. The Japanese are to be credited with devising and implementing a very effective counter insurgency programme in Portuguese Timor. They first neutralised the Australian threat to Dili and then manipulated the human environment to remove the support base for the guerrillas. That they were constrained in implementing this programme until August appears to be due to the lack of military resources available to them to do so. Once it began, however, the

---

47 AWM, AWM54 571/1/9, DCGS 17 Oct 42.
48 AWM, AWM54 571/1/9, Relief of 2 Ind Coy in Timor, HQ Northern Territory Force, 11 Oct 42.

progress to a successful conclusion was relentless and ultimately achieved the objective of ridding Timor of the enemy. From the Australian perspective there certainly was no strategic imperative for a guerrilla campaign on Timor. It occurred more by accident than design. Its impact on the enemy is problematic. The number of Japanese killed is invariably given as 1,500 in many sources, these being based presumably on the estimate given by Bernard Callinan.[49] In reality, however, this number is only a guess. Given the nature of the war being fought, one of hit and run ambush and raid, it could be nothing else. Official Australian records claim 300 dead Japanese from the period March to July 1942, apart from those killed in the initial landings.[50] The same source acknowledges that following that period no estimate of enemy casualties has been attempted, but does acknowledge that ambushes which were conducted were highly successful.[51] It is unquestionable that the Australian guerrillas on Timor killed numerous Japanese, certainly many hundreds, but it is debatable exactly how many this was. Throughout November and December 2/4th Independent Company almost exclusively fought against Timorese pro-Japanese war-bands.[52] Thus it can be asked how many of the claimed 1,500 killed, if we assume this number to be correct, were in fact Timorese.

There has also been a claim made that the Commandos on Timor distracted the attention of the Japanese at a critical time and that the Commandos occupied a considerable number of Japanese troops so that they could not be used elsewhere.[53] When one considers the relative inactivity of the Japanese in taking decisive action against the Commandos until August and the actual numbers of Japanese troops committed to Portuguese Timor those claims cannot be substantiated. The total Japanese garrison of Timor was approximately 12,000. This was a Divisional sized force, but it was not a unified force. One half of the force, some 6,000, garrisoned Dutch Timor and these were not immediately concerned with events in Portuguese Timor. The balance of the force, another 6,000, was in Portuguese Timor. The question must be asked how many of those troops were front line combat soldiers? It was normal Japanese procedure during its campaigns in the South West Pacific to included detachments of construction and maintenance troops with forces that seized isolated locations. Indicative of this was that the Japanese invasion force that landed in Portuguese Timor in February consisted of 1,000 Naval Infantry and 4,000 *other* troops; there was no explanation of just who these other troops were.[54] As we have seen Japanese concerns that they did

---

49 Callinan, *Independent Company*, p. xxviii.
50 AWM, AWM54 571/1/9, Relief of 2 Ind Coy in Timor, HQ Northern Territory Force, 11 Oct 42.
51 Ibid.
52 AWM, AWM54 571/4/55, Timor – Report on Operations.
53 Klemen, Forgotten Campaign: The Dutch East Indies Campaign 1941–1942, The fighting on Portuguese East Timor, 1942 <https://dutcheastindies.webs.com/timor_port.html> (consulted 27 Oct 2018).
54 AWM, AWM54 571/4/55, Timor – Report on Operations.

not have enough troops to counter the guerrillas in Portuguese Timor were given as a reason for them not taking action until August. This implies that Japanese forces prior to August were not as combat capable as they could have been, and that consequently Timor was not a staging post for forces destined from further aggressive adventures in the South West Pacific. Even when numbers were reinforced, with combat capable troops, allowing the August offensive to occur, only 2,000 troops were deployed. This hardly supports the claim that the Commandos were responsible for a significant diversion of Japanese military resources.

It is certainly the case that the Timor Commandos deserve praise. They were a remarkable, determined and organised small force that resisted against all the odds. Alone amongst the formed Allied units that had been overrun by the Japanese military in the early stages of the Japanese offensives they refused to surrender. This alone was an outstanding feat of arms and one for which those who participated in it can be forever proud. That the enemy prevailed in the end is beside the point as it demonstrated a spirit of courage, resilience, self-determination and fortitude which, when the story was finally released to the general public, offered a ray of hope in what was a very dark time in Australia's history.[55]

---

55 The Army did not release information about the Commando campaign on Timor until early 1943 see: P. Dean, *Australia 1942 – In the Shadow of War* (Cambridge University Press, Port Melbourne, 2013), p. 201.

5

Kanga Force – The 'Ragged Arsed Fifth'

On 8 March 1942 in a move to secure the southern approaches to the major Japanese base at Rabaul some 3000 men of the Japanese Naval 7th Base Corps which was part of Army South Sea Detachment landed at Lae.[1] At the same time a detachment landed and secured Salamaua. Both were on the north coast of New Guinea. All civilians had been evacuated from Salamaua on 22 January following an air raid the previous day.[2] Only a small force of locally recruited New Guinea Volunteer Rifles (NGVR) was in both places and as one NGVR man observed 16 Japanese ships sailing into Lae harbour while the rest withdrew into the surrounding jungles.[3] In accordance with a predetermined 'Plan G' the NGVR were to remain in the jungle and observe the Japanese until food supplies were exhausted, or further orders were received.[4] In the weeks that followed the Japanese made no move to expand their foothold and contented with preparing the airfields at Lae and Salamaua for their use. At the same time they reduced their garrison in Lae to some 1,200 with some 200–300 in Salamaua.[5] When circumstances permitted it the NGVR ambushed and killed the occasional Japanese, but left with little option they could do no more than get as close as they could to the Japanese and watch them. To assist them do so they constructed the DAWN observation post on a platform in a tree overlooking Salamaua, the TOJO observation post close to Lae and an observation post about 300 metres from Heath's

1 AWM, AWM54 779/3/119, Answers to Questionaire [sic] on New Guinea (Feb.42 to 22nd Jan 43) Milne Bay, Wau-Salamaua (Feb to Sept 43) + Huon Peninsula Offensive. Complied by Japanese Officers.
2 AWM, AWM67 2/1, Gavin Long notebooks, interview with Pte. H.W. Forrester NGVR.
3 AWM, AWM67 2/33, Gavin Long notebooks, interview with Lt. G. Whittaker ex.NGVR – Nadzab 6 Dec 43.
4 AWM, AWM54 741/5/15, Kanga Force, Reports on reconnaissance and observation Patrols and appreciations, – 1942–1942 Lae-Markham and Salamaua areas.
5 AWM, AWM54 779/3/119, Answers to Questionaire [sic] on New Guinea (Feb.42 to 22nd Jan 43) Milne Bay, Wau-Salamaua (Feb to Sept 43) + Huon Peninsula Offensive. Complied by Japanese Officers; AWM, AWM67 2/1, Gavin Long notebooks, interview with Pte. H.W. Forrester NGVR.

Plantation near Lae.⁶ Communicating via a system of flags, runners, horseback riders and homemade radio the NGVR reported Japanese activity at each location and guarded the tracks leading inland to Wau and the Bulolo Valley.⁷ They continued to do so as a platoon of the 2/1st Independent Company, who by fortunate chance had not been sent to New Ireland with the rest of their company, arrived. The Japanese remained in their Lae and Salamaua enclaves and while they were seemingly satisfied to remain inactive, the response of the Allied High Command to their presence was to be very different.⁸

General Douglas MacArthur, coming from the debacle that had overwhelmed American and Filipino forces in the Philippines, arrived in Australia by air on the night of 17 March 1942. He was welcomed as something of a saviour and immediately made supreme commander of all Allied forces in the South West Pacific area. In that role MacArthur cast an eye over developments in New Guinea. On 1 May he identified Lae and Salamaua as targets for a limited offensive against the Japanese, with the object of destroying installations there as well as possibly retaking them.⁹ The Commander in Chief of the Australian Army and Commander of Allied Land Forces, Lieutenant General Sir Thomas Blamey followed this up by identifying 2/5th Independent Company as being available.¹⁰ MacArthur responded to this by telling Blamey to conduct the operation as soon as possible, once the Coral Sea situation allowed it.¹¹ Plans for an aggressive move against Lae and Salamaua proceeded accordingly. The character of this operation was decided in a conference held in Port Moresby on 21–24 April, when Australian Major General George Vasey and US Army Air Force Lieutenant General George Brett, decided to form a guerrilla force to be known as Kanga Force and send it to Wau some 51 Kilometres West of Salamaua. The peculiarly Australian title 'Kanga Force' was the idea of Colonel D.D. Pitt attached

---

6   Warrant Officer Peter Ryan in a 30 Nov 44 interview with Gavin Long mentions the code names for the observation posts at Lae and Salamaua see: AWM, AWM 67 2/117, Records of Gavin Long, General Editor, Notebook No 117 (Fenton) – [notes on Kanga Force], Peter Allen Ryan 30 Nov 44; in AWM67 2/34 Gavin Long notebooks Maj. J. McAdam ex.NGVR – Lae 19 July 44, McAdam describes construction of a platform in a tree overlooking Salamaua; In AWM67 2/33 Gavin Long notebooks Captain H. Lyon ex-NGVR – Lae 6 Dec 43, Lyon describes establishing an observation post 300 yards from the Japanese at Heath's Plantation.
7   AWM, AWM 67 2/117, Records of Gavin Long, General Editor, Notebook No 117 (Fenton) – [notes on Kanga Force], Cpl Pl A.M. Wood NGVR, 9 Dec 44.
8   For a good account of the history of the NGVR see: Ian Downs, *The New Guinea Volunteer Rifles NGVR 1939–1945 A History*, Pacific Press, Broadbeach Waters, 1999.
9   MMA, Box 190 Historical Index Cards (Actual) Record Group 3 Index 3, MacArthur to Blamey 1 May 1942, General Headquarters Southwest Pacific Area (SWPA).
10 MMA, Box 189 Historical Index Cards (Actual) Record Group 3 Index 15, Blamey to MacArthur May 1942 (no date), General Headquarters Southwest Pacific Area (SWPA).
11 MMA, Box 190 Historical Index Cards (Actual) Record Group 3 Index 1, MacArthur to Blamey 4 May 1942, MMA, General Headquarters Southwest Pacific Area (SWPA).

to headquarters New Guinea Force.[12] Kanga Force would consist of those NGVR and the platoon of 2/1st Independent Company already in the area, a section of mortars and service personnel, but its main combat element would be 2/5th Independent Company. There was, however, no consistent idea amongst Australian high command on what the role of Kanga Force was to be. Vasey and Brett saw Kanga Force as a guerrilla force to harass the enemy. MacArthur and Blamey intended Kanga Force to be used aggressively to recapture Lae. Undeterred MacArthur's directed that Kanga Force attack and recapture Lae and Salamaua, and destroy artillery, radio stations, aircraft, and supply dumps in both areas.[13] It was expected that with the fall of Lae and Salamaua both places could be reinforced with Allied troops and that Allied aircraft could operate from them. By doing so it was hoped that any Japanese moves against Port Moresby could be delayed.[14]

The choice of 2/5th Independent Company for this task was not, however, a moment of sudden epiphany from the Australian Army. Rather it was a response to the Commander in Chief South West Pacific's desire for some form of timely combative action against the Japanese. As it so happened 2/5th Independent Company was available at a time when very few other trained troops were on hand. Even so the choice of 2/5th Independent Company did at least indicate that the Army recognised the tactical, and strategic, potential of such companies, a great improvement from its attitude in 1941.

The threat of a Japanese assault on Port Moresby delayed the deployment of Kanga Force. This was resolved following the Battle of the Coral Sea during which the Japanese invasion fleet was turned back and the threat of a seaborne assault on Port Moresby annulled. Subsequently 2/5th Independent Company and its attendant mortar section was flown to Wau on 23 May, the first time a significant number of Australian troops had been airlifted into a combat zone. Kanga Force Head Quarters, under the command of Major Norman Fleay, was established in Wau on 31 May.[15]

With Kanga Force on the ground it soon became apparent that the orders it had been issued to recapture Lae and Salamaua were impractical. Kanga Force's strength at its peak was approximately 500. Japanese garrisons in Lae and Salamaua numbered between 600 and 1500 depending upon the source consulted.[16] The disparity in numbers

---

12   AWM, AWM 67 2/117, Records of Gavin Long, General Editor, Notebook No 117 (Fenton) – [notes on Kanga Force], Maj Gen B Morris (CO NGF 42), 23 Nov 44.
13   McCarthy, *First Year: Kokoda to Wau*, p. 85; Bottrell, *Cameos of Commandos*, p. 142.
14   MMA, Box 190 Historical Index Cards (Actual) Record Group 3 Index 1, Draft memo from Col. E.L. Sheehan to A. C/S, 25 May 42, General Headquarters Southwest Pacific Area (SWPA). From G-3 GHQ.
15   McCarthy, *First Year: Kokoda to Wau*, p. 89.
16   Japanese strength in Lae was 6–800 and in Salamaua Was 100–200 see: MMA General Headquarters Southwest Pacific Area (SWPA) Box 190 Historical Index Cards (Actual) Record Group 3 Index 1, From G-3 GHQ draft memo from Col. E.L. Sheehan to A. C/S, 25 May 42; AWM, AWM54 779/3/119, Answers to Questionaire [sic] on New Guinea (Feb.42 to 22nd Jan 43) Milne Bay, Wau-Salamaua (Feb to Sept 43) + Huon

between Kanga Force and the Japanese, the physical demands of campaigning in an undeveloped tropical environment, and the likelihood of the local indigenous people disclosing Kanga Force's intentions, all conspired to render a successful surprise attack on Lae-Salamaua unworkable. Blamey had already informed MacArthur in May 1942 that Lae and Salamaua even if recaptured could not be supplied, and thus any garrison in those places would be untenable.[17] Colonel E.L. Sheehan of MacArthur's staff made the same point in a memo of 25 May 42 when he wrote that there would be no chance of reinforcing Kanga Force.[18] When confronted with the realities of the situation New Guinea Force, which had command authority over all Allied troops in New Guinea, responded with commendable flexibility and issued Kanga Force with new orders. The intention to storm and occupy Lae and Salamaua was abandoned. Kanga Force was now to harass and destroy enemy personnel and equipment in the Markham District, which included Salamaua.[19] It was hoped that by it mere presence Kanga Force would provide the means of tying up large numbers of enemy troops.[20] This would mean that Kanga Force would adopt the role of guerrillas, resurrecting Vasey and Brett's original intention.

The choice of 2/5th Independent Company for this task was a significant moment in the history of the Australian Independent Companies. This was the first time a deliberate and definite operational instruction had been issued for an Independent Company which reflected the whole range of the unconventional capabilities of the Company. It was an important milestone in the Army's developing understanding of and management of the Independent Companies.

The geographic region into which Kanga Force had been sent was most challenging. Kanga Force was to be based in Wau, a small gold mining town established at an elevation of 1,079 meters on high ground adjacent to the Bulolo Valley. The area Kanga Force was responsible for stretched from Lae some 74 kilometres to the North East to Salamaua some 51 kilometres to the East. Within that region between Lae and Wau lay the mostly unfordable Markham River and its valley, and numerous ranges of precipitous mountains clad in thick jungle intersected by deep fast flowing streams. The climate was tropical, the rain incessant and the dangers from diseases such as malaria, not to mention every other ailment the tropics harboured, extreme. When it arrived in Wau 2/5th Independent Company began to replace the NGVR in

---

    Peninsula Offensive, complied by Japanese Officers, states that the combined Japanese force in Lae-Salamaua was 1500.

17   MMA, Box 189 Historical Index Cards (Actual) Record Group 3 Index 15, Blamey to MacArthur May 1942 (no date), MMA General Headquarters Southwest Pacific Area (SWPA).

18   MMA, Box 190 Historical Index Cards (Actual) Record Group 3, Index 1, General Headquarters Southwest Pacific Area (SWPA). From G-3 GHQ draft memo from Col. E.L. Sheehan to A. C/S, 25 May 42.

19   McCarthy, *First Year: Kokoda to Wau*, p. 90.

20   AWM, AWM54 587/6/2, Kanga Force Operations Wau Salamaua 1942.

the forward areas, retaining only a few NGVR personnel as guides.[21] Those NGVR who remained with 2/5th Independent Company taught the newcomers the skills they would need to operate and survive in the jungle environment. With no experience of operating in the jungle the company certainly required lessons and teaching the company those skills fell to the old New Guinea hands of NGVR. One of these tutors was Private H.W. Forrester who despaired of what seemed to him the newcomer's total lack of knowledge of the basics of moving through the jungle.[22] Another, Sergeant Jim Cavanagh, observed that the company's personnel did not know how to conceal themselves, and advertised their presence because of the poor track discipline.[23] Learning the skills necessary to operate and survive in the jungle would be a priority for 2/5th Independent Company.

Throughout the first weeks of June Kanga Force conducted patrols south of the Markham River, and south and west of Salamaua.[24] At the same time plans were made to raid the enemy. Conducting raids was a fundamental aspect of the classic commando repertoire, and given their instruction to harass the enemy, was a natural focus for Kanga Force. Raids would not only harm the enemy but serve to distract their attention away from other Allied activities in New Guinea, such as the construction of airfields in places such as Buna.[25] Making a move on Lae was still an intention for Kanga Force, even if the intention was no longer to storm and occupy it. To this end attention was paid to Heath's Plantation which was some 14 kilometres from Lae and connected to it by road.[26] Eliminating Heath's would remove an obstacle in the way of an assault on Lae if any such was ever mounted.[27] Salamaua with its airfield and radio station was also identified as the target for a raid. As the days of June passed, planning to raid both Heath's Plantation and Salamaua commenced. By the end of June reconnaissance and planning for raiding both had been completed.

The raids conducted by Kanga Force at Salamaua on the night of 29 June and Heath's Plantation on 1 July were very much raids in the classical commando style. It is clear that the concept for both raids owed much to the commando ethos established by British Commandos during 1940–42. Kanga Force Intelligence Officer Lieutenant B. Dawson acknowledged this when he observed that the raids would be conducted in, 'the true spirit in which Commando troops were conceived'.[28] To this end the raiders were to appear unexpectedly, hit hard, cause maximum mayhem to the enemy and

---

21 AWM, AWM67 2/1, Gavin Long notebooks, interview with Pte. H.W. Forrester NGVR.
22 Ibid.
23 AWM, AWM67 2/34, Gavin Long notebooks Sgt Jim. Cavanagh ex.NGVR.
24 AWM, AWM54 587/6/2, Kanga Force Operations Wau Salamaua 1942.
25 MMA, Box 190 Historical Index Cards (Actual) Record Group 3 Index 3, General Headquarters Southwest Pacific Area (SWPA), 17 July 42.
26 AWM, AWM54 587/6/2, Kanga Force Operations Wau Salamaua 1942.
27 McCarthy, *First Year: Kokoda to Wau*, p. 99.
28 AWM, AWM54 587/6/11, 2/5 Independent Coy, Operations in New Guinea 25 October 1942.

just as quickly depart. As it eventuated the raid on Salamaua would be an outstanding success and the raid on Heath's Plantation a costly disappointment. An examination of each raid reveals how this was so.

Salamaua had been occupied by the Japanese since they landed there on 8 March. Since that time they had worked on the airfield and begun using it as a base for aircraft in transit between New Britain and Lae. Various defences had been constructed including weapon pits with mortars and machineguns on the isthmus connecting Salamaua town to the mainland, as well as a 6-inch naval gun emplaced on the peninsula.[29] The Salamaua raiding force consisted of 56 men, made up of half 2/5th Independent Company and half NGVR.[30] The raiding party began moving from Wau on 14 June and by 17 June had made camp at a site named Wireless Camp. While there Captain Norman Winning, the raid commander, and NGVR Sergeant and chief scout James McAdam conferred. It was decided that not enough reconnaissance had been conducted of Salamaua and both Winning and McAdam set out to do so. With the assistance of an indigenous guide they made their way through the jungle, negotiating a stream for two miles, crossing the Francisco River at a thigh high ford, and eventually found a site to act as an advanced base camp from which the raid could be launched. They then, in an exemplar of skilful field craft, infiltrated closer to Salamaua, taking up a hiding place in a building at the west end of the airfield. From there they stole into Kiela Village on the outskirts of Salamaua. Hidden they watched and counted the Japanese. On 25 June the main party moved closer to the site that Winning and McAdam had chosen for the advanced base camp. It transpired that insufficient rations had been provided for the raiding party, and a delegation had returned to Mubo, a village which lay to the East of Wau, to arrange resupply, but without success. Winning once he had completed his close reconnaissance also returned to Mubo to hasten the dispatch of rations. The failure of the rations to reach the raiders was later blamed on poor staff work, an indirect criticism of the Commanding Officer of Kanga Force Major Fleay whose responsibility it was to ensure that rations were available. The lack of food was becoming acute, even when supplies brought in by indigenous carriers reached the raiders on 26 June there was no time to distribute them.[31] Nevertheless the force pressed on. By 28 June they had arrived at Butu, the site of the advanced base camp. It was there that briefing for the raid commenced in earnest. The raiding party was divided into seven groups, each with its own objectives and responsibilities. Using a sand table model and aerial photographs every aspect of the raid was carefully explained. Rehearsals by each group for the tasks they were to undertake were conducted. Zero Hour for the raid was set for 3.15 a.m. 29 June.

---

29   AWM, AWM SO4152 Part 2, Mick Sheehan, 2/5 Independent Company, Interview by Neil MacDonald, 12 Jan 1986.
30   Ibid.
31   Ibid.

Between 9.00 p.m. and 10.30 p.m. on the night of 28 June, the ground leading up to objective was checked for booby traps and none were found. It was raining torrentially when groups began to move with one group occupying an abandoned house at the end of the airfield, where amazingly they slept until 12.30 p.m. Each group having moved into place settled and waited for Zero Hour.[32] The rain ceased about midnight. As it transpired Zero Hour would occur slightly prematurely. Shortly before time a Japanese sentry, who had been sitting on a log, got up and meandered over to where one of the raiders was waiting in the shadows to urinate. The Japanese soldier encountered Private 'Paddles' Hatfield and lunged at him with his bayonet. Hatfield parried the bayonet with his rifle. As that happened a Commando stepped forward and without hesitation fired his Tommy gun into the Japanese.[33] When that happened every Tommy gun with a target opened up, and raiders ran forward with grenades and bombs to houses in which Japanese were known to be. In the words of Norman Winning this resulted in, 'dreadful havoc'.[34] Some of that havoc was inflicted by Sergeant Mal Bishop who had worked his way into a position where he could see a group of Japanese inside a hut enjoying themselves in the company of two indigenous women. The moment the shooting started he and his comrades, which included one indigenous man, ran to the hut in which the Japanese were screaming like banshees. The Japanese soldiers, now aroused were scrambling to get through the front door of the hut.[35] In Bishop's right hand he held a sticky bomb which had two slabs of TNT attached to boost its power, and he fired his pistol from his left hand. The Japanese were fighting each other to get through the door. Bishop looked at his bomb and suddenly realised that he had no idea if he had pulled the pin to ignite the fuse on the bomb or not. With only seven seconds before it exploded he threw his pistol away, which being on a lanyard around his neck flicked around to hit him in the back. He fumbled in a panic to find the pin and then in desperation threw the bomb and turned for cover. The bomb erupted blowing the roof off the hut and collapsing its walls. Bishop was hit in the back from a round fired, he guessed from a Japanese soldier in the hut prior to the explosion. Taking cover behind a seawall an indigenous man who had been with Bishop all the time excitedly thrust a Tommy gun into Bishop's hands and cried, 'Masta killim Japan, killim Japan'. Firing his Tommy gun and now bleeding heavily he leaped up and ran back towards the now blazing hut.

---

32 AWM, AWM54 419/1/11, Operation Reconnaissance + Intelligence Reports from Nos 3 + 5 Independent Company, Signed by Capt N.I. Winnng. No 2 Company report on Salamaua Raid – July 1942. No 3 Company Report New Caledonia – Dec 41 to July 1942.
33 Pirie, 'Commando – Double Black', p. 73.
34 AWM, AWM54 419/1/11, Operation Reconnaissance + Intelligence Reports from Nos 3 + 5 Independent Company, Signed by Capt N.I. Winnng. No 2 Company report on Salamaua Raid – July 1942. No 3 Company Report New Caledonia – Dec 41 to July, p. 4.
35 AWM, AWM SO4152 Part 2, Mick Sheehan, 2/5 Independent Company, Interview by Neil MacDonald, 12 Jan 1986.

The Japanese were running about and screaming as Bishop shot them down.[36] The role of indigenous men in the raid is an interesting one. Lieutenant Michael Sheehan recalled that the indigenous men who were with the raiders were absolutely loyal and hated the Japanese. He reported that it was difficult to dissuade them from joining the raid. The problem for the raiders in this was that it was feared that the indigenous men would take the opportunity to massacre the Japanese with their machetes and tomahawks. Just why this was a problem was not explained although it may have been that the Japanese would have taken vengeance on the local indigenous people if they had suffered casualties to what was obviously indigenous weaponry. Disrupting the local indigenous population in this manner would have not been in the interests of the company. Rather than allow the indigenous men to actively participate in the fighting they were used as carriers.

While this was occurring other raiders were making their mark. There was a float plane in the harbour. The pilot was attempting to get back to his aircraft when he was shot and killed and a satchel he was carrying was recovered. One of the raiding groups was a mortar section and this, sited on high ground overlooking the town, lobbed bombs onto the weapon pits at the isthmus. The dreadful havoc went on for 57 minutes when with Japanese resistance stiffening and Japanese machineguns becoming more dangerous by the minute Winning ordered a withdrawal. This was successfully achieved despite Japanese tracer fire from six Japanese machineguns cutting the air just above the raider heads.[37]

The raid was an outstanding success. Casualties inflicted on the Japanese could only be guessed. For the cost of three raiders slightly wounded Winning claimed 100 dead Japanese from his own estimates and reports he received from NGVR scouts and indigenous witnesses in the days following.[38] Japanese sources admitted to various totals with one naval infantryman claiming 16 of his platoon killed and 11 wounded, another from the Naval Defence Unit in Lae claiming 24 killed and 7 wounded.[39] Tuai, an indigenous man of the Sepik district was in Salamaua during the raid. The next day he counted 56 dead Japanese and heard of five more that had been killed.

36   Mal Bishop, interview with Dr Peter Williams, 2004.
37   AWM, AWM54 419/1/11, Operation Reconnaissance + Intelligence Reports from Nos 3 + 5 Independent Company, Signed by Capt N.I. Winnng. No 2 Company report on Salamaua Raid – July 1942. No 3 Company Report New Caledonia – Dec 41 to July 1942, 'N.G. Force Intelligence Report No. 35 Appendix A6. Report from G. Archer (Guide to Lieut. O'Loughlin's party'.
38   McCarthy, *First Year: Kokoda to Wau*, p. 96; AWM, AWM SO41173, Michael Sheehan 2/5th Independent Company interviewed by Neil MacDonald, no date.
39   AWM, AWM55 1/6, ATIS SWPA Bulletins Nos 426–455 27 Sept to 13 October 43, B439 5 Oct 43, Item 14, 4705. Diary of Fireman 1st Class Wasaburo Ito – Miyata Buto Tanaka Tai Uraguchi Tai, 15 Nov 40–21 Jul 42, AWM55 1/6; ATIS SWPA Bulletins Nos 526–565 24 Nov to 18 Dec 43, B546 6 Dec 43, Item 1 7001, Mimeographed file in diary form 25 Jun 42–30 May 43–82 Defence Unit LAE (Naval).

He said he had seen all the bodies and had seen them burned by the Japanese.[40] Mala another indigenous man from Wanimo said that he had heard that 30 Japanese had been killed.[41] A most important result of the raid was the capture of documents contained in the Japanese pilot's satchel. The actual content of these documents has been credited in numerous accounts both primary and secondary as being plans for the Japanese landings at Buna, and plans for the Japanese assault on Milne Bay.[42] This was not the case. The Document in question, which became known in Allied Intelligence circles as the 'Kanga Document', was in fact a list of dates and locations which troops from the No.14 Construction Unit and part of the No.5 Sasebo Special Naval Landing Party would land and construct infrastructure most likely airfields beginning 16 July. These locations were Kavieng, Guadalcanal, Lae and Eastern New Guinea. As the Japanese did not yet have a presence in Eastern New Guinea Allied intelligence assumed that this referred to either Buna or Milne Bay.[43] Such information was useful in that it indicated Japanese interest in Eastern New Guinea and intentions. It was not, however, a revelation of an imminent invasion or of a location for that invasion. Allied High Command was already aware of Japanese plans to establish themselves in Eastern New Guinea. MacArthur had written to Blamey on 1 May advising him of Japanese plans to soon move against the north east coast of New Guinea emphasising the need for the navy and air force to resist such moves.[44] Buna and Milne Bay, both in Eastern New Guinea, had already been recognised as sites of strategic interest. Steps had been taken as early as June to begin preparing Milne Bay for defence and development of an airbase at Buna had been earmarked for similar attention. The 'Kanga Document' did add to this general concern, and recommendations were made to assemble a force to intercept any attempt by the Japanese to land.[45] Such recommendations were never actioned, thus calling into question the ultimate value of the 'Kanga Document'.

On the night of 1 July Heath's Plantation was raided. Heath's Plantation was situated some 14 kilometres to the southwest of Lae and connected to Lae by road. It had since the Japanese landing at Lae, been garrisoned by a Japanese force which from

40   AWM, AWM54 587/7/20, Report on Japanese Attack on Mubo Interrogation of Native wounded and captured from Japanese patrols July 1942.
41   Ibid.
42   Michael Sheehan, who took part in the raid, claims that the plans were for the attack on Milne Bay, see: AWM, AWM SO4152 Part 2, Mick Sheehan – 2/5th Independent Company, Interview by Neil MacDonald, 12 Jan 1986; Pirie, *Commando Double Black*, p.78 claims that the Japanese pilot had plans for the invasion of New Guinea and that his satchel contained maps of the invasion.
43   MAA, Box 190 Historical Index Cards (Actual) Record Group 3, Index 3, General Headquarters Southwest Pacific Area (SWPA).
44   MAA, Box 190 Historical Index Cards (Actual) Record Group 3 Index 2, General Headquarters Southwest Pacific Area (SWPA) McArthur to Blamey 1 May 42.
45   MAA, Box 190 Historical Index Cards (Actual) Record Group 3 Index 3, General Headquarters Southwest Pacific Area (SWPA).

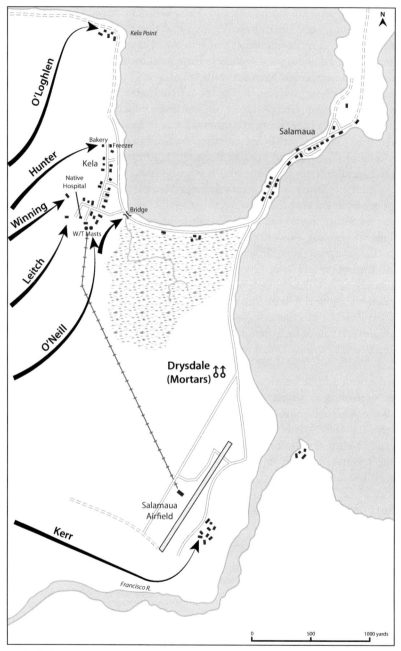

Map 3 The Salamaua Raid 28 June 1942. 2/5th Independent Company and the New Guinea Volunteer Rifles raided Salamaua on the night of 28 June in a highly successful operation against an enemy force many times greater than their own.

about 24 April included a light artillery gun.⁴⁶ Since the Japanese landings in March Heath's had been under constant observation by elements of the NGVR. On 15 June patrols conducted close reconnaissance.⁴⁷ It was originally intended for Heath's to be the first place raided, but this was not to be.⁴⁸

The raiding force consisted of 54 men mostly from 2/5th Independent Company accompanied by several NGVR who acted as guides and scouts.⁴⁹ The force was under the command of Major Paul Kneen, who we have met before as an intelligence officer on New Caledonia in June 1941, and who was now the commanding officer of 2/5th Independent Company. The objective of the raid was to destroy Japanese soldiers and equipment and capture documents.⁵⁰ It was, like Salamaua, to be a classic commando raid. The intention was to infiltrate as close as possible to the Japanese in the early hours of the morning, attack suddenly, kill as many Japanese as possible, destroy the plantation house and the light artillery piece which was there, and then withdraw. The party would also blow up the bridge on the road from Lae. An air attack on Lae had been promised the day following the raid to disrupt any Japanese plans to pursue the raiders.⁵¹ While he fortified his men with a nip of Scotch liberated from a NGVR dump, and allowed the men to have a smoke, Kneen studied the sand table model of the Plantation that had been prepared.⁵²

Unfortunately for the raiders several factors conspired to thwart their plans. The first of these was the late return of one of the forward scouts, who had been forced to lie motionless beneath a log as Japanese sat on it. He only managed to return to the raiding party at 10.30 p.m. which delayed the planned time for the raid to commence. The second was the bright moonlight of that night. Two men whose task was to kill Japanese sentries could not get close to their targets because of the moonlight. The third was a dog which began barking when it sensed the approaching raiders and woke the Japanese in the Plantation house. This forced one raider group to go to ground.⁵³ Not knowing that one group had been delayed the raiders tasked with killing the sentries attacked with fire and grenades at 2.20 a.m. This caught the group which had been delayed by the dog by surprise. Not knowing what else to do they withdrew to re-join Major Kneen and then began to fire into the Plantation house. There was a mist and some Japanese, mistaken in the confusion for the group of raiders who had withdrawn due to the dog, ran into it and escaped. About this time the bridge, which had been prepared for demolition by one raider party, exploded. The Japanese artillery gun began firing sending in a period of about fifteen minutes two or three shells

46 McCarthy, *First Year: Kokoda to Wau*, p. 63.
47 Ibid, p. 97.
48 Ibid, p. 89.
49 Ibid, p. 97.
50 Pirie, 'Commando – Double Black', p. 85.
51 McCarthy, *First Year: Kokoda to Wau*, p. 97.
52 Pirie, 'Commando – Double Black', p. 85.
53 McCarthy, *First Year: Kokoda to Wau*, p. 98.

towards the raiders. As fate would have it one of these shells struck Kneen in the chest exploding on impact and killing him instantly.[54] It was at that moment that the raid began to unravel. Because of a dispute with the NGVR contingent, prior to the raid, in which the NGVR refused to accept a 2/5th Independent Company officer as second in command, there had been no second in command appointed and subsequently no provision made for the eventuality of the loss of Kneen.[55] Left without a leader, confusion reigned. A Japanese machinegun somewhere behind the raiders began to fire.[56] With tracer rounds coming at them it was decided to abandon packs and retreat and this occurred in a shambolic fashion.[57] Any plans to destroy the artillery gun were abandoned. The confusion continued until Lieutenant Mal Wylie assumed command and ordered a withdrawal. They did so carrying two wounded with them and leaving Kneen's body behind.[58]

The raid on Heath's Plantation raid was not a success. The physical results of the raid were inconsequential. The destruction of the artillery gun, a primary objective, was not achieved. Not nominating a second in command, dividing the raiding party into separate groups with no ability to communicate with each other, and not considering the problems of bright moonlight all compromised the integrity of the mission. Such failings highlighted the inexperience of the raiders. The official score of Japanese killed in the raid was 43, although this was later acknowledged was purely guesswork and could not be substantiated.[59] The Japanese 82 Defence Unit LAE (Naval) reported that 16 enlisted men killed in action in the Lae area on 1 July. It also reported that 4 had been despatched to the base hospital aboard ship.[60] It is not certain that this refers to the raid on Heath's but the date matches and 'Lae area' does indicate this to be so. In his official history *First Year: Kokoda to Wau* Dudley McCarthy goes to pains to cast the raid in a positive light by observing that an unexpected blow in the guerrilla

---

54 AWM, AWM54 589/7/81, Report on Operations in the Lae Markham Area – Effect of raid on Heath's plantation Observation by Medical Officer.
55 Downs, *The New Guinea Volunteer Rifles NGVR 1939–1943*, p. 211.
56 McCarthy, *First Year: Kokoda to Wau*, p. 99; AWM, AWM54 589/7/81, Report on Operations in the Lae Markham Area – Effect of raid on Heath's plantation Observation by Medical Officer.
57 AWM, AWM54 589/7/81, Report on Operations in the Lae Markham Area – Effect of raid on Heath's plantation Observation by Medical Officer.
58 McCarthy, *First Year: Kokoda to Wau*, p. 99.
59 AWM, AWM 54 511/7/2, Observation Reports Kanga Force, Lae July 1942. Fleay reports 'at least 41' Japanese killed in the raid, this number was later changed to 43 which has become the standard claim for casualties inflicted in the raid: see for example McCarthy, *First Year: Kokoda to Wau*, p. 99, and Bottrell, A, *Cameos of Commandos*, p. 142; It was recognised, however, that such claims could not be substantiated. AWM 54 578/9/1, The History of Kanga Force Account of the activities of New Guinea Volunteer Rifles an Kanga Force from, March 1942 to January 1943, states that, 'There is no basis for numbers of enemy claimed to be have been killed at Heaths'.
60 AWM, AWM55 1/9, ATIS SWPA Bulletins Nos 526–565 24 Nov. to 18 Dec 1943, B546 6 Dec 43, Item 1 7001.

tradition had been struck at the invaders.⁶¹ Despite McCarthy's upbeat assessment it is difficult to identify any positive outcomes from the raid. The raid certainly did not compromise or discomfort the Japanese occupation of Lae or even Heath's Plantation in any way. It was the case that the raid provided the raiders with combat experience, but this had been mismanaged and its value questionable. Perhaps the only positive outcome was that if nothing else it provided an example of what not to do next time.

In response to the Salamaua raid the Japanese bombed Mubo and Komiatum, two significant features between Salamaua and Wau. They also conducted air raids on Wau and Bulolo. They flew aircraft low over the mountain trails and send a patrol or 90 men out into the foothills. Kela village adjacent to Salamaua was converted into a strongly held position, 200 reinforcements were brought over from Lae to Salamaua, and by 16 July it was estimated that the Salamaua garrison was 400–500.⁶² More pointedly the Japanese took out their vengeance on hapless indigenous people who happened to venture near Salamaua shooting a group, who had paddled their canoes into the waters nearby, and bombing and strafing other canoes.⁶³ Soon after the raid, a Japanese patrol, led by indigenous guides, moved towards Mubo. The patrol was ambushed by elements of 2/5th Independent Company and a number of Japanese and their guides were killed.⁶⁴ In reaction to this the Japanese began to patrol more cautiously and only in significant numbers. This made it difficult for Kanga Force to strike at the Japanese, other than by sniping.⁶⁵ Such developments were seen by some as a counterproductive outcome of both the raids. Sergeant McAdam of NGVR was convinced that with a few more men the raiders could have captured Salamaua, and by failing to capture it only incited the Japanese to increase their activities which resulted in Kanga Force being unable to conduct effective reconnaissance patrols.⁶⁶ The Japanese response to the raid at Heath's Plantation was energetic. They sent out aircraft to strafe and bomb tracks leading out from Heath's sending at one stage a Zero airplane and 30–40 men to hunt down any raiders still lurking in the area.⁶⁷ Other air attacks were made against the Ngasawapum and Nadzab areas which were

---

61   McCarthy, *First Year: Kokoda to Wau*, p. 99.
62   McCarthy, *First Year: Kokoda to Wau*, p. 100; Allan Walker, *The Island Campaigns, Australia in the War of 1939–1945*, Series Five Medical, Volume III, Australian War Memorial, Canberra, 1957, p. 129.
63   AWM, AWM54 419/1/11, Report on Japanese Attack on Mubo Interrogation of Indigenous wounded and captured from Japanese patrols July 1942; AWM, AWM54 419/1/11, N.G. Force Intelligence Report No.35 Appendix A3 (4–11 JULY 42). To C.O. Kanga Force Ex Sgt. McAdam. J.B.
64   McCarthy, *First Year: Kokoda to Wau*, p. 100.
65   AWM, AWM54 587/6/11, 2/5 Independent Coy, Operations in New Guinea 25 October 1942, Lieut. B. Dawson 2/22 Bn and I.O. Kanga Force.
66   AWM, AWM67 2/34, Gavin Long notebook 34, Maj. J. McAdam ex.NGVR – Lae 19 July 44.
67   AWM, AWM67 2/33, Gavin Long notebooks interview with Captain H. Lyon ex.NGVR – Lae 6 Dec 43.

further inland.⁶⁸ Although they caused no casualties to Kanga Force one consequence of these air attacks was that it frightened the indigenous carriers who deserted in large numbers and created a major supply problem for Kanga Force.⁶⁹

Despite the problematic practical outcome of the raids they did offer a moment of optimism for the Allied cause. The Salamaua raid was the first occasion in which Allied land forces had taken the war successfully to the Japanese since the beginning of the war in the South West Pacific. This provided a morale boost for both Allied headquarters and the general public. The Australian press drew parallels between the Salamaua raid and the raids by British Commandos, and extolled the raid as signifying a change of the fortunes of the Allied cause since the fall of Singapore.⁷⁰ Further afield the Editorial of the *New York Times* hailed the Salamaua raid as a possible precursor to an offensive against the Japanese.⁷¹ There were even suggestions that such raids should occur on a grand scale and that by doing so, 'the Allies could smash the enemy and seize control of all of New Guinea.'⁷² There was, however, no indication that the army's high command was about to embark on a campaign of commando offensives against the Japanese. There were several Independent Companies available by mid-1942 and the army made no use of them in such a role, indeed all but 2/5th Independent Company, and 2/2nd and later 2/4th Independent Companies on Timor, sat idle in Australia until August 1942 when one only was released for service along the Kokoda track.

When the Japanese landed at Gona and Buna on 21 July 1942 and began their overland campaign aimed at Port Moresby Allied High Command was forced to respond with all its strength to that mortal threat. All thoughts of operations outside the immediate Papuan area were pushed to the side. Kanga Force being located at Wau, far from the primary theatre of operations was quickly relegated to a sideshow. It is with this second phase of its experience that the Kanga Force narrative continues.

For Kanga Force the six months following the raids on Salamaua and Heath's Plantation were characterised as months of frustration. During this period the role of Kanga Force devolved to one of defending its own supply lines and trying to coax the enemy to stretch his own lines of communication and by so doing open himself to

68 Pirie, 'Commando Double Black', p. 96.
69 Downs, *The New Guinea Volunteer Rifles*, p. 211.
70 *Maryborough Chronicle, Wide Bay and Burnett Advertiser*, Friday 3 July 1942, p. 2, 'Salamaua Raid is Omen of Greater Offensives to Be'.
71 New York Times Editorial, *Cairns Post*, Friday 3 July 1942, p. 4, 'Raid a Beginning'.
72 *Sunday Mail*, Sunday 5 July 1942, p. 2, 'Too Soon For Major Move From Australia – Bigger U.S.A. Force Essential'. Examples of other articles related the story of the Salamaua raid can be found in *The West Australian*, Wednesday 7 October 1942, p. 3, 'Jungle Heroes. Salamaua Raids. Guerillas (sic) Return. Stories of the Fighting'; *Maryborough Chronicle, Wide Bay and Burnett Advertiser*, Wednesday 7 October 1942, p. 3, 'Japs Outclassed at Lae and Salamaua'; *The Daily News*, Monday 12 October 1942, p. 3, 'Commandos Tell Of Salamaua Raid'.

attack.[73] This was hampered by the Japanese refusal to expose their troops and lines of communication. The consequences of this were that Kanga Force had to adopt the role of ineffectual observers. Kanga Force had in fact killed many more Japanese than it had lost itself. Such numbers meant little though, as the Japanese still far outnumbered Kanga Force.[74] The inactivity rankled with the men of the company.[75] The inability to strike at the enemy through July and August was compounded by health and logistics issues, the greatest challenge for troops operating in tropical jungles. The cumulative strain of operating in the tropical environment, poor and insufficient food, and having to be constantly alert for the enemy wore the men down.[76] The health of the Company was of particular concern with a 98% incidence of malaria, and 30% of the company expected to come down with boils and tropical ulcers. An unrelieved diet of Bully Beef, which was made up of minced corned beef and gelatine, and biscuits with few vegetables and almost no fruit as supplements, caused both poor health and morale.[77] By 31 August 181 men of the original 303 were fit for service, a loss rate of 44%.[78] By October, gastritis and diarrhoea brought on by the diet was a serious problem. While full blown malaria was common many were suffering from malarial 'low fever' brought on by inadequate malaria protection. Septic sores from infected scratches were also a problem.[79] The lack of dry clean clothes to change into was resulting in an epidemic of contagious skin conditions.[80] The medical situation had a significant impact on Kanga Force operational capacity with the number of officers and Non Commissioned Officers who succumbed to illness forcing those men in the ranks who remained relatively fit to take on extra responsibilities. This resulted in some forward patrols being commanded by corporals and privates.[81]

Logistics for Kanga Force was an acute problem. Supplying troops in forward areas was a major challenge. The supply of indigenous carriers, without which adequate amounts of supplies could not be transported, was always problematic. All distances had to be covered on foot at speeds no faster than terrain and weather conditions permitted. This often meant a two week round trip from supply dumps at Wau to the most forward positions. Japanese patrol activity following the Salamaua raid frightened many of the indigenous carriers who deserted, a problem compounded by the

---

73 AWM, AWM54 587/6/11, 2/5 Independent Coy, Operations in New Guinea 25 October 1942, Lieut. B. Dawson 2/22 Bn and I.O. Kanga Force.
74 AWM, AWM54 587/6/11, 2/5 Independent Coy, Operations in New Guinea 25 October 1942, Lieut. B. Dawson 2/22 Bn and I.O. Kanga Force.
75 AWM, AWM54 587/6/11, 2/5 Independent Coy, Operations in New Guinea 25 October 1942.
76 Walker, *The Island Campaigns*, p. 129.
77 AWM, AWM54 587/6/11, 2/5 Independent Coy, Operations in New Guinea 25 October 1942, Lieut. B. Dawson 2/22 Bn and I.O. Kanga Force.
78 McCarthy, *First Year: Kokoda to Wau*, p. 104.
79 Walker, *The Island Campaigns*, p. 131.
80 Pirie, 'Commando Double Black', p. 217.
81 Ibid, pp. 233–34.

Japanese discovering several reserve food dumps.[82] The consequences for those troops in the forward areas were severe. At once stage 72 men had to subsist on only 11 cans of soup and seven pounds of rice.[83] Lieutenant Michael Sheehan observed that procuring supplies of food was very difficult, and that what they had had to be supplemented by eating sweet potato. At one stage the only vegetable that was available was cabbage which led Private Lyn Noakes of the NGVR to recall that, 'Everyone stank – farting. One man stepped in a bloated dead horse, everyone laughed as it smelled worse than the cabbage farts.'[84] Private Tommy Tucker remembered when he received a serve of cheese it consisted of a small portion and two army dog biscuits. This was meant to last the whole day.[85] Rice was available but in limited amounts. Lieutenant John Kerr wrote in December 1942 that he had 40 lbs of rice left, and that was all there was and it was not likely that there would be any more.[86] There was no salt or sugar.[87] In one uncharacteristic moment of largesse several thousand cans of 'fruit' arrived which on inspection all turned out to be carrots.[88] Sheehan had no doubts that the shortage of adequate rations contributed to the health of men deteriorating rapidly and as a consequence men were becoming unfit for hard work.[89]

Supplies of other items, such as tobacco, which was considered essential, were also inadequate. A major problem for supply was the pillaging of supplies before they reached the frontline troops. Major General Basil Morris commanding officer of New Guinea Force in early 1942 was unsympathetic to Kanga Forces food situation. He claimed that there were large amounts of food stored at Wau, enough he claimed for 18 months. Morris suggested that the problem of supply was caused solely by theft and pillaging.[90] Lieutenant Richard Littlejohn echoed Morris's concerns and was most bitter about the theft of tobacco by rear area troops which resulted in the company receiving none, whether this was in Port Moresby or Wau was never explained.[91] For some eight months razor blades were unavailable, nor had there been any scissors to cut hair, and many members of the company sported magnificent beards.[92] The availability of medical supplies was another pressing issue. Quinine was available but it was

82   Walker, *The Island Campaigns*, p. 129.
83   Ibid.
84   AWM, AWM SO4152 part 2, Lyn Noakes NGVR, interviewed by Neil MacDonald, 12 Jan 1986.
85   Pirie, 'Commando Double Black', p. 209.
86   Ibid, p.231.
87   Ibid, p.324.
88   AWM, AWM SO 4161, Interview with an Independent Company soldier (Ray Burbury?) by Neil MacDonald (no date).
89   AWM, AWM SO4152 part 2, Michael Sheehan, 2/5 Independent Company 12 Jan 1986, interviewed by Neil MacDonald, and Pirie, 'Commando Double Black', p. 228.
90   AWM, AWM 67 2/117, Records of Gavin Long, General Editor, Notebook No 117 (Fenton) – [notes on Kanga Force], Maj Gen B. Morris (CO NGF 42) – 23 Nov 44.
91   McCarthy, *First Year: Kokoda to Wau*, p. 103.
92   Pirie, 'Commando Double Black', p. 324.

at Wau, of little use to men in forward positions for whom a march to the airstrip at Wau for medical evacuation if necessary would take five days.[93] The supply of iodine was not good, and complaints were made that what did get through had often been 'ratted' by those in the rear areas.[94] Mail was delivered erratically. At Christmas 1942 the men in the forward areas received no parcels and no mail to help them celebrate the day.[95] There was no provision to answer mail, no post office and no stamps. Nor was there any ink. Letters, if written at all could only be done on scraps of paper using a pencil.[96] Added to this was the maladministration by Kanga Force headquarters of mail when it did appear. One Section had not received any mail for ten weeks. In September they found their mail 'strewn all over the place' at a location they had never been to before.[97]

During all this time no effort was made to significantly resupply, reinforce or relieve Kanga Force. This was despite Major General Morris reversing his previous claims of adequate supplies on hand for Kanga Force, and reporting to Army Headquarters on 3 August that the supply situation for Kanga Force was most serious and that forward troops were liable to starvation.[98] In a sign that the interests of Kanga Force had been well and truly pushed down the list of priorities nothing came of this. Members of 2/5th Independent Company felt that they had been 'dumped' and that Port Moresby had 'wiped its forehead' and forgotten them.[99] Such observations were not far from the mark with one official report stating that Kanga Force was not important as the main job was to defend Port Moresby against the Japanese, who at the time were pushing in that direction down the Kokoda Track.[100] The virtual abandonment of Kanga Force from July to October 1942 by New Guinea Force, even if unconscionable, was excusable if only because doing so was beyond the capacity of New Guinea Force. Kanga Force's fate was a consequence of the very real strain the logistical infrastructure of the Australian Army was suffering under at the time. A review of the transport assets available to New Guinea Force reveals why this was so. There were at the commencement of the Papuan Campaign, only 30 transport aircraft in all of Australia. Of these only half would be serviceable at any one time. The requirement to supply Allied forces in Papua was 50,000 lbs per day, and for Kanga Force 5,000 lbs per day. New Guinea Force wanted to build up a reserve of 20 days materiel for Papua.[101] Air-dropping was the primary means of delivering supplies to troops on the

93 AWM, AWM SO4152 part 2, Michael Sheehan – 2/5 Independent Company interviewed by Neil MacDonald 12 Jan 1986.
94 Pirie, 'Commando Double Black', p. 231.
95 Ibid, p. 225.
96 Ibid, p. 235.
97 Ibid, p. 149.
98 McCarthy, *First Year: Kokoda to Wau*, p. 140.
99 Pirie, 'Commando Double Black', p.304.
100 AWM, AWM54 587/6/2, Kanga Force Operations Wau Salamaua 1942.
101 McCarthy, *First Year: Kokoda to Wau*, p. 100.

Kokoda Track. The normal payload of a C-47, the most common type of transport aircraft, was 5,000 lbs, although in an emergency it could carry 7,000 lbs.[102] Wastage of supplies that were air-dropped, could be as high as 60%, thus requiring multiple extra flights to ensure that the required amount of supplies could be delivered.[103] With the limited number of transport aircraft available this would ensure that those which were available would prioritise their sorties to resupplying the main force on the Kokoda Track. The number of transport aircraft available would improve with time, but it becomes readily apparent that in the latter half of 1942, there would be very few aircraft available to service a secondary theatre such as Kanga Force at Wau. The situation was therefore straight forward; in the competition for aircraft to carry supplies Kanga Force would be trumped every time by the requirements of the Papuan campaign. There was also an attitude that supply by air for Kanga Force was only to be used in an emergency and that alternative supply methods should be used.[104] The only alternative supply method was indigenous carriers, which had to negotiate the route to Wau along the rugged Bulldog track. Such methods were time consuming, and due to difficulty of gathering and retaining carriers, and the physical strain of negotiating the Bulldog track, could never deliver the appropriate capacity of supplies.[105] Headquarters Kanga Force reported that the indigenous carriers were disinclined to operate in forward areas and frequently deserted when they heard that the Japanese were approaching. This hampered the movement of stores. This resulted in the troops having to carry and this was considered to be too severe for Europeans in the tropics. The consequences of this were that the range patrols could penetrate was significantly restricted.[106] Further contributing factors to the logistical challenges faced by Kanga Force, were the less than adequate staff work by Kanga Force headquarters in managing those supplies that were available. The problem was that Kanga Force headquarters never did have enough personnel to conduct efficient staff work. This was acknowledged by New Guinea Force with the excuse given that nothing could be done about it because no one was available to send.[107] As has been noted Kanga Force in any event generated very little interest for New Guinea Force, and at no time did any senior officer from New Guinea Force visit Kanga Force to advise or assist in its administrative operations.[108]

---

102 C-47 Aircraft <https://www.britannica.com/technology/C-47> (consulted 9 March 2018).
103 McCarthy, *First Year: Kokoda to Wau*, p. 308.
104 MacArthur made this very point to Blamey see: McCarthy, *First Year: Kokoda to Wau*, p. 197.
105 McCarthy, *First Year: Kokoda to Wau*, p. 544.
106 AWM, AWM54 741/5/15, Headquarters Kanga Force report, Sept 42, AWM54 578/7/5; Report on Raid on Salamaua Jun 1942.
107 AWM, AWM 67 2/117, Records of Gavin Long, General Editor, Notebook No 117 (Fenton) – [notes on Kanga Force], Maj Gen B. Morris (CO NGF 42) – 23 Nov 44.
108 Ibid.

Inadequately fed, chronically sick, indifferently administered, unable to effectively harm their enemies, and feeling abandoned by the Army it was little wonder that the troops of 2/5th Independent Company came to call themselves the 'Ragged Arsed Fifth'.[109]

While Kanga Force endured their situation activity on the Salamaua front did not remain static. On 21 July, the same day that Japanese troops landed at Gona and Buna, the Japanese sallied out of Lae and Salamaua. The force from Lae pushed up the Markham Valley, and that from Salamaua advanced to Mubo, about half way between Salamaua and Wau. By the end of August some 900 Japanese troops occupied Mubo.[110] The sudden upsurge of Japanese activity incited an extraordinary response from Kanga Force commander Norman Fleay. Presuming that the Japanese intended to capture both Wau and the Bulolo Valley, and convinced he was unable to halt or even delay such a move Fleay, who had been promoted to Lieutenant Colonel, decided that the Japanese moves were a precursor to an all-out assault on Wau and the Bulolo Valley. Subsequently he decided to withdraw Kanga Force and destroy the domestic infrastructure of both Wau and the Bulolo Valley. This decision ran counter to reports from a patrol led by Norman Winning that found accounts of any so called Japanese offensive were nothing but unsubstantiated indigenous rumour.[111] Winning's information was reinforced by a report from an independent Army Intelligence Bureau (AIB) patrol. The AIB was an organisation distinct from the Army whose role was to gather intelligence and to manage the indigenous populations in areas not under Australian control. In this case the AIB patrol had been operating in the Markham Valley without Fleay's knowledge. The patrol reported that there was no evidence of aggressive Japanese movement in the Markham Valley area.[112] Fleay ignored both reports, indeed, piqued by the presence of the AIB patrol operating independently in his domain he ordered that it be arrested.[113] The Japanese actually had no plans to assault and occupy Wau or the Bulolo Valley.[114] This was of course unknown to Fleay, who persisted with his intention to evacuate Wau and the Bulolo Valley and destroy the infrastructure in both placers.

The evacuation was conducted in a hasty manner, earning the sobriquet 'Bulldog Derby' by those who took part in it.[115] Buildings, stores and equipment at Wau and

---

109 Pirie, 'Commando Double Black', p. 235.
110 AWM, AWM54 741/5/15, Kanga Force Operation and Patrol Reports 1942, Report on Raid on Salamaua June 1942.
111 McCarthy, *First Year: Kokoda to Wau*, pp. 105–7.
112 Alan Powell, *The Third Force – ANGAU's New Guinea War* (Oxford University Press: South Melbourne, 2003), p. 33.
113 Ibid.
114 AWM, AWM55 1/8, Allied Translator and Interpreter Section, South West Pacific Area Bulletins 1942–1943, Nos 492–525 3 Nov. to 24 Nov 43, Bulletin 515, 18 Nov 43, Item 6 6416.
115 Pirie, 'Commando Double Black', p. 150.

in the Bulolo valley were destroyed. Loaded with gear to the point that they had to abandon their grenades to reduce the weight, the men of 2/5th Independent Company made their way out of Wau.[116] In a mark of the ongoing inadequate staff work that characterised Kanga Force Headquarters several patrols, including Winnings, did not receive the instruction to withdraw, and were left isolated. Fleay did not communicate with New Guinea Force, who had no idea why Wau was burning or the airfield there had been rendered unusable. Eventually Kanga Force, after having demolished what it could of Wau, relocated to a new position at the head of the Bulldog Track. There it waited for the Japanese onslaught, which never came. Fleay's actions at the time were controversial and have remained so since.[117] With no sign of any Japanese interest in Wau or the Bulolo Valley Kanga Force had, by the end of September, made its way back to both places.

Having returned to a now battered Wau, Kanga Force revisited its desire to inflict harm on the Japanese. The opportunity to do so came in October when a raid against Mubo, led by Winning, was conducted. Unlike the raid on Salamaua the October raid on Mubo, the first of two against Mubo which would be conducted, was a failure resulting only in confusion and achieving nothing. The reasons for this had much to do with the disruptive intervention of Lieutenant Colonel Fleay, who had decided to accompany the raid, choosing for his own reasons to do so as an 'observer' rather than as the commanding officer. This arrangement proved to be disastrous. As the raiding party drew near to Mubo two men activated booby traps wounding themselves. Fleay shouted loudly for the men to withdraw and save themselves. Winning attempted to rally his men, but to no avail. Great disruption and confusion ensued. Having caused the fiasco Fleay then fled into the jungle accompanied by one other man. He did not return to Kanga Force for one week.[118] The raiding party, having achieved nothing withdrew back towards Wau. It was only in October when reinforcements in the form of the 2/7th Independent Company finally reached Kanga Force that plans could be made to strike back at the Japanese. Once again Mubo was chosen as the target. This raid which occurred on 11 January 1943 was conducted to distract Japanese attention away from 17 Brigades planned move to the nearby Nadzab region. This time Fleay did not accompany the raid which was successfully conducted and resulted in many Japanese casualties.[119]

116 Ibid.
117 Pirie, 'Commando Double Black' devotes a chapter to the evacuation with numerous firsthand accounts of what occurred; P. Bradley, *The Battle For Wau* (Cambridge University Press: Melbourne, 2008) is also very critical of Fleay's decision to evacuate and demolish Wau.
118 The command of Kanga Force by Norman Fleay and the influence this had upon the relationship with the troops under his command will be examined in Chapter.
119 AWM, AWM54 583/6/4, Operational Plans, Wau – Lae – Salamaua Appreciations of Situation in North east Area – Oct 1942 – Jan 1943.

The 2/5th Independent Company served in the tropical jungle and mountains, unrelieved from the end of May 42 until late April 43, 11 months service in an extraordinarily hash and taxing environment. Such an extended period physically ruined the men of the company. It was accepted that after one month of service in tropical forest men begin to lose form, and that after 90 days units so deployed needed to be relieved.[120] The surprising thing was that the company managed to survive such an extended term, even if it was in an extremely debilitated condition when it was finally withdrawn. Leaving a force in such conditions, with minimal support, for such an extended time, demonstrated that the Army chose to treat the company as little more than a piece on the game board which was the Papuan campaign. It evidenced no genuine concern for the welfare of the company and despite the fact that there were unemployed Independent Companies in Australia that could have relived 2/5th Independent Company it preferred to keep the company in place. This was not unprecedented as the army had a history of consigning units to unsupported situations, witness the fate of the troops committed to the Island Barrier forces. Its treatment of 2/5th Independent Company during 1942 was very much in this fashion.

When assessing Kanga Force's role in New Guinea it is questionable as to the degree it achieved its intended objectives. Kanga Force was unable, due to its strength relative to that of the enemy, to storm and occupy Lae and Salamaua. When its mission was changed to that of harassing and destroying Japanese forces in the Markham area, it was only able to effectively do so for a period of about three weeks at the end of June and early July 1942. Following that, apart from one raid at Mubo in October 1942, it was unable to take the war to the enemy in any appreciable way. The Australian official response was to credit Kanga Force with a range of accomplishments which in fact it did not achieve. On 27 October 1943 Major General George Vasey noted that Kanga Force activity had resulted in the Japanese 'facing inland' rather to the sea, but goes on to contradict himself by saying that this had not distracted the Japanese from their seaboard defences. In effect Vasey was saying that Kanga Force had very little practical impact on the Japanese deployments at Lae-Salamaua.[121] On 20 September 1942 Lieutenant General Sydney Rowell, commander of New Guinea Force, reported that Kanga Force was engaging the attention of a considerable enemy force, as well as ensuring a flow of valuable information.[122] Dudley McCarthy in the official history *First Year: Kokoda to Wau*, observed that the force posed a constant threat to the Japanese at Lae and Salamaua. He went on to state that despite their disappointments and hardships Kanga Force had in the final analysis done what they were sent to New

---

120 AWM, AWM67 1/3, Diary No.3 Gavin Long Official History, 9 November 1943; Shelford Bidwell, *The Chindit War – Stillwell, Wingate and the Campaign in Burma: 1944* (MacMillan Co, Inc. New York, 1979), p. 68.
121 AWM, AWM54 583/6/4, Operational Plans, Wau – Lae – Salamaua Appreciations of Situation in North east Area – Oct 1942 – Jan 1943, Appreciation of the Situation Lae Salamaua Area, 27 Oct 42, General Vasey GOC 6 Div.
122 McCarthy, *First Year: Kokoda to Wau*, p. 536.

Guinea to do.[123] While Vasey's appreciation indirectly acknowledges Kanga Force's limited impact on the enemy, both Rowell and McCarthy's assessments are overly generous. By 'engaging the enemy' it is presumed that the Japanese had intentions to employ their numbers in some action to the disadvantage to the Allies, perhaps seizing Wau, and that Kanga Force somehow distracted them from this. The Japanese during 1942 had no intention of moving against Wau and thus Kanga Force's presence offered no distraction. As for engaging considerable numbers of enemy troops, it is a moot point if this was so as Japanese numbers in Lae and Salamaua following the reduction in numbers after the initial landing remained at approximately 1,600 and never varied much during 1942. There certainly were fears that the Japanese intended to employ their troops at Lae and Salamaua as part of an assault against Port Moresby. An intelligence situation report of 27 May reports the potential for the Japanese to land troops by air in the rear of Wau and Salamaua as part of a plan for an overland assault on Port Moresby. This was despite reports from Kanga Force indicating no apparent preparations from the Japanese to do so.[124] Claims that Kanga Force was engaging the attention of considerable enemy forces are therefore somewhat meaningless.

Following its raids on Salamaua and Heath's Plantation, Kanga Forces record was in fact uninspiring. Apart from a brief moment during the second raid on Mubo, on 11 January 1943, Kanga Force was after the third week of July 1942 in effect reduced to impotence and unable to seriously inconvenience the enemy in any significant way. Compelled by its numerical inferiority and debilitating physical and logistical situation Kanga Force was compelled to adopt a relatively low profile. The members of Kanga Force were aware of this and the more hopeful amongst them rationalised Kanga Force's reluctance to engage the enemy as a deliberate ploy, intended to not provoke the Japanese and incite them to make a push against Wau.[125]

The claim that Kanga Force sent valuable information depends very much on the period which is considered. From March until July a great deal of information on Japanese troop, shipping and air movements was sent back to New Guinea Force firstly by NGVR during March and April and from May onward by Kanga Force. Intelligence such as the 'Kanga Document' captured during the Salamaua raid was timely, and even if not acted upon directly did provide information on enemy intentions. The type of information did change from July onward, however, reflecting the difficulty Kanga Force found in mounting reconnaissance patrols following the Japanese reaction after the Salamaua raid. An examination of the reports sent back to New Guinea Force from Kanga Force during this period, reveal that the information

---

123 Ibid, p. 544.
124 MAA, Box 189 Historical Index Cards (Actual) Record Group 3 Index 2, General Headquarters Southwest Pacific Area (SWPA); AWM, AWM54 578/7/5, Headquarters Kanga Force Report, Sept 1942; AWM, AWM54 741/5/15, Kanga Force Operation and Patrol Reports 1942; MAA, Box 189 Historical Index Cards (Actual) Record Group 3 Indexes 3, 4, 5, 6, 8, General Headquarters Southwest Pacific Area (SWPA).
125 Pirie, 'Commando – Double Black', p. 229.

was invariably routine in nature, with no significant revelations of Japanese, numbers, dispositions or movements. During this period Kanga Force certainly did not ensure anything like a flow of especially valuable information.[126]

That Kanga Force did what they were sent to New Guinea to do is debateable. They were initially sent to New Guinea to protect Port Moresby, a role that in no way required them to use their unconventional warfare skills. That role changed in May 1942 when they were tasked with capturing Lae and Salamaua, and changed again in early June when they were ordered to harass the Japanese. In October 42 that role was refined to include defending the airfields in the Bulolo Valley.[127] Just what the Force had been sent to New Guinea to do is thus open to interpretation depending on what period of their deployment one examines. Perhaps the greatest achievement for Kanga Force was that it represented an Australian presence in the Lae-Salamaua area. McCarthy correctly points out that at the time Kanga Force was 'A very small group of men who, alone in the whole of the South-West Pacific Area, except for those on Timor, were actually facing the Japanese invaders on the ground'.[128] Kanga Force demonstrated that the Australian resolve to confront the invader was indisputable. In this sense Kanga Force did fulfil its role and did do what it had been sent to New Guinea to do.

In an indirect way Kanga Force did have an influence on the operations on other components of the A.I.F. A 23 September 1942 document titled 'Training Notes Tropical and Jungle Warfare', gives Kanga Force's raid on Salamaua as an exemplar of how to conduct operations in the Jungle. One of three examples used, the others being the fighting on the Kokoda Track-Milne Bay and the campaign in Malaya, Kanga Force is signalled out for special mention. There is no way of knowing how widely disseminated this paper was or how well it was received, especially as it goes on to discuss the employment of motor transport in the jungle, a thoroughly impractical idea.[129] What the paper did do, however, was to acknowledge Kanga Force and offer it as an exemplar for other AIF units. It seems ironic that the Army would recognise the unique skills of the Force in this way but offer minimal support for it to actually carry out such a role.

It could thus be argued that Kanga Force failed in its mission. It was unable to achieve a great deal of its originally intended objectives and spent most of its time posing little danger to the enemy. While technically correct this would in fact be too harsh a judgment. Kanga Force's ability to carry out its mission of harassing the

---

126 AWM, AWM54 578/7/5, Headquarters Kanga Force Report. Sept 1942; Kanga Force Operation and Patrol Reports 1942 AWM54 741/5/15; MAA, Box 189 Historical Index Cards (Actual) Record Group 3 Indexes 3, 4, 5, 6, 8, General Headquarters Southwest Pacific Area (SWPA).
127 McCarthy, *First Year: Kokoda to Wau*, p. 538.
128 Ibid, p. 588.
129 AWM, AWM54 937/3/37, Training Notes Tropical and Jungle Warfare Nos 1 and 2 First Australian Army training Instruction No 3 – 23 Sept 42.

enemy was demonstrably negatively influenced by it becoming a victim to the exigencies of war. Due to the Kokoda Campaign it found itself reduced to a sideshow and of little interest to the Army which was totally committed to the necessity to defeat the Japanese threat to Port Moresby. Thus denied adequate administrational and logistical support Kanga Force could do little more than it did. In the final analysis Kanga Force did what it could; to its great credit its men persevered and continued to face the enemy despite every hardship.

When assessing the significance of Kanga Force in the history of the Independent Companies the most significant achievement of Kanga Force, had little to do with its military record or achievements, it was that Kanga Force represented a milestone in the evolution of the Independent Companies. For the first time an Independent Company had been selected by the Army for a specific task in keeping with Independent Company training and the role originally intended for the Companies. The original orders Kanga Force had reflected this being succinct and unambiguous; to assault and capture specific strategic objectives, and then to harass the enemy by using guerrilla tactics. Kanga Force led the way in the utilisation by the Army of an unconventional force for a specific role in 1942 and this experience would not be forgotten in the year to come.

The guerrilla campaign waged by Kanga Force in the Lae – Salamaua region was not the sole experience of the Independent Companies in New Guinea in 1942. Another company, 2/6th Independent Company, would embark on its own campaign in the mountains, jungles and coastal flood plains of Papua, a campaign that would be dramatically different in both role and practice to that of the 2/5th Independent Company. The following chapter will examine the experiences of 2/6th Independent Company in these campaigns.

6

Kokoda-Buna

The year 1942 was one in which the Army managed its Independent Companies in a very uneven manner. The previous chapter examined how 2/5th Independent Company fared as Kanga Force. This chapter will examine the employment of the 2/6th Independent Company during the Papuan Campaign. The manner in which this company was managed, and the tasks it was given, was notably different to Kanga Force with 2/6th Independent Company being given a number of important tasks which were directly related to ongoing operations. The manner in which 2/6th Independent Company was utilised during this period represented a move, albeit a limited one, towards a more fully developed appreciation for Independent Companies by the Australian Army.

The 2/6th Independent Company arrived in Port Moresby on 7 August 1942. It received no orders when it arrived, but was told to be ready to move by aircraft at one day's notice.[1] Just where it was to be moved to remained a mystery. This mystery was resolved five days later when the company was inspected by Lieutenant General Sydney Rowell and Lieutenant Colonel Norman Fleay of Kanga Force, in the expectation that the company was to be attached to Kanga Force.[2] This, however, was not to be for a number of reasons. As it transpired the aircraft to be used for the move to Kanga Force in Wau were damaged on the airstrip during a Japanese air raid. Kanga Force also declined to be reinforced as it was, at that time in no condition to maintain another Independent Company.[3] Thus the Company remained in Port Moresby. This

---

1　AWM, AWM52 25/3/2, 2/6 Independent Company War Diary, 8 Aug 42.
2　Ibid, 12 Aug 42.
3　Ibid, 9 September 1942; AWM, AWM54 587/6/11, A report by Lt. B. Dawson 2/22 Bn I.O. Kanga Force 2/5 Independent Coy. Operations in New Guinea, 25th Oct 1942. In this report Dawson requests that no reinforcements be sent to Kanga Force because Kanga Force did not have the resources to maintain extra personnel. The date of this request is somewhat obscure. Dawson's message reached LHQ on 7 Nov 42 but it must have been written before this date. 2/7 Independent Company arrived in Wau in late October 42 and it seems that this may have been a factor in deciding not to send 2/6 to Wau.

109

was in fact a far more practical outcome considering the strategic situation that was unfolding.

To describe the circumstances in Papua in August 1942 as a crisis would be an understatement. In late July the Japanese had landed on the north coast of Papua at Buna and Gona, and immediately begun to advance down the Kokoda Track across the Owen Stanley mountain range, their objective to capture Port Moresby. Countering this offensive required the commitment of every available resource from the Army and on 27 August 2/6th Independent Company was assigned as a mobile reserve for 7th Division then engaged with the Japanese along the Kokoda Track.[4]

The tasks allocated to 2/6th Independent Company by 7th Division were both appropriate to the company's training, and of immediate relevance to the strategic and tactical situation. Typically Independent Companies seldom operated as a complete company sized unit, with components of the company being sent off to perform varied tasks. This was how 7th Division chose to employ the Company. As such throughout September-October the company was divided into four sections. These individual components operated at great distances from each other, and were entirely independent, illustrating both the capacity of the company to sustain such a deployment, and the qualities of sub-unit leadership and initiative inherent within the Independent Company. The tasks allocated to each of these sections reflected the diversity of the work Independent Companies were required to undertake.

On 19 September the threat to the left flank of the Australian forces on the Kokoda Track was increasing. It was imperative to discover the enemy's intentions on that flank. Consequently 2/6th Independent Company was ordered to search out information on enemy activities to the North West of Kokoda. They were to pay special attention to any possible flank approaches from that direction the Japanese might exploit towards Port Moresby.[5] To do so the Company was to patrol jungle tracks and report if the enemy are using the Mambrare or Yodda rivers to transport stores. They were to prevent any enemy penetration from the Yodda Valley. They were to do so as quickly as possible so as to allow 7th Division planners to be assured of the security of their left flank.[6] The knowledge of the areas into which 2/6th Independent Company was sent was scanty at best. Maps which were available were generally found to be hopelessly inaccurate, little more than glorified sketches and useless from a military point of view.[7] Typical of these maps were examples which had large blank spaces on them stamped with such useful information as, 'no information available', and more

4 AWM, AWM52 25/3/2, 2/6 Independent Company War Diary 27 Aug 42 and 9 September 1942.
5 Ibid, 19 Sept 42.
6 AWM, AWM52 25/3/2, 2/6 Independent Company War Diary 7 Division Operational Instruction No. 8 of 5 Sept 42.
7 AWM, AWM 54 1/5/42, Australian Military Forces Army Headquarters and Unit History Diaries, 1939–1945. Bena Force; AWM, AWM67 2/34, Gavin Long notebook 34, Captain Owens NGF ex.NGVR – Lae 20 July 44.

disturbingly, 'suspected cannibals'.[8] Without accurate maps infantry patrols could only move at their peril, larger formations could not move without risk of encountering impassable terrain, and that the lines upon which an enemy may move would remain unknown.[9] It was vital that this unknown terrain was examined. It was just the type of task for which an Independent Company had been trained. This was understood by 2/6th Independent Company and it seemed that by August 1942 influential elements within the Army had recognized this as well.[10]

In a mark of the unique operational style of the Independent Companies the patrolling process to the left flank of the Kokoda track was conducted in as clandestine manner as possible. To avoid detection by the enemy, and as a means of approaching their objective indirectly, the 32 men of 'A' Patrol who had been tasked with the reconnaissance mission boarded a lugger and sailed to Yule Island 100 kilometres west of Port Moresby. From there they crossed to the mainland and trekked inland to examine all the tracks in the Chirima and Yodda River Valleys. From there they would penetrate the Japanese held area around Kokoda.[11] Operating remote from any source of supply air dropping was employed. This was not always successful with much of what was dropped being damaged or lost in the jungle. Consequently the ration situation became critical, but nevertheless the patrols pushed on. Ultimately their persistence was rewarded. On the morning of 25 October, taking advantage of the early morning fog, a three man patrol led by Lieutenant Frederick Winkle, entered Kokoda which was, at that time, well behind Japanese lines. Ironically and indicative of the difficulty of establishing exact locations in the jungle, the patrol did not realise they had arrived at Kokoda. So far behind the lines were they that they encountered no Japanese sentries or guards. Undetected they settled down under cover to watch a group of Japanese soldiers gathered around a camp fire. Having done so for some time, they quietly withdrew and crossed what was later determined to be the overgrown and disused Kokoda airstrip. Continuing towards Efogi, which was in the direction of the front line between Australian and Japanese forces the patrol heard intermittent mortar and small arms fire nearby. Undeterred they pressed on until they were fired at from a position on top of a nearby ridge. It was only then that it was realised they were actually in amongst the Japanese front line. With this they pulled back, and by

---

8   Stephen Murray-Smith interviewed by Hazel de Berg in the Hazel de Berg collection [sound recording] 1961 <http://nla.gov.au/nla.obj-214336861> (consulted 22 August 2016).
9   TNA, WO106/4841, Observations of the New Guinea Campaign by William Courtenay British War Correspondent, WO106/4841.
10 AWM, AWM54 583/7/4, Tropical Service of an Independent Coy Based on experience of 2/5 Australian Independent Coy. Kanga Force – 1943 Written by INT Sgt W.A. Chaffey 2/5 Indep Coy, 20 July 1943.
11 Syd Trigellis-Smith, *The Purple Devils – A History of 2/6 Independent Australian Commando Squadron* (Australian Military History Publishers: Loftus, 2008), pp. 17–19.

the night of 26 October had returned to Yodda.¹² This mission illustrated just what a well handled Independent Company patrol, acting with stealth and craftiness could achieve.

The patrolling by 2/6th Independent Company to the left flank of the Kokoda Track resulted by the end of September in the Company being able to confidently report that there was no evidence that the Japanese were moving in strength to the Western flank of the Kokoda track.¹³ The value of such intelligence to the strategic decision making process cannot be understated.

While the patrol to the left flank of the Kokoda Track was progressing, other patrols of the Company pushed deep into the country immediately to either side of the track. This resulted in unexpected dividends with the discovery of Australian soldiers from the 2/14th and 2/27th Battalions who had been cut off and lost in the jungle since the fighting around Isurava on 26 to 31 August. These men, who had been isolated in the wilderness since that time, were emaciated and in poor condition, and were taken in hand and reunited with their units.¹⁴ On 11 September 'E' Patrol was detailed to join a force known as 'Honner Force'. This force was commanded by Lieutenant Colonel Ralph Honner, who had commanded the 39th Battalion during the fighting at Isurava. 'Honner Force' consisted of one company from each of the 39th, 49th and 55th Battalions, some 500 men in all.¹⁵ The role of Honner Force was to gain control of Kokoda through to Deniki by moving around the enemy right flank and into the rear of the enemy, thus cutting their line of communication and by so doing support the move by 25 Brigade to halt the Japanese advance. At the same time Honner Force was to protect the left flank of the Australian main force. The role of 'E' Patrol was to act as scouts and forward troops for the force.¹⁶ As it was the expectations for 'Honner Force' were far too optimistic. Many of the force's members were unfit and generally of poor quality, they failed to achieve even the most basic standards expected of soldiers engaged in such work. Patrols would go out and return a short time later, the men exhausted, shaken by their encounter with the deep jungle, and having abandoned equipment to lighten their loads. The men of 'E' Patrol could do little more than look on at the wretched sight.¹⁷ The use of 'Honner Force' for what was an Independent Company task, indicates that the army had accepted that mobile lightly equipped forces intended to conduct guerrilla like raids and harassment of the enemy rear areas, was a viable tactic to use in the jungle. Just why untrained and ill-prepared standard infantry should be used for such a role, when both 2/8th Independent Company, then marking time in the Northern Territory, and 2/7th Independent Company sitting idle

---

12 Ibid, pp. 22–23.
13 Ibid, p. 21.
14 McCarthy, *First Year: Kokoda to Wau*, pp. 593 and 597; Powell, *The Third Force*, p. 52.
15 AWM, AWM52 25/3/2, 2/6 Independent Company War Diary 7 Division Operational instruction N0.10 19 Sept 42.
16 AWM, AWM52 25/3/2, 2/6 Independent Company War Diary, 11 Sept 42.
17 Ibid, 12–16 Sept 42.

in Queensland were both available remains a mystery. Local commanders, who set up Honner Force, certainly understood the value of unconventional forces, but this was obviously not shared by higher echelons in the Army. From this it was apparent that the Army as an institution still had a great distance to go before it fully developed the mechanisms or appreciation for making full use of its Independent Companies.

Despite this during September 2/6th Independent Company was kept busy by 7th Division. On 22 September the Company was instructed to conduct protective patrols on the left flank of the Division and to mount offensive patrols forward towards Efogi as far as their supply circumstances permitted. It was understood that should the Japanese breakthrough in on the left flank it would be the Company's role to harass them and act as guides to lead friendly troops to positions of tactical advantage.[18] On the same day the company was issued orders to conduct a reconnaissance of the Mount Asquith area, locate enemy movements in the area, capture prisoners, destroy any enemy found there, and watch an important creek junction.[19] It was obvious that Major General Arthur Allen, the commander of 7th Division, certainly understood how to best employ an Independent Company in support of his operations.

The collection of accurate terrain intelligence requiring collecting all information possible was a primary purpose of the Company's patrolling.[20] The comprehensive nature of the reports generated by these patrols illustrated the attention to detail and reconnaissance prowess of the Independent Company personnel. The 16 September 1942 report of Lieutenant Nichols's 'D' Patrol illustrated this. Nichols's report focussed on an extensive list of subjects ranging from topographical features, vegetation, tracks, indigenous people, and logistical potential of the country.[21] In a mark of the dual nature of the patrols aggression, while not their primary purpose, was not discouraged. Patrols were instructed they did not need to ask permission to attack, which acknowledged the degree of initiative expected from them.[22] In compliance with this on 25 Sept 'C' Patrol raided a Japanese mountain gun which had been causing casualties to friendly troops. The patrol killed the 12 Japanese serving the gun.[23]

The reports made on the absence of a Japanese presence to the left flank of the Kokoda Track was not the only strategic contribution made by 2/6th Independent Company during the Papuan Campaign. Victory in the battle of Oivi-Govari which occurred 10 November 1942 was achieved by Australian forces outflanking and

18   Ibid, 11 Oct 42.
19   Ibid, 22 Sept 42, Operational instruction to Lt Bullock.
20   AWM, AWM52 25/3/2, Tropical Service of an Independent Coy Based on experience of 2/5 Australian Independent Coy. Kanga Force – 1943 Written by INT Sgt W.A. Chaffey 2/5 Indep Coy, 20 July 1943.
21   AWM, AWM52 25/3/2, 2/6 Independent Company War Diary, 16 Sept 42, Report of "D" Patrol By LIEUT NICHOLS.
22   AWM, AWM52 25/3/2, 2/6 Independent Company War Diary 2/6 Operational Instruction to Captain R.S. Belmer (not date but most likely late Sept 42).
23   AWM, AWM52 25/3/2, 2/6 Independent Company War Diary, 25 Sept 42.

enveloping the Japanese defenders. Such a move could not have been made without accurate topographical and terrain intelligence. 'D' Patrol of the Company was operating in the Oivi-Govari area at the time and was perfectly placed to secure and provide topographical and terrain intelligence. It was claimed after the war that information provided by this patrol, 'Was partly responsible for the successful outflanking of the Jap positions by 16 Brigade.'[24] There is no direct evidence to support this claim but when the activities of 2/6th Independent Company patrols at the time are examined it does suggest that the claims may have been correct. On 6 October 7th Division ordered 'D' Patrol of the company to move to Sirorata which lies along the Kokoda track north of Kokoda and in the area in which the Oivi–Gorari battle occurred.[25] The patrol conducted reconnaissance of the area and reports were made to 7th Division.[26] The danger in doing so, was illustrated by the fate of one four man reconnaissance patrol consisting of three 2/6th Independent Company men and an indigenous Policeman. Only one man, the signaller who had been operating his radio from a different location, survived and managed to make his way back to base camp, having abandoned all his equipment except his weapon and cipher key. The other members of the patrol vanished and were presumed to have been killed by hostile indigenous people.[27] The report on the patrol from the signaller sole survivor was duly despatched directly to 7th Division.[28] Unless these reports were ignored, which is unlikely, they must have contributed in some way to the planning made by the Division for the assault on Oivi-Govari. It is thus reasonable to claim that the efforts of 2/6th Independent Company contributed to the success of the Oivi-Govari operation.

The Papuan experience of 2/6th Independent Company was certainly diverse. Split into independent sub-units, each with its own tasks, and operating across a widely dispersed geographic area, the company exemplified the adaptability and resilience characteristic of the Independent Companies. The experience also indicated that influential elements within the army were aware of and willing to employ an Independent Company in roles for which it had been trained. Such a development was a vast improvement from the mismanagement that the companies had experienced during 1941 and the early months of 1942.

24 Trigellis-Smith, *The Purple Devils*, pp. 32–3.
25 AWM, AWM52 1/5/14/31, 7 Division General Staff Branch October 1942 Part 2 Appendices, 6 Oct 42.
26 AWM, AWM54 577/7/11, Message Form B64 2025 4 To D PATROL 6 Ind Coy – rptd 6 Aust Div – 7 Aust Div – 32 US Div (no date); Message 8141/1230/42 Message Passed to NGF by 7 Aust Div, Messages and reports relating to 2/6 Independent Company Patrol – September 1942.
27 Trigellis-Smith, *The Purple Devils*, pp. 32–5.
28 AWM, AWM52 25/3/6/5, 2/6 Independent Company War Diary, Nov 42, Short Report By NX86139, Sig. McIntosh of 'D' PATROL of Lieut. W.H. Nichols (Oi/c 'D' Patrol) Last patrol before he was reported "missing". This report of one element of 'D' Patrol, from which three of the four men in the patrol went missing presumed killed, attests to danger of the work being done.

Operating along the Kokoda Track was not the only task 2/6th Independent Company participated in during the Papuan campaign. From October to December 1942 elements of the company were attached to the US 32nd Infantry Division, and in that role participated in the battle for the Buna beachhead. During this time the company exemplified its adaptability, resilience and consummate skills of reconnaissance and communication in a foreign military milieu. Just how an Australian company came to be attached as an integral sub-unit to a US Division is worthy of a digression. On 8 October 1942 a component of 2/6th Independent Company was attached to what was known as 'Hatforce', at Wanigela, which was on the east coast of Papua.[29] New Guinea Force intended 2/6th Independent Company to conduct reconnaissance and minor offensive actions in support of Hatforce from Wanigela towards Buna, and to find suitable points on the coast for landing supplies and small craft. The intention was to eventually raise Hatforce to brigade strength by despatching the AIF's 18 Brigade to Wanigela. This, however, did not happen because 17 Brigade which was to replace 18 Brigade at Milne Bay had not yet arrived, and the Air Force preferred to fly troops to and from Port Moresby rather than directly to Milne Bay. Thus it was decided that the US 128th Infantry Regiment, which was part of the US 32nd Division, and was in Port Moresby and thus more conveniently transported by air, would provide the troops sent to Wanigela.[30] The 32nd Division subsequently despatched the 1st Battalion of the 128th Infantry Regiment (1/128) and the 3rd Battalion (3/128), as well as the Headquarters of 128th Regiment to Wanigela. Once there the troops came under the command of US Brigadier General Hanford McNider. When 1st Battalion US 126th Infantry Regiment (1/126) arrived Hatforce metamorphosed into 'Warren Force', named after the home county of the Division commander Major General Edwin Harding.[31] The Australian Army, rather than withdraw and redeploy the 2/6th Independent Company personnel already at Wangeli, conceded to the practicality of the situation and formally attached the company to Warren Force and thus under US command. The role of 2/6th Independent Company as part of Warren Force was to provide

---

29 NARA, RG 319 Bulk File #3 to Victory in Papua – Milner, Box 5, Records of the Army Staff, Center of Military History, Victory in Papua, Interviews –Folder: New Guinea Operation Instruction New Guinea Force Operation Instruction #7. NG Force OP Instruction No.35 – 8 Oct 42.

30 NARA, RG 319 Bulk File #3 to Victory in Papua – Milner, Box 5, Records of the Army Staff, Center of Military History, Victory in Papua, Interviews –Folder: New Guinea Operation Instruction New Guinea Force Operation Instruction #7. NG Force OP Instruction No.35 – 8 Oct 42'; MMA, Intelligence Folder 1, 'Studies in the History of General Douglas MacArthur's Commands in the Pacific "Establishment of the Southwest Pacific Area and the Papuan Campaign 7 December 1941–22 January 1943."

31 DDEA, Box 885, Headquarters 32nd Infantry Div APO 32 March 1945, Public Relations – History of 32nd Division, 32nd Inf Div. 'Warren Force' was named after Warren County Ohio the home county of the commanding officer of 32nd Division Major General Edwin Harding.

the capabilities of experienced scouting and reconnaissance, skills that were sadly lacking amongst the untested US troops.

To this end 2/6th Independent Company acted as guides and a flank guard for the American battalions as they made their way along the coast to Buna. As it transpired the rugged terrain, and the flooding of the Musa River inland from Wanigela, conspired to dissuade the US troops from venturing too far into the wilderness, and on 22 October they retreated to the coast where they awaited transport by sea.[32] This isolated the 2/6th Independent Company, which had pushed ahead to the far side of the flooded Musa. In a reflection of an almost obsessive desire by Australian commentators to criticise American forces engaged in the Buna campaign, historian Dudley McCarthy asserts that, 'Americans made no provision for supplying 2/6 once it got cut off by the floods'.[33] Reinforcing this, the Company history *The Purple Devils* claims that as far as the Americans were concerned once the company had moved out from Wangeli it was 'out of sight out of mind'.[34] The withdrawal of 3/128 back to Wangeli did complicate the company's supply situation, as that battalion had been responsible for the supply chain to the company. Subsequently rations for the company ran short.[35] There was, however, no deliberate negligence by US forces in regard to supplying the company, in fact the opposite applied. On 17 October Major Harry Harcourt, the CO of 2/6th Independent Company, informed 3/128 that rations for the company were urgently needed.[36] The battalion subsequently informed Warren Force Head Quarters of the Company's situation emphasising that supplies be rushed as they were badly needed. With this 3/128 informed the Company that rations would be air dropped to them the next day, which occurred.[37] As it happened many of the supplies, which consisted of six pound tins of Bully Beef and bags of rice, were damaged during the drop, a not at all uncommon occurrence at that stage of the war.[38] Aware that this had occurred 3/128 informed Warren Force Head Quarters the same day and repeated that the company must have its rations.[39] This reminder was repeated on 23 October, with a direct enquiry made by 3/128 as to had the company been supplied.[40] It is apparent

---

32 MMA, Box 190 Historical Index Cards (Actual) Record Group 3 Index 7, General Headquarters Southwest Pacific Area (SWPA).
33 McCarthy, *First Year: Kokoda to Wau*, p. 360.
34 Trigellis-Smith, *The Purple Devils*, p. 86.
35 Ibid, p. 86.
36 DDEA, Box 1348, Journal of 1st Bn 128th Infantry, September – November 1942 (incomplete), Harcourt to Miller 17 Oct.
37 Ibid, Journal of 1st Bn 128th Infantry, September – November 1942 (incomplete), Miller to McNider 20 Oct, McNider to Miller 20 Oct.
38 Ibid, Journal of 1st Bn 128th Infantry, September – November 1942 (incomplete), Miller to Harcourt 21 Oct, McNider to Miller 20 Oct; Trigellis-Smith, *The Purple Devils*, p. 86,
39 DDEA, Box 1348, Journal of 1st Bn 128th Infantry, September – November 1942 (incomplete), Miller to McNider 20 Oct.
40 Ibid, Journal of 1st Bn 128th Infantry, September – November 1942 (incomplete), Miller to McNider 23 Oct.

that 2/6th Independent Company had not in fact been forgotten by the Americans, and was certainly not 'out of sight out of mind'. Indeed if anyone could be accused of ignoring the companies supply situation it was the Australian Army. On 2 November with men suffering from sores due to prolonged fatigue, poor food, and no sleep and unable to mount patrols due to a lack of boots and socks Harcourt flew back to Port Moresby to follow up on why no supply requests from the Australian Army had been met since 15 October. He was told that stores would arrive by 4 November. The stores did not arrive. Boots and rations were eventually supplied from US sources.[41] It did seem that, in a familiar refrain, the welfare of an Independent Company was once again a low priority for the Australian Army. Therefore Australian criticisms of any American supposed disregard for 2/6th Independent Company's wellbeing are entirely unwarranted.

The intention was for Warren Force to move overland along the coast to Buna. Even though the Japanese were withdrawing there was still a perceived threat to the left flank of the force. To this end 2/6th Independent Company was tasked to cover Warren Force's left flank.[42] The Company performed this task while gathering intelligence at the same time. Working with the Intelligence Section and patrols of the US 126th Infantry Regiment, the company scouted ahead to locate any Japanese and locate sites for airfields.[43] By 5 November the company had reached Pongani, a village further along in the direction of Buna. At Pongani the company received orders from Lieutenant Colonel McCoy of 3/128 to patrol the tracks to the north, and to place small groups as outposts on those tracks.[44] The company did this until 12 November when orders were issued to prepare to move by boat to a point on the coast to the east of Buna. The relationship between the company and Warren Force was still very new, and the liaison between the two still awkward. The order to move by boat was one example of this, and despite Harcourt and his second in command attending a meeting at Warren Force Head Quarters for instructions on 15 November both left with what they described as, 'absolutely no information obtained'.[45] Rather than wasting time waiting for orders, the company began Bren and Thompson sub

---

41 AWM, AWM52 25/3/6, War Diary of 2/6 Independent Company, November 1942, General Report, 2–6 Nov 42.
42 NARA, RG319 Box 7 ARC 1D 2205874 P Entry 53, Records of the Army Staff, Center of Military History, Victory in Papua, G-3 Reports – September 1942 to December 1942, Field Order #4, 0800L.
43 NARA, Box 8805 Folder: 332-INF (126) – 09 (3422) 126TH CT-5-2 S-3, WWII Operations Reports, 1940–48 32nd Infantry Division 332-INF (126) – 0.7 DEC 1945 TO 332-INF (126) – 0.9, "Reports on Trail Operations" Buna (Papuan) Campaign 17 Oct–8 Nov 42.
44 DDEA, Box 1348, Journal of 1st Bn 128th Infantry, September–November 1942 (incomplete).
45 AWM, AWM52 25/3/6, War Diary of 2/6 Independent Company, November 1942, General Report, 15 Nov 42.

machinegun recapitulation training.⁴⁶ Eventually the situation resolved itself and on 17 November Harcourt received orders to take the force that had gathered at Pongani and move overland to Buna, all thoughts of the proposed move by boat having apparently been cast aside. The constitution of the Pongani force was significant in two ways. Firstly it was a mixed force of Australian and US troops consisting of 117 men of 2/6th Independent Company and A Company, and part of C Company, and part of Head Quarters Company of US 126 Infantry Regiment.⁴⁷ Secondly Harcourt, an Australian officer was given command of the force. Placing US troops, who far outnumbered Australians in the Pongani force, under foreign command was an uncommon occurrence for US Forces. Such an appointment could only have occurred if McNider the commander of Warren Force trusted Harcourt, which says much for Harcourt's personal attributes as well as his diplomatic skills. Harcourt's force arrived at Buna on 20 November, and joined Warren Force, which had arrived there earlier by boat, as reinforcements.⁴⁸ From that moment 2/6th Independent Company would be engaged intimately in the brutal conflict that characterised the fight for Buna.

The Japanese force which had retreated along the Kokoda Track had lodged in the two coastal enclaves of Gona and Buna. There they had been reinforced by fresh troops. Working tirelessly they had constructed elaborate and sophisticated networks of fieldworks and bunkers which took advantage of every aspect of the local terrain to channel any attack into carefully prepared fields of machinegun fire. Faced with this formidable obstacle the tactical situation which confronted the Allied forces moving against them was one in which there was no room for subtlety or finesse. Consequently 2/6th Independent Company found itself thrown directly into a fight where a determined enemy could only be confronted by frontal assault. This resulted in the Company forced by circumstances to at first operate in the unaccustomed and unpopular role of infantry. Gradually though, as they acclimatised to the task confronting them, and US commanders became more aware of the attributes that the company offered them, the role of company began to change. Instead of close assault the company began patrolling, seeking out the cunningly camouflaged enemy bunkers and reporting their locations. They moved out onto the flanks of the US battalions guarding them from surprise by the enemy and very importantly ensuring that the battalions were aware of just where they were in the tangled tropical wilderness and swamps which characterised Buna. By inserting elements between the US battalions the Company also provided a reliable link between the battalions, an important

---

46   Ibid, 16 Nov 42.
47   NARA, Box 1348, NARA RG319, Box 7, ARC 1D 2205874 P Entry 53; Records of the Army Staff, Center of Military History, Victory in Papua, G-3 Reports – September 1942 to December 1942, Field Order #4, 0800L, RG319 Box 7 ARC 1D 2205874 P Entry 53; DDEA, Box 1348, Col Horne to Maj Harcourt 2/6 Ind Co 17 Nov 42, Journal 1st Bn, 128th rgt. 332-70.3 Nov 19, Journal of 1st Bn 128th Infantry, September – November 1942 (incomplete).
48   DDEA, Box 1348, Journal of 1st Bn 128th Infantry, September–November 1942 (incomplete).

service as in the physical environment of Buna it was easy for units to become separated from each other. At other times the Company would assault Japanese positions relieving US troops of the necessity to do so. Of all of these tasks patrolling would was the most valuable contribution the company made to the operations of Warren Force. Harcourt summed this up when he observed that virtually all of Warren Force's patrols were done by his company.[49]

The reasons patrolling was important, and the company was so important for patrolling, at Buna were twofold. Buna was a battle in which the enemy had skilfully concealed himself from view and could quite literally only be discovered by stumbling upon him. Soldiers lamented that they, 'Sure did wish they could see the yellow bastards so they could shoot them'.[50] The problem for Warren Force was the very poor capacity of the US infantry to conduct effective patrolling. Much of this inadequacy was not because of any fundamental failing by the troops concerned, but much more to do with the nature of the US troops who had been sent to Buna. The 32nd Division had been trained for conventional warfare. Its primary purpose had originally been to assist defend Australia from invasion. Even then its training cycle had been constantly interrupted by being continually moved from one location to another while in Australia. Without any effective retraining for Jungle warfare it had been redeployed to New Guinea. The brutal tropical environment of New Guinea came as a savage shock to the men of the Division, many of who were National Guard troops from the rural states of Michigan and Wisconsin. In the jungle the men of the Division were complete novices. US commanders acknowledged this, commenting that their troops lacked the fundamental requirements of patrolling. They openly lamented that their patrols brought back meagre and inaccurate information and that, 'If you have poor scouts your mission is very hard to accomplish.'[51] It was acknowledged that so poor were the US troops at patrolling, that knowledge of the enemy was only gained by them when they actually contacted the enemy.[52] Major General Harding summed

---

49 AWM, AWM67 2/8, Gavin Long Notebook 8, Maj. Harcourt 2/6 Indep Coy – Cairns Jul 43.
50 NARA, RG 319 Bulk File #3 to Victory in Papua – Milner, Box 5 to Intelligence and Supply – Bulk File #3, Box 4, Entry 53, Records of the Army Staff, Center of Military History, Victory in Papua, 32nd Division Reports – Bulk Package #2Interviews, Report of Col. Harry Knight "Observation of the Battle of Buna", p.4.
51 NARA, RG407 Box 7885 Entry 427 HMFY 2007, Records of the Adjutant General's Office WW11 Operations Reports, 1940–48 32nd Infantry Division 332-3.2 Nov 42 to 332-3.2 Papuan Dec 1942, Message 2684 9 Dec To C.O. Urbana Force Rpt Warren Force; NARA, Records of the Army Staff, Center of Military History, Victory in Papua, 32nd Division Reports – Bulk Package #2Interviews – Bulk File #3 to Victory in Papua – Milner, Report of Col Herbert B. Laux "Report of Military Observer in Southwest Pacific"; NARA, RG 319 Box 5 to Intelligence and Supply – Bulk File #3, Box 4, Entry 53; DDEA, Box 1342, Summary of Lessons Learned, 126th Regt After Action Reports, (no date).
52 NARA, RG 319 Bulk Package #2Interviews – Bulk File #3 to Victory in Papua – Milner, Box 5 to Intelligence and Supply – Bulk File #3, Box 4, Entry 53, Records of the Army

up his Division's inability to patrol and operate effectively when he admitted that his troops were, 'Weak in patrolling and self-reliance'.[53] Compounding this was that there was a lack of adequate maps and aerial photographs. Consequently patrol leaders did not know where they had started and where they had been once they finished their patrols. In such a situation the value of the careful systematic reconnaissance offered by 2/6th Independent Company was invaluable.

The patrol reports from the company were routinely detailed and precise. A reconnaissance report of 23 November 1942 from Harcourt to McNider illustrates the quality of such reports. In his report, which was accompanied by a detailed sketch, Harcourt indicates the location of enemy machineguns, adding that those who discovered them are attempting to silence them. He goes on to report on vegetation, movement of enemy and the position of an observation post that the company had established.[54]

Reports were precise and detailed, an example of this was the 30 November description given of Japanese positions:

> All emplacements appeared to be made of coconut logs laid lengthwise with others placed on the bearers forming the roof. The whole was then camouflaged according to the country in which they were situated. In the case of those to the west of the strip kunai grass festooned all over them with small bundles standing upright in front, while at the eastern end ...[they] were covered with coconut leaves, bits of scrub and heaps of fallen coconuts or husks. In most cases the loopholes were hidden to view by the screen of bush or camouflage, although vision from inside out was still possible, and in nearly every case the pillbox or emplacement was not discovered until you were right on to it. The openings were difficult to see from the front and only in two cases – those near the bridge – were they located, nor could the width or size of the loopholes be ascertained.[55]

Reports on enemy activities were carried by company runners back to Warren Force Head Quarters.

In addition to the reconnaissance role another important task of 2/6th Independent Company was to secure the flanks of US units. Battalions would come to rely on the Company to protect their flanks.[56] Complementary to flank protection was acting as

---

Staff, Center of Military History, Victory in Papua, 32nd Division Reports – Basic Intel Report, 32nd Division Papuan Campaign.
53   Leslie Anders, *Gentle Knight The Life and Times of Major General Edwin Forrest Harding* (The Kent State University Press: Ohio, 1981), p. 255.
54   NARA, Box 7885, WWII Operations Reports, 1940–48 32nd INFANTRY DIVISION 332-3.2 NOV 1942 – 332-3.2 PAPUAN DEC 1942.
55   AWM, AWM52 25/3/6, 2/6 Independent Company War Diary, 30 Nov 42.
56   NARA, Box 7, ARC 1D 2205874 P Entry 53, Records of Army Staff, Center of Military History, Victory in Papua G-3 Reports – September 1942 to December 1942, Field Order #4, 0800L.

Patrol report Harcourt to McNider, 23 November 42. This is the type of report that 2/6 Independent Company was producing for 32nd Division during the Buna campaign on a regular basis. At this stage of the war in New Guinea US troops did not have the experience or skills required to produce such a report. (NARA, Records of the Army Staff Center of Military History Victory in Papua G-3 Reports – Sept 1942 to G-3 Reports – Dec 1942. RG319 Box 7 ARC ID 2205874 P Entry 53)

a communication link between battalions. It was very difficult to locate the flanks of units in the jungle and swamps of Buna. The dangers posed to battalions by this of surprise Japanese attacks were taken very seriously.[57] To facilitate the accurate identification of flanks and ensure communication between battalions 2/6th Independent Company was posted in the space between 1/128 and 1/126. Operating in small patrols it was able to keep both battalions informed of their positions, and provide a secure communication link as well as provide flank protection.

It was not surprising that in an environment in which operating styles and military cultures were very different, 2/6th Independent Company would encounter a degree of friction when operating with US troops. The first such incident occurred during the very first day of operations on 21 November. Harcourt surmised that the positions that 1/128 had marked for its positions on their operational maps were in fact incorrect, as they showed the battalion positions some 200–300 yards north of the eastern end of the New Strip, an airstrip built as a ruse by the Japanese and located to the east of the more established Old Strip. Harcourt, who had conducted a personal reconnaissance of the position, advised 1/128 that they were in fact not occupying the positions they thought they were. He was ignored.[58] On the same day the battalion moved against the New Strip and Harcourt's advice would prove to be prescient. The advance on the New Strip was a bitterly contested exercise. The terrain was such that swamps channelled all moves and Japanese machineguns skilfully camouflaged in bunkers dominated every approach. The attack working as it was from inaccurately marked maps soon bogged down and halted. It had been intended that 2/6th Independent Company would advance in concert with the battalion to protect it flank. This the company did only to find the battalion falling further and further behind, with the result that the company found itself exposed between both US and Japanese forces and taking fire from both. With no option the company went to ground and did not move. Being caught in advance of US troops would become a perennial problem for the company throughout the campaign.[59] In another incident US troops complained that the company's habit of hunting Japanese snipers was 'Stirring up the Japs' and could the company stop doing so.[60] Two fundamentally different military cultures were at loggerheads, one which was aggressive and actively sought out the enemy and another which caught in an environment that was for it as perplexing as it was terrifying sought to minimise risk. Harcourt was fully aware of the role his company must play. For him it was a simple task. He knew it was his role to prepare the way for US

57 NARA, RG319 Box 7885WWII Operations Reports, 1940–48 32nd Infantry Division 332-3.2 NOV 1942 – 332-3.2 Papuan Dec 1942.
58 AWM, AWM52 25/3/6, 2/6th Independent Company, War Diary 21–2 Nov 42.
59 McCarthy, *First Year: Kokoda to Wau*, p. 378.
60 AWM, AWM67 2/8, Gavin Long Notebook 8, Maj. Harcourt 2/6 Indep Coy – Cairns Jul 43.

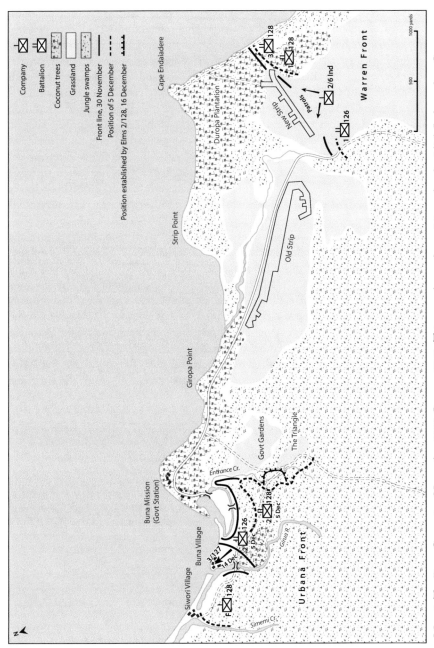

Map 4 The Buna Campaign November 1942–January 1943. This map shows the position taken by 2/6th Independent Company between two battalions of the US 126 and 128 Infantry Regiments during the campaign November to December 1942.

troops, and in doing so he needed to take any chance to inflict casualties on the enemy and by doing so open avenues for the US troops to advance through.[61]

Despite all of this 2/6th Independent Company's interaction with US troops was generally a positive one. US senior officers certainly appreciated what the company had to offer. Harcourt, a company commander, attended conferences of senior Warren Force officers, indicating that his opinion was respected and sought after.[62] One such conference occurred on 20 November the day Harcourt arrived at Buna with his force from Pongani. At the conference were McNider, and Warren Force Battalion commanders McCoy and Courier and their staffs.[63] McNider made it clear that he intended to use the company in the unconventional role it was originally intended for.[64] It was also acknowledged that the company could provide valuable reconnaissance work. Subsequently all the officers of Warren Force were instructed to regularly visit Harcourt's Head Quarters to get up to date information.[65] The primary component of the citation for the award of the US Silver Star to Harcourt made for his contribution to the Buna campaign stated that he was 'Able to secure information of great value to the commander of the force'.[66] A further indication of the value 32nd Division put on the services of 2/6th Independent Company is evident in their response to a 5 December 1942 message from New Guinea Force requesting the return of the Company to Australian command.[67] The reply of the Division was immediate and to the point informing New Guinea Command that the company could not be relieved because it was needed on the present mission.[68] This was followed up by a message from General Albert Waldron, then commanding 32nd Division, after Harding was relieved from command on 2 December 1942, to the Commander of 1 US Corps Lieutenant General Robert Eichelberger which repeated that 2/6th Independent Company could not be relieved from its present mission.[69] By this time

61 McCarthy, *First Year: Kokoda to Wau*, p. 376.
62 DDEA, Series II Library Reference Publications, Box 21, Report of the Commanding General, Buna, Forces on the Buna Campaign, 1 Dec 1942–25 Jan 1943, FILE #1, Collection of 20th Century Military Records, 1918–1950.
63 DDEA, Box 1348, Journal of 1st Bn 128th Infantry, September–November 1942 (incomplete).
64 NARA, RG319 Box 9, ARC 1D 2205874 P Entry 53, Records of Army Staff, Center of Military History, Victory in Papua, Australia to New Guinea Operations, 3rd Bn 128th Inf Jnl, 20 Nov 42, MacNider [sic] to Miller.
65 DDEA, Box 1348, Journal of 1st Bn 128th Infantry, September – November 1942 (incomplete).
66 NARA, RG496 Box 907, Records of General Headquarters, South West Pacific Area and United States Army Forces, Pacific, Adjutant General, General Correspondence, 1942–45 200.6, RG496 BOX 907, General Headquarters Southwest Pacific Area General Orders No.7 January 15, 1943.
67 NARA, Box 7885, WWII Operations Reports, 1940–48 32nd INFANTRY DIVISION 332-3.2 NOV 1942 – 332-3.2 PAPUAN DEC 1942, BOX 7885.
68 Ibid.
69 Ibid.

the Company's strength had fallen to 27 effectives, but obviously these were a highly regarded remnant.[70]

The contribution of the company to the campaign to destroy the Japanese force at Buna was studiously ignored by both official US and high level Australian sources. The official US report on the battle for Buna makes no mention of 2/6th Independent Company despite having the company marked on the maps that accompany the report.[71] This may have been because General Robert Eichelberger, the overall commander of the US Buna operation, who was known not to recoil from embellishing his own reputation, perhaps considered that the contribution of a non-US sub-unit to the success of US forces under his command did not serve the interests of his reputation.[72] In the Australian case it indicates the relative low importance the Australian high command ascribed to Independent Companies in the broader scheme. Indeed Blamey expressed his low opinion of 2/6th Independent Company to Herring on 10 December 1942, the day it was relieved from Buna, which may have coloured official Australian attitudes towards the company.[73]

The company was relieved from its duties with 32nd Division on 10 December and moved back to the Australian 7th Division. Despite prior claims by New Guinea Force that a suitable role had been found for the company no immediate task was allocated, which would have come no doubt as a welcome relief to the remnants of the company. In this case New Guinea Force cannot be criticised too harshly, as with the overtly conventional nature of the battle for Gona and Buna opportunities to use the company in an unconventional role would not be readily apparent. This would be especially so for Australian commanders who were not aware of the role the company had played at Buna and the value that the company could have added to Australian operations. As elements of 'A' and 'D' patrols re-joined, the company spent its time 'clearing up' and 'going through stores'. It was given mundane tasks such as guarding prisoners of war, protecting a dump from Japanese marauders, scouting a tank route to Soputa, and patrolling quiet back areas for signs for the enemy. On 18 December the company still had not be allocated a task. It remained this way until 20 December when a phone call from 7th Division requested that the company send a patrol behind enemy lines to blow up enemy stores, dumps and guns, a true Independent Company task. Preparations were made, explosives prepared and passwords issued. The patrol set forth on the night of 22 December, Harcourt being forbidden to accompany the patrol. As it transpired the patrol was to spend a very wet night in impassable swamps

---

70 Ibid.
71 DDEA, Series II Library Reference Publications, Box 21, Report of the Commanding General, Buna, Forces on the Buna Campaign, 1 Dec 1942–25 Jan 1943, FILE #1, Collection of 20th Century Military Records, 1918–1950.
72 NARA, RG 319 Records of the Army Staff Center of Military History Victory in Papua Interviews Bulk File #3 to Victory in Papua – Milner, Box 5, Entry 53, Lt. Gen. Richard K. Sutherland to Major Gen. Ward, Chief Military History – 6 Apr 1951.
73 AWM, AWM 3DRL/6643, Blamey to Herring, 10 Dec 1945.

and achieved nothing, apart from gathering indigenous rumours that the Japanese were short of food and shells for their guns. On 24 December the company's time on the front line in Papua came to an end, and it was flown back to Port Moresby.[74]

The experiences of 2/6th Independent Company during 1942 presents an example of the growing realisation within New Guinea Force of the strategic and tactical value of Independent Companies. Prior to this the only other deployment of an Independent Company that showed evidence of any serious war planning was that of 2/5th Independent Company to Wau in May 1942. It was fortunate for 2/6th Independent Company that it was engaged in a campaign which was at the centre of the army's commitment at that stage of the war. This ensured that the company's role would receive due consideration, and that those tasks allocated to it were designed to support ongoing operations. In true Independent Company style various patrols performed diverse tasks, the value and importance of which varied. Confirming that there was no Japanese presence on the left flank of 7th Division during the Kokoda Campaign was a significant contribution, while the work done at Buna alongside US forces provided a valuable asset to those forces.

Overall the army did much better with its management of 2/6th Independent Company than it had with any preceding Independent Company. The company's activities were conducted over a widely dispersed geographic area and conducted concurrently, indicating that the army was capable of managing such a deployment. There was no example of any deliberate tactical misuse of the company by the army during the Papuan campaign. The company was allowed to contribute its skills of reconnaissance and patrolling to its best ability. If there was one weakness with the Army's management of 2/6th Independent Company it was in the area of maintenance. Supplying the company was still handled in an uneven manner, an ongoing weakness in Staff work related to Independent Companies which, while not decisively debilitating to 2/6th Independent Company's operations, in part thanks to US intervention, revealed that there was still a great deal of improvement to be achieved in that area. It was true, at least, that in general the maintenance of 2/6th Independent Company was handled more effectively than that of 2/5th Independent Company and certainly infinitely better than had been that of 2/3rd Independent Company on New Caledonia.

The experiences of 2/6th Independent Company during the 1942 Papuan Campaign was a watershed in the Army's growing development of an appreciation for how to best employ Independent Companies. Unlike the earlier experiences the Army demonstrated an understanding of how to exploit the skills of the company in support of higher formations. The consequence of this was that the company contributed significantly to both the Kokoda Track campaign and the support of Allied forces at Buna. This evolving ability to manage Independent Companies would mature in 1943, and lead to the most effective employment of the companies at any time during the Second World War, the story of which will be recounted in the following two chapters.

74 AWM, AWM52 25/3/6, 2/6 Independent Company War Diary, Dec 42.

7

Jungle Cavalry – 1943

The Japanese threat to Papua and the Solomon Islands had been defeated by the end of 1942. 1943 would be the year of pushing back the Japanese from areas in New Guinea they had seized during their offensives in 1942. Australia was not, however, the master of its own destiny in this regard with overall strategy being determined by Washington and London. The focus of these two was firmly fixed on the war with Germany. What occurred in the South West Pacific was very much of secondary concern for them. Australia, as a junior partner in the alliance had no option but to comply with what was decided by Washington and London.[1] The initial aspiration for the South West Pacific campaign had been an Allied counter offensive to recapture Rabaul, but due to a lack of resources allocated this was changed to objectives confined to New Guinea and the Solomon Islands.[2] As part of this campaign the intention was to break the barrier between the New Guinea Mainland and New Britain presented by the Dampier and Vitiaz Straits. This would isolate Rabaul. To this end plans were made to capture airfields on Kiriwina and Woodlark islands and to capture Lae and Salamaua.[3] Australia was designated to provide the majority of troops for these operations. The Japanese interrupted these plans when they launched an offensive against Wau in January 1943, but when this was defeated the Allies were able to move over to the offensive. The subsequent operation Postern to capture Lae and Salamaua would involve 3rd Australian Division, with later US assistance, moving against Salamaua and 9th and 7th Australian Divisions against Lae. The plan was that following the capture of Lae and Salamaua, Allied forces would push on up the Markham and Ramu River valleys towards Madang.[4] Japan was aware of the threat and had resolved to defend Lae and Salamaua. The subsequent campaign

1 Peter J. Dean, *Australia 1943 – The Liberation of New Guinea* (Cambridge University Press: Port Melbourne, 2014), pp. 29–33.
2 Ibid, p.32.
3 Ibid, p. 54.
4 Dean, *Australia 1943*, presents a concise yet comprehensive account of this crucial year.

promised to be hard fought.⁵ This offensive focus by Australian forces would see the employment of Independent Companies in a number of roles that were eminently suited to.

1942 had been a year of mixed returns for the Independent Companies in New Guinea. The Army had managed the companies with a mixture of relative astuteness in the case of 2/6th Independent Company and, because of strategic circumstances, indifference in relation to 2/5th Independent Company. It would be very different in 1943.

By the beginning of 1943 the Army, or more accurately influential individual elements within the Army, had developed the confidence and competence to employ the unconventional Independent Companies in a manner commensurate with their unique attributes. Independent Companies during this period would be employed as strategic and tactical assets. Companies were granted the autonomy and materiel support necessary for them to operate effectively and achieve success. The year 1943 would represent the apogee of the Independent Companies service during the war.

There were two theatres of operation and one specific action in which Independent Companies excelled during 1943. In each case the operational and strategic advantages gained by successful Independent Company operations were significant. The first of these was on the Wau-Salamaua front where 2/3rd Independent Company, working first with 17 Brigade, and then 3rd Division, contributed notably to the conduct and outcome of that campaign. The second theatre was on the Bena Bena plateau to the west of Lae where the 2/2nd Independent Company, having returned from Timor, and the 2/7th Independent Company kept at bay Japanese forces threatening the strategically vital plateau. Subsequent to these operations the 2/6th Independent Company, now reunited and released from its travails at Buna, in an extraordinary battle seized and held the important airfield at Kaiapit, facilitating the rapid progress of 7th Division towards Lae. In each case Independent Companies contributed to achieving successful and significant strategic outcomes. This chapter and the following chapter will examine how this high point for the Independent Companies manifested itself in the AIF's campaigns in New Guinea in that year.

In January 1943 the Japanese offensive in Papua lay in ruins and the remnants of the Japanese army which had landed in Papua in July 1942 were being systematically eliminated from what remained of their Sanandana-Buna beachhead fortifications, albeit at a high cost in Allied casualties. With the threat to Papua removed the focus of Allied attention shifted westward towards Lae and Salamaua, just as Japanese attention also shifted in that direction.

With their plans to capture Port Moresby by advancing through Papua thwarted the Japanese army, in the last week of January 1943, launched an offensive from Salamaua against Wau. The reasons for this offensive were to circumvent what the Japanese

---

5   Ibid, p. 84; AWM, AWM063813, T. Yoshihara, trans. D. Heath, *Southern Cross: account of the Eastern new Guinea Campaign*, pp. 41–2.

presumed to be Allied plans to establish an airbase at Wau from which they could threaten Lae and Salamaua. The loss of Lae and Salamaua would render the Japanese position in that region of New Guinea untenable and thus it had been resolved to defend both places vigorously. Capturing and neutralising Wau would achieve this.[6] Unaware of Japanese intentions against Wau New Guinea Force still harboured plans to seize Lae. To this end it identified 17 AIF Brigade, then in Milne Bay, to move to Wau to undertake the task. The lead elements of 17 Brigade began to arrive in Wau in mid-January, which by sheer luck coincided with the Japanese offensive. The Japanese assault against Wau consisted of some 3,500 men of the Okabe Force, named after the commander General Okabe. These moved out from Salamaua and Mubo on 31 January. Shadowing their advance were 2/5th and 2/7th Independent Companies, who could do nothing to hinder it. Luckily for the defenders of Wau 2/6th Australian Infantry Battalion, which was part of 17 Brigade, had arrived in Wau and was able to confront the Japanese on the tracks leading from Mubo. In a series of hard fought engagements they managed to slow the Japanese advance. This delay of the Japanese offensive allowed the remainder of 17 Brigade to be flown into Wau. This was done even as Japanese troops pushed up to the outskirts of the town and directly threatened the airfield. Attached to 17 Brigade was 2/3rd Independent Company, which arrived in Wau aboard transport aircraft on 31 January, to be greeted by Japanese sniper fire as they disembarked.[7]

It was not certain that 2/3rd Independent Company would be of any use when it returned to Australia from its sojourn in New Caledonia in August 1942. The company arrived back in Australia wearing American uniforms and carrying American carbines, the consequence of the AIF's failure to maintain the Company while it was on New Caledonia.[8] Nine months living in small groups in New Caledonia, and being forced by Australian parsimony to fend for themselves had destroyed whatever unit discipline there was. Lieutenant John Winterflood describing the company at the time recalled that 'We were a rabble of 240 men spoiled by NC French and wine'.[9] The state of the company incited the wrath of their new Company Commander Major George Warfe. Warfe, a veteran of the Middle East and Greece, was an idiosyncratic, charismatic, tough and uncompromising soldier. He would by sheer force of personality and resolve come to stamp his mark onto the company in the months to come. Warfe initial introduction to the company was typical of the man. On calling the men out on parade Warfe was infuriated by the slovenly attitude they exhibited, the affair was in the words of one witness very much a 'Paddys Market'.[10] There are two versions of

---

6   Yoshihara, *Southern Cross*, p. 3.
7   Bottrell, *Cameos of Commandos*, p. 139.
8   AWM, AWMSP4155, Scotty McMillan 2/3 Independent Company interviewed by Neil MacDonald interviewed 1985–1991.
9   AWM, AWM S04156, Lieutenant John Winterflood interviewed by Neil MacDonald (no date).
10 AWM, AWM SO4158, John Lewin interviewed by Neil MacDonald (no date).

the story in the manner in which Warfe handled this situation. The first, as told by Lieutenant John Lewin, has Warfe calmly tell his Sergeant Major that he did not like the way the men had fallen in and to have them do it again.[11] The second story, told by one member of the company who was there has Warfe, on seeing the right markers shamble out and be made fun of by other members of the company bellowing 'You Bastards! Welcome back to the AIF you bastards, you are no longer in the American army, you are back in the Australian Army!'[12] Warfe was a strict disciplinarian and a hard task master and he set to weeding out the undisciplined individuals.[13] This was not resented by the men of the company, on the contrary Lieutenant John Winterflood's reaction to Warfe's regime was 'Bless him we all loved it – sent from heaven'.[14] Months of relentless training followed during which the companies discipline, morale and self-confidence was restored. By October the company was ready for deployment and found itself attached to 17 Brigade. When, as part of 17 Brigade, the company arrived in Wau it did so in the middle of a battle. Japanese snipers, who had worked their way to the edge of the airfield, fired at the men of the company as they alighted from their transport aircraft. With no time to spare Brigadier Murray Moten the commander of 17 Bde, faced with a situation where he needed every man available on the front line, threw the company into combat, not concerned at all what type of unit it was. As a consequence 2/3rd Independent Company fought its first action, an assault on a feature known as Woody Island, as conventional infantry.

Woody Island was a copse of trees distinct from the Jungle scrub that surrounded it; hence it was a 'Woody Island'. The Japanese had fortified themselves inside Woody Island, and posed a threat to the flank of the Australians resisting the Japanese push on Wau. From that position they also protected the flank of the Japanese force. It was 2/3rd Independent Company's task to capture Woody Island and expel the Japanese there. The fight would take three days. On the first two days Warfe assaulted with his company working in small groups as per their training. The Japanese repelled each assault, despite Warfe and his Head Quarters personnel joining in the attack on the second day.[15] On the third day, unimpressed with the company's failure to capture Woody Island General Frank Berryman, the Chief of Staff of New Guinea Force, who was in Wau at the time, instructed Moten to send the company in again. This was done according to Berryman 'In order to show them how easily it could be done if properly prepared'.[16] Warfe acting on his new instructions changed tactics, and following an intense artillery bombardment attacked in what was to be the only full strength company attack by the company of the campaign. Formed into formal

11   Ibid.
12   AWM, AWMSP4155, Scotty McMillan 2/3 Independent Company interviewed by Neil MacDonald interviewed 1985–1991.
13   AWM, AWM SO4158, John Lewin interviewed by Neil MacDonald (no date).
14   AWM, AWM S04156, John Winterflood interviewed by Neil MacDonald (no date).
15   AWM, AWM 204158, John Lewin, interviewed by Neil MacDonald (no date).
16   AWM, AWM67 3/30, T/LT Gen. F.H. Berryman [Part 2].

assault lines the company advanced with fixed bayonets and captured the position.[17] This third assault, was watched by all of 17 Bde many of who cheered the company on.[18] During the battle for Woody Island Lance Corporal Leopold Lasgourgues, who was a member of a section led personally by Warfe, encountered heavy fire at a range of fifty metres from six light machineguns, a heavy machinegun and rifles. Lasgourgues charged forward capturing a Light Machinegun and killing its two man crew. Picking up the machinegun he fired it from the hip killing four more Japanese. He came under heavy fire and was wounded in the chest but he kept firing until weakness from loss of blood forced him to drop the machinegun. He lay on the ground surrounded by the enemy and threw grenades at them until he lost consciousness, by so doing preventing the Japanese from surrounding his section. Lasgourgues's selfless and heroic action saw him awarded the Distinguished Conduct Medal.[19] For the loss of two officers and 12 soldiers killed and one officer and 21 soldiers wounded 2/3rd Independent Company experienced its baptism of fire.[20] A grand spectacle it may have been but for the men of the company it was a rude introduction to combat, one participant describing the experience as being akin to being used as storm troops.[21] Another reflected 'Talk about Commando tactics in jungle warfare! It was more like an attack in France in WW1!'[22]

The commander of 17 Brigade, Brigadier Murray Moten, was an officer noted for his, 'coolness and smooth efficiency'.[23] He was an experienced infantry commander having led 2/27th Battalion in the Middle East and taken over 17 Brigade from General Stanley Savige on 17 December 1941 when Savige moved on. He had been awarded the DSO and mentioned in dispatches for gallantry. Moten was, however, an example of the uneasy nature of the relationship that existed between the mainstream army and the Independent Companies. It was a relationship which Robert Hancock, a Captain with the Company, encapsulated in a letter to his parents in January 1943 where he wrote, 'We are a good working combination and everyone understands each other. Unfortunately this does not go higher'.[24] Moten's attitude towards the Independent Companies reflected Hancock's misgivings. A very conservative commander, Moten scathingly referred to Independent Companies as, 'Incorrectly trained. The "bearded gentry" – hit and run, mostly run'.[25] He went on to

17 Garland, *Nothing is Forever*, p. 69.
18 AWM, AWM PR91/002, Moten, Murray John (Brigadier b.1899 d.1953), An account of the fighting at Wau – 'Woody island Attack', Folder 16.
19 Garland, *Nothing is Forever*, p. 416.
20 Ibid, pp. 62–3.
21 AWM, AWM 3DRL/6766, Arden, John PH 'Jack'.
22 Garland, *Nothing is Forever*, p. 70.
23 William Bins Russell, *There Goes a Man – The Biography of Sir Stanley Savige* (Longmans: Melbourne, 1959), p. 276.
24 AWM, AWM PR91/052, Hancock. R.
25 AWM, AWM93 50/2/23/387, Records of the War 1939–45, Brig. M.J. Moten.

state that he was forced to retrain the Independent Companies under his command in elementary infantry tactics.[26] The Commandos reciprocated Moten's attitude calling him 'Mudguts' presumably in reference to an incident which occurred when Moten at one time decided he wished to see the Commandos in action. To do this Private Brian Walpole was detailed to escort Moten to the front lines. True to his unwavering regular army disposition Moten arrived at his rendezvous with Walpole wearing an impeccably pressed uniform. Walpole sensing he had better behave in a proper manner snappily saluted, something he admitted he seldom did. As they proceeded out into the jungle Walpole and Moten came across a group of Commandos firing at something to their front. Walpole shouted 'down sir' and with that pushed Moten face down into the mud. He then suggested to Moten that with the shooting and activity just to their front it wasn't safe to continue any further. Firing a burst from his Tommy Gun Walpole then extracted the Brigade commander and withdrew, returning to Moten's headquarters. Moten who by that time was in a decidedly dishevelled and muddy state did not reprimand Walpole but instead thanked him for showing him the front line and said that he now had a better appreciation for the situation.[27] There was in this incident a glimmer of hope that Moten's perception of his Commandos may have somewhat moderated, but as it turned out it did not, and he remained as contrary to them as he ever had been.

In January Moten assumed command of Kanga Force, which had expanded to include 17 Brigade as well as the units which had composed the original Kanga Force. With this Moten inherited both the 2/5th and 2/7th Independent Companies. Moten's attitude to his new charges was immediately derogatory. He described 2/5th Independent Company as unreliable, and that the company's officers lacked basic infantry training. He considered the discipline in the company to be poor, that they straggled on the march and lacked the basics of hygiene and sanitation. He considered the commander of the company to be ineffective, and that the company needed a strong commander to weld them into an effective team.[28] Moten's criticisms were those of a conservative conventional infantryman and reflected the wide gulf that existed between the conventional mainstream military mind-set and the Independent Companies. Moten took little account that the company was at the end of an extremely arduous and physically ruinous lengthy term of service in the jungle.[29]

26 Ibid.
27 Brian Walpole, *My War, Life is for Living: An Australian Commando in New Guinea and Borneo 1943–1945* (ABC Books: Sydney, 2004), p. 21.
28 AWM, AWM PR91/002 Folder 4, Moten, Murray John (Brigadier b.1899 d.1953).
29 Walker, *The Island Campaigns*, pp. 137–8. Walker states that the General Health of 2/5 Independent Company was the subject for investigation at the time. 114 Officers and men examined and classified 8 as fully fit. 27 as partially fit, 56 as temporarily unfit and recommended that 12 be evacuate or sent for medical board, 11 were left for a later decision. 18 months service in tropical conditions (which includes their time in Port Moresby prior to deployment to Wau) endemic disease: chronic malaria and dietary

He ignored concerned medical reports on the company considering them to be exaggerations.[30] Consequently Moten ordered 2/5th Independent Company to spend three weeks with 2/7th Battalion to rest and be 'retrained', a process that was completed to Moten's satisfaction on 25 March.[31] Moten's attitude to 2/3rd Independent Company was similar. He initially dismissed the company as being 'just as bad', but nevertheless considered that the company needed to be retrained and that 'I had to make them or break them and finally made them'.[32] Moten made no public comments regarding 2/7th Independent Company, but it is hard to imagine he would have regarded it any more favourably than the other two companies.

The process by which Moten 'made' 2/3rd Independent Company must have been an interesting one. This was especially so considering the respective personalities of Moten and Warfe. In contrast to Moten's conservative nature George Warfe was very much the extrovert. He was described by those who knew him as possessing 'incredible daring confidence' and 'like a pirate on the high seas searching for loot and plunder'.[33] Brian Walpole, who had taken a demotion to private so that he could join 2/3rd Independent Company, said that Warfe was like a coiled spring, full of power and energy.[34] Warfe's prowess as a combat officer was summed up by one officer who observed that 'He would make your blood go cold at his superlative courage and cool savagery'.[35] Warfe was never reluctant to take on any task, fight any fight and to tell anyone who would listen when he achieved success, even if he was accused of exaggerating his achievements at times.[36] Despite all of this Warfe was a stickler for battalion discipline.[37] His personality and manner of command were the direct antithesis of Moten. Despite this, Moten did concede, 'that one could not help liking the blighter'.[38] It is perhaps this wary respect on Moten's part and Warfe's innate regard for discipline and superior authority, which allowed two such disparate personalities to work with each other.

---

deficiency, Vitamin B deficiency, boredom and constant threat and tension due to superior enemy numbers all contributed this state; 2/5 was a physical wreck when it returned to Australia from New Guinea, it was declared a B class unit and attached to 3 Militia Division; Treichel, *Commando Army Service 1941–1946*, pp. 15–16.
30 AWM, AWM PR91/002 Folder 2, Moten, Murray John (Brigadier b.1899 d.1953).
31 Ibid.
32 AWM, AWM93 50/2/23/387, Records of the War 1939–45 Brig. M.J. Moten.
33 AWM, AWM S04158, John Lewin, interviewed by Neil MacDonald (no date); Russell, *There Goes a Man*, p.276; Garland, *Nothing is Forever*, p. 96.
34 Walpole, *My War*, p.16.
35 Phillip Bradley, *Hell's Battlefield – The Australians in New Guinea in World War II* (Allen and Unwin: Sydney, 2012), p. 215.
36 Russell, *There Goes a Man*, p. 276; AWM, AWM93 50/2/23/387, Records of the War 1939–45, Brig. M.J. Moten.
37 AWM, AWM 204158, John Lewin, interviewed by Neil MacDonald (no date).
38 AWM, AWM93 50/2/23/387, Records of the War 1939–45, Brig. M.J. Moten.

Nevertheless applying restraints on Warfe was a feature of Moten's relationship with his impetuous subordinate. Characteristic of the difficulty for a conservative higher commander to manage the impetuosity of Warfe was an incident when Warfe personally lead a small group out on what he called a 'marauding expedition'.[39] After the Japanese offensive on Wau had been defeated and the Japanese retreated back along the jungle tracks towards Mubo it was time to pursue the beaten enemy. To do this 2/3rd Independent Company was divided into three sections each covering a different track leading out from Wau. These sections set to pursuing the defeated Japanese but inevitably given the rugged terrain and scattered nature of the enemy the company's pursuit became a tangle of sub units intermixed with the enemy.[40] This suited Warfe, whose desire was always to 'go get the bastards'.[41] The most vigorous pursuit of the Japanese occurred along what was euphemistically called the 'Jap Track', where elements of the company caught up with many Japanese and killed them.[42] During this period Warfe absented himself for three days, on his marauding expedition, taking a party of men out to hunt and kill Japanese. Private Brian Walpole was part of Warfe's marauding force. He and 12 others set out down the track. Within two days they had lost radio contact, but continued nevertheless, during which they ambushed and killed numerous Japanese. Food was running short and the men were hungry. There was no hope of finding rations and they began to wonder what was to become of them. It was at that moment that climbing a spur they spotted a large group of Japanese cooking a meal. Warfe told his men to wait and watch until the Japanese had finished cooking and then 'we shoot the bastards and eat it ourselves'. After one hour the Japanese cooked their meal and the Commandos opened fire killing them all. They then ate the meal which Walpole said that despite being poor fare was the best food he and his comrades had eaten in days.[43] Typically during this expedition everyone in the company camp and at Brigade Headquarters was deeply concerned with Warfe's absence, except George Warfe.[44] It was around this time that Warfe informed 17 Brigade that he was prepared to 'bash' Bobdubi ridge, a strategically significant ridge which ran parallel to the main Japanese line of Communication from Salamaua to Mubo. He was restrained by Moten from doing so.[45]

---

39 AWM, AWM 204158, John Lewin, interviewed by Neil MacDonald (no date).
40 Garland, *Nothing is Forever*, p. 73.
41 AWM, AWM 204158, John Lewin, interviewed by Neil MacDonald (no date).
42 AWM, AWM S04156, John Winterflood interviewed by Neil MacDonald (no date). The 'Jap Track' was a track which had been surveyed by the Germans (both miners and missionaries have been credited with the surveying) in 1926 and not being used was subsequently reclaimed by the jungle. Its existence was revealed to the Japanese by a European, possible a Swiss named Hoffsetter, who was collaborating with them. Using the 'Jap Track' Japanese troops were able to approach Wau more quickly and from an unexpected direction.
43 Walpole, *My War*, p. 22.
44 Garland, *Nothing is Forever*, pp. 87 and 91.
45 AWM, AWM93 50/2/23/387, Records of the War 1939–45, Brig. M.J. Moten.

Despite Warfe's impetuosity and unpredictability Moten continued to tolerate him, indicating that there was some recognition of the value of Warfe's contribution to ongoing operations. Even so there were suspicions within the company that Moten planned to relieve Warfe of command because of his insubordinate impetuosity, but there is no evidence Moten ever considered doing so.[46] If nothing else the relationship between Moten and Warfe illustrates the ability of two very disparate commanders to work together for their mutual benefit, when circumstances made it wise to do so. This was, in its own way, a reflection of the pragmatism of two professional military commanders and a precursor to what would later, in 1943, become an effective utilisation of Independent Companies in the wider operations of the Army.

There were, however, limits to Moten's capacity to bear with the Independent Company manner of waging war. One such incident occurred when Moten ordered Lieutenant John Lewin to leave wounded men on a track and make haste to another position. Lewin refused the order and instead brought his wounded back into camp. There could be no clearer example of the conflict of presumptions between the mainstream army mindset of unquestioning obedience and compliance and that of the Independent Company culture of individual responsibility and loyalty to the group. For Moten an order issued by higher authority in time of war was an order, which was not to be questioned. For Lewin such an order was meaningless if complying with it would force him to abandon his wounded to an unknown fate in the jungle. Such an action went against the fundamental ethos of the Independent Companies who prided themselves on looking after their mates and not abandoning them, even if dead. When Lewin returned to Brigade Head Quarters, Moten demanded to know why he had come back. Lewin, who was himself ill, replied that he had sick and wounded and would not abandon them. Unsympathetic Moten told Lewin he should have left them, to which Lewin retorted directly to Moten that he would never do such a thing.[47] Such mutually incompatible states of mind sorely challenged military relationships.

Despite this, and the obvious incompatibility between Moten's understanding of operational conduct and discipline and that of 2/3rd Independent Company's concept of how things were done, on balance Moten's handling of the company appears to have been both professional and prudent. The instructions he issued were both appropriate for an Independent Company and realistic.[48] One example of this was the deployment of the company during April out to the far left flank of 17 Brigade to a position where it could threaten Japanese lines of communication, a task eminently suited to an

---

46   Garland, *Nothing is Forever*, p. 88. Garland claims that Moten was preparing a dossier of Warfe's indiscretions to use to secure Warfe's relief of command. This may have been the case, but an examination of Moten's extensive personal papers reveals no evidence of any such dossier.
47   Ibid, p. 79.
48   AWM, AWM PR91/002 Folder 2, Moten, Murray John (Brigadier b.1899 d.1953).

136   Jungle Cavalry

Independent Company.⁴⁹ Moten's handling of 2/3rd Independent Company demonstrates that at that stage of the war there was no intention, even from officers who were not enamoured of the Independent Companies, to completely discount whatever unconventional contribution the companies could make. This was a great improvement from the dismissive attitudes of 1941, and reflected the growing appreciation for the qualities of the Independent Companies which had manifested in 1942. Just how influential others, such as Warfe, were in determining the nature of his company's tasks at this time is unknown. Warfe was certainly not above suggesting ideas to his superiors and was acknowledged by none other than Lieutenant General Edmund Herring, who from October 1942 until August 1943 was the commander of New Guinea Force and would eventually become commander of 1st Australian Corps, as being, 'full of good ideas'.⁵⁰ Such advice may well have been offered by Warfe and conceded to by Moten. Perhaps the best acknowledgement of Moten's ability to manage for the better what had the potential to be a quite adversarial relationship was that by 22 April 2/3rd Independent Company's aggressive patrols had for the loss of 5 killed in action and 17 wounded killed 257 Japanese and wounded many others.⁵¹

On 23 April Kanga Force was disbanded and Major General Stanley Savige with 3rd Division assumed command on the Wau-Salamaua front. 2/5th Independent Company was finally relieved and sent back to Australia for much needed rest and recuperation. At the same time 2/7th Independent Company was redeployed to operate as part of Bena Force on the Bena Bena Plateau, the story of which will be related in the following chapter. This left 2/3rd Independent Company, as the sole Independent Company in the Wau-Salamaua area. Savige's appointment would prove to be a turning point for the operational contribution 2/3rd Independent Company would make to the campaign to capture Salamaua. Unlike Moten whose tolerance of Independent Companies was strained, Savige had a finely tuned appreciation for how to employ the unconventional attributes of an Independent Company to support larger formations. Savige's concept of war owed much to his First World War experiences. He had during 1918 been a member of Dunsterforce, during which he and a party of five officers and 15 Non Commissioned Officers, operated independently in northern Iran to protect 80,000 Assyrian refugees from the depredations of Kurds and Ottoman troops. Such an experience, operating in an unconventional military environment in a campaign with no hard and fast rules, would have given him the personal experience to both appreciate and understand the nature of small scale

49   McCarthy, *First Year: Kokoda to Wau*, p. 585.
50   AWM, AWM 172, 10, David Dexter interview with Herring – 6 April 1951. Herring suggested that the idea of the attack on Bobdubi ridge in May 1943 may have been made by Warfe.
51   AWM, AWM54 587/6/2, Analysis of operations (or lessons learnt) Report on Doublet T. (Salamaua.) Report by 2/6 Bn on action Lababia Ridge 20/24 June. – Report on operations in the Mubo Area by 2/7 Australian Infantry Battalion 13th April to 2nd June. 1943.

unconventional operations.⁵² Furthermore his experiences on the Western Front had taught him the futility of frontal attacks, and as a consequence he always sought the indirect approach to defeat his foe. This was very much his approach to fighting the Japanese in which he stressed no frontal attacks because of the certainty of heavy casualties to the attacker, and to pin down the enemy and find his flanks. This was because, as he said, the Japanese would invariably 'bolt' when they were surrounded or partially surrounded.⁵³ Fighting with limited resources in the dense jungle, where large scale manoeuvring in the manner of conventional combat was impossible would make such tactics de rigueur. Savige accepted this acknowledging that war in the jungle simply could not be fought in the manner of war in 'civilised countries'.⁵⁴ For Savige, the Independent Company provided the tool he could employ to achieve success in such a setting.

Savige alone amongst all the senior field commanders in the AIF during the Second World War wrote down his thoughts on the use of unconventional forces in the jungle. On 29 April 43 he produced an appreciation urging the employment of Independent Companies and equating the Companies to the role of cavalry in the jungle by securing forward areas, harassing the enemy's line of communication, and retarding enemy advances.⁵⁵ In later years Savige would go further and formally proclaim his ideas for the use of Commandos in the jungle. His *Tactical and Administrative doctrine for jungle warfare applicable to all formations under command 2 Aust. Corps (AIF)* included a section specifically addressing Commandos. In this Savige continued his association between Commandos and cavalry with their usefulness as scouts and to outflank and harass the enemy. He concluded by stating that in the jungle 'cavalry' was even more valuable to a commander than in Europe or the Western Desert.⁵⁶ This idea of the Independent Companies being cavalry became firmly fixed in the mind of the Companies and they came to refer to themselves as 'Jungle Cavalry'.⁵⁷ While Savige's appreciations were his own, his senior rank and field command responsibilities made it sure that his ideas became doctrine for those under his command. It was Savige's understanding of the value of Independent Company operations in the jungle that would provide the context in which 2/3rd Independent Company would operate during the Wau-Salamaua campaign.

52 For a detailed account of Savige's experiences with Dunsterforce see: Russell, *There Goes a Man*, pp. 101–118.
53 AWM, AWM67 2/40, Gavin Long Notebook 40.
54 Russell, *There Goes a Man*, p. 260.
55 AWM, AWM52 1/5/4 3, Australian Division General Staff Branch (3 Aust Div GS Branch) May 1943 Part 1, Appreciation of the Situation by GOC 3 Aust Div at 0300 hrs 29 Apr 43.
56 Stanley Savige, *Tactical and Administrative doctrine for jungle warfare applicable to all formations under command 2 Aust. Corps (AIF)*, HQ 2 Aust. Corps (AIF) (N.G. Press Unit: New Guinea, 194, p. 38.
57 AWM, AWM52 2/2/58, 2/6 Commando Squadron War Diary November to December 1943.

From the first Savige began to utilise 2/3rd Independent Company in a strategic role. Rather than simply support the tactical operations of a larger formation, which had been the case for 17 Brigade, the Company was allowed the autonomy to conduct tasks which directly contributed to the combat value of the Division as a whole. Part of the reason for the use of the Company in this way was the makeup of 3rd Division itself. For want of a better description 3rd Division was an 'unbalanced' Division. The Division consisted of two Brigades, 15 Brigade and 17 Brigade. 17 Brigade was a fully formed three battalion veteran AIF brigade while 15 Brigade consisted of only two battalions the 24th and 58/59th, both inexperienced untested militia battalions. Savige deployed his experienced 17 Brigade against the fortified Japanese positions at Mubo, and 15 Brigade out to his left flank to cover the approaches from the Markham River Valley. Needing to screen the tracks leading from Markham resulted in the 24th Battalion being split into company sized groups and ordered to patrol those tracks. This left just the 58/59th Battalion as the sole force available for 15 Brigade to cover the immediate left flank of the Division. The reliability of the 58/59 Battalion was questionable. As Militia its training for jungle warfare left much to be desired and its officers were both inexperienced and described by one source as incompetent.[58] To bolster 58/59th Battalion Savige attached 2/3rd Independent Company to 15 Brigade and deployed it to Missim, a dominant point on the left flank. From there the company, acting as a 'cavalry' flank guard could dispute any Japanese moves in that direction, conduct offensive raids against the Japanese line of communication between Salamaua and Mubo, and gain information of enemy strengths, dispositions and movements.[59] Savige knew Warfe from his time in the Middle East, and understood Warfe's aggressive impetuous temperament.[60] By posting Warfe to Missim, some distance from the main force, he was giving Warfe the opportunity to act autonomously.

Once at Missim the company immediately embarked on patrols during which numerous Japanese were encountered and killed, including one group surprised while they were swimming and sunbathing.[61] In a very short time the Japanese became aware that a force was stalking them and took steps to protect themselves. Japanese soldiers were instructed to keep on the alert for the slightest sound and to watch not only the front but the rear. They were warned to be alert and aggressive, for it was only in this way that they could stamp out 'the "guerrilla" activities of the enemy'.[62] The

---

58 Walpole, *My War*, p. 48.
59 AWM, AWM 54 587/7/12, Part 2, p.5, Report on Operations of 3 Australian Division in Salamaua Area from 22 April 1943 to 23 August 1943.
60 Phillip Bradley, *To Salamaua* (Cambridge University Press: Melbourne, 2010), p. 54.
61 AWM, AWM 54 587/7/12 Part 2 p.5, Report on Operations of 3 Australian Division in Salamaua Area from 22 April 1943 to 23 August 1943.
62 AWM, AMW55 1/3, Allied Translator and Interpreter Section, South West Pacific Area Bulletins 1943, 'Instructional Reference – approach manoeuvres in the jungle' Moto 2803 Butai – stamped Otake 28 Apr 1943, Bulletin 255 26 Jul 1943, Item 2776.

Japanese came to call the company the 'fierce bearded barbarians', from the beards many of the Company tended to wear after spending extended periods in the jungle.[63]

By late April Company patrols had determined that Bobdubi ridge, a significant feature that ran from the west of Mubo virtually all the way to Salamaua, was lightly held.[64] Warfe who was concerned that his company be employed aggressively before health issues reduced its effectiveness to do so, suggested that the ridge be attacked and occupied.[65] Such a move would directly threaten the Japanese line of communication to their main defensive positions on Mubo, and possibly result in them abandoning those positions. Warfe's enthusiastic plan was to employ all of the company to capture the ridge, and at the same time make use of two companies of 24th Battalion to move through the nearby Malalo area. Savige agreed with the suggestion to attack Bobdubi, but placed a limit of one platoon to attack although he conceded that Warfe could make use of elements from company Head Quarters.[66] Warfe accepted the restraint assuming that it was due to Savige's concerns over having to divert resources to maintain a larger attacking force.[67] On 3 May, a date that coincided with 3rd Divisions plans to move against Mubo, the Company attacked Bobdubi ridge. Warfe was determined to give the Japanese a 'bloody nose' and went about the task with cunning enthusiasm. He sent out parties to the front and flanks and to infiltrate behind the Japanese on the ridge.[68] Once all were in place he attacked, feinting to the front and flanks, and then when the time was right assaulted from the rear. By 9 May the Japanese had been driven completely from many positions on the ridge including the important Old Vickers position, which overlooked the Komiatum track, the main Japanese line of communication between Salamaua and Mubo. With the Japanese who remained on the ridge the company decided to indulge in some very unconventional tactics. On the night of 9 May a 'terror type raid' was carried out on the last Japanese defenders. This tactic involved creeping up on the Japanese at night and inflicting a barrage of noise on them. 'Flares, lots of screaming and yelling', as well as grenades and small arms fire

---

63 Peter Pinney, *The Barbarians, A Soldier's New Guinea Diary* (University of Queensland Press: St Lucia, 1988); Joe Wills, 2/3 Independent Company veteran interview, 26 September 2016.
64 AWM, AWM 54 587/7/12, Part 2, p. 6, Report on Operations of 3 Australian Division in Salamaua Area from 22 April 1943 to 23 August 1943,
65 AWM, AWM93 50/2/23/489, Records of the War 1939–1945, Warfe to Gavin Long 6 Dec 1956 from Jungle Training School Canungra.
66 Garland, *Nothing is Forever*, p. 118.
67 AWM, AWM93 50/2/23/489, Records of the War 1939–1945, Warfe to Gavin Long 6 Dec 1956 from Jungle Training School Canungra. The origin of the idea for the attack on Bobdubi ridge on 4 May is the subject of some disagreement. Savige in a 10 April 1951 interview with David Dexter claimed the idea was his, Herring states that he is unsure who suggested it but would not have been surprised if it had been George Warfe.
68 Garland, *Nothing is Forever*, pp. 116 and 118.

assaulted the senses of the entrenched Japanese.[69] Private Brian Walpole recalled the men screaming their heads off, throwing verbal abuse, whistling, throwing flares and grenades, and firing bullets.[70] In doing so the company was imitating the Japanese tactic of 'firing and shouting' at night time.[71] Patrols the next day detected no movement from the enemy and on 11 May it was found that the Japanese had abandoned their positions and departed, thus surrendering all of Bobdubi ridge.[72] Warfe, typically, had ignored Savige's admonishment to restrain the numbers he employed and eventually in addition to the one platoon allowed, had employed Engineers, Signallers, Medical and members of the transport section as well.[73] He was not reprimanded for this, no doubt because the mission was successful. Bobdubi ridge had been captured in an operation that 3rd Division staff acknowledged to be as unconventional as it was effective.[74]

Once present on Bobdubi ridge the company did not hesitate to make its presence felt. It was very much the case 'he who holds the ridges, holds the country'. The Komiatum Track was repeatedly raided by parties from the ridge and 68 Japanese were killed.[75] Vickers Machineguns, which were not officially part of their table of equipment, but had been acquired when on New Caledonia and kept, were placed on vantage points which overlooked the track and harassed any Japanese who were spotted. As it would eventuate these Vickers guns would prove to be valuable assets in many of the company's engagements.

The presence of 2/3rd Independent Company on Bobdubi ridge created a strategic threat to the Japanese forces occupying Mubo. Enemy forces occupying Bobdubi ridge directly threatened the Japanese line of Communication to Mubo, and the ability to reinforce and supply to that position. Raids by the Independent Company along that line of communication had led to the desertion of native carriers forcing Japanese troops to carry their supplies to their forward troops, no small imposition in the

---

69 Ibid, pp. 122–23. These tactics became known as 'Nerve Tactics' and were promulgated through the army as one means of discomfiting the Japanese see: AWM, AWM54 937/3/4, Tactical Directive No.7, The Development and use of "Nerve Tactics" in Jungle Warfare.
70 Walpole, *My War*, p. 26.
71 AWM, AWM55 1/7, ATIS South West Pacific Area Bulletins Nos 446–490 14 OCT. TO 3 NOV. 1943, ASA No.2086 Force, Takeo Ono, 'Directive on ending instructions based on experience in combat', Bulletin 484 30 Oct 43, Item 17, 5917.
72 Garland, *Nothing is Forever*, pp. 122–23; AWM, AWM52 25/3/3/9, 2/3 Independent Company War Diary, 9–11 May 43. It is possible that the enemy had evacuated their positions prior to the terror raid as there was no response from the Japanese to the raid.
73 Garland, *Nothing is Forever*, p. 119.
74 AWM, AWM52 1/5/4, 3 Australian Division General Staff Branch (3 Aust Div GS Branch) May 1943 Part 1.
75 'Battle of the Ridges', *The Australian Army at War*, Brochure Number Three, Army Directorate of Public Relations, Alfred Henry Pettifer Acting Government Printer, 1944, p. 6; AWM, AWM 54 587/7/12, Report on Operations of 3 Australian Division in Salamaua Area from 22 April 1943 to 23 August 1943 Part 2.

jungle.⁷⁶ Consequently the Japanese responded to the challenge forcefully. On 14 May, using a phone line laid by 2/3rd Independent Company to guide them towards the company, the Japanese counter attacked. The force that attacked the ridge consisted of 50 Naval troops from Salamaua, 200 men from the YAMAGATA force, 130 men from the 1st infantry company of the Markham garrison and 10 unattached army troops, some 390 men in total supported by heavy machineguns, mortars and artillery.⁷⁷ With no intention of holding the ground and under orders from 3rd Division not to risk casualties, the Company broke contact with the enemy and withdrew.⁷⁸ The following day 30 Japanese 'light' bombers, and 9 'attack planes' escorted by 40 fighters, bombed the area in which the company had been but which was now occupied by the Japanese.⁷⁹ The men of the company sitting safe at a distance watched with amusement as the Japanese set to 'belting themselves on the head'.⁸⁰

The impact of the seizure of Bobdubi ridge by the company should not be underestimated. In capturing Bobdubi ridge 2/3rd Independent Company had delivered a significant strategic blow against the Japanese defenders facing 17 Brigade at Mubo. The tactical decisiveness of the company's assault on the ridge and their subsequent relentless aggression against the Komiatum track had convinced the Japanese that up to 800 Australians had occupied the ridge.⁸¹ Such numbers could not be ignored. Even when they recaptured the ridge the Japanese assumed that 300–400 Australians were lurking in the jungle nearby.⁸² This ability of Independent Companies to create

76   Garland, *Nothing is Forever*, p. 131.
77   AWM, AWM PR91/002, Allied Translator and Interpreter Section South West Pacific Area – Enemy Publications No. 145 Part I, July 1944 – Intelligence Reports, maps and Sketches Operations in New Guinea Apr 43 to Aug 43, in: Moten Murray John (Brigadier b.1899 d.1953) folder 19; AWM, AWM54 587/6/2, Analysis of operations (or lessons learnt) Report on Doublet T. (Salamaua.) Report by 2/6 Bn on action Lababia Ridge 20/24 June. – Report on operations in the Mubo Area by 2/7 Australian Infantry Battalion 13th April to 2nd June, 1943.
78   AWM, AWM52 25/3/3/9, 2/3 Independent Company War Diary, May to June 1943, 14 May 43.
79   AWM, AWM PR91/002, Allied Translator and Interpreter Section South West Pacific Area – Enemy Publications No. 145 Part I, July 1944 – Intelligence Reports, maps and Sketches Operations in New Guinea Apr 43 to Aug 43. Intelligence Record No.98 16 May 43', Moten Murray John (Brigadier b. 1899 D. 1953) folder 19–28; AWM, AWM52 25/3/3/9, 2/3 Independent Company War Diary – May to June 1943, 15 May 43. 2/3's diary entry for the bombing claims the Japanese had 24 twin engine bombers escorted by 30 Zeros. The figures quoted in the text are from the Japanese Intelligence report of the bombing raid.
80   Garland, *Nothing is Forever*, p. 130.
81   AWM, AMW55 1/4, Allied Translator and Interpreter Section, South West Pacific Area Bulletins 8 August – 14 September 1943, Bulletin 332 5 Sept 43, Item 7, 3428.
82   AWM, AWM PR91/002, Allied Translator and Interpreter Section South West Pacific Area – Enemy Publications No. 145 Part I, July 1944 – Intelligence Reports, maps and Sketches Operations in New Guinea Apr 43 to Aug 43. Intelligence Record No.98 16 May 43, Moten Murray John (Brigadier b.1899 d.1953), folder 19.

an illusion of greater strength than they actually were was a consistent feature of Independent Company operations. That the Japanese had been forced to divert a considerable force from the front line to deal with the threat, and then to maintain a garrison on the ridge was of value to the overall operations of the Division. A further factor adding to Japanese discomfit was that Major General Okabe who had commanded the offensive against Wau and was the senior Japanese officer in the area was wounded in the foot by a booby trap at Bobdubi on 14 May. He was evacuated to Lae and then back to Rabaul.[83] The capture and then withdrawal from Bobdubi ridge was an excellent example of a most effective use of economy of force to strike behind enemy lines in support of the strategic objectives of the main force, a tactic entirely in keeping with the operational concept of 'Jungle Cavalry'.

For the remainder of May the Company concentrated on defending the Hote area. This sat to the north of Missim and offered a good approach if the Japanese wished to threaten the main carrier supply line across Double Mountain. The Japanese began to build up their numbers in Hote and a move by them seemed imminent. A combined force of 24th Battalion infantry and a 2/3rd Independent Company Vickers machinegun were posted to cover the approach from Hote. The 24th Battalion troops were inexperienced never having been in action before. At 7.00 a.m. on 20 May the Japanese attacked, their approached being heralded by the sound of booby traps exploding. With that the Vickers gun and infantry rifles opened fire. There were approximately 150 Japanese at Hote. It is not known how many of these attacked but their number eventually told and fearing being outflanked the 24th Battalion infantry withdrew. The Vickers gun, which had, it was estimated killed 50 or 60 Japanese, was disabled and abandoned. There were reports of 55 stretcher cases carrying Japanese wounded back to Salamaua.[84] Two Australians were wounded in the fight.[85] Despite their success the Japanese did not press their advance against Missim, but shifted their attention towards Mubo, which may always have been their intention. Australian troops occupied Hote soon after.

During June many of the Company rested at Missim. One company of the 58/59th Battalion, and one company of the 24th Battalion, came to Missim and were placed under the command of 2/3rd Independent Company. Patrols continued to go out, but these met with limited success and indeed suffered reverses. One such example was when a patrol led by Lieutenant John Lewin intended to raid Malolo village was surprised unprepared in camp by Japanese and following a savage close quarter fire-fight managed to escape but in a disordered state. This near disaster had come about because Lewin had neglected to post sentries which had allowed the Japanese

---

83 AWM, AMW55 1/3, Allied Translator and Interpreter Section, South West Pacific Area Bulletins 1943, Bulletin 273 4 Aug 1943, Item 8, 2933.
84 Garland, *Nothing is Forever*, p. 141.
85 Ibid, pp.139–40; AWM, AWM52 25/3/3/11, 2/3 Independent Company War Diary, 20 May 43,

to creep up on him. Pulling in his sentries had only been for 15 minutes, but as with all such things it was during those 15 minutes that the Japanese had arrived.[86] Why Lewin, and experienced officer would commit such an error has never been explained, although it was suspected that he had been betrayed by an indigenous guide who was with his patrol.[87] Another patrol, under the command of Sergeant Bob Swan, a consummate stalker who had once spent the night underneath a hut in which Japanese soldiers were, set out to destroy Japanese artillery guns which had been shelling the company lines from a hill.[88] The patrol has six men. When the patrol reached a point from which it could observe the well defended Japanese gun position it was fired on by Japanese light machineguns and mortars and realised that it did not have the strength to carry out its mission.[89] Both these patrols were failures, the first due to the officer in charge not carrying out correct procedures and the second because the designated target was too strong for the patrol detailed to attack it, implying inadequate reconnaissance had been conducted. June would prove to be a disappointing time for the company with very little achieved.

One aspect of Warfe's temperament that diminished the image of the consummate warrior to a degree was over-confidence which at times verged on arrogance. This trait did assist him to create a charismatic persona, but it did have its drawbacks. An example of this occurred on 6 July 1943 when the company was to move in a column from Namling into country closer to Mubo. The company was to move stretched out along jungle tracks through a region that was no so heavily timbered. Warfe was told that this route was open to observation by the enemy. Warfe, who was utterly contemptuous of Japanese military skills, ignored the warning. The consequences of this were that the Japanese, who had seen the company's movement from their positions at Orodubi, attacked the centre of the column at a site that would subsequently be called Ambush Knoll which would play an important part in events related to the Company in the near future. The indigenous carriers with the column warned of the attack, and came running back shouting 'Japan man stapim klostu' (Japanese are near). Private 'Curly' Tregaskis was killed and two men, Privates Alan Ives and Alan Besley were wounded. The indigenous carriers dropped their loads and ran into the jungle, and the company lost all its reserve supplies of food and ammunition, two Vickers machine guns, a 3-inch mortar, medical supplies and its war diary. Heavier casualties were only prevented by the thickness of the bush which provided cover. The Japanese ambush split the company into two separate sections isolated from one another, and also revealed to the Japanese the location of the company and its strength. This was a devastating blow with the potential to reduce the company's operational capabilities

86 Garland, *Nothing is Forever*, pp. 146–49.
87 Ibid, p. 141.
88 Garland, *Nothing is Forever*, p. 154.
89 Ibid. p.149; AWM, AWM52 25/3/3/11, 2/3 Independent Company War Diary, 29 June 43.

significantly. Warfe's soldiers were aware of their commanders capacity to ignore advice and act without due consideration of danger. Even though they respected him greatly, they were inclined not to always accept everything proposed by Warfe without a degree of scepticism, their attitude being that they 'had been conned by George before'.[90]

Unfazed, even though it was his actions which caused the setback, Warfe ordered each section of the now split column to probe towards the site of the ambush at the centre of the column, in the hope of locating and rescuing the lost supplies and equipment. These patrols clashed with Japanese still in the area. Orders to harass the Japanese lines of communication to Mubo still stood, but now the company with only 60 effectives in the leading section, no support weapons, limited amounts of food and ammunition and no medical supplies would have a difficult time achieving that. Despite this, in the next few days Warfe pushed aggressively sending out patrols which located the Japanese and engaged them. During these operations some of the lost stores, including the Vickers Machineguns and 3-inch mortar were recovered.[91] What this incident revealed was the danger of underestimating the enemy, which Warfe habitually did. It also illustrated the reluctance of Warfe to accept advice which ran counter to his preconceived ideas. Warfe was an outstanding leader but certainly did have his limitations.

On 19–20 July the company became involved in a battle which while being entirely conventional in every aspect illustrated the resilience and sheer bloody minded doggedness of the Independent Companies. The battle was for a rising hump of ground, which became known as Ambush Knoll. The knoll was located to the immediate west of Mubo sitting between 15 and 17 Brigades and was the site of the successful Japanese ambush on the Company on 6 July. The Japanese occupied the knoll on 12 July threatening to drive a wedge between 15 and 17 Brigades and thus cut the lateral line of communication between the two Brigades, which would effectively cut 3rd Division in half and thus compromise the Division's operations against Mubo.[92] Being the nearest unit on hand, 2/3rd Independent Company was given the task of ejecting the Japanese from the Knoll, despite having only 40% of its men available due to casualties and sickness.[93] The fight would be conducted in true Independent Company style, with a frontal assault to distract and fix the enemy, followed by an assault from the rear by troops who had infiltrated behind the enemy position. Consequently 24 men, taking advantage of every scrap of concealment and cover offered by the jungle, pushed up to in some places within five metres of the Japanese positions and exchanged Tommy gun and machine gun fire. During this fight Corporal Keith

---

90   Garland, *Nothing is Forever*, p. 159.
91   Garland, *Nothing is Forever*, pp. 161–81; AWM, AWM52 25/3/3/11, 2/3 Independent Company War Diary, 7 Jul 43.
92   AWM, AWM54 587/7/12 Part 1, Report on Operations of 3 Aust. Div. in Salamaua Area From 22 April 43–25 Aug 43.
93   Garland, *Nothing is Forever*, p. 181.

No.7 Infantry Training Centre, Tidal River, Wilson's Promontory 1941.
(Courtesy Keith Reynolds)

Men of the 2/5th Independent Company during training at No.7 Infantry Training Centre,
Tidal River 1941. (Australian War Memorial)

2/3rd Independent Company men on New Caledonia 1942. It is apparent that their time on New Caledonia was far more comfortable than that of their comrades of 2/1st Independent Company in the islands north of Australia or 2/2nd Independent Company on Timor. (Arden family photograph collection. National Library of Australia)

2/2nd Independent Company allied with local Timorese people burn down huts belonging to pro-Japanese Timorese, Timor 1942. A great deal of the fighting that took part in Timor from November 1942 until January 1943 was against pro-Japanese Timorese. (Australian War Memorial)

Two men of 2/6th Independent Company patrolling through the jungle on their advance towards Buna, November 1942. The style of dress and automatic weapons accurately reflect the appearance of Independent Company soldiers at this period of the war. (Australian War Memorial)

Major Harry Harcourt 2/6th Independent Company, wearing the beret, in conference with Brigadier General Hanford McNider of the U.S. 32nd Infantry Division, centre wearing helmet, and staff during the move towards Buna November 1942. Harcourt frequently met with McNider and other senior U.S. officers during 2/6th Independent Companies deployment with U.S. 32nd Infantry Division. (Australian War Memorial)

A portrait by war artist Ivor Hele of Signaller Peter Pinney 2/3rd Independent Company, during the Salamaua campaign. Pinney would later say that this image accurately captured both his combat worn dishevelled appearance and state of mind at the time, and was a far more realistic portrayal than any photograph. (Australian War Memorial)

Vickers guns were employed by 2/3rd Independent Company to harass the Japanese along the Komiatum track during the Salamaua campaign. In this image Private 'Stumpy' May fires his Vickers gun at a Japanese mountain gun some 1900 metres distant, in an effort to distract the gun from firing on Australian positions. (Arden family photograph collection. National Library of Australia)

'A' platoon of 2/3rd Independent Company wait to attack Timbered Knoll as the knoll is pounded by artillery and mortars and raked by Vickers machineguns, 29 July 1943. This photo depicts the men wearing the mixture of gear they would normally take with them into combat. The string of grenades attached to the belt of the man on the right of the photo and the bandolier of ammunition he also wears is typical of this. (Arden family photograph collection. National Library of Australia)

Early in the attack on Timbered Knoll, by 'A' Platoon of 2/3rd Independent Company, Private Bill Robins has been seriously wounded, shot through both lungs. Corporal Roly Good, the Company medic prepares a field dressing for Robins and reaches out to him. This photo, which is a still from a film taken by combat cameraman Damian Parer, was taken ten seconds after Robins had been hit. (Arden family photograph collection. National Library of Australia)

Private Leonard Mahon of 2/3rd Independent Company during the assault on Timbered Knoll. The style of dress of the Independent Companies has evolved with jungle green uniforms, and gaiters. Automatic weapons remain predominant. (Australian War Memorial)

On the summit of Timbered Knoll following the battle. From left to right Major George Warfe, Lieutenants John Barry, John Lewin and Syd Read. (Arden family photograph collection. National Library of Australia)

Shooting Japanese wounded following the battle of Timbered Knoll. War artist Ivor Hele captured this moment as photography of such action was forbidden. As Ron Garland an officer with 2/3rd Independent Company admitted there was no option but to methodically destroy the Japanese as even their wounded would attempt to kill Australian soldiers. Such was the brutal nature of the Jungle War. (Australian War Memorial)

Men of Bena Force, 2/2 Independent Company, July 1943. Bena Force conducted a campaign of patrolling and harassment which denied the Japanese access to the strategically important Bena Bena Plateau from May until September 1943. (Australian War Memorial)

Members of 2/4th Commando Squadron stand to one side as a Matilda tank rolls past them on Tarakan, May 1945. Matildas provided invaluable support for the Squadron in its assault on Tarakan Hill. (Australian War Memorial)

Major Norman Winning of 2/8th Commando Squadron, standing to the right, liaises with indigenous guides, Bougainville, June 1945. In their relentless unconventional campaign against the Japanese on Bougainville 2/8th Commando Squadron worked closely with indigenous people. (Australian War Memorial)

McEvoy leading a section against the centre of the Japanese position found himself left with only one comrade after the other four men with him were wounded. McEvoy pushed forward engaging the Japanese at very short range and forcing them out of their forward trenches. The Japanese hit back with considerable machinegun fire and grenades but McEvoy hung on for the remainder of the day harassing the enemy.[94] In an equally bold action Private Claude Wellings was advancing up a steep spur with his section when it came under heavy light machinegun and rifle fire. Wellings with his Bren gun at his hip ignored the enemy fire and rushed forward to three metres from a Japanese pillbox. Firing his Bren he knocked out the light machinegun in the pill box. This enabled his section to seize the local high ground and consolidate their gains. As dusk came the sound of automatic fire erupted from behind the Japanese positions when Lieutenant Winterflood, who commanded the thirty two man infiltration party, attacked. The Japanese attempted to relieve their troops now cut off on the knoll, but although this attempt was driven off the Japanese defenders stubbornly held on. Night came on and the Independent Company troops pulled back some forty meters to consolidate. They could hear a 'tremendous commotion' coming from the Japanese. Assuming it was because the Japanese were improving their defences they banished thoughts of what this meant for the next day, and settled down to get what rest they could. In the morning they patrolled forward, only to find that the Japanese had abandoned the knoll during the night. Ten dead Japanese were found in trenches on the knoll. Abandoned equipment, documents and other detritus littered the ground.

Having captured the knoll two sections were posted to hold the knoll and the remainder of the company began patrolling in the direction of the Japanese main force engaging them at a site called 'Graveyards' and killing five of them. The Japanese were not, however, finished with Ambush Knoll. There were three approaches to Ambush Knoll an attacker could take. The Eastern approach was cut by a number of re-entrants and narrow ridges which favoured the defender. The ground on the Western approach dropped away steeply. The northern approach was dominated by a steep razor back ridge, and thus an unlikely direction. The Southern approach was, however, not hampered by any undue topographical obstacles and was thus the most likely avenue from which an attack could be made. The two sections on the Knoll, commanded by Lieutenant Ron Garland and pipe smoking Lieutenant Hughie Egan, placed listening posts out on the tracks leading to the knoll. They booby trapped the tracks. As dusk descended on 19 July Garland looked out into the jungle and saw what to him looked like one thousand little lights winking away. He figured that these must be the light from Japanese cigarettes. At 8.15 p.m. firing broke out on the track as one of the outposts engaged the enemy. The Japanese were moving on Ambush Knoll.

Only Ron Garland and his No.8 Section, squatting in their weapon pits stood in the way of the enemy. Garland had only seven men. A full moon had risen, which offered some visibility. Three men of the outpost ran back, and joined Garland's section.

94   Ibid, pp. 416–17.

All was silent, as the Japanese move stealthily ever closer. Garland ran through his options. Retreat was out of the question. He had to stand and fight. The question was how best to do so. He knew that if he could inflict maximum casualties on the attackers he could stop them, and that once stopped the Japanese would find it almost impossible to get their men moving forward again. To do this he would utilise what he described as 'the old-fashioned broadside principal'.[95] By this he meant to hit the attackers with a crashing blow of automatic fire which would cause casualties to the attacking troops as well as their second wave which must be close behind. Garland section had one Bren gun and what he described in an understated manner as 'more Tommy guns than rifles'.[96] Shadows in the jungle concealed any sight of the Japanese, so the defenders listened. Garland knew the Japanese style of fighting, and that he had to stop them before they could break cover from the jungle and get close enough to throw grenades or rush and overwhelm his section. He waited. A metallic click sounded out to the front, it was ignored as it was a well-known Japanese trick to draw fire. Then came the sound of bushes being carefully and quietly pushed aside, and a twig cracking came from his left side. He squeezed the trigger and his Tommy gun exploded into a frenzy of fire. All the section fired. There was no cover for the attackers and they withdrew. Immediately, one man from the section crept forward, to act as a listening post. Garland knew that the sound of his firing would bring other men from the Company to the Knoll, and was both surprised and very pleased when three men carrying a Vickers gun came up from behind. The gun was quickly set up to cover the approaches. There was already another Vickers gun in place, this one commanded by Hughie Egan and set up to cover the track leading to the Knoll from the south. Both guns would add formidable firepower to the defence. Shortly after the Japanese attacked again, and were again repulsed by the concentrated automatic fire of Tommy guns and Vickers guns. The Japanese fell back. By dawn the defenders of the Knoll had been reinforced by the 50 men of Winterflood's 'B' Platoon. Garland and his men routed through the debris left behind by the Japanese when they withdrew. One item they prized were the steel cleaning rods from Japanese rifles. They used these to push out .45 calibre rounds which had jammed in the chambers of their Tommy guns. The Japanese attacked again at 9.20 a.m. A broadside of automatic fire once again repulsed them. Throughout the morning the Japanese peppered the Knoll with fire from a 70mm mountain gun and a number of Woodpecker machineguns that had on nearby Sugarcane Ridge. Hughie Egan's Vickers gun which was situated on a high point on the Knoll responded and engaged the mountain gun in something of a duel. At the same time, the third of the companies Vickers guns which was some distance away at the Company Headquarters began firing. At 12.40 p.m. the Japanese struck again, this time in large numbers. Pressed together by the narrow ridge up which they had to come, the attackers presented an easy target to the automatic broadsides and were cut

95 Ibid, p. 207.
96 Ibid.

down. In a pattern which was typical of Japanese troops they persisted in their attacks, coming on repeatedly but always using the same tactics. After suffering heavy casualties the assault was repulsed. At 1.20 p.m. the Japanese assaulted the knoll again, this time along the entire defender's front. Described as frantic these attacks were also beaten back. Throughout the day the Japanese launched twelve attacks, alternating their attacks with a continual bombardment of the knoll. Ammunition was being used at a prodigious rate, Garland estimated he and his men were firing 500 rounds a day from their Tommy guns. With this Garland ordered his men to fire only short bursts during their broadsides, and shoot only at identified targets. Night came and the Japanese attacked at 3.00 a.m. and at 4.00 a.m. During these attacks, with the Japanese pressing in close, Garland's Tommy gun jammed with a bullet lodged in its chamber, and he had to use a cleaning rod to knock it loose. The soldier by his side quipped 'what have you got their boss, a muzzle loader?' Following these attacks with the supply of ammunition now critically short an order came through to switch automatic weapons to single shot. Supply was a major concern, not just for ammunition but food and especially water which were both running short. The situation was resolved shortly after dawn when men from the company, who had come up a track on the Northern face which was unknown to the Japanese, appeared on the Knoll fully armed and loaded down with stores. Bursting into song Garland's section began to sing 'Praise the Lord and pass the ammunition'. Mail also arrived but for Garland it was a mixed blessing as the only letter he received was from the New South Wales Income Tax Commissioner, informing him that he was in arrears for four shillings and six pence, and if he did not pay it by 1st February 1943, legal action would be taken. Aware that he was now six months overdue to pay his arrears Garland resigned himself to his fate fully aware that the absurdities of life were in no short supply on Ambush Knoll. The next day at 1.00 p.m. the Japanese assaulted again. They were thrown back, but in the chaos of the battle Hughie Egan was killed when a mortar shell hit him on the back killing him instantly. The fight was getting desperate. The defenders had not slept since the night of 18 July and it was now 22 July. Lack of sleep was beginning to scramble their thoughts and challenge their ability to stay alert. In one incident a soldier was knocked out by a mortar bomb. When he came too he was confused and unaware where he was. He wandered for a while, found a track and was so tired he lay down and went to sleep. He woke to hear two men speaking nearby. They were Japanese, one of who was urinating. He lay still. One of the Japanese spoke to him and he grunted an answer. He then crawled away and made his escape. The Japanese made their own contribution to the psychological pressure on the defenders by shouting out the names of soldiers in the company. This was a trick they often used. They would call out personally to men, with calls such as 'Tom Kidd, are you there Tom Kidd'.[97] The hope would be that a soldier would answer and by doing so reveal his

---

97   AWM, AWM S04158, John Lewin Interviewed by Neil MacDonald.

position. The Japanese had captured the medical files of the company in the ambush previously described, and most likely learned the names from those files.

Casualties were thinning the defenders ranks. There was no question of them giving ground or surrendering the knoll, but relief was nearby. A platoon of 2/6th Infantry Battalion from 17 Brigade had fought its way towards Ambush Knoll. It had been stopped by the Japanese before it had arrived, and forced to dig in. Yet it was there, not too far away, and the knowledge of that gave the defenders of the knoll the determination to outlast their attackers.

Fire from the Japanese mountain gun, Woodpeckers, rifles and mortars continued to fall on the knoll. Japanese light machineguns began to snipe at the Vickers guns, concentrating their fire on the Vickers every time they fired. Maybe in the knowledge that relief for the defenders was at hand and that the knoll must therefore be captured without delay, Japanese attacks were becoming more ferocious and began to take on the characteristics of the traditional Banzai assault. These assaults threw themselves at the knoll's defenders at 6.15 p.m. and again at 10.10 p.m., and 1.30 a.m. and 4.30 a.m. in the early morning of 23 July.

As dawn approached movement could be heard in the jungle. The bone weary defenders prepared for yet another Japanese attack. It was, however, not to be and at 6.00 a.m. George Warfe came down a track, a platoon of 2/6th Infantry Battalion following him. Ambush Knoll had been relieved. Faced now by the leading element of an Infantry Battalion as well as the stubborn defenders of Ambush Knoll the Japanese withdrew. The battle was over.

The Japanese had launched twenty attacks on Ambush Knoll. For the cost of three killed and seven wounded 2/3rd Independent Company had resisted every one of them. Sixty seven Japanese graves were found although there was no real way of knowing how many Japanese had been killed or wounded. For the men of the company the defence of Ambush Knoll had been a traumatic experience. When it was over some of them had been awake for three to four days. Their eyes had seemed to have sunken into the backs of their heads, they were unwashed, unshaven and their clothes were filthy. Yet they were victorious.

The defence of Ambush Knoll was an extraordinary feat of arms. A small light infantry force without access to artillery or mortars, had resisted repeated assaults from a determined enemy, who both outnumbered them and enjoyed artillery, heavy machinegun and mortar support. It was not the type of warfare for which the company had been trained, and certainly not what the men expected they would have to fight. Winterflood recalled that it was 'not our cup of tea', and that for the company to fight such a fight was 'quite wrong', but that they did do it.[98] Even so, it proved to sceptical regular army units that Independent Companies could hold ground against determined enemy pressure. The fight for Ambush Knoll proved to such doubters that 2/3rd Independent Company could effectively engage in conventional operations and

98 AWM, AWM S04156, John Winterflood interviewed by Neil Macdonald.

operate as 'proper infantry'. Most importantly the successful defence of Ambush Knoll had secured the link between 15 and 17 Brigades, and ensured that 3rd Division's campaign against the major Japanese defensive positions at Mubo could continue uninterrupted.[99]

One aspect of Independent Company operations was that they were never completely out of contact with the enemy. Patrolling was constant and at any one time one or more elements of the company would be engaging or closely observing the enemy. It was estimated that the average Australian soldier in close combat with the enemy very rarely actually saw the Japanese.[100] This was certainly not so with the Independent Companies whose task was to maintain close contact with the enemy. To do this stealth was employed so as to get as close as practicable to enemy lines. In this way as much information as possible could be garnered without the enemy realising they had been compromised. This constant activity in close proximity to the enemy required the utmost stamina both physical and mental. The process was an unvarying feature of the Company's war in the jungle.

In the days that followed the Company established that the Japanese had built interlocked continuous defensive positions in the nearby area known as Goodview Junction, and pushed into these. They engaged the enemy in a series of savage little battles during which 50 Japanese were killed. Having overcome the enemy there the Company eventually established themselves at all points along the dominant ridges in the area.

On 29 July the Company became involved in its second conventional action within the space of two weeks. This new action was an attack on a fortified Japanese location on a ridge known as Timbered Knoll that flanked the Mubo feature. Lieutenant John Lewin commanded 'A' Platoon and it was his task to capture the Knoll. It was impossible to do a comprehensive reconnaissance, and because of this Lewin had no way of knowing just what was up on top of the Knoll. Planning a formal attack was out of the question, and also not at all the Indepdnent Company modus operandi. Lewin knew that this battle would have to be fought by intuition, and not by the book. Firstly he had to decide if he would go in 'all guns blazing' or use stealth. He chose to go in all guns blazing. He was fortunate that there was artillery and mortars to support his attack. There were also Vickers guns available and Lewin placed these off to a flank, determining to attack at right angles to their line of fire. The artillery bombardment began at 4.00 p.m. and soon after the attack went in. One Section advanced from the front, and another attacked from the right flank. It was not long before the attack ran into trouble, unable to make any headway against the entrenched and determined

---

99 Garland, *Nothing is Forever*, pp. 186–230. Garland gives an excellent detailed firsthand account of 2/3rd Independent Companies capture and defence of Ambush Knoll.
100 Mark Johnston, *Fighting the Enemy – Australian Soldiers and their Adversaries in World War II* (Cambridge University Press: Cambridge, 2000), p. 77, claims that this was the case in 75% of contacts.

Japanese. Thwarted Lewin reassessed his options, and in an example of the inspirational flexibility characteristic of the Independent Company ethos quickly shifted his axis of attack from the right to the left flank. He personally led the Section which had been attacking from the front around to the left flank. The terrain there was a very steep razor back ridge, and instinctively he felt that the Japanese would not expect an attack from that direction. Nevertheless, the Japanese responded with fire from pillboxes and trenches, and by rolling grenades down the slope. Lewin's men scooped the grenades up and threw them back. To this they added many of their own grenades, lobbing them over the lip of the high ground above them. Private John 'Lofty' Moran was frustrated trying to knock out one Japanese bunker. Every time he threw a grenade someone in the bunker would throw it back at him. 'Smart bastard' Lofty cursed, and then employed cunning to eliminate his enemy. He took a grenade and pulled the pin releasing its lever. The grenade had a four second fuse and Lofty waited for three seconds then threw it. The grenade did not come back and the bunker was taken.[101] Even then, however, with the enemy only metres away, the wellbeing of the men was not ignored and hot scones and a cup of tea suddenly appeared for them.[102] From where this pick-me-up came was never recorded, but obviously someone was paying attention to the soldier's needs. With their tea and scones consumed Corporal Percy Hooks shimmied up over the rise and disappeared into the Japanese position. He was heard to call out 'alright we're up', and was killed as he did so. With that Private Walter Dawson rushed forward with Tommy gun and grenades and despite being wounded in the head by a grenade killed several Japanese and knocked out the pillboxes and trenches to his front. Exploiting the breach made by Dawson, Lewin lead his section up onto the high ground. The Japanese they encountered had their backs to them, still shooting at the Section which was pressing on them from the right flank. In a bitter fight those Japanese were killed and the assaulting Sections linked up on the crest of the Knoll. The attacked had cost the company three dead, all Non Commissioned Officers. These were sorely missed.[103]

Exceptional as these two combats were, they were entirely conventional actions, fought in a traditional infantry manner, even if the sudden change in the direction of the attack at Timbered Knoll was a decidedly unconventional and impulsive move. Ron Garland observed that at that time it very much seemed that the company had been suddenly transformed from a guerrilla force into a shock force intended to smash Japanese defences but without any specialised equipment to help them do so.[104] It was true that these actions were not exemplars of the primarily irregular character Independent Company operations, nor corresponded to their primary function of

---

101 Garland, *Nothing is Forever*, p. 245.
102 Ibid, p. 245; NLA 3573411, Caption to photo.
103 AWM, AWM S04158, John Lewin interviewed by Neil MacDonald; Garland, *Nothing is Forever*, pp. 238–48.
104 Garland, *Nothing is Forever*, p. 232.

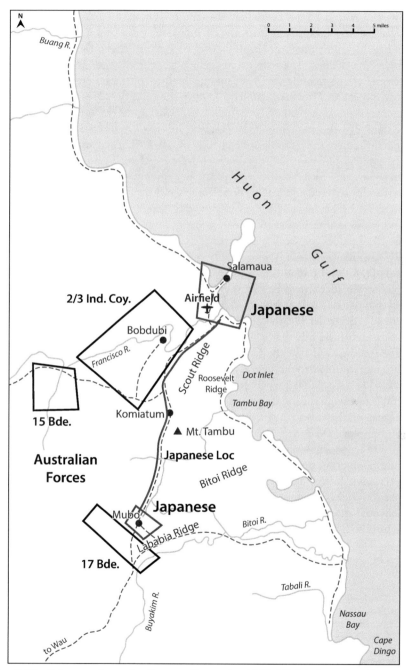

Map 5 The Salamaua Campaign January–September 1943. 2/3rd Independent Company ranged over a wide arc of territory out on the left flank of 3rd Division.

reconnaissance and harassment. It is also the case that this may have reflected the Division backing away from utilising its Jungle Cavalry as such, but it was more likely that the Company found itself used in such a way due to the lack of alternative manpower in the areas where these engagements occurred. Even if they were distractions from helping to understand the unique qualities of the Independent Companies Ambush Knoll and Timbered Knoll do confirm the exceptional resilience and capacity for combat of the Companies.

The nature of the war against the Japanese in New Guinea was one noted for the frequent brutality and merciless behaviour of all its participants. Such behaviour was the product of a conflict in which men were faced with constant danger from an unseen enemy, and forced to live and operate in a forbidding environment in which the slightest indiscretion could lead to disablement or death. This was for the Australians compounded by having to face an enemy who were racially and culturally distinctive and whose military ethos was seen as inexcusably murderous by the Australians. Within this broader context it is unsurprising to find that the Independent Companies attitude towards their enemy was equally ruthless, unforgiving, and pitiless.[105] Those participating in the conflict fully realised the nature of that conflict. Savige alluded to the type of war that would be fought by unconventional forces in the jungles of New Guinea as being one that would of necessity be different to how it was done in 'civilised countries'.[106] Brigadier Heathcote Hammer, the Commander of 15 Brigade summed up the nature of the war that was being fought when he described it as 'murder war'. Hammer pointed out that the Japanese would kill wounded Australians and anyone who attempted to aid them, his response was that the only answer was to be equally relentless.[107] In such a war, where resources and numbers were limited and constantly vulnerable to enemy and environmental threat, utilising any means possible to inflict as much harm on the enemy as possible became the norm. It was accepted that any means could be employed to do so.[108] For example one method used of killing Japanese officers by 2/3rd Independent Company was to steal into Japanese camps under cover of darkness and booby trap the toilet seats on the officer's lavatory. Japanese officers did not share the same latrine as the soldiers and the camp would be watched carefully until the location of the Japanese officer latrine could be established. The toilet seat in that latrine would then be booby trapped with a grenade so that when an officer visited he would be killed.[109] Such tactics were considered to be perfectly legitimate. The intimacy

---

105 For an examination of the attitude towards killing the Japanese enemy see: Mark Johnston, *Fighting the enemy: Australian soldiers and their adversaries in World War II* (Cambridge University Press: Cambridge, 2000); Tom Lewis, *Lethality in Combat: a study of the true nature of battle* (Big Sky publishing: Newport, 2012).
106 Russell, *There Goes a Man*, p. 260.
107 Dean, *Australia 1943*, p.204.
108 AWM, AWM 3DRL/6766, John Arden, 'Jack', p. 9.
109 Ibid.

of killing the enemy was a notable characteristic of the Independent Company.[110] Contact with the enemy was normally by ambush and raid in which the killing would be conducted within a few metres. Such a close proximity to the enemy generated intensely personal responses. Peter Pinney, then with 2/3rd Independent Company celebrated his 21st Birthday during the Salamaua campaign. Pinney recounted how as a birthday present he requested from Warfe that he be allowed to go out on a one man patrol so that he could 'bag a Jap'. Warfe refused him permission which disappointed Pinney greatly.[111] Captain Peter Tancred in a letter to his parents related how he got thrill of his life when he 'pipped his first Jap'.[112] Indeed killing Japanese became regarded as something of a sport.[113] That killing was frequently pitiless. Warfe would habitually kill wounded Japanese with a Japanese bayonet he carried with him.[114] At one time Warfe shot and killed a Japanese soldier encountered on a track without breaking his stride; he simply shot the man and walked on by.[115] Pinney explained the reasons for this merciless attitude in his partially autobiographical *The Barbarians, A Soldiers New Guinea Diary*, when he described the Japanese as 'not fair dinkum humans', and that there was a 'compelling greed' amongst his comrades for their total elimination.[116] It was an attitude shared even by non-combatants. War correspondent Damien Parer, was with 2/3rd Independent Company for a time during its operations during the Salamaua campaign. Parer was not a soldier but for a time he shared their experiences and established a close bond with them. He came to refer to the Japanese as 'vermin' whose battlefield prowess was due to 'low animal cunning'.[117] Discovering evidence of Japanese cannibalism hardened such attitudes. Private Brian Walpole came across a Commando who he personally knew lying face down in a stream. The Commando had been shot and killed and stripped naked. His buttocks had been sliced off. The presumption was that the Japanese had done this for food. This filled Walpole with an intense hatred and disgust for the Japanese.[118] In another incident Damien Parer describing finding a dead Australian soldier tied to a tree with the flesh cut from his thighs, and War artist Ivor Hele described finding Japanese corpses dismembered and mutilated by their comrades with the obvious intention of eating them.[119] When Lieutenant John Lewin was interviewed years after the war he asked for the recording

110 Johnston, *Fighting the Enemy*, p. 77.
111 University of Queensland, Freyer Library (UQFL), Papers of Peter Pinney, Box 13, UQFL288, Pinney to Mother and Father, 10 June 1943.
112 AWM, AWM PR91/052, R. Hancock, Letter to Parents, 14 Feb 43.
113 AWM, AWM 54 583/7/11, Operations of 2/3 Independent Company, subsequent to the battle of Wau, and pursuit of Japanese Forces to Mubo, covering the period March, April, May and June, 1943.
114 Neil McDonald and Peter Brune, *Kokoda Front Line* (Allen & Unwin: Sydney, 1994), p. 290.
115 Roly Good, 2/3rd Independent Company, interviewed by Barry Higgins, 2 February 2016.
116 Pinney, *The Barbarians*, pp. 124–5.
117 Macdonald and Brune, *Kokoda Front Line*, p. 293.
118 Walpole, *My War*, p. 20.
119 McDonald and Brune, *Kokoda Front Line*, pp. 293 and 297.

device to be turned off as he related the story of finding a soldier tied to a tree with the flesh from his thighs cut away.[120] Such incidents bred a violent animosity towards the Japanese.

There was, however, conversely alongside the gratuitous brutality towards the enemy a lingering sense amongst some of the Independent Company personnel of the inappropriateness of their behaviour. This sometimes led them to modify their actions. Warfe desisted killing wounded Japanese with his bayonet when Parer was with the company for several months during 1943, and Roly Good the medical orderly for the company, made of point of refusing to kill wounded Japanese even though he recognised that by not doing so he was condemning those men to a lingering death in the jungle.[121] Nevertheless, the dominant ethos was one of destroying the enemy without mercy and by any means, and it is this which most accurately characterises the actions of 2/3rd Independent Company during this period.

The fundamental contribution made to the Salamaua campaign by 2/3rd Independent Company was to act in the role of Savige's 'Jungle Cavalry', to provide the eyes and ears or his Division. Unlike the average soldier who complained that 'You can't see the little bastards … and certainly never claps eyes on a Jap', Independent Company troops frequently observed the Japanese and often from very close range.[122] This was achieved by establishing observation posts, and constantly patrolling behind Japanese lines. The ability of the companies to infiltrate areas held by the Japanese was considered even by the Japanese to be 'quite remarkable'.[123] Lieutenant Colonel H.G. Quinn of 3rd Division Staff recorded that, 'Patrols provided by 2/3 Indep Coy were excellent and gained valuable information as to enemy's strength and disposition'.[124] Reports by the company were valued as reliable and accurate, unlike reports from, for example, 58/59 Battalion which tended to exaggerate enemy numbers.[125] The number of such patrols mounted by 2/3rd Independent Company was extraordinary. In the first two weeks of September 1943 the company conducted 63 patrols. In comparison, 2/7th Battalion, a force three time the size of the Independent Company at the same time conducted 21 patrols.[126] If it is assumed that each 2/3rd Independent Company patrol during September operated over a two day period, a conservative estimate at best, then as an aggregate in the first two weeks of September the company

---

120 AWM, AWM SO4158, John Lewin interviewed by Neil MacDonald (no date).
121 Macdonald and Brune, *Kokoda Front Line*, p. 85.
122 Johnston, *Fighting the Enemy*, p. 77.
123 Kengoro Tanaka, *Operations of the Imperial Japanese Armed Forces in the Papua New Guinea Theatre During World War II* (Papua New Guinea Goodwill Society: Japan, 1980), p.166. Tanaka does not identify 2/3 Independent Company as the infiltrating force but is quite reasonable to presume that the force carrying out the majority of the infiltration in the Wau Salamaua area was 2/3.
124 AWM, AWM54 587/7/16, Patrol Records 2/3 Australian Independent Coy routine patrols Salamaua 1943.
125 Ibid.
126 Ibid; AWM, AWM52 8/3/7/37, 2/7 Battalion War Diary – September – December 1943.

conducted 126 days of patrolling. This would have provided ample opportunity to spy out Japanese positions.

The importance of patrolling was paramount. Major General George Vasey made the point that commanders were forced to execute plans 'on the most nebulous information', due to lack of information, and that the only way of securing that information was by infantry patrols.[127] In this context the patrols of 2/3rd Independent Company contributed essential information to 3rd Division. Savige would have been fully aware of the company's activities, as he was keenly interested in the patrol activity of the units under his command, and read every patrol report that was submitted.[128] Savige acknowledged 2/3rd Independent Company's value in this regard when he identified the company as the 'outstanding' unit of the campaign, an extraordinary accolade for a single company from within an entire Division. He stated that the information the company had provided gave him the confidence to conduct the campaign as he did.[129] Such praise confirmed the value an Independent Company if it was employed in the manner for which it was intended.

In the closing days of August, the Japanese found themselves defending an increasingly confined perimeter in defence of Salamaua. It was during this period that the nature of the land campaign for Salamaua began to change, an eventuality which would have a decisive impact on the operations of 2/3rd Independent Company. In the early days of the campaign contacts with the enemy had in general been at platoon and company level, often fought against a dug in and unseen foe, with minimal support from artillery or air. Independent initiative by small groups was what was required to achieve success in such circumstances. This was the type of warfare in which an Independent Company could excel. As the year progressed and the logistical profile of allied forces improved, the tactical situation changed to reflect this. Reliance on small unit tactics began to give way to the employment of overwhelming firepower and more set piece larger scale operations.[130] US Army Air Force General George Kenney epitomised this when he announced that he would, 'blow the Japs out of New Guinea by Christmas'.[131] The war diary of 2/6th Commando Squadron (formerly 2/6th Independent Company), during the later months of 1943 makes numerous references to large numbers of Allied aircraft flying overhead, 10 Marauder and 40 Mitchell bombers escorted by P38 and P40 fighters on one day alone.[132] The tonnage of bombs dropped on the Japanese in the Salamaua area increased dramatically from July 1943. During the months of February to

---

127 AWM, AWM54 937/3/33 p.2, Military Training Pamphlet No 23 Jungle Warfare comments on draft by Maj Gen G.A. Vasey.
128 Russell, *There Goes a Man*, p. 268.
129 AWM, AWM 172, 10, David Dexter Interviews Interview with Gen. Savige – 10 April 1951.
130 AWM, AWM54 1/5/4, 3 Australian Division General Staff Branch, 1943 Part 8 General Staff appendices.
131 AWM, AWM52 2/2/58, 2/6 Commando Squadron War Diary November to December 1943, 10 Oct.
132 2/6 Commando Squadron Diary November to December 1943, AWM52 2/2/58.

June 1943 the average monthly tonnage of bombs was 77.86. This increased dramatically from July until September with an average monthly tonnage of bombs of 850.6 with 1238.9 tons in the month of July alone.[133] On 29 July, the day of the fight for Ambush Knoll, American artillery, which had along with the US 41st Division, landed at Nassau Bay, fired 4000 shells at a Japanese position. In another attack the Japanese 115th Regiment was shelled by Australian artillery for 24 hours.[134] The weight of firepower directed against them was described as 'terrible' by one Japanese soldier and contributed to forcing the Japanese to abandon their defensive positions at Mubo and withdraw closer to Salamaua.[135] On 1 August 1943 the commander of Japanese 51st Division, seeking a way to protect his troops from the enemy artillery and aerial firepower, issued an order to construct deep strong points robust enough to withstand the bombardments. By concentrating his forces in heavily defended positions he compelled Allied forces to conduct set pieces assaults on them. This changed the nature of the campaign from clashes of small units of infantry, to one of heavily supported close assaults on well prepared Japanese positions.[136] With Japanese withdrawals into prepared positions the ability of the Independent Company to infiltrate behind Japanese lines was reduced and the range of country over which 2/3rd Independent Company could operate steadily diminished. In such a tactical environment, the uses for 'Jungle Cavalry' diminished. On 27 August, a conference determined the future employment of 2/3rd Independent Company, and on 29 August the Company became the 15 Brigade reserve. In a mark of the diminished requirement for an assertive autonomous Independent Company, Warfe who personified those attributes was relieved of command of the company in late August, promoted to the rank of Lieutenant Colonel and transferred to command 58/59th Battalion.[137] The Company continued to patrol and engage the enemy but effectively its unconventional independent contribution to the campaign had ended.[138]

The contribution of the Company to the overall campaign for Salamaua was indeed outstanding. A comparison of relative casualty figures suffered by the company is illustrative of the degree of commitment by 2/3rd Independent Company to the campaign. From the period 23 April until 13 September 1943 the company lost eight

---

133 AWM, AWMPR91/002 Moten, Murray John (Brigadier b.1899 d.1953.) Folder 22, Tonnage of bombs dropped 43 Wau-Salamaua area.
134 Tanaka, *Operations of the Imperial Japanese Armed Forces in the Papua New Guinea Theatre During World War II*, pp. 159–74.
135 AWM, AWM55 1/8, ATIS, 3 Nov to 24 Nov 1943, Diary of unnamed member of Waku unit in Nakamura Battalion. 28 Dec 42–11 Aug 43, Nos 492–525 Bulletin 541 3 Dec 43, Item 14 – 6944,; Tanaka, *Operations of the Imperial Japanese Armed Forces in the Papua New Guinea Theatre During World War II*, pp. 159–74.
136 AWM, AWM55 1/8, ATIS, 3 Nov to 24 Nov 1943, Commander 51st Division 17 July 43 on the construction of positions at the time of defence of Salamaua, issued 1 Aug 43 by MO Force Operation Sec, Nos 492–525 B493 4 Nov 43, Item 12 – 6067.
137 AWM, AWM54 587/7/11, Action Diary HQ 15 Australian Infantry Brigade, Operation Doublet attack on Bobdubi ridge, during Salamaua Campaign 1943.
138 Ibid.

officers and 105 other ranks. In comparison the highest losses for a battalion engaged in the campaign was 2/7th Battalion which lost 19 officers and 209 other ranks. Other battalion losses were 2/5th Battalion nine officers and 120 other ranks, 2/6th Battalion 6six officers and 125 other ranks, 24th battalion five officers and 34 other ranks, 57/60th Battalion three other ranks, and 58/59th Battalion 17 officers and 194 other ranks.[139] That a company sized unit exceeded the casualty rate for two battalions, was only marginally less for another two battalions and was exceeded by two battalions from an entire Division indicates the level of contact with the enemy the company engaged in during the period. George Warfe's Jungle Cavalry had truly been an exceptional unit and an essential ingredient of the Allied force which achieved the ultimate success of the campaign to capture Salamaua.

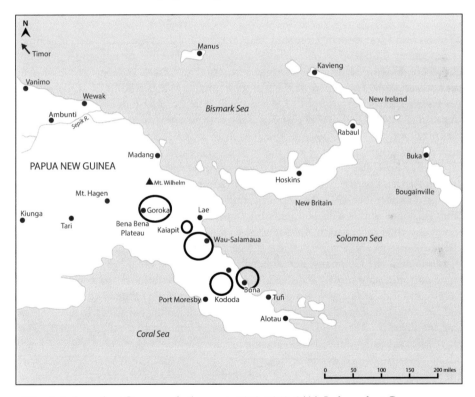

Map 6 Independent Company deployments 1942–1943. 2/5th Independent Company was deployed to Wau later joined by 2/7th Independent Company, 2/6th Independent Company to the Kokoda Track and Buna, 2/4th Independent Company joined 2/2nd Independent Company on Timor and 2/3rd Independent Company took part in the Salamaua campaign.

139 AWM, AWM54 171/2/28, Unit Casualties Wau – Salamaua 23rd April to 13th September 1943, Australian Military Forces – New Guinea.

8

Bena Force and Kaiapit

While 2/3rd Independent Company was engaged on the Wau Salamaua front other Independent Companies were contributing their expertise to ongoing operations elsewhere. Having returned from its service on Timor 2/4th Independent Company spent several months training at the Canungra Jungle Warfare School in Queensland. They were then sent to join 9th Division in its forthcoming move to capture Lae in September 1943. During this campaign the company provided flank and reconnaissance support for 9th Division. They did this with little trouble despite unfavourable weather, difficult terrain and the occasional clash with small parties of Japanese. Ironically the Company suffered its heaviest casualties during this operation not from its activity on the ground, but aboard landing craft heading for the beach near Lae on 4 September 1943. Japanese aircraft attacked and bombed the landing craft killing 28 men with six declared missing in action.[1] Following the capture of Lae the Company then took part in the campaign to take Finschafen, acting once again as the flank guards and reconnaissance element of 9th Division. Following the capture of Finschafen the Company, now officially a Commando Squadron, was engaged in some patrolling but mostly indulged in a variety of tasks around the main base such digging a bunker for the Divisional Commander and providing working parties to unload stores.[2] It seemed to the men of the squadron, having been mostly side-tracked into menial tasks, that the Division had no idea of how to utilize their talents.[3] From there the Squadron moved onto reconnaissance work on the Huon Peninsula, in which they discovered evidence of Japanese diggings and camp sites. Contact with the enemy was, however, infrequent and although some Commandos were wounded the Squadron did not engage in any major clashes with the Japanese.

---

1 Lambert, *Tidal River to Tarakan*, p. 267; AWM, AWM52 25/3/4/5, 2/4 Independent Company War Diary, 4 Sept 43.
2 Lambert, *Tidal River to Tarakan*, p. 298.
3 Ibid.

During this period two other Independent companies, 2/2nd and 2/7th, formed a group known as Bena Force, which had been established to secure and protect the airfields on the Bena Bena plateau. These companies were to perform a service of significant strategic value to ongoing operations in New Guinea during 1943.

The Bena Bena plateau was narrow, no more than 32 kilometres wide and extended some 209 kilometres from its start 160 kilometres west of Lae up into the highlands of Mount Hagen. The climate on the plateau was good, being described as offering a two blanket cool sleep at night and days warm enough to wear shorts.[4] Most importantly there were no mosquitoes and therefore less chance of disease. Even though many streams cut across the plateau and there were numerous valleys several crude airstrips had been built there. The army's intention was to improve and expand the size of these airfields for future use in its continual push along the coast against the Japanese. These improved airfields would provide alternatives to the Bulolo Valley airfields if they were lost, and also provide a point from which supplies could be distributed.[5] The Japanese were fully aware of the importance of the plateau, and their intelligence reports from June 43 mentioned the construction of airfields at Goroka, Hagen, Wilhelm and Bena Bena.[6] Japanese aircraft began to overfly the plateau and made several attacks on ground targets during May.[7] It was important that Australian forces prevent the Japanese from interfering with those airfields. This set the stage for the deployment of Independent Companies to disrupt any enemy intentions to threaten the strategically important Bena Bena Plateau.

The beginnings of Bena Force were modest. Established on 23 January 1943 it originally consisted of 56 men of 2/7th Battalion and two small units, one of ANGAU the Australian New Guinea Administrative Unit whose task was to manage the indigenous population for the war effort, and another a detachment of a RAAF communications and rescue unit accompanied them. Some personnel from the 'special New Guinea patrols', civilian patrol officers, were also present. The collective force's task was to establish a presence at the site of the Bena Bena airstrip and defend it if necessary.[8] By the end of April the men of 2/7th Battalion had conducted patrols. With the assistance of indigenous labourers they had constructed a comprehensive infrastructure around the airfield. The list of work was impressive and included amongst many

---

4 Ayris, *All the Bull's Men*, p. 400.
5 AWM, AWM54 583/6/4, Operational Plans, Wau – Lae – Salamaua Appreciations of Situation in North east Area – Oct 1942 – Jan 1943, APPRECIATION of Situation in N.E. Area for GOC NEW GUINEA FORCE as at 11 Jan 43.
6 AWM, AWM PR91/002, Enemy Publications No. 145 Part II, July 1944 – Intelligence Reports, maps and Sketches Operations in New Guinea Apr 43 to Aug 43; in Moten, Murray John (Brigadier b.1899 d.1953) folder 20.
7 Dexter, *New Guinea Offensives*, p. 238.
8 Dexter, *The New Guinea Offensives*, p.233. The New Guinea Patrols were patrols which were mounted by the civil authorities to maintain contact with and administer indigenous people. They were quite active during peacetime. It is not known just what function they performed during wartime.

other achievements Weapons pits, heavy type pill boxes, and a bomb proof Head Quarters.⁹ In May 2/7th Independent Company, now no longer part of Kanga Force, was deployed to Bena Bena.¹⁰ It had been originally intended to deploy a battalion to the plateau, but it was soon decided that there were not enough aircraft available to fly in such a force and once it was there was not enough air transport available to maintain a force of that size. Thus an Independent Company, which could be maintained, was chosen for the task.¹¹ It so happened that 2/7th Independent Company was in Port Moresby after having been relieved from Kanga Force. They were tired and needed a rest, but there were no other troops available and they were chosen for the task. On 29 May the Company was flown to the Bena Bena airstrip with the instructions to secure the airfield, deny Japanese freedom of movement and harass the enemy in the area.¹² Furthermore the company was to report directly to New Guinea Force, not 3rd Division which had by that time been established at Wau and was the closest senior Army formation to the plateau. New Guinea Force would thus take responsibility for managing the company and assume responsibility for the unconventional campaign which would occur. New Guinea Force was a higher level command echelon, superior to individual Divisional commands. For it to take on command of an Independent Company and manage its unconventional operations was a significant step in the evolution of the army's recognition of the value of unconventional forces. In June Bena Force grew to also include 2/2nd Independent Company less one platoon, one platoon of 2/7th Battalion, and one machinegun section from 2/7th Battalion. The two Independent Companies formed the primary active military contingent of the force and were deployed to two locations; 2/7th Independent Company being at the Garoka airstrip and 2/2nd Independent Company being at the Bena airstrip.¹³ As well as protecting the airfields on the plateau, Bena Force was given instructions to actively prevent the enemy from crossing the Ramu River and penetrating to the plateau. At the same time the companies were to construct a road and provide highly detailed maps of the terrain.¹⁴

The frontage of country that Bena Force was made responsible for was extraordinary. In all it measured approximately 200 kilometres, all of it undeveloped, uncontrolled, unmapped wilderness.¹⁵ Adequately covering such an area would have required a significant deployment of regular troops, which at that time was impossible. The 550 Independent Company personnel of the two Independent Companies on the Bena

9   AWM, AWM 54 1/5/42, Bena Force.
10 Dexter, *The New Guinea Offensives*, p. 238.
11 Ibid, p. 238.
12 AWM, AWM 54 1/5/42, Bena Force, New Guinea Force OP Inst, No 82 – 27 May 43.
13 AWM, AWM 54 1/5/42, Bena Force, New Guinea Force OP Inst, 12–25 June 43.
14 Ibid.
15 Dexter, *The New Guinea Offensives*, p. 241.

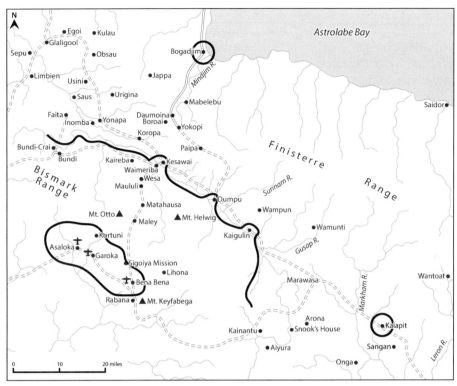

Map 7 The Central Highlands indicating the region protected by Bena Force and the approximate front line of Bena Force patrols from May until September 1943. Bogadjim the objective of Bena force patrols is also marked.

Bena plateau presented a much more economical means of securing the plateau.[16] It was also a task for which the autonomous, independent, small unit, innovative qualities of the Independent Companies were eminently suited.

Having been told to range out and harass the enemy the two Independent Companies of Bena Force set out to patrol the wilderness. In keeping with their normal practice they first found and mapped useable tracks.[17] These were of primary importance, as without knowledge of tracks, traversing the tangled jungle would have been impossible. Knowing where the tracks were also provided an idea from where the enemy may appear, as they too would be compelled to make use of them. The detail contained in these track reports was remarkable. One example was the report

16 AWM, AWM 54 1/5/42, Bena Force, Australian Military Forces New Guinea Force Headquarters Bena Force, 9 Nov 43, Closing Report.
17 AWM, AWM 54 1/5/42, Bena Force, patrol reports.

of Lance Corporal Evens of 2/7th Independent Company titled 'Geological, Physical and Botanical Report on Bena Plateau'. In this report Evens describes in detail rock formations, the sub soil, the climate, drainage and an itemised description of the plant life.[18] With reports such as Evens and many other similar ones a comprehensive profile of the region was established.

Throughout June the Japanese continued to bomb the plateau's airfields from the air, Allied fighter planes often intercepting the raiders.[19] During this incessant patrolling continued. Those who conducted the patrols would later recall that if you were not on patrol you would be either recovering from one or preparing for another one.[20] Many patrols resulted in no contact, or indications that the Japanese had recently departed which in itself was useful information. The nature of the patrols illustrated both the type of patrols necessary and the character of those patrolling. One example of this was a patrol mounted by one man of 2/7th Independent Company who swam naked and unarmed across both the Gusap and Ramu rivers to reconnoitre Japanese positions at the quaintly named location of Bum Bum.[21] The technique of patrolling was simple, but extremely cautious. The dense jungle reduced visibility at times to only metres. Two forward scouts would lead. They would leap frog each other, watching for any hint of the enemy.[22] There was the constant danger of being surprised by unexpected Japanese as happened to Private B.R. Roffe, originally a farmer from South Australia. Roffe was surprised while he was in an observation post. He was shot three times then attacked by a Japanese officer wielding a sword. He suffered cuts to his chest, head, arm, hand and wrist and was stabbed between the neck and shoulder. Stunned Roffe stood up and advanced on the officer shouting obscenities at him. He only escaped when the Japanese officer's pistol misfired and he managed to throw himself jungle and out of sight.[23]

The Japanese were not the only danger faced by patrols. River crossings ran the risk of attack by crocodiles, or 'puk puk', as the indigenous guides called them.[24] Checking the crossing points of the Ramu River was a constant chore, which was done by pairs of men taking turns to do two day patrols.[25] Patrols climbed up into the nearby Bismark Ranges to elevations of 2000 metres or more. The climbs were described by those who did them as an, 'absolute bastard of a climb'.[26] One important objective of the patrols was to locate suitable ambush sites on the tracks which the

18 AWM, AWM 54 1/5/42, Bena Force, patrol reports, LCpl E. Evens 2/7 AUST INDEP COY, Geological, Physical and Botanical Report on Bena Plateau, 7 July 43.
19 AWM, AWM 54 1/5/42, Bena Force War Diary, June-July 43.
20 Ayris, *All the Bull's Men*, p. 426.
21 AWM, AWM 52 1/5/42, Bena Force War Diary, August-November 43, 20 Sept 43.
22 Ayris, *All the Bull's Men*, p. 426.
23 Ibid, p. 402.
24 Ibid, p. 417.
25 Ibid, p. 405.
26 Ibid p. 409.

Japanese would have to use. The plan was to use the close terrain and ambush the enemy at point black range. Indigenous reports of Japanese were followed up with fighting patrols. Mapping parties continued to operate in all areas. During July and into August frequent clashes with Japanese patrols, and Japanese parties probing the defences kept everyone on their toes. Two men from 2/7th Independent Company and four Japanese were killed in a clash at a site known as Snook's House.[27] In another clash two Australians were wounded and three indigenous men were killed.[28] One attack saw some 60 Japanese assault one position five times on the same day, only to be driven off after losing 14 casualties including two officers. On 24 August a patrol of 2/2nd Independent Company contacted an enemy patrol of 10 men and killed six of them. Again on 27 August a patrol by the same Company led by Lieutenant Gerry McKenzie, who we have met before defending Dili airfield against invading Japanese, ambushed a Japanese patrol killing six of them. In both cases the ambushers suffered no casualties.[29]

In August there was concern that the Japanese may launch a parachute infantry attack to seize the Bena and Garoka airstrips.[30] Obstructions were placed on Bena, Mount Hagen and Ogelbeng airstrips, and an operational order was issued which stated that in event of an attack be enemy paratroops 'no withdrawal will be accepted.'[31] The fear of Japanese airborne assault was not an uncommon feature of concern in New Guinea at the time, even though in every such incident no such attack ever occurred.[32]

One characteristic of the Independent Companies which distinguished them from regular formations was their ability to conduct long range reconnaissance patrols deep into enemy country. One such patrol was to a site known as Bogadjim. The Japanese were building a road from Bogadjim to the Ramu Valley across the Finisterre Mountains. When completed this would provide them with a reliable overland line of communications to the Bena plateau, and if extended to Lae. On 13 July 1943, a two man patrol made up of a Corporal and an indigenous policeman undertook a patrol to observe this construction work. To do so they had to pass through unmapped wilderness and avoid enemy as well as unfriendly indigenous areas.[33] The patrol made its way to Bogadjim, and observing from a hidden post, reported the presence of 4000

---

27 Ibid.
28 Ibid, p. 406.
29 AWM, AWM 52 1/5/42, Bena Force War Diary August-November 43.
30 Dexter, *The New Guinea Offensives*, p. 243.
31 Dexter, *The New Guinea Offensives*, p. 243; AWM, AWM 54 1/5/42, Bena Force Operational Order No.14.
32 The report that Japanese were intending to land troops from the air behind Wau in 1942, mentioned in Chapter 5, is an example of the fear of Japanese airborne assault which excited New Guinea Command from time to time, See: MMA, Box 189 Historical Index Cards (Actual) Record Group 3 Index 2, General Headquarters Southwest Pacific Area (SWPA).
33 Dexter, *The New Guinea Offensives*, p. 247 refers to 'truculent' indigenous people posing a threat to one patrol to the Bogadjim road.

'coolies' working on the road, 1000 'coolies' carrying supplies, 60 motor vehicles and the presence of a tank. Ships were also seen unloading at night.[34] Four more two man patrols to Bogadjim were mounted through August to October.[35] Another such mission mounted in October was to a distant area known as Joesphstaal. The Patrol consisted of a Lieutenant and five Sappers from the 2/2nd Commando Squadron, as 2/2nd Independent Company had recently been retitled, a Warrant Officer from ANGUA, 32 indigenous carriers and five indigenous policemen. The patrol was given two objectives, the first to determine if there were any Japanese at or in the vicinity of Joesphstaal, and the second to determine if the existing Joesphstaal airstrip could be repaired and extended. The journey to Joesphstaal took nine days, avoiding known tracks to reduce the chance of contacting the Japanese. On arrival the patrol found no Japanese at Josephstaal, and evidence of only a light Japanese patrol presence. They did find marks which indicated a more significant Japanese movement through the area having occurred several weeks before the patrols arrival. It was also revealed to them by local indigenous people that the Japanese were in some strength at Ambele, not too far distant. The existing airfield had stakes driven into it by the Japanese to prevent its use, but it was determined that it could be returned to serviceable condition, by using indigenous labour, and even extended from its current 600 metres to 1,000 metres if surrounding rain forest was cleared. It was also determined that if the airstrip was moved a short distance to the west it could be extended to 1,300 metres. The survey conducted was comprehensive, and the soil was considered to be suitable for about 100 landings before it 'cracked up'. In all the patrol took thirty days, which in the conditions, required both endurance and resilience, especially as only 16 days of rations had been carried.[36]

In addition to reconnaissance patrols Bena Force, in keeping with its instructions to harass the enemy, mounted fighting patrols. The Japanese threat to the plateau had not diminished. On 10 August documents were recovered from a crashed Japanese aircraft that indicated the Japanese intended to attack the Bena Plateau during September or October, with three battalions of infantry and a battalion of mountain artillery.[37] On 26 September General George Vasey, the commander of 7th Division, assumed command of Bena Force. He wished to blunt the anticipated Japanese offensive and immediately gave Bena Force permission to cross the Ramu River and engage the Japanese encouraging the Companies to act vigorously and with all speed.[38] The Companies needed no better incentive to seek out and inflict harm on the enemy.

---

34 AWM, AWM52 1/5/42, Bena Force War Diary June-July 1943.
35 AWM, AWM 54 1/5/42, Bena Force August-November 1943, the patrol reports do not mention the inclusion of any indigenous police in the patrols.
36 AWM, AMW54 592/2/5, Patrol report Sepu to Jospephstaal Lieut G I Green – 2/2 Aust Cav (Commando) Sqn 28 October 43 to 26 Nov 43.
37 AWM, AWM 54 1/5/42, Bena Force, Interpretation of Translation of Documents taken from crashed Japanese plane at Tsili Tsili 10 Aug 43.
38 AWM, AWM 54 1/5/42, Bena Force War Diary August-November 1943, 1 October 43.

Captain David Dexter's ambush of 29 September, described earlier, was one example of the type of actions incited by Vasey's order. On 14 October 10 Japanese were killed in an ambush. There were further encounters on 18, 19 and 27 October in which an unknown number of Japanese casualties occurred, reflecting the difficulty of assessing enemy losses in the close jungle terrain. From May to November 1943 Bena force killed 230 enemies and successfully prevented any Japanese penetration onto the Bena Bena plateau. Every enemy patrol that crossed the Namu River was driven back with casualties. Every determined attack by the Japanese was repulsed with heavy casualties. In a delusion common to all Japanese encounters with Independent Companies, they became convinced that the Bena Bena plateau was occupied by significant numbers of Australians.[39] This deception was caused by the constant movement and aggressive presence of elements of the companies over a vast area. It was also aided by the operation of 23 radio stations transmitting from the plateau and the construction of four large marked hospitals added to the deception. This fooled the Japanese into presuming that the plateau was held by a large force. So much were the Japanese deceived that they planned to employ 6,000 troops to attack the plateau. Luckily for Bena Force this attack never did eventuate due to the Allied capture of Lae in September.[40] That a small force could achieve such a result over an extended period of time says a great deal for the resilience, autonomous independence, initiative and versatility which characterised the force's operational style.

One source of ongoing concern for Bena Force was its relationship with the indigenous People in the Bena Bena region. While the loyalty of some indigenous people had been an issue during the Wau-Salamaua campaign, the large number of Allied troops, relatively limited numbers of indigenous people, and more tightly controlled type of operations had never made indigenous relations more than a peripheral issue. Such was not the case on the Bena Bena plateau. Bena Force numbered at its best no more than 1,105 personnel much less than the indigenous population in the region.[41] The Chimbu people who lived in the highlands in the Mount Hagen area adjacent to the plateau, alone numbered 31,000 and provided 3,000 carriers and labourers for Bena Force. This does not take into account the families of those carriers who came with them. Numerous groups of other indigenous people lived in the region along the Ramu River valley[42] Establishing and maintaining a working relationship with the indigenous population was a primary concern for Bena Force. The relationship was to be a complicated one. It was forbidden to associate with indigenous people unless

---

39 AWM, AWM 54 1/5/42, Bena Force War Diary August-November 1943.
40 AWM, AWM54 595/7/19, Reports on Japanese Operations New Guinea Ramu Valley Campaign, Sept 1943 – April 44 History Compiled from Series of questionaries and interrogations answered by the Commander of the Japanese Army.
41 AWM, AWM 54 1/5/42, Bena Force War Diary August-November 1943 states the total personnel for Bena Force as 1105.
42 Dexter, *The New Guinea* Offensives, p. 233; AWM, AWM 54 1/5/42, Bena Force War Diary, June to July 1943, Appendix 7 to War Diary 30 July 43.

sanctioned by ANGUA. Indigenous people were not to be given presents of any kind as it was thought this would have a bad effect on the indigenous trade system through which Bena Force procured food and indigenous labour.[43] The loyalty of the indigenous people to the Australian cause was determined very much by the specific group of indigenous people in question. Competition between the Australians and Japanese for the amount of resources offered to indigenous people to compensate them for their cooperation was an ongoing issue. Another challenge was countering the impression amongst some indigenous people that the 'Japan Man' had humbled the 'White Master' and now dominated their world, and thus deserved their deference. The Chimbu who lived in the high country in the direction of Mount Hagen were in almost all cases friendly and accommodating to Bena Force, providing most of the carrying parties and labourers. Such was not the case with the indigenous people who lived along the Ramu River. Patrols in that area frequently reported local people to be hostile and what they called 'treacherous'.[44] There was a spirit of unrest through the district and clashes occurred with Australian troops in which indigenous people were killed.[45] Bena Force war diaries of June to November 1943 recount several incidents when patrols fired killing and wounding indigenous people. On 30 July 43 the diary states that 'any kanaka seen was shot immediately', 'kanaka' being a pejorative term used for indigenous people not under Australian control. Dexter's comment that he shot first and asked questions later implies that killing indigenous people was far more common than the War Diary records.[46]

On 12 August a patrol was ambushed by a hostile indigenous group while crossing the Ramu River, it fought back killing two of the attackers.[47] On 3 June Lieutenant Colonel Thomas MacAdie, the commander of Bena Force, reported that Ramu Valley indigenous people were guiding the enemy to Bena Force observation posts, cutting telephone lines and ambushing indigenous carriers.[48] On 11 July two Australians were killed and mutilated by an enemy patrol consisting of Japanese and Kaigulin indigenous people; it was suspected that the Kaigulin were responsible for the mutilation.[49] Indigenous raiders stole rifles from an ANGAU dump and fired them causing concern for patrols, who could not determine if the shots were from Japanese or indigenous sources.[50] When Lieutenant Claude Dunshea was returning from a patrol to the Bogadjim road he reported that his patrol was seen by indigenous people and shot at,

43 AWM, AWM 52 1/5/42, Routine Order Part 1, 10 Aug 43, Bena Force War Diary, August-November 43.
44 AWM, AWM 54 1/5/42, Bena Force, patrol reports; Dexter, *The New Guinea Offensives*, p. 241.
45 Dexter, *The New Guinea Offensives*, p. 241.
46 AWM, AWM 54 1/5/42, Bena Force War Diary, AWM 54 1/5/42.
47 AWM, AWM 54 1/5/42, Bena Force War Diary, June-July 1943.
48 Ibid.
49 Dexter, *The New Guinea Offensives*, p.244.
50 AWM, AWM 54 1/5/42, Bena Force, patrol reports, AWM 54 1/5/42; AWM, AWM 54 1/5/42, Bena Force, June to July 1943, 30 July 43.

then pursued by Japanese.⁵¹ Responding to what was seen as a serious threat to their existence the response from Bena Force was uncompromising. MacAdie ordered that all 'kanakas' were to be shot first and questions asked later. He later advocated the public hanging of any indigenous person caught guiding the Japanese.⁵² The shooting policy was followed energetically with whole districts being deemed disloyal, and any indigenous person seen within them shot on sight. As brutal as it was, this was considered the most effective way of dealing with the situation.⁵³ Managing relations with the indigenous population was an ongoing concern for Bena Force all through its history.⁵⁴

Supplying the commandos, unlike in 1942, was no longer an issue of concern. Air dropping was the most common means used of resupplying the Squadrons, with indigenous carriers, or 'Kai Trains' as they were called, delivering the goods to the scattered sections. The normal ration was the ubiquitous Bully Beef and biscuits, supplemented whenever possible by local produce such as sweet potato, taro and the occasional vegetable. Whenever possible, pigs, which were extremely important and valuable to the indigenous people, would be bartered for, even though the process of doing so was fraught with the potential for cultural misunderstanding.⁵⁵

On 5 September the US 503rd parachute infantry dropped onto Nadzab, which was on the plateau. This secured the site for the expansion of airfields which would enable 7th Division to begin flying in troops for the assault on Lae. This forced the Japanese to abandon any plans to attack the Bena Bena plateau. With the rapid build-up of regular formations on the plateau in the first weeks of September the denial phase of the Bena Force operation came to an end. The focus for Bena Force then changed to that of probing reconnaissance, interdiction of enemy forces and providing flank security in support of formations within 7th Division. Consequently the two Commando

---

51 AWM, AWM 54 1/5/42, Bena Force Routine Order No 23 Part 1, 10 Aug 43, reports that indigenous people more frequently than not used these rifles to kill other indigenous people.
52 AWM, AWM 54 1/5/42, Bena Force, June to July 1943, Progress Report Bena Force 21 July 43.
53 AWM, AWM 54 1/5/42, Bena Force War Diary, August-November 43, AWM 52 1/5/42; Dexter, *The New Guinea Offensives*, p.246; AWM, AWM 54 1/5/42, Bena Force, June to July 1943, Appendix 7 to War Diary 30 July 43.
54 Insights into the often acrimonious relationship between the Australian Army and New Guinea indigenous people can be gleaned from K.S. Inglis,, 'War, Race and Loyalty in New Guinea, 1939–1945', pp. 503–30 in K.S. Inglis (Ed.), 'The History of Melanesia – 2nd Waigan Seminar', The University of Papua New Guinea-The Research School of Pacific Studies The Australian National University, 1968; Rogerson, E, 'The "Fuzzy Wuzzy Angels": looking beyond the myth', *Australian War Memorial*, SVSS paper, 2012; K.C. Stead, 'Remembering Australia' Wars: Hangings of Papua New Guineans by Australian Soldiers in WWII Complicate our National Narratives' <http://aph.org.au/remembering-asutralia%e2%80%99s-wars-hangings-of-papua-new-guineans-by-australian-soldiers-in-wwii-complicate-our-national-narratives>.
55 Ayris, *All the Bull's Men*, pp. 428–9.

Squadrons of Bena Force moved along with 7th Division as it began to advance on the Japanese in the Markham and Ramu River Valleys protecting its line of communication from Japanese interference. The subsequent campaign of the Commandos, was one in which they patrolled ceaselessly and operated very much in the role of 'Jungle Cavalry'. The patrolling of Australian commandos during the last months of 1943 provided 7th Division with conclusive proof that the Japanese had given up any intentions of striking out across the Ramu River, and that the Japanese were in fact withdrawing.

Sometimes the Squadrons were required to adopt a static role, such as occupying a prominent feature, they nonetheless constantly searched for signs of the enemy and reported enemy movement and any signs they left.[56] These patrols were extensive and deep and paid particular attention to topography, especially timbered areas that may conceal small parties of the enemy. During this period the health of the men, always a concern in New Guinea, became a concern. The men's diet was limited lacking vegetables, and the disease beri beri was common. Leeches, which could infiltrate the stoutest protection, were a major concern and their bites would cause sores which would become septic. Luckily there were adequate supplies of Sulphapyridine antibacterial tablets, known colloquially as M and B tablets, available to counter the effects of suppurating leech sores.[57]

Inevitably patrolling and defending positions of tactical importance resulted in encounters with the Japanese. This was especially so in December, during which 'C' Troop of 2/6th Commando Squadron, which had joined the Commando force covering 7th Division, was attacked repeatedly by strong Japanese forces.[58] Even though they were operating on the fringes of the main Australian force the operations of Australian Commandos in the Ramu Valley did have an impact upon the enemy. Kenji Ueda a Non Commissioned Officer with the Japanese 78th Regiment, which was opposing the Australian 7th Division in the Nadzab region during September 1943, recalled that following the landing of US paratroops at Nadzab on 5 September and the Australian seizure of Lae on 9 September, his unit received no more supplies. He ascribed this to what he called 'Australian Commandos' operating behind his unit and attacking its supply line. Udea recalled one incident when his Regimental commander appeared riding his horse, and informed the regiment that because of the actions of the Commandos the regiment would be forced to pull back to its next defensive position, which in this case was Shaggy Ridge.[59] It is possible that Udea, who gave his account in 2006, may have misremembered, or exaggerated the importance Commandos played in deciding the actions of his unit, but the fact that he

---

56   AWM, AWM52 2/2/58, 2/6 Commando Squadron Diary October to December 1943.
57   Ayris, *All the Bull's Men*, p. 436.
58   AWM, AWM52 2/2/58, 2/6 Commando Squadron Diary December 1943.
59   Kenji Ueda 78th Infantry Regiment, interviewed by Dr Peter Williams, Hiroshima, 8 March 2006.

acknowledged Commandos at all indicates that he was aware of them and that they did feature as a conspicuous element of his wartime recollections.

The experiences of Independent Companies during 1943 cannot pass without mention of the actions of 2/6th Independent Company on the Bena Bena plateau from January to June, and at Kaiapit on 19–20 September. The experiences of the Company during this period clearly reflected the operational dexterity and versatility of the Independent Companies. The Bena Bena patrol of 2/6th Independent Company from January to June in 1943 was something of a special mission. On 24 December 1942 shortly after the company had emerged from its trials at Buna, twelve men were detailed to proceed to the Bena Bean plateau. Their mission was to hunt down and apprehend 'alien', that is German, missionaries operating in the area. These missionaries were known to be assisting the Japanese. The patrol would be operating alone. Bena Force as such had not yet been established, and the nearest friendly troops were some 200 kilometres distant with the original Kanga Force then facing the Japanese at Wau and Mubo. For seven months the patrol would act under the auspices of ANGAU, which with its intimate knowledge of the indigenous population would provide fundamental guidance and support. The twelve man patrol ranged from the mountains of the Bismarck Ranges down into the Ramu Valley. Highland indigenous people were used as carriers, because, in a precursor of what Bena Force would encounter, patrols found it difficult to recruit 'lowland' people, and as with Bena Force 'hostile' lowlanders were shot. During the patrol's operations several missionaries were taken into custody and handed over to ANGAU. In six months of patrolling the patrol lost one man killed in action, betrayed by a German missionary to the Japanese. In addition to apprehending the missionaries the patrol provided New Guinea Force with valuable track reports, and information on the movement of Japanese troops in the area. The Company's Bena Bena Patrol was an example of how an Independent Company sub-unit, with the capacity to operate autonomously and efficiently in a jungle environment, could provide valuable service for minimal outlay of manpower and resources. This was something that could not be expected from any regular unit in the conditions and circumstances in which the operation occurred.

The battle of Kaiapit occurred on 19–20 September 43. It was fought as the result of 2/6th Independent Company operating in direct support of 7th Division to facilitate the Division's advance to achieve its strategic objective. It was an example of how an Independent Company, as a self-sufficient and autonomous sub-unit, could be detached from the main force, and sent out some distance from that force as a spearhead to capture a strategic objective. The plan of 7th Division was to seize a disused airstrip at Kaiapit which lay ahead on its axis of advance to the Markham and Ramu River Valleys and eventual assault on the coastal enclave of Finschafen. If the Division had followed a conventional pathway it would have required the building of a road to Nadzab on the Bena Bena Plateau so as to establish a secure supply line. This would take two months. Such a delay was considered to be unacceptable and a quicker means of pushing ahead needed to be found. The solution, suggested by New Guinea Force Commander General Herring, was to secure enlarge and improve the airfield at Kaiapit, which lay ahead along the Division's axis of advance. Once this was done 21 and 25 Brigades of 7th Division could be flown in, thus hastening the Divisions move forward.[60] Major General Vasey, the commander of 7th Division, agreed with Herring's assessment and decided to make use of 2/6th Independent Company as 'Cavalry' to leap ahead of the main force and seize the objective.[61] Vasey's concept of the operation was to be a classic 'bite and hold' one.[62] There was some risk involved as there was no real knowledge of Japanese forces in the area and the Independent Company would be sent out far in front of the main force, beyond artillery range, and the ability of any other unit to support it. A sense of urgency prevailed, however, and although Vasey would later concede he had acted somewhat impetuously and that if he had known that the Japanese 78th Regiment had moved towards Kaiapit he would not have done so, he issued orders and the Company set forth.[63] On 17 September after waiting three frustrating days in Port Moresby for the weather to clear, the Company was flown to Leron 16 kilometres from Kaiapit.[64] There it linked with a company of a Papuan Infantry Battalion that had moved to the area with orders to come under the command of the Company.[65] With each man carrying 60 lbs of equipment as well as ammunition the Company undertook an arduous 10 hour march in sweltering heat, through waste high Kunai grass and scattered brush. Arriving on the afternoon of 19 September they halted some 1,200 metres from Kaiapit.[66] Kaiapit was in fact a general area in which there were three villages, titled on maps and in all correspondence related to the battle as No.1, No.2, and No.3 Village. This was all overlooked by high ground on what was called Mission Hill because of a Lutheran Mission hut on the hill. The previous day a forward scout group had established itself on high ground overlooking Kaiapit. From there they had observed the area, attempting to spot the positions of the Japanese. They saw very little of the Japanese, although they did see a group of Indigenous men led by Japanese. Having done their job the scout group withdrew but due to a misunderstanding failed to report what they had seen to the attack force. There were in fact some 65 Japanese troops in Kaiapit, being a mixture of headquarters troops and infantry.[67] Further Japanese troops had been ordered to

60   AWM, AWM52 1/5/14, Divisions 7 Australian Division General Staff Branch (7 Aust Div GS Branch) September 1943, 7 Aust Div Operation Instr No.6.
61   AWM, AWM52 2/2/58, 2/6 Commando Squadron War Diary, August to September 1943.
62   AWM, AWM52 2/2/58, 2/6 Commando Squadron War Diary, 1943–1944.
63   Dexter, *The New Guinea Offensives*, p. 426.
64   Dexter, *The New Guinea Offensives*, pp. 414–15; AWM, AWM52 2/2/58, 2/6 Commando Squadron War Diary August to September 1943, 5 September.
65   AWM, AWM52 1/5/14, 7 Australian Division General Staff Branch (7 Aust Div GS Branch) September 1943, 7 Aust Div Operation Instr No.6.
66   AWM, AWM54 595/7/14, 2/6 Australian Independent Coy Report on action Kaiapit 19, 20, 21 Sept 1943.
67   AWM, AWM55 1/6, ATIS SWPA Bulletins, Nos 426–455 27 Sept to 13 Oct 1943, Bulletin 434, 13 Oct 43, Item 3, 4825.

Kaiapit to prepare to attack Allied forces at Nadzab, part of the anticipated three pronged major attack against the Bena Bena Plateau, but these had not yet arrived.[68]

At 3.50 p.m. one platoon of the Company under the command of Captain Gordon King commenced the attack on Kaiapit. In a short sharp fight that lasted about 10 minutes the Japanese defenders were overcome with thirty being killed and the survivors fleeing.[69] Notable amongst the attackers was Private Sydney Graham who took a Japanese strong point killing all 10 Japanese occupying it.[70] By 5.00 p.m. the rest of the company had come up and a defensive perimeter had been established. During the night groups of Japanese soldiers, rifles slung and oblivious of their loss of Kaiapit wandered in. Six to ten of them were killed. An indigenous man carrying a note to what he thought was the Japanese garrison of Kaiapit was also killed. The note was written in Japanese and later translation revealed that it simply stated, 'we believe there are friendly troops in Kaiapit, if so how many and what units'.[71] The night, despite its interruptions would be a relatively peaceful interlude before the climatic events of the following day.

During the night considerable numbers of Japanese, who had marched overnight through what was for them unknown country, gathered just outside of Kaiapit. At approximately 6.30 a.m. on 20 September 500 of them attacked the North West perimeter of the company's position. The Japanese force which attacked Kaiapit consisted of the 8th and 9th Companies of the 3rd Battalion 78th Infantry Regiment, one machinegun platoon, one section of signals and one platoon of 37th Independent Engineer Company.[72] The Japanese came on with a deluge of fire and shouting.[73] The men of the Company quickly set to defending themselves.

It was soon noticed that despite their numbers and the noise they were making there was a noticeable lack of offensive spirit among the Japanese. The usual frenzied aggression typical of Japanese infantry assaults was absent.[74] This may have been because the Japanese troops were tired from having marched all night, but whatever the cause, this lack of offensive spirit was capitalised on by the Company. Acting with a characteristically aggressive spirit the Company set to countering the Japanese

---

68   Ibid, Bulletin 432 29 Sept, Item 1, 4420, AWM55 1/6.
69   AWM, AWM54 595/7/14, 2/6 Australian Independent Coy Report on action Kaiapit 19, 20, 21 Sept 1943; AWM, AWM52 2/2/58, 2/6 Commando Squadron War Diary 1943–1944.
70   Trigellis-Smith, *Purple Devils*, p. 166.
71   AWM, AWM54 595/7/14, 2/6 Australian Independent Coy Report on action Kaiapit 19, 20, 21 Sept 1943; AWM, AWM52 2/2/58, 2/6 Commando Squadron War Diary August to September 1943.
72   AWM, AWM54 423/4/33, Captured documents – Translations Japanese Operation Order.
73   AWM, AWM54 595/7/14, 2/6 Australian Independent Coy Report on action Kaiapit 19, 20, 21 Sept 1943; AWM, AWM52 2/2/58, 2/6 Commando Squadron War Diary October 1943.
74   AWM, AWM52 2/2/58, 2/6 Commando Squadron War Diary October 1943.

assault with its own, 'decisive offensive tactics'.[75] 'C' Platoon, spurred into action by a Whistle Blast from their commanding officer, immediately counter attacked driving the Japanese back on No. 3 Village. 'A' platoon also counter attacked and pushed the Japanese out of the area of the villages into the long Kunai wild grass surrounding Kaiapit. The fighting continued, and 'C' Platoon, running short of ammunition was held up at No.3 Village. Their situation was rectified when ammunition was carried forward by the Papuan troops attached to the company. Reinvigorated, 'C' Platoon then broke through the Japanese positions and drove them out of the village and back into the Kunai and Pit-Pit grass.[76] This assault, which pushed forward some 300 metres, devastated the Japanese facing it, with an estimated 100 being killed, including their commander Major Yonekura. While this fighting had been going on a Section from 'A' Platoon had made its way up onto Mission Hill overcoming the Japanese encountered on the way. That Section now with an uninterrupted view proceeded to assist and direct the efforts of 'A' and 'C' Platoons, shouting and 'barracking like football spectators at a big game'. The battle had been going for about half an hour when 'C' Platoon destroyed three Japanese machinegun posts with grenades and pushed on to link up with 'A' Platoon to their right flank. 'A' Platoon, then went on to destroy one more Japanese machinegun post killing twelve Japanese. It was then with the main Japanese resistance broken, that 'B' platoon, which had been in reserve, was unleashed and rushed forward to clear the area around the airstrip killing some 40 more Japanese without loss to themselves. By that time the Japanese force was in complete disarray and leaderless without Major Yonekura. Their morale broken they fled, running and crawling away into the grass, dumping their gear as they went.[77] The collapse of Japanese morale was extraordinary and emphasised the impact of the ferocity and competence of the Companies counter offensive. So disorientated by the assault were the Japanese that a Japanese Sergeant who was present at Kaiapit, and captured later, said that he and his comrades fled from what they feared was a flank attack by 300 paratroopers.[78]

By 10.00 a.m. only dead and dying Japanese remained. In keeping with the tight schedule that had been conceived for the operation, an American engineer officer was flown in by light plane at 12.50 p.m. and began organising the repair of the 1,200 yard airstrip which was to be ready by 11.00 a.m. the next day. While this was occurring, the Company set to patrolling to the west and south east.[79]

75 AWM, AWM52 2/2/58, 2/6 Commando Squadron War Diary 1943–1944.
76 Pit-Pit is very tall wild grass.
77 AWM, AWM54 595/7/14, 2/6 Australian Independent Coy Report on action Kaiapit 19, 20, 21 Sept 1943; Dexter, *The New Guinea Offensives*, p. 421.
78 AWM, AWM54 595/7/14, 2/6 Australian Independent Coy Report on action Kaiapit 19, 20, 21 Sept 1943; Trigellis-Smith, *The Purple Devils*, pp.161–184 gives a comprehensive blow by blow account of the battle at Kaiapit.
79 AWM, AWM52 1/5/14, 7 Australian Division General Staff Branch (7 Aust Div GS Branch) September 1943, 7 Aust Div Operation Instr No.6.

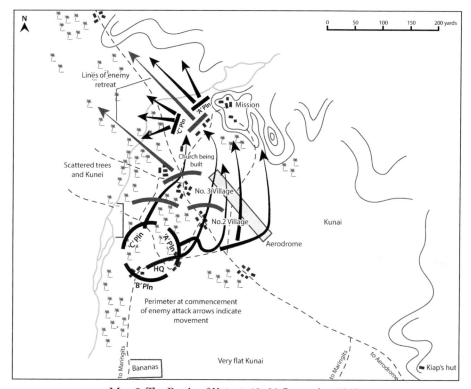

Map 8 The Battle of Kaiapit 19–20 September 1943.

So unexpected was the assault on Kaiapit that throughout the afternoon several Japanese were killed when they entered Kaiapit, apparently with no knowledge of what had occurred. For the loss of 13 members killed and 23 wounded, 2/6th Independent Company had killed some 143 Japanese with indications that at least 50 more had fallen. A very large amount of Japanese documents, weapons and equipment was captured. On 21 September, D Company of 2/16th Battalion was flown into Kaiapit.[80] On the same day General Vasey himself flew into Kaiapit stayed for a brief time and left, to be replaced by the commander of 21 Brigade.[81] Kaiapit had been secured, 2/6th Independent Company had won an outstanding victory and demonstrably assisted 7th Division achieve its objective. It later transpired that the Japanese force destroyed at Kaiapit had been one component part of the planned

---

80 F. Sublet, *Whatever Man Dares – The Second World War Memoirs of Lieutenant Colonel Frank Sublet DSO MC*, (Kokoda Press, 2013), p. 188.
81 AWM, AWM52 1/5/14, 2/6 Australian Independent Coy Report on action Kaiapit 19, 20, 21 Sept 1943.

Japanese offensive against the Bena Bena plateau. Its defeat had ruined those plans. The defeat also caused the Japanese to abandon defensive positions which had been established to delay 7th Division advance towards Lae.[82] The commander of US Fifth Air Force General George Kenney was so pleased with the Company's capture of the Kaiapit airfield that he offered the company a plane load of anything they wanted. The Company enthusiastically responded and lists were made up and sent.[83]

The action at Kaiapit illustrated the versatility of what an aggressive, experienced and well led Independent Company could achieve, as well as the valuable role such a company could play in the broader aspects of operations.

The year 1943 was the apogee of the Independent Phase of the Independent Companies during the Second World War. At no other time during the War were the Independent Companies tasked with missions that were as strategically significant as those they were given during 1943. At no other time during the war, with the single exception of 2/8th Commando squadron on Bougainville in 1945, were the companies granted the degree of autonomy to operate in a manner whereby they could exploit their unique qualities to the full. The operations of 2/3rd Independent Company, Bena Force and 2/6th Independent Company at Kaiapit contributed decisively to the overall strategic objectives of main force operations. Importantly for the evolution of unconventional operations within the Australian Army all three cases illustrated how, by 1943, the Army was prepared to discard preconceived ideas, to adapt to the tactical and environmental realities it was confronted with, and to acknowledge that unconventional forces provided a valuable asset which could be employed to address the challenges it faced. This mature, astute and perceptive understanding was a far cry from the ignorance which characterised the management of the Independent Companies during 1941, and the uneven behaviour which characterised 1942.

Despite these achievements, however, and despite elements within the Army being very much attuned to the potential for employing unconventional forces, the year 1943 also represented a time when the beginning of the end of the independent phase of the Independent Companies began to manifest itself. At its core the army had never accepted the independent ethos of the companies. As the nature of the war in the South West Pacific began to change from one of small unit infantry combat in forbidding jungle terrain to a war of materiel might along more open coastal areas, the army's interest in unconventional independent sub-units waned. This changing military milieu would in 1944–1945 result in a fundamental and radical reassessment of the Independent Companies and lead to their transformation into Commandos and initiate the Commando phase of the Australian 'Commando' experience.

---

82 Bottrell, *Cameos of Commandos*, p. 45; Malcolm Uren, *A Thousand Men at War – A History of the 2/16th Australian Infantry Battalion AIF* (Australian Military History Publications: Loftus, 2009), p. 198; Sublet, *Whatever Man Dares*, p. 190.
83 AWM, AMW52 2/2/58, 2/6 Commando Squadron War Diary August to September 1943.

9

"The Doldrums of War" – Atherton 1944–1945

By 1944 the strategic situation facing the Australian army had changed dramatically. The direct Japanese threat to Australia had long since passed, and US Forces under the command of MacArthur had begun to plan and prepare for the invasion of the Philippines. Australian forces were not to participate in the return to the Philippines, leaving the Australian army searching for a meaningful role to play. Thus during 1944 the majority of the Australian Army, including all but one of Australia's Commando Squadrons, was relegated from front line service, to the training grounds of the Atherton Tableland in Northern Queensland. It was during this period, of enforced passivity, that the Army moved away from the Independent Company model and redefined its concept of 'Commando'. In doing so it, for the first time, formulated a set of guidelines for the use of Commandos and their employment operationally.

While the Army never formally announced it had anything like a Commando doctrine, and no field manuals were produced related to Commandos, considerable thought went into formulating a theory of the functions of Commandos within the Army. The conclusions were written down and promulgated in official correspondence. In practical terms the redefined concept for Commandos was in every respect a doctrine. This was a radical departure from the previous lack of any such official documentation or interest from the Army in regulating its unconventional forces.

The difference between the new Commando guidelines, and what had gone before was profound. The Independent Companies had been characterised by voluntary enlistment, unorthodox tactical training, and rebuttal of mainstream military decorum, adaptive small and very small unit tactics, and little formal contact with other army sub-units. The commando doctrine ended voluntary enlistment, reinstituted traditional military decorum, concentrated on orthodox combined arms tactics at Troop and Squadron level, and maintained close liaison with other army units. The first step towards this change occurred when on 3 July 1943 an instruction was issued which changed the name of the Independent Companies to Commando Squadrons, although the actual change did not occur officially until 17 February

1944.¹ Free ranging 'Commando' units held a special appeal in the popular imagination, with such groups celebrated for their, 'rapier like thrusts at the enemy'.² That the Army recognised this and wished to associate it with the Independent Companies was evident by Independent Company soldiers when on leave in Australia wearing the title 'Commando' on their shoulder.³ Indeed 'Commando' was a much-used epithet in Australian newspapers during early 1942 in relation to the activities of the Independent Companies.⁴ 2/2nd Independent Company on Timor was consistently referred to as Commandos in a multitude of press reports.⁵ The term Commando had been used more and more in general to describe the actions of the Independent Companies, even if the tasks of the Independent Companies bore little similarity to the actions of the British Commandos.⁶ In a reflection of the extent to which the ideal of the 'Commando' had permeated the popular consciousness a notably silly piece in the *Hobart Mercury* commends Berger Paints for their 'Commando Toughness' and for being 'tough, weather fighting paint'.⁷ Another equally fatuous article in the *Bowen*

1 AWM, AWM 52/2/52 Box 44, 2/7 Commando Regiment War Diary, January to May 1944, 2/7 Aust Cav (Commando) Regiment Routine Orders, 17 Feb 44.
2 *The Sun*, Wed 9 Sep 1942, Page 4, 'Commandos for Striking Power'.
3 UQFL, UQFL288, Papers of Peter Pinney Box 13, Pinney to his Mother, Father and Maura, 13 August 1943.
4 Numerous Australian newspaper articles referred to the Australian Army training of Commandos see for example: *The Newcastle Sun*, Tuesday 10 February, 1942 p. 1 and *The Telegraph*, Tuesday 10 February 1942, p. 3, 'Commando Units in Australia; *The Advertiser*, Wednesday 11 February 1942, p. 3; 'Commando Units Training', *The Argus*, Wednesday 11 February, 1942 p. 2; 'Commando Duty. Training Special Men. Revealed by Army', *Cairns Post*, Wednesday 11 February, 1942 p. 4; 'Guerrilla Warfare Special Training in Australia', *The West Australian*, Wednesday 11 February 1942, p. 4; 'Commando Troops in Training'. A further use of the term Commando was the announcement of The Independent Company Raid on Salamaua in June 1942 which was reported as: *Adelaide News*, Wednesday 1 July 1942, p. 1, 'Commando Swoops on Salamaua', *The Armidale Express and New England General Advertiser*, Wednesday 1 July 1942, p. 4, 'Raid by Commandos on Salamaua 60 Enemy Casualties', *Tweed Daily*, Thursday 2 July 1942, p. 1; 'Filming the Timor Commandos Cameraman's Story of Visit to Island'.
5 *The Sydney Morning Herald*, Thursday 31 December 1942, p. 4, 'A.I.F. Commandos in Timor Small Band Holds Down Big Enemy Force'; *National Advocate*, Thursday 31 December 1942, p. 1, 'Fighting On Australian Commando in Timor A Little Story of Great Deeds Battling Against Odds of 100 to 1'; *Warwick Daily News*, Thursday 31 December 1942, p. 4, 'Timor A.I.F. Commandos Pinning Down Japs.'; *Lithgow Mercury*, Thursday 31 December 1942, p. 5, 'Epic Story Of A.I.F. In Timor Handful of Commandoes Pin Down Japs and take toll of 100 to 1 "You Alone Will Not Surrender to Us" Says Jap Commander'; *The Age*, Thursday 31 December 1942, p. 3, 'Commandos Defy Japanese Australian Heroes in the Wilds of Timor'; *Kalgoorlie Miner*, Thursday 31 December 1942, p. 2, 'A.I.F. Commandos Epic Resistance in Timor odds of 100 to One against West Australians and Tasmanians show How'; *The Argus*, Thursday 31 December 1942, p. 12, 'AIF Commandos Hold up Japs at Bay Heroic Resistance in Timor by "Lost" Force Dramatic Story of Fighting In Wild Mountain Country'.
6 Dexter, *The New Guinea Offensives*, p. 566 fn.
7 *Mercury*, Friday 12 February 1943, p. 5.

Independent refers to Queensland Boy Scouts instructing Volunteer Defence Corps (VDC) in their Boy Scout skills to assist the VDC in their 'Commando warfare'.[8] In March 1942 Blamey had referred to a 'certain amount of commando training' being instituted to inculcate an offensive spirit into the Australian Army.[9] In September 1942, the Australian Press followed this up with a clamour to have all soldiers trained as Commandos.[10] Despite his earlier allusion to the value of commando training Blamey's response to the suggestion was forthright, 'Wars are not won by guerrilla bands', an indicator of the shape of thing to come for the Independent Companies.[11]

The title Commando held various connotations and differed as to who interpreted it. There was for some no clear definition of the word, which could mean either a unit or an individual soldier.[12] It was generally understood that 'Commando' referred to a specially trained military force that cooperated with the navy but fought on land, very much the British model.[13] An alternative understanding was such as that of Captain David Dexter of the 2/2nd Independent Company who considered that the 'Commando' in the Australian context was akin to the Boer Commandos with their collective spirit, living and sharing everything, skill with arms and casual reference to rank.[14] Conversely in January 1942 several newspapers reported that the name 'Commando' was not popular with Australian troops as it was considered that what commandos did was what Australian troops did as part of their normal duties.[15] The title 'Commando' had a decided negative undertone for others especially those intimately affected by the title change. Opposition to the term 'Commando' was particu-

8   *Bowen Independent*, Friday 27 March 1942, p. 4. The Volunteer Defence Corps was the Australian version of the British Home Guard. It consisted of civilian volunteers who undertook military training to act as a local defence force in case of invasion.
9   *The West Australian*, Monday 30 March 1942, p. 6, 'General Blamey. A Stern Message. "We Live or Die As Nation."'
10 *The Argus*, Tuesday 8 September 1942, p. 2, 'Commando Spirit' and *The Telegraph*, Tuesday 8 September 1942, p. 4, 'We Must Develop Commando Spirit To Full'; *The Newcastle Sun*, Tuesday 8 September 1942, p.3, 'Testing-Time in New Guinea'; *The Argus*, Wednesday 9 September 1942, p. 2, 'Mass Commando Drill Answer to NG Reverses'; *The Telegraph*, Monday 14 September 1942, p. 2, "'Every Digger a Commando" Means Every Man an Attacker, The Way to Victory Lies Through Beating The Jap at His Own Audacious Game'; *The Argus*, Saturday 19 September 1942, p. 1, 'Our Commandos'; *Western Mail*, Thursday 10 December 1942, p. 10; *The Macleay Chronicle*, Wednesday 25 November 1942, p. 4, 'Digger A Commando'.
11 *The Sydney Morning Herald*, Wednesday 16 September 1942, p. 6, 'General Blamey's Report'.
12 *American Speech*, Vol. XIX, April 1944, Number 2, p. 90.
13 *The Australasian*, Sat 5 Sep 1942, p. 10, 'Francis Drake Would Have Loved Them: Exploits of Commandos: Nicknamed Churchill's Marines'.
14 David Dexter interviewed by Mel Pratt for the Mel Pratt collection [sound recording] 1976 <http://nla.gov.au/nla.obj-221579220> (consulted 14 July 2016).
15 *The Mercury*, Friday 9 January 1942, p. 1; *The Age*, Friday 9 January 1942, p. 1; *The Sydney Morning Herald*, Friday 9 January 1942, p. 8.

larly strong within the Independent Companies themselves. The opinion from the companies was that the name Commando was 'unfortunate'; a polite euphemism for what was in fact significant resentment.[16] The reasons for this were mixed. On one hand, there was a perception that the name 'Commando' implied an elite soldier 'the flower of the British army'. This apparently offended the egalitarian sensibilities of Australian Independent Company soldiers who saw themselves as 'merely a cross section of the Australian army'.[17] This was regardless of a certain perception amongst at least some Independent Company soldiers that they were indeed 'elite' or at least a cut above the average soldier. Ron Garland a Captain with 2/3rd Commando Squadron recalled that during the Squadron's time training on the Atherton Tableland it was only the thought amongst the veteran Commandos that other units were worse off when it came to combat experience, which assisted them to endure the routine and tedium. This attitude indicated that despite protestations that they were no different to anyone else there was indeed a perception that they were superior to other troops.[18] The adverse reaction went further with Independent Company members describing the average Commando as, 'a blatant, dirty, unshaven, loudmouthed fellow covered with knives and knuckledusters'.[19] Dexter in a more reflective mood commented that the term 'Commando' was alien to the Australian Army.[20] There was an understanding that the work of British Commandos bore little resemblance to that of the Australian Independent Companies. Where British Commandos would inflict as much damage as possible and withdraw immediately, Australian Independent Companies would remain in the field operating within the same general area as the enemy and continue to harass them.[21] It was suspected that choosing the term 'Commando' was done simply for the 'blatant glamour' of the name which was used as propaganda to attract volunteers to Commando units.[22] Peter Pinney of 2/3rd Independent Company echoed this when in a letter to his parents he wrote:

> We are now officially called Commandos, but it's just a farce to get the suckers to come in as reinforcements. We aren't even a parody of the Tommy Commandos – just an infantry guerilla [sic] show, + we resent the glorified farce of taking advantage of the Tommies good name. But I suppose it's good propaganda.[23]

16 AWM, AWM54 595/7/13, Report on Operations – Covering period Sept 1943 to March 1944 2/6 Aust Commando Sqd Markham – Ramu Valley Campaign Part 1.
17 Ibid.
18 AWM 3DRL/6766, Arden, John PH 'Jack', p. 46; Garland, *Nothing is forever*, p. 330.
19 AWM, AWM54 595/7/13, Report on Operations – Covering period Sept 1943 to March 1944 2/6 Aust Commando Sqd Markham – Ramu Valley Campaign Part 1.
20 Dexter, *The New Guinea Offensives*, p. 565.
21 AWM 3DRL/6766, Arden, John PH 'Jack', p. 46.
22 Dexter, *The New Guinea Offensives*, p. 566 fn.
23 UQFL, UQFL288, Papers of Peter Pinney, Box 8. Pinney to Mother 9 October 1944.

The manner in which the soldiers of the Independent Companies found out about the title change also varied. Andy Pirie of 2/5th Independent Company first heard of it enroute from Ballum to Wau in New Guinea when he encountered some troops from 2/6th Battalion who told them that they were now Commandos.[24] Arthur Botterell Chaplain to the 2/4th Independent Company at the time recalled that when the change occurred the commander of the unit was surprised and that the news was met with a mixture of dismay, amusement and pride.[25]

There was, however, a more consequential reason for the name change. The adoption of the term 'Commando' clearly marked the end of the Army's association with and tolerance for independent sub-units. The Army as an institution had never warmed to the idea of independent unconventional sub-units. At no time in relation to any of these examples did Army as an institution express any interest or desire to manage the Independent Companies in any way whatsoever. All management of Independent Companies had been at the localised level and entirely reliant on the attitudes of senior commanders on the spot. Savige during the Salamaua campaign, Herring with Bena Force and Vasey at Kaiapit were examples of this. When the Army did move to impose its will on the Independent Companies in late 1943 it was no surprise that it did so from an entirely conservative perspective. Thus with the transformation of the Independent Companies to Commandos the independent ethos which constituted the fundamental core of the companies was eliminated, and the function of Commandos was redefined as one more closely attuned to the needs of conventional warfare. Changing the title to Commando signalled this transformation.

There were in fact rational reasons for choosing this pathway even if by doing so the Army turned its back on utilising an asset which could have added value to its operations. By 1944 the war in New Guinea had physically moved out of the forbidding forested mountain ranges of the hinterland, which favoured small unit actions, and was now being fought along the coast where the country was much less forbidding. In this environment manoeuvring large formations supported by the heavy use of artillery, air power and tanks became the new standard. The war had evolved into one which had taken on the characteristics of overwhelming, crushing firepower, and assaults delivered by large conventional formations. In an example of the way in which the logistical profile and tactical thinking of the Army had changed was the planning for Operation Seagull in March 1945. In this Operation, which despite the voluminous amount of staff work it generated never did occur, the Army planned to allocate 216,000 artillery shells, 121 combat aircraft, amphibious tanks, a parachute battalion and a naval bombardment to achieve its ends.[26] In such a military environment it was thought that there was no place for small independent sub-units.

---

24   Pirie, 'Commando Double Black', p. 272.
25   Bottrell, *Cameos of Commandos*, p. 15.
26   AWM, AWM54 945/7/1, 'Operational Seagull', Part 1 and Part 14.

The Army carefully defined the new role of its Commandos. They were to conduct close reconnaissance for the infantry divisions and other formations as directed. They were to seize ground and hold it for limited periods of time. Most importantly Commandos were required to take their place in the line of battle as conventional infantry when and if required.[27] Interestingly given what would be the failure by the Army to actually allocate any such missions to Commandos during 1944–1945 Commandos were also to conduct long range independent patrols, 'special missions', sabotage and 'commando tactics'.[28] In reality the Army had no intention of employing its commandos in anything but a tightly controlled manner. Commandos were in effect to be used as well-trained light infantry to provide reconnaissance, vanguard and flank protection to larger formations, and when required to engage in conventional operations. This change was to be profound and was recognised as such by those who it most affected. Jack Boxall of 2/5th Commando Squadron understood that the Independent Companies had been transformed into what he called 'lightly equipped mobile infantry' and that the days of guerrilla fighting were over.[29]

It has been claimed that the formation of Commando Squadrons by the Army was an innovative step.[30] This was not so. There was nothing innovative in the introduction of light infantry. The role of light infantry was a well understood within British, and thus Australian, military tradition.[31] Unlike the original concept of Independent Companies the concept of light troops to provide close support in the role of reconnaissance, vanguard and flank was not particularly difficult for the Australian Army to understand, adopt and assimilate. One important element of the change from Independent Companies to Commandos which would make the change acceptable to the Australian Army was that it was a parochial decision. The idea was not the initiative of an outside agency, as had been the Independent Companies. Illustrative of this was that the Army increased the number of Commando Squadrons from seven to 11.

A further signpost that the Army was finished with the Independent Company ethos was that the practice of voluntary enlistment for the Independent Companies

27 AWM, AWM 52/2/52 Box 44, 2/7 Commando Regiment Outline War Diary June to December 1943, O.C. Coys 2 Aust Corps L.H.Q/ (Via) 2 Aust Corps, Training, 19 June 1943.
28 AWM, AWM 52/2/52 Box 44, Organisation of Indep Coys, 2 Aust Corps 20 June 43 – Organisation of Independent Companies; NAA, MP729/6 37/401/1714, 2/7 Commando Regiment Outline War Diary June to December 1943, Australian Military Forces, Organisation – A Cav Commando Regt, 2 Aust Corps, 19 July 43; AWM, AWM 52/2/51 Box 40, 2/6 Cavalry Commando Regiment War Diary, 2/6 Cav Commando Regiment – Appendices, 2/10 Commando Squadron War Diary Aug 1944, August to September 1944; AWM, AWM 52/2/52 Box 44, 2/7 Commando Regiment Outline War Diary, June to December 1943, O.C. Coys 2 Aust Corps L.H.Q/ (Via) 2 Aust Corps training 19 June 1943.
29 Pirie, 'Commando Double Black', p. 349.
30 Peter Stanley, *Tarakan an Australian Tragedy* (Allen and Unwin: St Leonards, 1997), p. 38.
31 See: David Gates, *The British Light Infantry Arm c.1790–1815* (B.T. Batsford Ltd: London, 1987).

was ended. Voluntarism has been a fundamental aspect of the original Independent Company recruitment process, but it would not be for the Commandos. On 23 February 1944 Army Headquarters posted a notice that stated, 'Reinforcements will not be provided by volunteers but provided in the normal manner'.[32] It was also stated that the number of reinforcements would not exceed 50 per month. Significantly the decision to do so was made by Blamey himself and indicated that at the highest levels the practice of voluntarism found no favour.[33]

The reasons for this were not necessarily any deep seated antipathy to the idea of voluntary recruitment but reflected the practical necessities of the time. The management of the allocation of manpower to service the various needs of the military and the national economy was an ongoing challenge throughout the later war years. At the time Australia's total manpower pool was 3,200,000. Of these 1,000,000 were directly engaged in the war effort either as members of the military or services directly associated with maintaining the military.[34] During 1943 the Army required to recruit 10,000 per month to maintain its operational capabilities.[35] This was however not being achieved with recruitment being one third below the target by June 1943.[36] By the end of 1943, at the time when the Independent Companies had been replaced by the Commandos, the Army against its wishes, continued to be compelled by the Federal Manpower Directorate to release personnel for the civilian economy.[37] The pressure for the Army to release personnel during the later war years was relentless, with 18,128 troops being lost to the civilian economy by June 1944 and a demand for a further 40,000 in October 1944 only being prevented by Blamey's determined protests.[38] Blamey linked the maintenance of the Army's manpower directly to strategic policy, and strongly resisted every attempt by the Manpower Directorate to reallocate army personnel to the civilian economy.[39] In such circumstances it is unsurprising that voluntary enlistment for the commandos, which by its very nature directly competed with the capacity of the army to allocate its increasing threatened manpower resource to where it wished it to be, was ended. Individuals who were part of the replacement pool could still volunteer for Commando service subject to the limitation on volunteer recruitment numbers, but the original system of volunteering from outside the official Army recruitment system no longer applied.

---

32   NAA, MP742 96/1/814, Reinforcement Training Independent (sic) Companies Aust Cav Commando TRG Sqn 7 Aust Cav Commando Regt.
33   Ibid.
34   Sydney James Butlin and Carl Boris Scheduin, 'War Economy 1942–1945, Australia in the War 1939–1945', *Civil*, Series 4, Vol. IV, *Australian War Memorial*, 1977, p. 348.
35   Ibid, p. 355.
36   Ibid, p. 357.
37   Ibid, p. 381.
38   Ibid, p. 387; Peter Dean, *Australia 1944–1945, Victory in the Pacific* (Cambridge University Press: Cambridge, 2016), p. 19.
39   Dean, *Australia 1944–1945*, p. 19.

Such a process ensured that the Commandos remained firmly under the Army's administrative control; it did little, however, to ensure that replacements for Commando squadrons were suitable. Many of those who came to the Squadrons were unsuitable material for Commando training even though they had been 'selected' and 'tested' prior to attachment to the Commando Squadrons. The Squadrons complained that the personnel they received were, 'neither better or worse than the general reinforcements to the infantry battalions', that some of those sent to them were 'mentally underdeveloped' and some so young that they were physically underdeveloped and incapable of putting up with the strain of the work.[40] At times 30% or more of the reinforcements were found to be unsuitable.[41] It was considered that when such reinforcements were received during operations it was impossible to bring them up to the required standard and that became liabilities to their units. Commando Squadrons were very firm on the notion that they 'cannot carry passengers'.[42] Contributing to this was the questionable quality of the process the Army employed to 'select' Commando recruits. Of particular concern was quality of the medical examination and selection of recruits which was frequently poorly managed and sometimes not occurring at all.[43] The standard of training Commando recruits had received prior to joining Commando Squadrons was also of concern. Recruits reported to the squadrons who had received substandard basic training and could not take their place in sections. It was noted that many recruits could not even cook themselves a meal, and had no idea how to keep themselves clean and healthy.[44] Whether or not Commando recruits were informed of what they had volunteered for was another issue. It was found that recruits did not understand the history and traditions of the Commandos, or had any idea of the 'Cavalry' role and were completely ignorant of all aspects of those subjects.[45] For some recruits the primary motivation for volunteering to join the commandos was the blatant glamour of the name 'Commando' and that those who joined for that reason were always undesirable.[46] Despite the difficulties it imposed on the Commando Squadrons the recruitment process persisted. What it demonstrated was that Commandos were now an integrated part of the army, and were to be managed and administered no differently than any other unit within the army. The exceptional status of the Independent Companies was ended.

Accompanying the title change was a change to the organisational structure of the Commandos as a whole with the formation of Cavalry Commando Regiments.

---

40 AWM, AWM54 595/7/13, Report on Operations – Covering period Sept 1943 to March 1944 2/6 Aust Commando Sqd Markham – Ramu Valley Campaign Part 1, Section II – Lessons Learned During the Campaign.
41 Ibid.
42 Ibid.
43 Ibid.
44 Ibid.
45 Ibid.
46 Dexter, *The New Guinea Offensives*, pp. 565–6.

On 4 April 1943 General Vasey received instructions to disband the 7th Division cavalry regiment, for which there was no use in New Guinea, and raise the 2/7th Cavalry Commando Regiment. The idea was to create an administrative centre to manage future Commando Squadrons. The date of April 1943 is significant as it illustrates that official moves to end the Independent Companies were in place in the early months of 1943, indicating that planning for such must have begun earlier. It can thus be assumed that sometime in late 1942 or in the first months of 1943 moves had commenced to end the Independent Company presence within the Australian Army, illustrating that there never was an intention to allow the companies any degree of longevity. There were at the time seven Independent Companies and although it was intended that the new Commando Regiment would be the home for three Commando Squadrons all seven Companies, now Squadrons, were allocated to it. A single Regimental Headquarters could not possibly cope with seven Squadrons. David Dexter observed in something of an understatement that 'the situation was very confused'.[47] Confusion was not just limited to unrealistic administrative workloads; there was also confusion as to the role of the new Regiment's Headquarters Squadron. As far as the Army was concerned the Commando Regimental Headquarters was to be purely administrative and have no operational role, but at the same time 2/7th Cavalry Commando Regiment Headquarters were informed that if it may become operational.[48] The contradiction here is obvious. The situation became even more befuddled when in January 1944, the 2/6th and 2/9th Cavalry Commando Regiments formed and six squadrons from the eleven squadrons now raised, who were at that time with 2/7th Cavalry Commando Regiment, were posted to them.[49] This left two squadrons, the 2/2nd and 2/8th unattached to any Cavalry Commando Regiment or by association any Division. No official reason for the exclusion of these two Squadrons exists, other than to speculate that the army wanted two 'Independent' Commando Squadrons in case special tasks not related to the operations of Divisions were required.[50] There was, however, fortunately at least one bright spot amidst the confusion. The Army did recognise that it needed to address the special requirements of the Commando Regiments. To facilitate this on 11 February 1944 Lieutenant Colonel Thomas MacAdie, was appointed as General Staff Officer II Commando 1st Corps.[51] MacAdie had commanded Bena Force with distinction and was thoroughly conversant with special operations and the needs of Commando type formations. MacAdie's role was to liaise with the Commando Regiments, discuss issues with them and relay

---

47 Ibid, p. 566 fn.
48 Ibid.
49 Ibid.
50 As it transpired 2/2nd Commando Squadron was posted to New Britain in 1945 to support the Australian Army force sent there and 2/8th Commando Squadron was posted to Bougainville in November 1944 to operate in support of 3rd Division.
51 AWM, AWM 52/2/52 Box 44, 2/7 Commando Regiment War Diary, January to May 1944.

subsequent decisions and recommendations to the Corps. MacAdie's appointment indicated that the army was aware that the knowledge and experience required to manage a special force such as the Commandos possessed a degree of distinctiveness, and thus needed to be managed accordingly. Even so their daily administration, maintenance and logistics were to be the province of the regular Army system.

Despite the Army's determination to redefine the Commando identity the change to Commando did not come as a sudden epiphany for the Independent Companies. There was no one moment when a unit's concept of itself suddenly transformed from Independent Company to Commando. The titles may have changed but the intellectual appreciation within those units, of just what the units were did not immediately alter. In August 1943 Lieutenant Colonel H.E. Bastin Commanding Officer of 2/7th Cavalry Commando Regiment gave a lecture in which he referred to how the attributes of the Independent Company, and he used that term, reflected the role and attributes of cavalry.[52] It was apparent that Bastin continued to apply the Independent Company attributes to the formation he commanded, even though it was now formally a Commando unit. This reluctance to adopt their new character would have a significant unsettling influence on the veteran Independent Company personnel when they began the process of training to transform them to their new Commando role.

Commando Training within the Cavalry Commando Regiments reflected the redefinition of the role of the Commandos within the army. Gone was the concentration on the unorthodox training that had characterised the training of the Independent Companies. The aim now was to create a force of infantry capable of fighting as part of a combined arms team in the line of battle and to fulfil the role of close reconnaissance and protection for Infantry Divisions.[53] To ensure this the training program was designed to concentrate on conventional skills. Notable amongst these was drill and 'smartness'.[54] Nothing could more emphasise the difference between the spirit of the Independent Companies and the Commandos than the reversion to this traditional military repertoire as a feature of the Commando training program.

Drill of course constituted only part of the training regime. There was a three-week syllabus for the training of the Commando Squadron. The first week involved weapon training, field craft (which bore no relation to the field craft training of earlier times), assault courses, route marching, swimming and interestingly 'hand hardening'. The second week involved shooting on the range, section level tactical training, river crossing, night patrols, compass reading and navigation by the stars. The third week involved more tactical training, patrolling and river crossings opposed

---

52 AWM, AWM 52/2/52 Box 44, 2/7 Commando Regiment War Diary, June to December 1943, Appendix 3, Functions of Cavalry, Lecture by C.O.
53 AWM, AWM 52/2/52 Box 44, 2/7 Commando Regiment Outline War Diary, June to December 1943, O.C. Coys 2 Aust Corps L.H.Q/ (Via) 2 Aust Corps, Training, 19 Jun 1943.
54 Ibid.

and unopposed.⁵⁵ Of interest was that bayonet fighting was a significant feature of the syllabus, emphasising once again the reversion to the more traditional combat style expected of the Commandos. Tactical training was another aspect which differed to earlier training. Unlike Independent Company training which focussed on autonomous small units, Commando training focussed on developing the skills necessary to fight and manoeuvre as Sections, Platoons and Squadrons in support of other formations.

In the new order represented by the Commandos the prior experience of the Independent Companies was considered by some to be a disadvantage. The experience of 2/7th Commando Squadron illustrates this. According to 16 Brigade, 2/7th Commando Squadron's tactical ability was not equal, in fact inferior, to other Commando Squadrons within its Regiment.⁵⁶ It is possible that after extensive unrelieved service in New Guinea 2/7th Commando Squadron, had lost its edge, but even if so, to consider its tactical ability inferior to the novice 2/9th and 2/10th Commando Squadrons, is extraordinary. Such a judgment, however, needs to be assessed within the context of the new Commando regime. Within that regime the expectations of Commandos bore no relation to the techniques which 2/7th Commando Squadron had practised as an Independent Company. It was thus necessary to retrain the Squadron and bring it up to what was now considered to be the appropriate military standard for a Commando Squadron. The training regime that was imposed on the squadron to achieve this included drill, route marches, obstacle course, weapon training, training at Section and Troop level, and jungle training.⁵⁷ Just what the Squadron could have been taught in regards to the skills of jungle warfare is problematic, considering the squadron's extensive experience fighting in the jungles of New Guinea throughout the latter months of 1942 and all of 1943. The army's capacity to teach jungle warfare skills was problematic at best. A jungle warfare centre was established at Canungra but veteran Independent Company personnel who experienced that training thought it was of little value due to the fact that many of the trainers had no or very limited jungle warfare experience and that in many cases the trainees were far more experienced in that mode of warfare. Private Brian Walpole of 2/3rd Independent Company, who was an Independent Company instructor at Wilson's Promontory and transferred to instruct at Canungra, when contrasting the jungle training rigours of Wilson's Promontory to that of Canungra recalled that Canungra was nowhere near as tough and was in comparison a piece of cake.⁵⁸ A jungle training school was set up at Danbula by Lieutenant General Savige which did employ jungle

---

55 AWM, AWM52 2/2/53 Box 45, 2/9 Aust Cav (Commando) Regt, Training Instruction No.10, 9 May 44.
56 AWM, AWM52/2/2/51, 2/6 Cav (Commando) Regiment Diary, 16 Aust Inf Bde Training Instruction No. 9 of 26 May 44.
57 Ibid.
58 Walpole, B. *My War*, p. 15.

warfare veterans as trainers, one of who was Ron Garland, but the training at this centre was restricted to Militia Battalions only.⁵⁹

Conversely, and typical of the cross currents within attitudes to Commando training, the prior experience of the members of the Commando squadrons was not necessarily always a cause for concern. The experience of the veteran squadrons was in fact seen as a bonus by some. 2/9th Cavalry Commando Regiment was composed of the newly raised 2/11th and 2/12th Squadrons, neither of which had seen active service. In April 1944 they were joined by the veteran 2/4th Commando Squadron. The Regimental Commanding Officer's report for May 1944 makes the point of welcoming 2/4th Commando Squadron stating that Squadron's experience would be a great help with the training the other two squadrons as 'foot cavalry'.⁶⁰ A further example of the army recognising the inherent experience and skills of the Commando Squadrons occurred on 23 September 1944 when 2/3rd Commando Squadron was detailed to conduct a demonstration ambush for the Command staff of 7th Division. Present to witness the demonstration was the Divisional Commander Major General Edward Milford, his three Brigadiers and every battalion commander in the Division. In this exercise the Commandos fired live ammunition from one Bren gun and five Owen guns and used half sticks of gelignite to simulate grenade explosions. Major General Milford expressed complete satisfaction with the ambush and the principles demonstrated in conducting it.⁶¹ A similar demonstration was conducted on 15 January 1945 by 2/5th Commando Squadron for the Platoon Command Cadre of 21 Infantry Brigade. The object of the exercise was 'to show the audience how it was done'.⁶² It was also the case that the type of training that Squadrons received could be modified according to the prior experience of the Squadron. In August 1944 Squadrons of 2/9th Cavalry Commando Regiment trained in how to conduct a Section attack. The novice 2/11th Commando Squadron undertook two training sessions, the equally inexperienced 2/12th Commando Squadron three training sessions and the veteran 2/4th Squadron only one training session.⁶³ During training 2/4th Commando Squadron provided instructors for the other squadrons, advising them how to carry their loads in the field.⁶⁴

59 Garland, *Nothing is Forever*, pp. 319 and 330.
60 AWM, AWM52 2/2/53, Box 45, 2/9 Cavalry Commando Regiment January to May 1944, C.O's Report and Comments on Month of May 44; AWM, AWM52 2/2/53, Box 45, 2/9 Cavalry Commando Regiment, War Diary, June 1944.
61 AWM, AWM52 2/2/55, 2/3 Commando Squadron War Diary September to October 1944, 23 September and OC TROOP ORDERS 13 Sep 44 (Lake Euramoo Ambush).
62 AWM, AWM52 2/2/57, 2/5 Commando Squadron War Diary January to February 1945, 21 Aust In Bde Pl Comd Cadre T.E.W.T and Ambush Demonstration, 7 Jan 45.
63 AWM, AWM52 2/2/53 Box 45, 2/9 Cavalry Commando Regiment July to August 1944, 2/9 Aust Cav (Commando) Regt, Training Instruction No.13, 1 Aug 44.
64 AWM, AWM52 2/2/53 Box 45, 2/9 Cavalry Commando Regiment January to May 1944, 2/9 Aust Cav (Commando) Regt, Training Instruction No.10, 1 Aug 44.

Even though the idea of independence was officially no longer part of the Commando repertoire Squadrons were theoretically granted a degree of independence in regards to conducting their own individual and tactical training. The rationale for this was that as Regimental Headquarters were non-operational they would have nothing to offer the squadrons in this regard. The reality was, however, somewhat different. Regimental Headquarters issued instructions for training and sports activities that interfered with or superseded Squadron plans. Officers were posted away from Squadrons by Regimental Headquarters to act as instructors at various schools and Non Commissioned Officers were placed in the 2nd Corps allocation pool without consulting or informing the Squadrons that this had occurred.[65] All of this hampered the Squadrons ability to independently conduct their training. Various other impositions also interrupted the overall program. Work parties affected all the Regiments often to the point of supplanting training altogether. During May of 1944 2/9th Commando Squadron spent 23 days on work parties building various parts of their camp. During this time only a limited amount of Commando training occurred, and only for those few not engaged on work parties. On 11 May the squadron war diary records 'Work parties as usual' indicating a degree of frustration with their situation.[66] The work undertaken involved digging latrines and erecting cook houses, hardly stimulating experiences. The training that did occur involved several sessions of bayonet training, in contrast to the lack of such training at Wilson's Promontory; Map reading; sub-machinegun and Bren gun training; compass marching; mock combat between parties; and Observation Post reports.[67]

Church Parades and numerous sports days did at least interrupt the work party tedium.[68] During May 1944 2/6th Cavalry Commando Regiment played nine hockey games, eight Australian Rules football games, four rugby games and one boxing match. One aspect of Church parades was that if a soldier did not want to attend Church parades his only alternative was to embark on a 24 kilometer route march. This resulted in almost everyone wanting to, 'hear the word of the Lord'.[69] On 7 May the 2/6th Cavalry Commando Regiment attended the cinema to watch three films; 'On Parade' which dealt with the benefit of good drill; 'Shoot to Kill' which showed the value of holding ones fire until the last moment; and 'Jungle Warfare' that showed the training at Canungra which all had experienced. Just what was learned from these films is questionable as a note made by the regiment following the 'Shoot Kill' film was that the first contact procedure shown in the film was incorrect and would not

---

65 Trigellis-Smith, *The Purple Devils*, pp. 213–15.
66 AWM, AWM52/2/2/51 Box 39, 2/6 Cav (Commando) Regiment Box 39, May 1944. The training that did occur involved several sessions of bayonet training, in contrast to the lack of such training at Wilson's Promontory; Map reading; submachinegun and Bren gun training; compass marching; mock combat between parties; and Observation Post reports.
67 Treichel, *Commando Army Service 1941–1946*, p. 17.
68 AWM, AWM52/2/2/51, Box 39, 2/6 Cav (Commando) Regiment, May 1944.
69 Treichel, *Commando Army Service 1941–1946*, p. 59.

be used by the regiment.⁷⁰ A further challenge for the regiments that significantly affected the ability to conduct meaningful training was that many personnel were on home leave during May 1944. The army's leave policy granted 24 days recreational leave to all personnel who had served 12 months in New Guinea. Accumulated leave separate to and in excess of 24 days was also permitted. In April 1944 a considerable number of soldiers had accumulated leave.⁷¹ It was not until the end of June 1944 that 2/6 Cavalry Commando Regiment had returned to near full strength.⁷² The 2/9th Cavalry Commando Regiment was unable to train effectively during February and March 1944 because most of its personnel were on home leave and when the troops did return in April they were put onto work parties to erect buildings in the camp.⁷³ Various distractions such as Squadron duties, light duties, and men relieved of duty, often reduced numbers available for training. At one time 2/6th Commando Squadron had only 8 soldiers able to train while 116 were otherwise engaged.⁷⁴ In a further distraction some Commandos were called out to help the local farmers bring in their corn crops.⁷⁵ Ceremonial parades at Divisional and Brigade level consumed significant amounts of time, with troops rehearsing and being inspected prior to them. During July 1944 General Blamey visited Atherton Tableland during which time he reviewed both the 6th and 9th Divisions in ceremonial parades. The war diaries of 2/10th Commando Squadron and 2/9th Cavalry Commando Regiment reported significant amounts of time being spent preparing prior to General Blamey's parades. The parade for Blamey was followed the next day by a Regimental parade and interestingly the day after by a Rodeo.⁷⁶ Other ceremonial parades also interrupted the training program. On 21 June 1944 2/9th Commando Squadron cut short a field training exercise by two days so it could return to camp and prepare for a Brigade ceremonial parade.⁷⁷

The field exercises conducted were often inconsistent in their intention and application. Some did not run for their planned number of days such as the 2/9th Commando Squadron experience, while others involved non-military activity. One such was Exercise 'Windward', held 9–26 April 1944. The exercise involved 18 Brigade with

---

70   AWM, AWM52/2/2/51, Box 39, 2/6 Cav (Commando) Regiment, May 1944.
71   AWM, AWM449/4/4, Leave Policy.
72   AWM, AWM52/2/2/51 Box 39, 2/6 Cav (Commando) Regiment May 1944.
73   AWM, AWM52 2/2/53 Box 45, 2/9 Cavalry Commando Regiment War Diary January to May 1944.
74   Trigellis-Smith, *The Purple Devils*, p. 215.
75   Pirie, 'Commando Double Black', p. 352.
76   AWM, AWM52/2/2/51, Box 39, 2/6 Cav (Commando) Regiment, May1944; AWM, AWM52 2/2/53 Box 45, 2/10 Sqn War Diary, June 1944; AWM, AWM52/2/2/51, Appendix No. vi, to War Diary, 2/9 Cavalry Commando Regiment, July to August 1944, 10–20 July; AWM, AWM52/2/2/51, Box 39, 2/6 Cav (Commando) Regiment War Diary, July 1944.
77   AWM, AWM52/2/2/51, 2/6 Cav (Commando) Regiment, June 1944, AWM52/2/2/51, Box 39; 2/9 Sqn War Diary June 1944.

2/7th Cavalry Commando Regiment attached. The role of the Regiment was to act as the advance guard for 18 Brigade, seize a razorback ridge, harass the 'enemy' from there, and then advance on specified objectives. One phase of the exercise involved a Brigade attack with artillery support. The exercise appeared to offer a sound tactical experience for all the troops involved. The reality was somewhat different. Troops found themselves trekking over a fixed route moving from one place to another, and spending a great deal of time resting and playing sport.[78] The poor value of such training, especially for veteran troops, is obvious. Route marching was a major feature of the Commando training programme. Long marches with full packs, rations, and extra boots strapped to their packs and halts conducted tactically with all round defence were common occurrences.[79] On 4 July 1944, 2/7th Commando Squadron route marched some 32 kilometres at the end of which they were ordered to dig trenches. The squadron was then marched some 72 kilometres on 10 July.[80] During August 1944 the 2/12th Commando Squadron was ordered to march 40 kilometres in one day to attend a four day exercise.[81] It eventually became apparent that Route marches were achieving very little, other than imposing tedious physical hardship on the troops, and an order was issued to avoid them and institute in their place more interesting training.[82] Ron Garland made the point that it took a long time 'for the penny to drop' in relation to excessive route marching, implying that there was not a great deal of attention being paid at higher levels as to the quality and value of the training that the Commandos were receiving.[83]

Commando squadrons often found themselves cast as the 'enemy'. Such a role would imply recognition that the Squadrons were capable of effectively operating in that role, and presumably allowed to exercise skills appropriate to their training and role. Such was not always the case. In such exercises the role of the 'enemy' was heavily scripted with every movement, location, contact, and post contact reaction being determined prior to the exercise. There was no place allowed for the 'enemy' to 'ad lib' and disregard the script. The instruction for Exercise 'Rampant' conducted in December 1944 was a good example of this. In this exercise 2/7th Cavalry Commando Regiment provided the enemy. It was clearly stated in the Instructions issued for the exercise that enemy tactics would be adhered to strictly in accordance with the scripted sequence of events and that nothing would be altered without approval of the chief umpire.[84] In

---

78 AWM, AWM 52/2/52 Box 45, 2/7 Commando Regiment War Diary, March to April 1945.
79 Trigellis-Smith, *Purple Devils*, p. 216; Ayris, *All the Bull's Men*, p. 468.
80 AWM, AWM52 2/2/56, 2/7 Commando Squadron War Diary, January to July 1944.
81 AWM, AWM52 2/2/53 Box 45, 2/9 Cavalry Commando Regiment War Diary, July to August 1944, Appendix No.vi To War Diary, Exercise 10–20 July.
82 Garland, *Nothing is Forever*, p. 330.
83 Ibid.
84 AWM, AWM52 2/2/7, 2/5 Commando Squadron War Diary December 1944, Instructions for Enemy Exercise 'Festive' Dec 45.

such circumstances the 'enemy' were little more than props in a pre-determined play. There was little value in such training for those playing the enemy.

The response from the Commando veterans to this imposed impotence sometimes led to friction with regular units. For example, when acting as the enemy during Exercise 'Rampant' 2/6th Commando Squadron engaged in a series of unscripted night actions in which they did not adhere to the sequence of events pre-determined for them. On a number of nights the squadron stole rifles and jeeps from the battalion it was working with. Tent ropes and telephone wires were cut. None of these actions were prescribed. The battalion, annoyed at the effrontery, paid them back by returning to camp by truck without telling the squadron and forcing the Commandos to walk back 12 kilometres.[85] During April 1944 2/7th Cavalry Commando Regiment deployed to play both friendly and 'enemy' for 18 Brigade in operation 'Westward'. During this exercise, the Regiment made use of vehicles including on 3 December 1944 some 46 three ton trucks – it is inconceivable just how such a vehicle heavy force was meant to operate as Commandos.[86]

It was not always the case that Commando training program was found to be uninspiring. In January 1945, 2/2nd Commando Squadron embarked on a training program designed and managed by itself. During this exercise, the Squadron was to act as the Advance Guard for an imaginary Brigade. Eight 'situations' had been devised for the troops to overcome. During the exercise, live rounds from Bren Guns were fired into the ground nearby. It was universally agreed amongst the participants that the exercise was the nearest thing possible in peacetime to the real thing, and the troops voted it the most interesting method of training.[87] 2/2nd Commando Squadron was able to organise this interesting and valuable training exercise because it was not attached to a Cavalry Commando Regiment which could potentially intervene to impose less interesting training. It was also the case that 2/2nd Commando Squadron had remained relatively unscathed by postings out of its original Independent Company personnel and thus could be confident that anything it arranged would be understood by all involved. 2/2nd was fortunate in this regard because a practical if somewhat cynical means of managing problematic issues arising from the resistance of old Independent Company men to the new Commando regime, was to transfer out the original Independent Company personnel and replace them with fresh troops. 2/6th Commando Squadron recalled that January and February of 1945 saw the face of the Squadron changing with many of the old hands being marched out or discharged and their places taken by fresh reinforcements. 2/6th Commando squadron lost 60%

---

85 Trigellis-Smith, *The Purple Devils*, p.220. Interestingly the 'enemy' force to which the Commandos were attached for Exercise Rampant was known as the 'Fuji Pyjama' Division, which at least indicates that someone at Divisional Headquarters had a sense of humour.
86 AWM, AWM 52/2/52 Box 45, 2/7 Commando Regiment War Diary, October to December 1944.
87 AWM, AWM52 2/2/54, 2/2 Commando Squadron War Diary, January to April 1945.

of its original members during January and February 1945 in this way.⁸⁸ Established officers were also moved on and new officers, most with no experience of Commandos or unconventional jungle warfare replaced them.

One of the subjects covered in Commando training which was of some practical value was tactical cooperation with aircraft. This was new to the Squadrons and would be of definite use in the field. The War Diary of 2/6th Cavalry Commando Regiment refers to air cooperation training frequently, but in an example of the inconsistency characterising the training of the Commandos, the War Dairy of 2/7th Cavalry Commando Regiment makes only a brief mention and no mention at all in the War Dairy of 2/9th Cavalry Commando Regiment. Nevertheless, such training did prove to be effective. When working with RAAF Boomerang aircraft 2/10th Commando Squadron practiced supply dropping from the air recovering 100% of the supplies dropped.⁸⁹ Radio Communication with aircraft was practised. There was no trouble experienced with this and reports stated that communication between ground and air occurred in less than three minutes and that reception was so good that the volume was turned down.⁹⁰ Message dropping from the air, deploying panels, understanding their codes, and identification of objects from air and ground also featured in the training.⁹¹ Troops on the ground, at least in 2/6th Cavalry Commando Regiment improved their capacity to work with aircraft to the point that it was felt that they were quite confident to use them for gaining information.⁹² Training also involved the squadrons travelling to Trinity Beach Cairns for Exercise 'Octopus', a two week practice in loading and embarking from landing ships.⁹³ 2/9th Cavalry Commando Regiment participated during August 1944 and 2/7th Cavalry Commando Regiment during October-November.⁹⁴ Contrary to this 2/6th Cavalry Commando Regiment had been sent to Aitape in New Guinea in October 1944 and did not participate in any amphibious training. Amphibious training for the Commandos received mixed reviews from them. Ossie Osborne of 2/6th Commando Squadron remembered

88 Trigellis-Smith, *The Purple Devils*, pp. 221–22.
89 AWM, AWM 52/2/51 Box 40, 2/6 Cavalry Commando Regiment War Diary, August 1944, 2/10 Aust Commando Sqn War Diary, 1–3 Aug 44, Appendix 2a Air Cooperation.
90 Ibid.
91 AWM, AWM 52/2/51 Box 40, 2/6 Cavalry Commando Regiment War Diary, August 1944, 2/10 Aust Commando Sqn War Diary, 1–3 Aug 44, Appendix 2a Air Cooperation; AWM, AWM 52/2/52 Box 45, 2/6 Cavalry Commando Regiment War Diary, August 1944; AWM, AWM 52/2/52 Box 45, 2/7 Commando Regiment War Diary, January to February 1945.
92 AWM, AWM 52/2/51 Box 40, 2/6 Cavalry Commando Regiment War Diary, August 1944, 2/10 Aust Commando Sqn War Diary, 1–3 Aug 44, Appendix 2a Air Cooperation.
93 AWM, AWM52 2/2/55, 2/3 Commando Squadron War Diary, November 1944 is mostly devoted to Exercise 'Octopus'.
94 AWM, AWM 52/2/52 Box 45, 2/9 Cavalry Commando Regiment War Diary, July to August 1944, AWM52 2/2/53 Box 45; 2/7 Commando Regiment War Diary, October to December 1944.

his time at Trinity Beach as a pleasant interlude.[95] Bill Powell of 2/3rd Commando Squadron, in a more negative reflection of everything at Atherton, remembered it as endless days of training which he and his mates got completely fed up with.[96]

In a sign of the new role for Commandos within the Army on 22 August 1944 all the available Officers of the 2/6th Cavalry Commando Regiment attended an Officers Cadre held in Regimental Chapel. Present at the meeting was a Signals Officer, and an officer from the Tank Attack Regiment. These two gave instructions on various aspects of their own individual rolls. The presence of a Tank Attack officer, whose roll was anti-tank warfare, to lecture to a meeting of Commando officers illustrates how the perceived role of the Commando had changed to one that was integrated much more closely with other heavy combat elements.[97]

Training did, however, incur its dangers. On 11 September 1944 an accident occurred when a Japanese anti-tank grenade being inspected by troops of 2/10th Commando Squadron, as part of a lesson to familiarise them with enemy weapons, exploded. The casualties were severe with one soldier killed outright, and 49 others wounded, some seriously.[98] While such accidents are part and parcel of military training, it did highlight the inherent dangers of their environment.

When everything was considered the overall training experience of the Commandos at Atherton was not a happy one. Troops resented being taught to, 'be soldiers again', with one Commando lamenting 'Why we had to be retrained I will never know'.[99] Adding to the sense of grievance was that this training was being conducted by officers who had no jungle experience, and subsequently who lacked the confidence and respect from their troops. For the old hands of the Independent Companies the training routine experienced on the Atherton Tableland was monotonous and for the most part meaningless. Endless route marches and tactical exercises that bore little resemblance to the realities of war did much to dampen enthusiasm. Interest and morale suffered accordingly. Many men hoped for a recurrence of their malaria so that they could get a break from the camp routine.[100] Chaplain Arthur Bottrell was fully aware that many Commandos resented the regimentation, drill and discipline of Atherton and were 'browned off'. Not even the Christmas Celebrations of December 1944, where the squadrons had been supplied with ample good quality food and alcohol, could alleviate the 'lack of verve and spontaneity', among the troops.[101] Bottrell was concerned that the frustration would bring, 'mental inertia and in some

---

95 Trigellis-Smith, *The Purple Devils*, p. 219.
96 Garland, *Nothing is Forever*, p. 325.
97 AWM, AWM 52/2/51 Box 40, 2/6 Commando Regiment War Diary, August 1944.
98 AWM, AWM 52/2/51 Box 41, 2/6 Cavalry Commando Regiment War Diary, October to December 1944, 2/10 Aust Commando Sqn War Diary – Personnel injured in accident in 2/10 Commando Lines 11 Sep 44.
99 Ayris, *All the Bull's Men*, p. 390
100 Bottrell, *Cameos of Commandos*, pp. 163, 170 and 136.
101 Ibid, pp. 163 and 170.

instances, moral rot'. The fundamental problem was that the veterans were 'itching to get back into action again'.[102] It was felt that with 'so many Japs to be beaten' the men were stagnating at Atherton.[103]

The endless training which for them was more often than not meaningless was very hard for the New Guinea veterans to take. Drill on the parade ground was particularly detested, and considered to be 'abhorrent' to men who had proved themselves at what they considered was their primary task of killing Japanese.[104] More than one veteran considered their time at Atherton to be the worst period of time they spent in the army. It was considered a waste of well trained, experienced troops when there was a war going on.[105] The editorial of the newsletter of the 2/3rd Commando Squadron expressed the frustration of the members of the squadron at being kept from action when it wrote:

> We would like to be in the fun and games, Doug, even if tho' we are such a trivial little crowd…so please Doug, would you let us go in first just once.[106]

The 'Doug' referred to was General Douglas MacArthur.

As something of a panacea to maintain the interest and morale of the troops, sport of all types was relentlessly pursued. Sporting activities included: Australian Rules football, rugby league, rugby union, soccer, basketball, softball, cricket, baseball, hockey, lacrosse, tennis, tug o' war, swimming, boxing, running, and jumping.[107] Sport was popular. Jack Duncan of the 2/3rd Commando Squadron said that the only real pleasure he got out of his time at Atherton was when he got to play rugby with his Squadron's team.[108] The Medical Officer of 2/5th Commando Squadron reported in September 1944 that the cessation of the football season may cause some unrest.[109] Other distractions such as the Cinema, concert parties, and fairly infrequent local leave, all provided a chance to alleviate the boredom of life in a static camp. Commandos were also not above finding ways to entertain themselves. In one case troops of the 2/5th Commando Squadron stole 10 chickens from a local farmer. The farmer complained but the chickens could not be found. In an act of bravado the thieves invited their officers to a meal. The meal consisted of chicken, hot vegetables, corn on the cob, peaches and cream washed down with beer. The beer had been stolen

---

102 Trigellis-Smith, *The Purple Devils*, p.223; Garland, *Nothing is Forever*, p. 324.
103 Garland, *Nothing is Forever*, pp.33 and 331.
104 Pirie, 'Commando Double Black', p. 353; Garland, *Nothing is Forever*, p. 325.
105 Trigellis-Smith, *The Purple Devils*, p. 221.
106 AWM, AWM52 2/2/55, 2/3 Commando Squadron War Diary, January to March 1945, *2/3 Broadcaster* Vol.1 Copy 5 Thursday 8 Mar 1945.
107 Pirie, 'Commando Double Black', p. 383.
108 Garland, *Nothing is Forever*, pp. 315–16.
109 AWM, AWM52/2/7, Report of the Health of 2/5 Commando Sqn for the month of Sep 1944, 2/5 Commando Squadron War Diary, August to September 1944.

from the officer's mess and the chickens were those stolen from the farmer. It was never said if the officers guessed where the largesse came from, but nonetheless they enjoyed their meal.[110] In another incident 2/3rd Commando Squadron stole Lieutenant General John Lavarack's staff car from Brisbane and drove it to Atherton. They kept it there until Lavarack visited the Squadron at Atherton when they returned the car to him.[111] There was no official follow up to the theft, Lavarack obviously accepting the incident for the prank that it was.

The two Squadrons who were not included in the Commando Regiment organisation; the 2/2nd and 2/8th Commando Squadrons had different experiences during the Atherton phase. As we have seen 2/2nd Commando Squadron managed its affairs in a relatively independent manner. Nevertheless there was a moment when the army's bureaucracy intervened to cause some angst within the squadron. The army did not recognise the battlefield commissions awarded to men of the 2/2nd Commando Squadron during their service on Timor when they were the 2/2nd Independent Company. The army insisted that if the awardees wished to retain their commissions that they must complete a formal Officer Cadet course. This was not an extraordinary demand in itself, as all those promoted to commissioned rank were required to attend Officer Cadet School, but was nevertheless received with scant enthusiasm by those concerned. Two members of 2/2nd Commando Squadron, Kevin Curran and Doug Fullerton, who had both received field commissions while in Timor, were sent to undertake the officer trainee course. During the course Curran who had used a bayonet against the Japanese at Dili Aerodrome was told by a bayonet instructor that he as too big and clumsy to be able to use the bayonet effectively. Curran dropped the instructor on the spot. Fullerton took a Sergeant who had been riding him hard outside the mess hall and beat him up. Both men were sent back to the Squadron to await discipline, which never happened. Learning its lesson the officer training school told the Squadron that it did not want any more officer candidates from 2/2nd Commando Squadron. Even so, the army then informed the Squadron that the field commissions would be allowed to stand.[112] In another incident 2/2nd Commando Squadron got angry with Frank Forde, the Minister for the army, when at a squadron parade Forde addressed them in what the troops considered to be 'a very patronising tone'. There was a distinct 'ripple in the ranks', which only subsided when the Officer Commanding the Squadron, Major Geoff 'Bull' Laidlaw, a veteran of Timor and Bena Force turned and glared at the troops. Those who were there recalled that things could have turned nasty that day but the men held back for Laidlaw's sake.[113] The experience of 2/8th Commando Regiment was entirely different. Alone amongst all of the Commando

110 Pirie, 'Commando Double Black', p. 401.
111 AWM, AWM SO4160, Neil MacDonald interview, 2/3rd Independent Company interviewee – no name, no date.
112 Ayris, *All the Bull's Men*, p. 391.
113 Ibid.

Squadrons 2/8th Commando Squadron was not posted to Atherton. This would have a fundamental impact on the character of the squadron. During 1942 and into the first half of 1944 the squadron had been left to stagnate in the Northern Territory, being required to do nothing more than conduct monotonous patrols in backcountry. In August 1944 isolated and with its numbers depleted the Squadron advertised to 2/5th Commando Squadron that it was seeking men to bring it up to full strength. 2/8th Commando Squadron was at that time commanded by Major Norman Winning, the commander of the 1942 Salamaua raid and Commander of 2/5th Independent Company from July 1942 until September 1943. Winning's appeal was directed at his old Company, the members of which held him in the highest regard. Almost every old hand from the squadron volunteered to transfer to 2/8th Commando Squadron. Such a mass exodus was forbidden by the 2/5th Commando Squadron commander Major Ian Kerr and 2/7th Cavalry Commando Regiment commander Lieutenant Colonel Norman Fleay, who nonetheless took the opportunity to shift 23 men they found difficult to control to the 2/8th Squadron.[114]

Maintaining military discipline with the veterans of the Independent Companies was always a challenge. While acknowledging the need for a formal chain of command such troops were not adverse to expressing their opinions or taking action to protect their interests when they felt them to be abused or threatened. Incidents previously related in which explosives were used to demolish an officer's wet mess and to punish an unpopular warrant officer attest to this. It was no surprise that such attitudes were manifested during the Commandos time on the Atherton Tableland. One such incident occurred in November 1944 when a group of 2/5th Commando Squadron refused to mount Regimental Guard duty and were charged and convicted of mutiny. It so transpired that the Squadron had been mounting Regimental Guard for an extended period and were due to hand over to 2/6th Commando Squadron the next day. The night before the handover the Squadron was told that they were to do one extra day of Regimental Guard duty because 2/6th Commando Squadron was to conduct a dance in town that evening. 2/5th Commando Squadron was to embark on a field exercise the day following which would mean that those on Regimental Guard duty would get no rest and little sleep before they had to march out for the exercise. Consequently, the troops refused to comply with the order to do Regimental Guard duty. The Squadron commander Major Kerr was not a veteran Commando officer, and had to his annoyance been called back from a reconnaissance task to deal with the insubordination. He was unsympathetic to the miscreants. The Regimental Sergeant Major on the other hand did manage to discuss the matter with the troops and organise for them to at least be on parade the next day. At the parade Kerr brusquely ordered the troops to mount guard. They unanimously refused to do so. Significantly amongst the 'mutineers' were veterans of Wau-Salamaua 'the most true and tried members of the squadron'. The Court Martial was in fact sympathetic to the

---

114 AWM, AWM52 2/2/57, 2/5 Commando Squadron War Diary, August to September 1944.

accused troops and not at all sympathetic to Major Ian Kerr the Commanding Officer of 2/5th Squadron. The mutineers received the minimum sentence of ninety days and were released from field punishment after fifty-nine days for 'good behaviour'.[115] It was obvious that the Independent Company veterans would take just so much of the newly imposed 'regular' military discipline and no more.

Some indication of the effect on the mood of the squadrons caused by the circumstances the troops were enduring can be found in a report on the state of the squadron lines published in 2/6th Cavalry Commando Regiment Routine Orders for 31 May 1944. The report noted a 'shocking state' of untidiness with gear and rubbish strewn all over the site. The report went on to demand that it was the personal responsibility of every Non Commissioned Officer to ensure that correcting these failings receives immediate attention.[116]

General Thomas Blamey did indicate he was aware of the malaise afflicting the troops at Atherton by telling a parade of 6th Division he addressed on 17 July 1944 that they would have to make the best of it.[117] The commander of 7th Division Major General Edward Milford acknowledged in his 1944 Christmas message to his troops that he had hoped they would have been in action by now and that he did not think that the Division seeing action would be long delayed.[118]

The mood of the Squadrons was not helped by changes in command. On 9 February 1944 Bastin retired relinquishing his command of 2/7th Cavalry Commando Regiment to Lieutenant Colonel Norman Fleay. Fleay was on the surface a logical choice for such a command. His record was that of an experienced Independent Company commander having commanded Kanga Force during its time at Wau-Salamaua from May 1942 until January 1943. Fleay had been awarded the Distinguished Service Order (DSO) for his command of Kanga Force at the time of the Salamaua raid, his citation reading for 'Personal gallantry and leadership'. He had received the personal and public endorsement of Blamey himself who lauded Fleay as possessing 'vision, enthusiasm, and the utmost determination'.[119] Others spoke well of Fleay's bravery, ability and leadership qualities.[120] Official army circles recognised Fleay as an authority on unconventional warfare engaging him to deliver lectures on Commando

---

115 Pirie, 'Commando Double Black', p. 374; Bottrell, *Cameos of Commandos*, p. 161.
116 AWM, AWM52/2/2/51 Box 39, 2/6 Cav (Commando) Regiment War Diary, May 1944, Routine Orders 31 May.
117 AWM, AWM52/2/2/51 Box 39, 2/6 Cav (Commando) Regiment War Diary, July 1944.
118 AWM, AWM52 2/2/7, 2/5 Commando Squadron War Diary, December 1944, Routine Orders 23 Dec 44.
119 AWM, AWM52 2/2/57, 2/5 Commando Squadron War Diary, Oct1943; AWM, AWM 191 301/954 Box 6, Honours and Awards.
120 AWM, AWM 67 2/117, Records of Gavin Long, General Editor, Notebook No 117 (Fenton) – [notes on Kanga Force], Maj Gen B Morris (CO NGF 42) – 23 Nov 44; AWM, AWM54 587/6/11, Lt. Bob Dawson Intelligence Officer of the 2/22nd Battalion, 2/5 Independent Coy, Operations in New Guinea, 25th Oct 1942.

operations at the Atherton training area during April 1944.[121] This would appear to be an adequate resume to assume command of a Commando Regiment, yet this was not so. Unfortunately for the smooth functioning of 2/7th Cavalry Commando Regiment Fleay's appointment to command was less than an astute move by the army.

It was a fact that many of those who had been under Fleay's command or had worked closely with him held him in poor regard. One NGVR soldier described Fleay as 'a big youthful looking guy…but I don't think there was much between the ears'. Another more pointedly declared that Fleay was a 'shocking leader … the bastard should be in Hollywood not here'.[122] Jack Boxall of 2/5th Commando Squadron and former member of 2/5th Independent Company observed that Fleay's 'ineptitude, ego, and self-protection caused untold hardships and misery on all members of the Fifth Coy in New Guinea', and went on to recall that Fleay 'appeared to have a particular dislike for the Fifth, and these feelings were reciprocated by the men'.[123] Major General Basil Morris commander of the 8th Military District and Commander of New Guinea Force at the time had described Fleay's appointment to command Kanga Force as a mistake which he had argued against.[124] Such criticisms were not unfounded. Fleay's relationship with his troops had been at times most troubled. During the evacuation of Wau in September 1942, which Fleay had ordered, he had accused some of the men of 2/5th Independent Company of cowardice and desertion and ordered them to be brought back to him under armed guard. Captain Hugh Marsden the Medical Officer of 2/5th was despatched to bring back the 'deserters'. When Marsden found the men in question, he realised that the reason for their separation from the main body of Kanga Force was due to an order for 'everyman to look after themselves' that had reached them during the 'total confusion' that accompanied the precipitate withdrawal from Wau. After the situation was explained to them the 'deserters' obediently complied with Marsden's orders and moved forward again.[125] In a self-serving move Fleay ordered that the signal ordering the men to be brought back under arms not be recorded in 2/5th Independent Company records. Major General Basil Morris commander of New Guinea Force did however see it, even though he conceded that he was not supposed to.[126] In May 1943 details of Fleay's activities with Kanga Force were released by the army to the press. The press duly reported Fleay's heroic exploits which included personally infiltrating Lae and counting the Japanese there and conducting a similar reconnaissance of Salamaua the night before the raid

---

121 AWM, AWM SO4160, Neil MacDonald interview, 2/3rd Independent Company interviewee – no name, no date.
122 Powell, *The Third Force*, p. 33.
123 Pirie, 'Commando Double Black', p. 353.
124 AWM, AWM 67 2/117, Records of Gavin Long, General Editor, Notebook No 117 (Fenton) – [notes on Kanga Force], Maj Gen B Morris (CO NGF 42) – 23 Nov 44.
125 Pirie, 'Commando Double Black', p. 152.
126 AWM, AWM 67 2/117, Records of Gavin Long, General Editor, Notebook No 117 (Fenton) – [notes on Kanga Force], Maj Gen B Morris (CO NGF 42) – 23 Nov 44.

in June 1942. Fleay's participation in the October 1942 Mubo raid was described as selfless and heroic when he had deliberately acted as a decoy for the Japanese so that his men could withdraw, subsequently leading the Japanese on a hunt for him through the Jungle for days.[127] It was for such heroics Fleay was awarded a DSO. Such claims were in fact preposterous fantasies and bore absolutely no relationship to reality. As seen in chapter 4, Fleay never went anywhere near Lae and during the Salamaua raid had remained in Wau having only marginal and not helpful influence on that operation. It was in fact Winning not Fleay who conducted the reconnaissance of Salamaua the night before the raid. As previously noted Fleay's involvement in the October Mubo raid was anything but heroic with his panicked bellowing for every man to look after himself just before he ran off into the jungle causing confusion and chaos. Such press reports infuriated those who knew what had actually occurred. Captain Peter Hancock who at the time was second in command of 2/3rd Independent Company was scathing of Fleay writing to his parents on 23 June 1943:

> There is only one flaw in the press reports and that is any reference to the exploits of Fleahy [sic] himself. He is not a trained commando and his name has a distinct odour amongst our predecessors here – to say the least. His own accounts of himself are so widely different from others I have heard that I am inclined to think that he is an absolute imposter and if so I only hope he is properly exposed.[128]

Fleay was an entirely manufactured hero, presumably created for propaganda purposes. This was not lost on those who knew him and the men he had commanded. The 2/5th Commando Squadron War Diary states that Fleay's award of the DSO was based on a false claim and that Fleay had taken the credit for the service of other officers and men while 'sitting in comfort in Wau'.[129] The matter was not let to rest by the Squadron and at their behest Mr. Daniel Mulcany a Labor member of Federal Parliament formally requested the Army Minister Forde conduct an investigation into the matter. Fleay's formidable support network then mobilized and in response General Thomas Blamey publicly praised Fleay in the press for his gallantry, vision, enthusiasm and determination. Consequently Forde dropped any idea of an investigation and no more was heard of the matter.[130] That the members of 2/5th Commando Squadron held Fleay in low regard was confirmed in telephone conversation this author had with Neil MacDonald the author of *Kokoda Frontline*. In his preparation for his book MacDonald had interviewed members of the Independent Companies including

---

127 UQFL, UQFL288, Papers of Peter Pinney, Box 6, *Digest of Digests* September 1943, 'Mubo Land of Ambush'.
128 AWM, AWM PR91/052, Hancock to Parents 23 June 1943.
129 AWM, AWM52 2/2/57, 2/5 Commando Squadron War Diary, October 1943 Appendix "J".
130 Ibid.

several from 2/5th Independent Company. During an interview with a member of the Company the subject of Fleay came up and the interviewee asked MacDonald to turn off the tape recorder. MacDonald said that this was because the interviewee wanted to express his opinion that Fleay did not deserve the DSO he was awarded which in the opinion of the interviewee should have instead been awarded to Norman Winning who actually led the Salamaua raid.[131] Given Fleay's acrimonious relationship with 2/5th Independent Company in particular it would have been assumed that the Army would not renew the relationship between the two. This was not to be, and the Army no doubt operating under the presumption of Fleay's officially recognised qualities of Commando leadership appointed him to command of 2/7th Cavalry Commando Regiment with the result that he would command the veteran 2/3rd, 2/5th and 2/6th Commando Squadrons. Fleay's unsettled and often acrimonious relationship with the personnel of these Squadrons would be a feature of his command of the regiment and would result in some notable breaches of discipline.

Many of the original Independent Company officers for who the troops had great respect had been posted out of the Commando Squadrons and new untried officers replaced them. The relationship between these new officers and the men was trying especially in the veteran squadrons of Fleay's command. In January 1944 a soldier from Fleay's Regiment was asked by an officer to repeat his name and shot back with, 'You fucking well heard' and then refused to practice with the bayonet as he had been instructed to do.[132] In February, a soldier detailed to guard some prisoners refused, saying he would not do so as they were his mates.[133] In the same month, another soldier struck a provost Corporal in the face escaped from his escort and then when apprehended and asked his name gave it as, 'Smith… 1 2 3 4 5 6 7'.[134] Another soldier struck a provost Corporal in the face shortly after in the same month.[135] During March, a soldier refused to be locked in the guardroom exclaiming, 'I'm fucked if I'll sleep in the boob tonight. You try to put me in it'. The same man accused an officer of being too drunk to stand up during a field exercise publicly calling the officer a 'bastard'.[136] During the same month an acting Sergeant refused to stop men making 'an undue noise in the mess' when told to do so by a Major. Angered, the Sergeant shouted out, 'Let me get at the bastard – I'll soon clean him up' and then struck the Major in the face.[137] On 10 October 1944 a soldier who was wearing Lieutenant badges of rank attempted to gain access to the officers mess and hit a Lieutenant in

---

131 Telephone conversation between the author and Neil MacDonald, 15 November 2015.
132 AWM, AWM 52/2/52 Box 44, 2/7 Commando Regiment War Diary, January to May 1944, Routine Orders, 17 Feb 1944.
133 Ibid.
134 Ibid.
135 Ibid.
136 AWM, AWM 52/2/52 Box 44, 2/7 Commando Regiment War Diary, January to May 1944, Routine Orders, 14 Apr 44.
137 Ibid.

the face.¹³⁸ In November 1944 a trooper told a Lieutenant, 'You're a dead cunt and a fucking rotten cunt', and, 'I'll get you and hammer you one of these days'.¹³⁹ In December of the same year, another trooper confronted the same officer with, 'you had better put me on a charge sheet too. You're a cunt'.¹⁴⁰ The same Lieutenant, who obviously had not established any kind of rapport with his men, was upbraided by another Trooper who when told to report to the cookhouse told him, 'I may as well be on a charge sheet too, I won't be there'.¹⁴¹ These three troopers were all members of the veteran 2/3rd Commando Squadron. Perhaps the most insubordinate action occurred on 28 March 1945 when Trooper Alan Enchell of 2/3rd Commando Squadron went AWL. When he was caught and paraded before Fleay he said directly to Fleay, 'I am sick of the army. Sick of you, and you are a fucking possum, get fucked'.¹⁴² Two soldiers of 2/3rd Commando Squadron George Head and 'Rusty' McEwan, both veterans of the Middle East and the Wau-Salamaua Campaign, decided that because of the endless boredom at Atherton they would desert. Both had craved action but on the Atherton Tableland that was denied to them. The manner in which they deserted indicated the mood within the squadron at the time, and also the bond that existed between the members of the Squadron. Both packed their belongings and said goodbye to their friends. They also formally said goodbye to the Squadron Commander Captain Peter Tancred, who like them was a veteran of the Wau-Salamaua Campaign. They then just simply disappeared. Tancred understood why Head and McEwan had done what they did, and took no action as he considered punishing them for their act would have been unjust.¹⁴³ A further example of the scorn with which the veteran soldiers of 2/7th Cavalry Commando Regiment held some of their superiors while at Atherton was that whenever 2/3rd Commando Squadron came anywhere within earshot of Fleay they would loudly sing 'I don't want to set the world on fire'. They did this because Fleay had in their opinion, as well as the opinion of many others, unnecessarily burned down Wau in 1942. Fleay threatened to charge them if they continued to do so.¹⁴⁴ Fleay was obviously aware of the disquiet within the Regiment. At one time he ordered a 112 Kilometre route march for the Regiment as a means to suppress the 'unrest amongst the troops', that route march was at least cancelled by Division.¹⁴⁵ Fleay's poor reputation elicited a

---

138 AWM, AWM 52/2/52 Box 45, 2/7 Commando Regiment War Diary, October to December 1944, Routine Orders 10 Oct 44.
139 AWM, AWM 52/2/52 Box 45, 2/7 Commando Regiment War Diary, October to December 1944, Routine Orders 14 Nov 44.
140 Ibid.
141 Ibid.
142 Ibid.
143 Garland, *Nothing is Forever*, pp. 326–7.
144 AWM, AWM SO4160, Neil MacDonald interview, 2/3rd Independent Company interviewee – no name, no date.
145 Bottrell, *Cameos of Commandos*, p. 165.

very personal response from at least one of his peers. At some time during April 1944 Fleay had been giving lectures on Commando Warfare in the Atherton area. During these lectures he had publicly referred to 2/5th Independent Company as 'rabble' and 2/3rd Independent Company as 'Warfe's Mob'. George Warfe now a Lieutenant Colonel, and equal in rank with Fleay, was at Atherton at the time and heard about this. He determined that he would confront Fleay outside the officer's mess and 'beat him up' for insulting 2/3rd Commando Squadron. Fleay heard about Warfe's threat and was seen to get into a jeep and leave Atherton not to return there again until Warfe had left.[146] All the Commando Regiments experienced the same sense of frustration caused by the Atherton experience. It was very much a period characterised by Chaplain Bottrell as, 'The Doldrums of War'.[147] Even so, similar incidents to what occurred in 2/7th Cavalry Commando Regiment are not recorded by 2/6th or 2/9th Cavalry Commando Regiments. There were of course concerns expressed but these tended to be relatively trivial such as admonishing the troops for not folding their greatcoats in the regulation manner and leaving their dry clothing on clothes lines inviting theft.[148] There was one incident in 2/9th Cavalry Commando Regiment when someone broke into the cook house of 2/7th Commando Squadron and when no culprits confessed all the Other Ranks in the Regiment had their leave cancelled for 10 days.[149] Cases of AWL also occurred but none of this was out of the ordinary for any unit in wartime. Unlike 2/7th Cavalry Commando regiment, both 2/6th and 2/9th Cavalry Commando Regiments maintained a working relationship and degree of decorum with their troops. Unique amongst the Commando Regiments 2/7th Cavalry Commando Regiment made a point of publishing explicit details of court martial cases in Regimental routine orders, perhaps as a deterrent to dissuade further offences, although this obviously did not work. The incidents of indiscipline within the Regiment were indicative of the challenges to morale and discipline imposed on the Commandos by their time at Atherton. These incidents illustrated how the exceptionally individualistic veteran Independent Company troops, forced to endure a monotonous training regime and compelled to deal with officers for who they had little regard or respect manifested their discontent.

To its credit the Army was not completely unaware of the unsatisfactory relationship between officers and soldiers within 2/7th Cavalry Commando Regiment. Major General Vasey, the Regiment's Division commander, had commented on the mutiny incident concerning 2/5th Independent Company, saying that the troops were simply

---

146 AWM, AWM SO4160, Neil MacDonald interview, 2/3rd Independent Company interviewee – no name, no date. The date for this may have been early April 1944 as AWM52 2/2/55 2/3 Commando Squadron War Diary, January to April 1944, notes a visit to the Squadron by Warfe on 1 April 44.
147 Trigellis-Smith, *The Purple Devils*, p. 216.
148 AWM, AWM52/2/2/51, 2/6 Cav (Commando) Regiment War Diary, July 1944, Appendices, 2/9 Commando Squadron War Diary, July 1944.
149 AWM, AWM52/2/2/51, 2/6 Cav (Commando) Regiment War Diary, 7 May 1944.

'jacking up' and that a good officer would have handled it in a much less confrontational manner.[150] It is also worthy of note that the sentence of 90 days field punishment the mutineers received was the least severe sentence for mutiny the courts martial could impose, indicating that the officers of the court sympathised to a degree with the mutineers.[151] The cancellation of Fleay's 112 kilometre punishment route march by Division was another indicator that higher authorities were paying attention to the troubled management of the regiment. Removing Fleay was not an option given his support from such as Blamey, but in late 1944 the Army took a step to alleviate the situation and appointed Major Harry Harcourt as second in command of the regiment.[152] Harcourt had commanded 2/6th Independent Company with distinction during 1942 and the early part of 1943. He was a deeply experienced and highly decorated combat officer, being awarded the DSO and Military Cross for his First World War service, Imperial Russian awards for his service against the Bolsheviks in North Russia in 1919, a bar to his DSO and the US Silver Star for his service with 2/6th Independent Company in New Guinea. Harcourt was 51 years old when he was appointed to 2/7th Cavalry Commando Regiment. His age precluded him from an active combat command, but he was obviously highly regarded.[153] Importantly, his presence within the Regiment would provide a buffer between Fleay and the men. An added bonus would be that as second in Command of the Regiment he would renew his relationship with his old Independent Company now a Commando Squadron within the regiment. The army was also aware that continual training with no relief was having a negative impact on the troops. In June 1943, 2nd Australian Corps issued a directive warning against overtraining the men so as not to put the men in the wrong mood.[154] This applied to Commando Regiments equally to the remainder of the Army.

The period the Commandos spent on the Atherton Tableland was a time that both transformed and challenged them. The transformation of the Independent Company to the Commando Squadron as the Army instituted its Commando guidelines and trained its Commandos in the methods and standards those guidelines required was necessary. Historian Adrian Threlfall characterises the Atherton Tableland training for the mainstream Australian Army as leaving Australian soldiers 'much better prepared of the challenges of jungle warfare than had previously been the case'.[155] This may well have been the case for regular troops but is debateable where the Commandos are concerned. Just how better prepared Commandos were for the challenges of jungle

150   Pirie, 'Commando Double Black', p. 374.
151   Pirie, 'Commando Double Black', pp. 374–75
152   Botterell, *Cameos of Commandos*, p.168.
153   AWM, AWM PR87/224, Papers of Maj Harry Harcourt DSO & Bar, MC, OBE.
154   AWM, AWM 52/2/52 Box 44, 2/7 Commando Regiment Outline War Diary, June to December 1943, O.C. Coys 2 Aust Corps L.H.Q/ (Via) 2 Aust Corps, Training, 19 June 1943.
155   Threlfall, Adrian, *Jungle Warriors* (Allen and Unwin: Crows Nest, 2014), p. 207.

warfare after their training at Atherton depended very much on the prior experience of the Squadrons and the individual soldiers. It is certainly true that the newly raised Commando Squadrons; 2/9th, 2/10th, 2/11th and 2/12th had no prior experience of jungle warfare, indeed no prior experience of combat of any kind. For those squadrons it would be perfectly valid to claim that the training at Atherton assisted them to prepare for jungle operations. On the other hand, it would be asking far too much to claim that the training at Atherton improved the preparedness for jungle warfare of the veteran Independent Company personnel. Such veterans were past masters at operating effectively in the jungle. That they had done so in an unconventional and independent manner and not the manner that Atherton was teaching is beside the point.

In one aspect the training at Atherton did prepare Commandos for the type of warfare they would engage in. Commandos were taught that they were to operate in close support of higher formations and that their role could be to take their place on the line of battle as infantry. They were taught to operate as part of larger groups and formations. Exercises in Troop and Squadron tactics, in and out of a jungle setting, were a constant feature of training. This was something the veterans of the Independent Companies were not accustomed to. Such training did acclimatise Commandos to this new role and prepare them for the type of warfare the Army was to practice during 1944 and 1945.

What was the overall value of the Atherton Tableland experience for the Commandos and where does it fit within the evolutionary history of Australia's Second World War Commandos? From the perspective of many of the veteran Independent Company personnel who underwent training at Atherton it was a waste of time, and very much a regression in how they perceived their worth and value to the Army as a whole. From the perspective of the army, however, the Atherton period was essential to transform the Independent Companies, for which there was no longer any perceived use, into Commando Squadrons for which there was a perceived use. In this sense the evolution of the army's appreciation for Commandos had come full cycle from a base where there was literally no official policy or interest to one where there was an official policy represented by a firm set of guidelines for the tactical employment of Commandos. What the time at Atherton did do for the Commando Squadrons was to acclimatised them, both as individuals and as units, to the requirements of their new 'Commando' function. They ended their time at Atherton as well prepared as they could be for this new task. The ability of the Commandos to carry out this role would be put to the test in the later part of 1944 and into 1945 when the Commandos would, after their very long hiatus, be sent into action again.

10

"The Little Bastards were Dug in to Stay" – Aitape-Wewak Campaign 1944–1945

The strategic situation facing Australia in 1944 was one in which political, not military, factors dominated decisions made to deploy Australian forces. Having been excluded from participation in the upcoming Philippines campaign it was imperative for Australia's military to find a role to play in the War effort. The primary reason for this was so that Australia would have a credible voice at post war peace talks. A supplementary motivator was a distinctly colonial one, in that formerly Australian ruled territories in New Guinea and Bougainville needed to have it impressed on them that Australia had defeated the Japanese occupiers, and by doing so Australian prestige among the indigenous people who would be under Australian authority was not diminished.[1] There had been some debate as to just how the campaigns should be fought. Blamey was of the opinion that the Japanese should be driven from the areas in which they were sustaining themselves and destroyed. This should be done by aggressive patrolling and carrying out offensive operations with small forces.[2] Such a campaign would be suited to Commando style operations. Blamey's view was not, however, to prevail and ultimately the decision of how to fight the war was removed from the purview of the military and became a political one. The War Cabinet decided that the enemy must be destroyed, with the important caveat of ensuring light casualties to Australian forces. This presaged a manner of warfare which would be both methodical and risk adverse in relation to personnel, not at all conducive for free ranging Commando operations.[3] It would be a style of warfare which in New Guinea in particular, would have a direct impact on the manner in which the Army employed its Commandos.

---

1   AWM, AWM DRL/6th6th43, Blamey to Chifley 18 May 1945, Appreciation of Operations of the AMF in New Guinea, New Britain and the Solomon Islands – 13 May 1945.
2   Ibid.
3   John Robertson and John McCarthy, *Australian War Strategy 1939–1945* (University of Queensland Press: St. Lucia, 1985), pp. 410–11.

The three squadrons of the 2/6thth Cavalry Commando Regiment; 2/7th, 2/9th and 2/10th Commando Squadrons trained at the Atherton Tablelands from December 1943 until October 1944 in the case of 2/9th and 2/10th Commando Squadrons, and in the case of 2/7th Commando Squadron from January to October 1944.[4] Of the three Squadrons only the 2/7th Commando Squadron had previous service experience, having been an Independent Company operating in New Guinea from October 1942 until January 1944. During their time at Atherton all three squadrons assimilated the operational expectations for Commando squadrons inherent within the Army's Commando guidelines.

As part of Australia's 1944 commitment the 2/6thth Cavalry Commando Regiment arrived at Aitape, New Guinea on 21 October 1944 as the vanguard of 6th Division. This role as advance guard was one for which the Commandos had been repeatedly trained during their time at Atherton. While it was on route to Aitape, Australian First Army issued an operational instruction that identified the tasks for the Regiment. These were to relieve US troops already there, support and assist ANGAU, scout for a site for a forward base, prevent Japanese infiltration, report the presence of Japanese and all Japanese movement, and destroy all Japanese encountered.[5] It was also considered that the best use of Commandos would be to use them as a reserve on the right flank of 19 Brigade, which would land later.[6] By using them to scout out the country, and protect the flank of 19 Brigade Commandos were being allocated light infantry tasks for which the new Army Commando regime had trained them. The instruction to establishing contact with ANGAU would of necessity anticipate some interaction with the indigenous population, even though as it transpired the degree of such interaction that would occur in the case of 2/6th Commando Regiment would be nominal at best.

When it arrived at Aitape the Regiment was the only Australian unit present, and consequently came under the command of the US 43rd Division. During 27 to 28 October the Commandos relieved US troops in a number of forward outposts and began patrolling immediately.[7] The prospect of active service came as a relief to the Commandos who following ten months of training at Atherton were looking forward to action and making a good name for themselves.[8] Eleven patrol routes were established, five being daily patrols, one every two days, four twice weekly, and one

---

4   AWM, AWM52 2/2/59, 2/7 Commando Squadron War Diary January-July 1944.
5   AWM, AWM 52/2/51 Box 41, 2/6 Cavalry Commando Regiment War Diary, October to December 1944, Appendices First Australian Army Operation Instruction No.48 to CO 2/6 Aust Cav (Commando) Regt 17 Oct 44.
6   AWM, AWM54603/7/27 Part 1, Appreciation of the Situation at Driniumor River on 5 Oct by Brig JEG Martin, Commanding 19 Bde, Sixth Australian Division Report on Operations – Aitape-Wewak Campaign 26 Oct 1944 ~ 13 Sep 1945, HQ 19 Aust Inf Bde, Oct 44.
7   AWM, AWM 52/2/51 Box 40, 2/6 Cavalry Commando Regiment War Diary, October 1944.
8   AWM, AWM 52/2/51 Box 41, 2/6 Cavalry Commando Regiment War Diary, November 1944, 2/10 Cdo Squadron Summary of Suain-Luain Operations.

weekly.⁹ The first contact with the enemy occurred on 3 November during which one Japanese soldier was killed, and two were captured. The next day the first Commando casualty occurred with one Trooper of 2/10th Commando Squadron being wounded by a Japanese Light machinegun. It was during this patrol phase that a considerable number of captured Japanese documents were forwarded to the Head Quarters of US 43rd Division.[10] With the arrival of 6th Division at the beginning of November patrolling assumed increased importance.[11] For 6th Division the Commandos provided its eyes and ears. Commando patrols were to range out and discover all that could be found about terrain, topography, enemy presence and intentions. This would assist the Division plan for its extension of operations in the future.[12]

The Commandos set to their task with energy and enthusiasm. During November 1944 to February 1945 150 Commando patrols were recorded. Of these, 100 were reconnaissance patrols to contact indigenous inhabitants, report on terrain, observe and contact the enemy, correct and add to maps, locate lines of communication routes and possible camp sites. There were thirteen clearance patrols designed to clear an area of the enemy, 30 were fighting or harassing patrols whose purpose was to locate and attack any enemy found, and seven were patrols to contact other units, provide local security and provide protection for other parties.[13] In a decidedly non-military action, but one that fulfilled the requirement to liaise with ANGAU 2/9th Commando Squadron was despatched on a mission to check on a complaint that indigenous houses had been destroyed.[14] Not all patrols conducted during this period are listed in the Squadron War Diaries. In January 1945, 2/10th Commando Squadron was caught in a flash flood of the Danmap River, three men were drowned and all the squadron's stores and records for the month, which included the record of all patrols, were lost.

The manner in which the patrols were conducted reflected that the squadrons were adhering to the Army's Commando guidelines of providing 'close' support. Unlike in the past where patrols would often extend over a number of days, or even weeks and range far from any other formation, all patrols conducted during November 1944 to

9   AWM, AWM 52/2/51 Box 41, 2/6 Cavalry Commando Regiment War Diary, November 1944, Appendices, Intelligence Summary No.1, AWM 52/2/51 BOX 41.
10 AWM, AWM 52/2/51 Box 40, 2/6 Cavalry Commando Regiment War Diary, November 1944.
11 AWM, AWM 52/2/51 Box 41, 2/6 Cavalry Commando Regiment War Diary, November 1944, Appendices, 2/6th Aust Cav (Commando) Regt to OC 2/10 Sqn, 4 Nov 1944.
12 AWM, AWM 52/2/51 Box 41, 2/6 Cavalry Commando Regiment War Diary, October to December 1944, Appendices, Operation Order No.A1.
13 AWM, AWM52 2/2/59, 2/7 Commando Squadron War Diary, November to December 1944 and January to May 1945; AWM, AWM52 2/2/62, 2/10 Commando Squadron War Diary, November to December 1944 and January to May 1945. In the war diaries, the purpose of patrols is stated directly, but in some cases, this has had to be inferred from the description of the patrol's object.
14 AWM, AWM 52/2/51 Box 40, 2/6th Cavalry Commando Regiment War Diary, November 1944.

February 1945 were one-day patrols. This ensured that Commandos did not venture too far from the main force, and also that the Commandos would be kept under close supervision, on a leash so to speak. The patrols for the novice 2/9th and 2/10th Squadrons were also mostly of section strength or larger, not patrols of five or less which had been characteristic of earlier times.[15] This, however, was not echoed by the vastly more experienced 2/7th Commando Squadron, who frequently sent out patrols of only a few and at one time only one man.[16]

In November a further objective was added to the Commandos tasks, which was to clear all enemy from west of the Danmap River area, prior to 6th Division move in that direction. The Commandos set to the assignment with gusto killing an average of six to eight Japanese per day as they advanced toward the river. During this period 67 Japanese were killed and seven captured for the loss of one Commando killed and one wounded.[17] It was reported that the Japanese who were encountered were disorganised, suffering poor morale, scattered in small groups, and short of food and arms.[18]

By the closing days of November the aggressive vanguard role of the Commandos was curtailed somewhat, and two Troops of Commandos were deployed as the mobile reserve of 17 Brigade. The role of this mobile reserve was to defend the Brigades line of communication and to hold itself ready to act as a counter attack force.[19] The reasons for this may have been to fill a temporary shortage of men within 17 Brigade at the time, but nevertheless it placed a sub-unit trained to undertake specialised tasks in a situation where it could not practice its special attributes.[20] Nevertheless it was a case

---

15 AWM, AWM52 2/2/59, 2/7 Commando Squadron War Diary November to December 1944 and January to May 1945; AWM, AWM52 2/2/62, 2/10 Commando Squadron War Diary November to December 1944 and January to May 1945.
16 AWM, AWM52 2/2/59, The War Diary of 2/7 Commando is excellent in listing the numbers of soldiers included in each patrol. These numbers are often quite small, at one time only one man, which harkens back to the days of the Independent Companies operating style. Hardly surprising when one considers that 2/7 Squadron was a veteran Independent Company.
17 AWM, AWM 52/2/51 Box 40, 2/6th Cavalry Commando Regiment War Diary, November 1944, Appendices, "A" Aust FS Det at Baibiang GIII (i) 6th Aust Div, 21 Nov 44, Copy to 2/6th Aust Cav (Commando) Regt; AWM, AWM 52/2/51 Box 41, 2/6th Cavalry Commando Regiment War Diary, November 1944, for action 43 US Div for information 6th Aust Div Also 71 Wing RAAF, 21 Nov 44.
18 AWM, AWM 52/2/51 Box 41, 2/6th Cavalry Commando Regiment War Diary, November 1944, Appendices, CO's Observations 2/10 Commando Sqn, 18–21 November 1944. This assessment was confirmed by numerous interviews with Japanese Prisoners of War who spoke of severe depredation and hardship suffered by Japanese troops, see: AWM, AWM 52/2/51 Box 41, 2/6th Cavalry Commando Regiment War Diary, November 1944, Prisoner of War Interrogation Report,.
19 AWM, AWM 52/2/51 Box 41, 2/6th Cavalry Commando Regiment War Diary, November 1944, Appendices, 17 Aust Inf Bde OP Instr No.2.
20 AWM, AWM 52/2/51 Box 41, 2/6th Cavalry Commando Regiment War Diary, November 1944, Appendices, 6th Aust Div Operation Order 1, 27 Nov 44. The commander of 17 Brigade was Brigadier Murray Moten. It is tempting to speculate

of Commandos being employed in the role of infantry, which was in compliance with Army Commando guidelines. In January 6th Division restricted its Commandos even further, informing them that they were only to conduct short patrols for local protection. It was also decided that Commandos would open a new line of communication and defend that line, which would place them in the rear of the Division and thus no longer with any opportunity to seek out the enemy.[21] Such tasks did, however, ensure that Commandos were kept firmly under the immediate control of the Division.

Throughout this period the style of operations the Commandos chose reflected conformity to army doctrine and certainly exhibited no independent aspirations. Illustrative of this were the observations of Major Allen Goode, formerly of 1st Independent Company and now the commanding officer of 2/10th Commando Squadron, who in December 1944 wrote that it was the objective of the squadron to dominate the enemy line of communication with the most economy of manpower, and that to do this would require the maximum use of air power.[22] Goode latter added that artillery and mortars could be used to neutralise all surrounding areas and control the tracks leading to them.[23] This was a far cry from the manner in which the Independent Companies had used ambush and harassment to control areas and tracks in the past. In a demonstration of just how determined the Commandos were to make use of airpower the Squadron called in seventeen airstrikes during the first 22 days of March alone.[24]

Through December 1944, 6th Division continued to employ the Commandos as light infantry in immediate support of higher formations. They fulfilled this role efficiently and effectively and by mid-December had killed more than half the enemy killed by the Division as a whole.[25] As 6th Division began its push forward in January 1945 the role of 2/6thth Cavalry Commando Regiment changed from that of an advance guard to that of protecting the right flank of 19 Brigade. To do this the regiment was to occupy the village of Walum, and patrol the area about it.[26] Extensive topographical

    just how much his previous negative appreciation of the Independent Companies and everything they stood for may have influenced his decision to use Commandos in this way.
21 AWM, AWM 52/2/51 Box 41, 2/6th Cavalry Commando Regiment War Diary, January 1945.
22 AWM, AWM52 2/2/59, 2/7 Commando Squadron War Diary, December 1944, Appreciation of the Situation by Major A.L. Goode O.C. 2/7 Aust Commando Squadron, 14 Dec 44.
23 AWM, AWM52 2/2/59, 2/7 Commando Squadron War Diary, December 1944, Addition to Appreciation of Tong Sector 16th Dec 44.
24 AWM, AWM52 2/2/62, 2/10 Commando Squadron War Diary, January to May 1945.
25 AWM, AWM54 603/7/27 Part 1, Sixth Australian Division Report on Operations – Aitape – Wewak Campaign 26th Oct 45; 6th Division had killed 136 enemy, 71 of these had been killed by the Commandos.
26 AWM, AWM 52/2/51 Box 41, 2/6th Cavalry Commando Regiment War Diary, January 1945, Appendices, AWM52 2/2/59; 2/7 Commando Squadron War Diary, January to February 1945.

reconnaissance was conducted by 2/7th Commando Squadron. The squadron moved along the Japanese line of communication, and up to the banks of the Danmap River. During this time it contacted and killed numerous Japanese including one notable engagement on 12 January when 36 Japanese were killed for the loss of one officer and one indigenous policeman wounded.[27] This aggressive patrolling experience was not, however, shared by every Squadron demonstrating that 6th Division had no intention of unleashing its Commandos as a whole force on the enemy. The less experienced 2/9th Commando Squadron found itself restrained to acting as flank guards, and providing close forward reconnaissance for 2/8th and 2/3rd Infantry Battalions. At the same time two Troops of 2/10th Commando Squadron were given the role of 19 Brigade reserve, effectively neutralising them as Commandos.[28] It is not possible to deduce what the uncommitted Troop of 2/10th Commando Squadron was doing during January due to the loss of records that occurred in the previously mentioned flash flood of the Danmap River. Curiously while 2/10th Squadron remained inactive, infantry battalions were sent out to conduct reconnaissance. On 10 January 2/7th Infantry Battalion was sent on a patrol to survey a new line of communication and to assess its suitability for motor vehicle traffic. On 17 January 6th Division created 'Jock Force' from 2/2nd Infantry Battalion and sent it on a two week patrol to report on enemy strengths and movements. During January 2/5th Infantry Battalion was sent on a deep patrol to the south, with the object of cleaning up enemy pockets who are within striking distance of the main force.[29] There was no specific reason given by 6th Division for its use of infantry battalions to conduct these long range missions which were essentially Commando tasks, while the Division's Commandos were not being employed. The Commandos were certainly not doing anything which prevented them from doing so. The attitude towards the campaign as a whole of Major-General Jack Stevens, the commanding officer of 6th Division, may explain this. Stevens, the same officer who had commanded Northern Territory Force in 1942 and at that time referred to the condition of 2/2nd Independent Company as 'rooted' considered the campaign as a 'heartbreaking' needless exercise, which would contribute nothing to the successful outcome of the war, and only result in needless casualties for those under his command. Consequently he had resolved that it was his task to accomplish the mission he had been given, but in doing so ensure that his command would suffer the minimum casualties.[30] Given the potential harm which could be inflicted on smaller Commando patrols, Stevens' considerations may explain why 6th Division

---

27 AWM, AWM 52/2/51 Box 41, 2/6th Cavalry Commando Regiment War Diary, January 1945, 12 Jan 45.
28 AWM, AWM 52/2/51 Box 41, 2/6th Cavalry Commando Regiment War Diary, January 1945, Appendices, 19 Aust Inf Bde OP Instr No. 5, 6th Jan 45.
29 AWM, AWM 52/2/51 Box 41, 2/6th Cavalry Commando Regiment War Diary, January 1945, Appendices, 6th Aust Div Operation Order 3, 17 Jan 45.
30 Dean, *1944–1945 Victory in the Pacific*, pp. 228–9.

deployed larger infantry formations to carry out what were essentially Commando tasks.

During February 2/6th Cavalry Commando Regiment came under the command of 17 Brigade. The commanding officer of 17 Brigade was Brigadier Murray Moten. We have met Moten before denouncing Independent Companies during the Wau Salamaua campaign. It did not seem that he had moderated his attitude towards Commandos in the 22 months which had elapsed since then. True to form Moten restricted the range at which Commandos could operate, by insisting that patrols were not to go beyond the range of artillery and mortar support. There would be no long range autonomous Commando ventures under his command. Moten was, however, a competent, if conservative, infantry commander, and the manner in which he employed his Commandos reflected this. He used Commandos to clear the enemy from specific areas, to cover his line of communications, conduct limited patrols, and to cover Walum village.[31] True to form he instructed Commandos that when they discovered enemy positions they were to directly attack those positions, the ideas of stealth and reconnaissance not being part of his agenda. In this he was no doubt ensuring that his Commandos behaved as 'proper infantry'. One such action occurred on 20 February, when 2/10th Squadron staged a deliberate attack on a fortified Japanese position at Kualagem. The attack failed with the loss of two officers killed and two men wounded. Max Luff a Trooper with 2/10th Commando bitterly described the attack as, 'Rotten show today. The Little Bastards were dug in to stay, let us get in & then outflanked.'[32] Kualagem was attacked for a second time on 22 March but once again, the attack failed despite the repeated bombing of the position by aircraft. It was reported by an indigenous policeman that the Japanese were furiously digging in. It was later reported by another indigenous policeman that the Japanese at Kualagem numbered, 'ten fella twelve Japan Man', which translated to 120 Japanese or in Luff's opinion 'a lot of angry men'. This explained why the attacks had been unsuccessful as the fighting patrols ordered by Moten to capture the site consisted of only nine to 12 men.[33] Despite this set back the Squadron did not relent and continued to patrol within the Vicinity of Kualagem. This patrolling resulted in clashes with the Japanese. Luff relates one such encounter:

> We hadn't been in our poss ... for more than 5 mins when they came sauntering into our trap ... We were itching to bowl them but had to hold our fire as we wanted to get them all right inside our ambush before springing it. One Nip gave Mo & I heart failure, he stared straight at us but apparently never saw us. At last

---

31 AWM, AWM 52/2/51 Box 42, 2/6th Cavalry Commando Regiment War Diary, February 1945, 17 Aust Inf Bde OP Instr No.10, 21 Feb 45.
32 George MacAfie 'Max' Luff Diary: 7 Section 2/10 Commando Squadron, 2/6th Cavalry Commando Regiment, 6th Australian Division, 1 February–5 October 1945, 9 February – 9 March 1945.
33 George MacAfie Diary: 9 Feb – 9 Mar 45.

they were in; Mo & I being on the end had the pickings as we caught any trying to run back down the track. It seemed to be only a second for the stampede to begin. Four of them came pounding back down the track yelling & squealing in terror. They died screaming.[34]

One result of these encounters was the rescue of Indian Prisoners of War. The Indians had been drafted by the Japanese to act as porters. 2/10th Commando Squadron found them in very bad condition, emaciated and mistreated by the Japanese. The troops of the squadron did what they could for the Indians. Major Goode became as 'mad as a hatter' at the treatment that the Indians had received at the hand of the Japanese, with the consequence that he declared 'open slather' on the Japanese from that day on.[35] By this Goode meant no mercy was to be shown to the Japanese, yet another manifestation of the ruthless nature of the war fought by the Commandos against the Japanese.

One feature of operations that did not change from the time of the Independent Companies was that the Commando Squadrons seldom operated as a unified entity. Unlike the companies of a standard infantry battalion, elements within the squadrons of the Commando Regiment would be allocated diverse tasks, which meant that they operated at some distance from each other. The same applied for the squadron's relationship to other squadron's within the Regiment. While 2/10th Commando Squadron was fighting it battles around Kualagem, 2/9th Commando Squadron was under the command of 2/3rd Infantry Battalion. Its role was to prevent enemy infiltration, and prevent the enemy moving across the front of 16th Bde. This eventually changed to clearing the enemy within an area forward of 16th Bde, and to patrol forward areas up to the air force bomb line.[36] This work was conducted offensively with 16 of the 35 Patrols conducted for the month being fighting patrols, and resulted in destroying several enemy stragglers and small parties.[37] Just what 2/7th Commando Squadron was doing during February remains a mystery as the Squadron war diary for that month is missing and the Regimental war diary makes no mention of the squadron at that time.

During February 2/10th Commando Squadron had engaged the enemy in unsuccessful conventional battle at Kualagem. One consequence of the conventional engagements at Kualagem was that the Commandos, unlike earlier times when stealth and concealment were a fundamental attribute of the Independent Companies, openly revealed themselves to the Japanese. From this the Japanese were able to establish a generally accurate estimate of the numbers of Australian troops they faced, and

---

34 George MacAfie Diary, 29 Feb– 3 Mar 45.
35 George MacAfie Diary, 23–24 Feb 45.
36 The bomb line was the line on the map inside of which aircraft would not bomb.
37 AWM, AWM52 2/2/61, 2/9 Commando Squadron War Diary, February 1945, AWM52 2/2/62 Part 1; 2/9 Commando Squadron War Diary, February1945 Part 2 (i).

concluded that there were not a significant numbers of Australians in the area.[38] The comparison to earlier times when the more stealthy tactics of the Independent Companies repeatedly fooled the Japanese into over estimating their numbers is evident. During this time 2/10th squadron's strength was 13 officers and 203 other ranks, this from a war establishment of 263 of all ranks. Due to its reduced numbers the Squadron was hard put to meet all of its responsibilities, as the squadron's war diary put it 'There was in all cases too much to be done and too few to do it.'[39] The consequences of this were that the squadron frontage was thinly stretched, with troops being too distant from each other to provide mutual support. Squadron Troops would be required to manage their own affairs and if it came to it fight their own battles. In March the Japanese took advantage of the situation and pushed hard into the area patrolled by 2/10th Commando Squadron. This brought on a major clash at Mapobma Creek, where for five days 'B' Troop holding the Milak Knoll repulsed attack after attack. The fight began on 13 March when indigenous sentries came running into the Troop's position frantically warning 'Japan man he come plenty'.[40] The first attack came soon after with the Japanese using mortars and placing light machineguns up in trees to fire down into 'B' Troop's position. Using sling shots they lobbed demolition charges at the defenders. The Commandos had dug themselves deep pits and were able to avoid any harm. That night the Japanese prowled around the defence perimeter setting off the booby traps the Commandos had placed out to their front. Shortly after sunrise on the second day the Japanese attacked again, this time driving indigenous men, women and children ahead of them as shields. Unwilling to shoot in the milling mass of screaming indigenous people the Commandos were unable to prevent twelve Japanese getting in amongst them. Lieutenant Neil Redmond, the officer on the spot, shouted, 'Get those bastards', and the Commandos set to killing all of the 12 Japanese. After 50 minutes or so the Japanese attack was driven off. Thirty four dead Japanese were counted for the cost of four dead Commandos. The next day supplies were air dropped, which were sorely needed as the Troop was running short of food. At least one canister containing food landed in front of the Japanese. The Japanese recovered the canister, but were immediately counter attacked by the Commandos. Dropping the canister the Japanese withdrew and the Commandos recaptured it, one of them remarking 'some war this is, having to fight the bloody Japs for our tucker.' Even so the Japanese managed to secure three of the eight canisters dropped.[41] The following day grenades were amongst the stores air dropped which were sorely needed as only thirty

---

38 AWM, AWM52 2/2/61, 2/9 Commando Squadron War Diary, January to May 1945, March 1945.
39 AWM, AWM52 2/2/62, 2/10 Commando Squadron War Diary January to May 1945, March 1945.
40 Gavin Long, 'The Final Campaigns, Australia in the War of 1939–1945', *Australian War Memorial*, Series One Army Volume VII, Canberra, 1963, p. 307.
41 Long, *The Final Campaigns*, p. 307.

grenades remained for the Troop.[42] Grenades were in fact the preferred weapon to use as the Japanese at night, as the Japanese would attempt to get the Commandos to fire and reveal their positions. Throwing a grenade generated no tell-tale flash for the Japanese to focus on. In one such incident two Troopers who went by the nicknames 'Shorrock' and 'Shorty' heard Japanese movement very close to them. 'Shorrock' told 'Shorty' that he could hear a Japanese breathing he was so close. He pulled the pin from a grenade and released the lever waiting three seconds before he threw it. In the morning they found a dead Japanese soldier one and half metres from their slit trench.[43] Air support also came in the form of ground attack with fighter aircraft strafing the Japanese only 50 metres from the Commandos positions.[44] Attached to 'B' Troop was single 3 inch mortar which had been despatched from 2/7th Infantry Battalion. This mortar proved to be invaluable in the battle against the attacking Japanese. Stripped down of all attachments including the base plate the mortar was aimed and held by hand. This allowed bombs to be dropped to within thirteen metres of the Commandos positions.[45] Throughout the battle the number of dead Japanese lying close to the Commando lines began to prove a problem as the bodies began to decay in the tropical heat. The smell threatened to become overwhelming. To alleviate this, the Commandos during breaks in the fighting buried whatever bodies they could. The Japanese had during their assault not cut the Commandos line of communication and it was used to evacuate indigenous people. Patrols also worked their way along the line securing it and establishing links with the rear area and thus the possibility of support. When this happened, the Japanese pressure on Mapobma reduced and by 19 March their assaults ceased.[46] The number of Japanese killed during the fight at Mapobma Creek could only be guessed at, although in the following days it was felt that the casualties the Japanese suffered weakened them and compelled them to withdraw their forces south.[47] At the same time they attacked at Mapobma Creek the Japanese also threatened 'C' Troop, but made only one serious attack which was repulsed. 'A' Troop experienced nothing out of the ordinary, illustrating the distance between the Troops.[48] As memorable as the fight at Mapobma Creek may have been it was in every way a conventional action, owing nothing at all to Commando training.

42 George MacAfie 'Max' Luff Diary, 10–11 Apr 45.
43 'The True Story of Shorrock and Shorty', 2/6 Cavalry Commando Regiment and 2nd Cavalry Regiment <http://www.26cavcommando.org.au/index.php?option=com_content&task=view&id=2673&Itemid=74> (consulted 1 Dec 2018).
44 Long, *The Final Campaigns*, p. 308.
45 'The Eventful Patrols of "B" Troop', 2/6 Cavalry Commando Regiment and 2nd Cavalry Regiment, <http://www.26cavcommando.org.au/index.php?option=com_content&task=view&id=2673&Itemid=74> (consulted 1 Dec 2018).
46 Ibid.
47 AWM, AWM52 2/2/62, 2/10 Commando Squadron War Diary January to May 1945, March 1945.
48 Ibid.

This was, however, perfectly consistent with the official requirement of Commandos to act as infantry whenever the circumstances dictated that they do so.

The conventional nature of the war enveloping the Commandos was not confined to 2/10th Commando Squadron alone. On 4 March 2/9th Commando Squadron unsuccessfully attacked a well dug in Japanese position in which three Commandos were killed. Adding insult to injury an airstrike called in the next day hit the Commandos instead, wounding five of them, and encouraging the Japanese to attack when the air strike had concluded. A further unsuccessful attack on the same Japanese position on 7 March resulted in another Commando being killed.[49] On 9 March artillery harassed the Japanese position for half an hour followed by an airstrike. The Commandos working alongside troops from 2/3rd Machine Gun Battalion occupied the Japanese position without opposition. A follow up patrol by 2/9th Squadron killed four Japanese.[50] It was the case that more and more the Commandos of 6th Division were finding themselves adopting the role of conventional infantry.

Active operations for 2/9th Commando Squadron ceased on 14 March, and on 23 March the Squadron was shipped to Pogreta Bay at Aitape where it went into camp and spent its time on construction duties and playing sport.[51] Patrolling occupied 2/7th Commando Squadron in the first ten days of March, but unlike 2/10th and 2/9th Commando Squadrons, 2/7th Commando Squadron did not engage in any deliberate conventional actions. On 19 March the Squadron was shipped to Aitape where it also went into camp.[52] 2/10th Squadron joined the other Squadrons at Aitape by the end of the month.[53]

Despite serious Japanese efforts to savage them the actual amount of work the Commandos were called upon to undertake during February and March was remarkably constrained. Commando Max Luff remembered six days during February when he was engaged in active duties; two days attacking Kualagem, one day on a Recce Patrol, and three days on an Ambush, the one described above. March was slightly more active with twelve days involving some type of action ranging from the fight at Mapobma, an ambush, assaulting a position known as 'Housecopp', an OP patrol, a Reconnaissance Patrol and harassing the Japanese line of communication. The remainder of the time Luff spent tramping about the jungle from one point to the other for what he considered to be no apparent reason, or escorting officers and wounded.[54] In fact in the two months of February and March 1945 Luff recalled that he was involved in 18 days of active service. When not so engaged a considerable amount of the time was spent sitting around the camp, playing cards,

---

49   AWM, AWM52 2/2/61, 2/9 Commando Squadron War Diary, March 1945.
50   AWM, AWM52 2/2/61, 2/9 Commando Squadron War Diary, 9 Mar 45.
51   AWM, AWM52 2/2/61, 2/9 Commando Squadron War Diary, March1945, March 45.
52   AWM, AWM52 2/2/59, 2/7 Commando Squadron War Diary, March to April1945, 19 Mar 45.
53   AWM, AWM52 2/2/62, 2/10 Commando Squadron War Diary, January to May1945.
54   George MacAfie Diary, Mar 45.

attempting to procure enough tobacco to make cigarettes, and generally relaxing.[55] As noted during the second half of March two of the Commando Squadrons were withdrawn from the line, and by the end of the month all of the Squadrons had been withdrawn.

All of April for 2/9th and 2/10th Commando Squadrons, was spent in camp. Likewise 2/7th Squadron spent most of April in camp, although towards the end of the month two Troops were sent out to patrol a relatively safe area, and one Troop was placed in 19 Brigade reserve. The reason for the stay in camp was to prepare the Commandos for the role they were to play in the offensive against Wewak which as to occur in May. This offensive would consist of two parts. The first was an amphibious assault against Dove Bay some 16 kilometres east of Wewak. The second was an overland advance along the coast toward Wewak. The Commandos would participate in each. The role of the 2/9th and 2/10th Commando Squadrons was as 'Assault Troops' assigned to Farida Force, as the landing force was called. They were to seize and hold a perimeter on the Dove Bay beachhead.[56] The role of 2/7th Commando Squadron was to accompany 19 Brigade as it advanced along the coast towards Wewak.

On 11 May Farida Force landed its troops at Dove Bay heralded by a heavy naval bombardment and airstrikes.[57] The troops came ashore but as with all such landings not everything went smoothly and 2/10th Commando Squadron found itself wading into a swamp consisting of chest deep water, matted vines and rotting logs.[58] Luff described this as, 'A Filthy Stinking hole; with no cover.'[59] Despite this the squadron soon established a beachhead and dug in. Just how this was done in a swamp was never explained other than, 'One just had to ly(sic) down in it & stick it Out.'[60] The 2/9th Commando Squadron avoided the swamp, pushed inland for 200 yards and dug in. Very light opposition was encountered, that which was being dealt with by the Commandos or silenced by naval gunfire.[61] There was no attempt to significantly expand the perimeter beyond what had been seized on the first day. Local patrols and the calling in of naval gunfire support characterised the role of the Commandos until 26th May.[62] By the end of the month some 23 Japanese had been killed for the loss of one Commando.[63] Other than that the Commandos swam, sunbaked and enjoyed themselves on the beach.[64] The squadrons were down on the strength at the time,

---

55   Ibid.
56   AWM, AWM 52/2/51 Box 42, 2/6th Cavalry Commando Regiment War Diary, May 1945, FARIDA FORCE O.O. No.1, 9 May 45.
57   AWM, AWM52 2/2/62, 2/10 Commando Squadron War Diary, May1945, 11 May.
58   Ibid.
59   George MacAfie Diary, 27–28 May 45.
60   Ibid.
61   AWM, AWM52 2/2/61, 2/9 Commando Squadron War Diary, May 1945.
62   AWM, AWM52 2/2/62, 2/10 Commando Squadron War Diary, 12–18 May 45.
63   AWM, AWM52 2/2/61, 2/9 Commando Squadron War Diary, May 1945.
64   AWM, AWM52 2/2/62, 2/10 Commando Squadron War Diary, 19–21 May 45.

2/10th Commando Squadron having nine officers and 146 other ranks, which was 108 short of its war establishment.⁶⁵ It may have been that this was why they were not used more assertively at that time. The Japanese never launched a counter attack against the landing at Dove Bay and little else happened there until 26 May when 19 Brigade arrived after advancing along the coast. At that time 2/10th Commando Squadron was moved to the Mandi Creek beachhead where it dug in and commenced patrolling. During this time, the Squadron killed only one Japanese but lost one Commando killed and one wounded in contact with the enemy. It also lost one Commando killed, one who died of wounds, and two wounded when the Japanese shelled their camp with artillery on 27 May.⁶⁶

While 2/9th and 2/10th Commando Squadrons were partaking of their beach experience 2/7th Commando Squadron was engaged in a campaign of a very different type. Attached to 19 Brigade the Squadron acted as the vanguard of the Brigade. In this role it was to aggressively patrol forward clearing any enemy they encountered.⁶⁷ This required the squadron to employ both its unconventional patrol skills, and in a mark of consistency with what was expected of Commandos under the Army's guidelines, it also found itself committed to deliberate infantry assaults on prepared enemy positions. The most notable of these assaults was the assault upon the Sauri Villages, of which there were three, where the Japanese had established a rearguard covering their withdrawal from Wewak.⁶⁸ In a series of assaults the Squadron captured the three villages one by one. To do so they employed Mortars, air strikes, artillery and flamethrowers. In such circumstances the standard operating procedure for the Army at that time was to employ massive firepower to overwhelm the enemy. Employing such resources in New Guinea had at times unique challenges. In preparation for the assault on the villages the artillery received directions from an indigenous policeman who had been acting as a scout. His instructions delivered in Pidgin language were:

> 'Loose 'im lik lik. Bomb e' mus sit belong arse belong dewai long arp,'em 'e good too mus, 'em 'e got to pella road. Yapan man 'e got hole belong pight, mus put 'em plenty bomb.'

Luckily one gunner understood and translated it as,

> Range down slightly, then bomb will fall at base of big tree along the ridge; at this point there is a track junction. The Japanese are dug-in, numerous foxholes and a good target for artillery.⁶⁹

---

65   AWM, AWM52 2/2/62, 2/10 Commando Squadron War Diary, 11 May 45.
66   AWM, AWM52 2/2/62, 2/10 Commando Squadron War Diary, 25 May 45, 27 May 45, 31 May 45.
67   AWM, AWM52 2/2/59, 2/7 Commando Squadron War Diary, May 1945, 11 May 45.
68   Long, *The Final Campaigns*, p. 347.
69   Bottrell, *Cameos of Commandos*, p. 260.

The target was subsequently shelled.

The Commandos were, quite naturally, not inclined to forego such support and not reluctant to make use of the firepower available to them.[70] The method used to capture No.3 Sauri Village by 'B' Troop decisively illustrates this. A frontal assault was considered to be too exposed to enemy fire, so while the rest of the Squadron raked the village with fire 'B' Troop guided by an indigenous policeman took two flamethrowers and made a half circuit around the village. They came up close to the village from the rear and attacked with the flame throwers.[71] The flamethrower used by the Australian Army was the American model M2-2, which were called 'juke boxes' by the troops. It used compressed nitrogen as a propellant, compressed hydrogen as the ignition gas and was ignited by a battery. The flamethrowers morale effect upon Japanese troops was devastating with many of them fleeing in the face of it. Terrified by the flame assault the morale of the Japanese defenders shattered and many of them killed themselves with their grenades. 'B' Troop then took the village without any significant casualties.[72] At the end of the fight for the Sauri villages two Commandos had been killed and four wounded, sixty four dead Japanese were found.[73] The use of Flamethrowers supported by overwhelming firepower illustrates the conventional nature of tactics the Commandos were employing at the time. Following the capture of the villages the Squadron then went on to cut the main road leading from Wewak inland.[74] Now reduced to 12 officers and 117 other ranks, less than half of its war establishment, the Squadron continued its advance repelling several attempts by the enemy to infiltrate its positions.[75] It continued in this role until 19 Brigade reached Dove Bay, and the squadron was released from Brigade command and took over responsibility for the Dove Bay beachhead perimeter.[76]

The nature of the war being fought at Dove Bay in which much time was spent not actively seeking out and engaging the enemy had a debilitating effect on the spirit of the Commandos. This was recognised and on 25 June a conference resolved that the aggressive spirit needed to be encouraged and that it was essential to build up within the men the concept of the 'Superman', which was thought to have suffered.[77] This in itself was an acknowledgement that there was a distinctiveness associated with the Commandos, whether or not the Commandos actually thought of themselves as Supermen.

On 26 May 2/10th squadron was deployed to Mandi Creek a short distance up the coast from Dove Bay where it dug in. The Japanese responded by shelling the Squadron

---

70 AWM, AWM52 2/2/59, 2/7 Commando Squadron War Diary, 11–20 May 45.
71 George MacAfie Diary, 27–28 Jul 45.
72 Bottrell, *Cameos of Commandos*, p. 262.
73 Ibid.
74 Walker, *The Island Campaigns*, p. 5.
75 AWM, AWM52 2/2/59, 2/7 Commando Squadron War Diary, 23–25 May 45.
76 AWM, AWM52 2/2/59, 2/7 Commando Squadron War Diary, 30 May 45.
77 AWM, AWM52 2/2/59, 2/6 Cavalry Commando Regiment War Diary, 25 June 45.

with 105mm artillery killing one man and wounding two.[78] The Squadron countered with a series of standing patrols which made liberal use of artillery support.[79] This use of artillery to support what were essentially small sub-units was symptomatic of the manner in which Commandos were being employed by 6th Division at the time. The insistence on using artillery was, when considering Commandos, not as uninspired as it may appear to be. By this time the Squadron had been reduced to 10 Officers and 67 other ranks, a shadow of its full strength.[80] In such circumstances and combined with the overriding intention to minimise casualties it is understandable that artillery would have been employed as a substitute for risking the lives of what was becoming a rapidly diminishing resource. Subsequently the squadron set to employing artillery as much as it could, and on 3 June following an artillery barrage of 800 rounds delivered with 10 minutes, it overran a Japanese bunker position.[81] Artillery coon became a central aspect of the Squadron's operational method. On 18 June a patrol contacted Japanese near Koanumbo village, withdrew and called down artillery fire. On the same day a patrol to Parom Village engaged the enemy and withdrew before calling down artillery fire.[82] On 23 June the Squadron again attacked Koanumbo capturing the position after an artillery barrage.[83] On 27 July a patrol advanced preceded by a bombardment of 190 artillery shells.[84] The difference to earlier Independent Company tactics is clear. Nevertheless, in an infrequent example of a Commando raid, one notable success came on 23 June when a patrol crept within 10 metres of an enemy bivouac and killed 15 Japanese. In a similar ambush on 13 January 2/7th Squadron killed 38 Japanese who were caught utterly by surprise and did not fire a shot in reply.[85] At least this demonstrated that the stalking and ambush skills of the Commandos, or at least those of the veteran 2/7th Commando Squadron, were still intact. On 5 July 2/7th Commando Squadron, relieved 2/10th Commando Squadron.[86] As with the previous Squadron Artillery work occupied much of 2/7th Commando Squadron's time, with patrols going out to register Japanese targets and escort Forward Observers to suitable observation posts.[87] These actions did not, however, come without a cost.

---

78 AWM, AWM 2/2/62, 2/10 Commando Squadron War Diary, 28 May 45.
79 AWM, AWM52 2/2/62, 2/10 Commando Squadron War Diary, Patrol Report, 27, 29, 30 May 45.
80 AWM, AWM52 2/2/62, 2/10 Commando Squadron War Diary June 1945, June 45.
81 AWM, AWM52 2/2/62, 2/10 Commando Squadron War Diary June 1945, 3 June 45.
82 AWM, AWM52 2/2/62, 2/10 Commando Squadron War Diary June 1945, 18 June 45.
83 AWM, AWM52 2/2/62, 2/10 Commando Squadron War Diary June 1945, 23 June 45.
84 AWM, AWM 52/2/51 Box 43, 2/6 Cavalry Commando Regiment War Diary July 1945.
85 AWM, AWM 52/2/59, 2/10 Commando Squadron War Diary June 1945, 23 June 45, AWM 52/2/62; 2/7 Commando Squadron War Diary January 1945, 12 Jan 45.
86 AWM, AWM52 2/2/61, 2/7 Commando Squadron War Diary, June to August 1945; AWM, AWM52 2/2/62, 2/9 Commando Squadron War Diary June to August 1945; AWM, AWM52 2/2/62, 2/10 Commando Squadron War Diary June 1945.
87 AWM, AWM 2/2/59, 2/7 Commando Regiment War Diary June to August 1945.

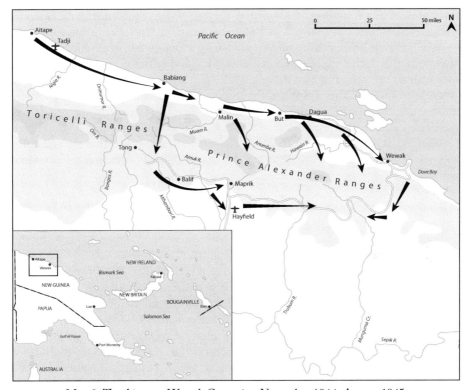

Map 9 The Aitape – Wewak Campaign November 1944–August 1945.

The Japanese had begun using buried aerial bombs as command detonated mines and in two incidents four Commandos were killed.[88]

While 2/10th Commando Squadron was operating around Mandi Creek 2/9th Commando Squadron was deployed to Brandi Plantation not far from Mandi Creek. There they established a defensive perimeter over a wide area. Heavy timber in the area had been cleared which gave the Commandos a good field of fire. Japanese 105mm artillery soon found the Squadron forcing 'C' Troop to relocate behind some rising ground to conceal themselves from observation. The Squadron made liberal use of Japanese slit trenches which they had found as protection from the shelling. Night time infiltration raids by Japanese were a constant threat and Lieutenant Doug Daniels was mortally wounded during one of them. In the same raid the Japanese got to within twelve metres of the tent of Major Tom Nisbet the Squadron commander. Having to remain constantly alert to the threat from the Japanese had a deleterious effect on the morale of the Squadron. Chaplain Botterell, who was with them at the

---

88   AWM, AWM 52/2/51, Box 43, 2/10 Commando Squadron War Diary, 24 and 30 June 45.

time, noticed that they lacked the zest and alertness so synonymous with members of Commando Squadrons.[89] He put this down to the amount of time the Squadron had been in the front line for seven months with only a total of five weeks break. He was also aware that such demands were not unusual. Another factor at work was that the men realised that the campaign they were taking part in was in no way decisive to the outcome of the war. They suspected that they were participating in what was essentially a political exercise and did not want to risk their lives for such a venture. It was accepted that if needed the Squadron would fight hard but there was no enthusiasm for doing so. It must be remembered that what was also at play was that the Squadron was one of those raised in late 1943 and was inexperienced in the rigours of coping with extended operational periods.

One example of 6 Division employing Commandos in an appropriate 'commando' manner was during June when two Japanese raiding parties began to harass Australian formations in the hope of drawing attention away from the main Japanese force. In an appropriate use of Commandos 2/6th Cavalry Commando Regiment was given the task of hunting down these groups.[90]

During July the campaign for Wewak entered its final stage with the Japanese being driven away from the coast and into the mountains.[91] Patrolling by Commandos attempted to maintain contact with the enemy, but engaged in no significant actions. The nature of the campaign had changed to one where 6th Division had achieved its primary objectives and was now engaged in grinding down the remnants of the Japanese forces in the area. In such an environment the Division could find no further practical use for the Commandos other than as standard infantry. Subsequently the task allocated the Commandos was to garrison and hold the Dagua-Hawain area.[92] The most prominent feature in the area was the Jikkoku Pass which was considered to be of prime importance and the Squadrons were instructed to hold the pass 'at all costs'.[93] Just why the order to hold the pass had been phrased with such hyperbole is unclear, as the Japanese had been driven back into the hinterland and posed no serious threat. Nevertheless it was and the Commandos were allocated the task. Settling into a static role the Commandos, operating uncharacteristically for the first time as a full Regiment with all Squadrons in the same area, patrolled the pass and its environs. The enemy were still active in the area, but limited themselves to night time harassment.[94] This was a period when the active presence of the Commandos was reduced markedly, no doubt with the intention of minimizing their risk of sustaining casualties.

---

89   Bottrell, *Cameo of Commandos*, p. 269.
90   Long, *The Final Campaigns*, p. 381.
91   Long, *The Final Campaigns*, p. 354.
92   AWM, AWM52 2/2/62, 2/10 Commando Squadron War Diary, 6th Aust Div Operational Order No.7 of 4 July 1945.
93   AWM, AWM52 2/2/61, 2/9 Commando Squadron War Diary June to August 1945, 2/6th Cavalry Commando Regiment Operation Order No.1, 14 July 1945.
94   AWM, AWM52 2/2/62, 2/10 Commando Squadron War Diary, July 1945.

Patrol activity was significantly reduced. ANGAU took over the patrolling area of 2/10th Commando Squadron, resulting in the Squadron not patrolling at all. Patrols for 2/7th Commando Squadron took on the character of local reconnaissance and artillery spotting, and for 2/9th Commando Squadron patrols were escort and local security only.[95] The idea of ranging out to find and destroy the enemy was no longer part of the equation. Indigenous personnel were used more and more for longer range patrols, with the Commandos patrolling when they did patrol, doing so closer to home.[96] All was not totally inactive, however, and there were some moments of action when 2/10th Commando Squadron unsuccessfully attacked a Japanese position on 3 July, which resulted in one Trooper Missing in Action. On 24 July 'A' Troop assaulted a strong Japanese position at Machoun, during which four Commandos were killed. Artillery shelled Machoun two days later and the Japanese evacuated the position.[97] Those patrols which did take place encountered the occasional Japanese, with one that Luff participated in working its way into a position 25 metres from a Japanese camp and observing the enemy.[98] Luff recalled that:

> They were sitting around in two Parties of Six around their fires cooking smelly rice; Whilst a big fat piggish Jap was sitting up on an old Tub watching the Antics of 3 or more of them who were jigging & dancing around laughing & joking.[99]

The Commandos waited concealed and silently observing until they were given he order to fire. When that occurred Luff estimated 2,000 rounds of automatic fire tore into the camp in two minutes killing all of the Japanese.

Apart from such actions July generally proved to be a decidedly sedentary time for the Commandos. There was tactical reconnaissance for the purpose of bringing down harassing artillery fire on the enemy, but generally the troops ensured the security of their posts and in compliance with instructions avoided unnecessary casualties. The Commando camp steadily became a permanent one of barbed wire defences, with booby traps set to instantaneous fuses, and stockpiles of stores, ammunition and rations.[100] The Squadrons continued in this role until mid-August when Japan surrendered and the war came to an end.[101] When hostilities ceased 2/6th Cavalry

---

95 AWM, AWM52 2/2/61, 2/7 Commando Squadron War Diary, June to August 1945; AWM52 2/2/59, 2/9 Commando Squadron War Diary, July 1945.
96 AWM, AWM52 2/2/59, 2/7 Commando Squadron War Diary, June to August 1945.
97 AWM, AWM52 2/2/62, 2/10 Commando Squadron War Diary, July 1945.
98 George MacAfie Diary, 27–28, 20 Jul 45.
99 Ibid.
100 AWM, AWM52 2/2/59, 2/7 Commando Squadron War Diary June to August 1945, 2/6th Cav (Commando) Regt 10 July 45 Conference Agenda.
101 During August indigenous patrols took over the patrol work of the Commandos who remained in camp only venturing out for immediate security patrols or on the occasional

Commando Regiment had killed 778 enemy troops, found 363 of them already dead and captured 23 Prisoners of War. This was accomplished for the cost of 48 Commandos killed and 119 wounded.[102]

The employment of the Commandos by 6th Division was an exercise in adapting the role of the Commandos to the guidelines which had been established by the army for their employment. In this context there was no fixed role set for Commandos, be it light infantry reconnaissance and flank protection, assault troops, or conventional infantry. All roles made their appearance at different times. The army's accepted guidelines for Commandos, which were suitably broad encompassed every task the Commandos were assigned. This was even if that employment did not always make use of the unique skills and attributes of the Commandos. It was not as if 6th Division did not understand how to utilise these skills and attributes. During the opening stages of the campaign Commandos were employed to carry out scouting and advanced guard functions. This was a role they were particularly suited for. This role lasted for as long as the Division perceived the need for such activity. Following this the requirement for a Special Forces contribution to the campaign diminished. Consequently Commandos were employed as flank guards, and then as conventional infantry. In this latter role they were used to assault enemy positions, or hold positions against enemy attacks. Throughout the campaign 6th Division was facing significant manpower shortages. In this context the Commandos represented a manpower asset that could be utilised to plug whatever gaps appeared in the order of battle. The frequent posting of Commandos as Brigade reserves and their use to garrison Jikkoku Pass are examples of this.[103] It was a combination of the nature of the war being fought by the Australian Army in 1944–1945, the specific instructions from their political masters, and best use of limited manpower resources, that determined how Commandos would be employed by 6th Division during the Aitape-Wewak campaign. In compliance with these circumstances, and influenced by the personal reluctance of its commander to risk the lives of his men, 6th Division resolved to use its overwhelming firepower to achieve its mission. Given all these caveats there was no place for free ranging Commandos.

Whether or not using Commandos in a more inspired manner where they could employ their unconventional distinctiveness may have added value to the Division's operations is a moot point. A post war report by Japanese staff officers who fought 17 Brigade during the campaign were critical of the Brigade for being what they called 'over cautious' and not repeating the tactics of infiltrating behind Japanese lines and threatening their supply lines which had been used earlier such as in the Salamaua campaign. The Japanese officers stated that if this had occurred and they felt their rear

reconnaissance for an artillery mission.
102 AWM, AWM 52/2/51 Box 44, 2/6th Cavalry Commando War Diary, August 1945.
103 Long, *The Final Campaigns*, p.354.

areas to be threatened it would have forced the Japanese forces to retreat.[104] Perhaps if 6th Division had used its Commandos in such a manner the campaign could have been brought to an earlier end.

Nevertheless during the Aitape-Wewak campaign the Commandos efficiently carried out the diverse roles 6th Division allocated to them. It mattered little that many of those roles had very little to do with the style of operation and combat their title 'Commando' implied. They carried out each task competently and efficiently according to the Commando guidelines established by the army. These guidelines were the final stage of a transformative process away from the Independent Company ethos which had by the first months of 1944 had, at least in theory, become the common protocol for the employment of Commandos as integral sub-units within the army. By operating according to this protocol the Commandos contributed to the final successful outcome of the Aitape-Wewak campaign.

104 Johnston, *Fighting the Enemy* p. 128; Long, *The Final Campaigns*, p. 369.

11

"Spreading our Gospel" – The Commandos on Bougainville

The commando squadron which operated on Bougainville; 2/8th Commando Squadron, was a unique case. So great indeed was the difference between the operational style of 2/8th Commando Squadron from that of the mainstream Commando squadrons, that it was in fact something of an anomaly within the 1944–1945 Australian Army's Commando community. As such it presents an excellent alternative model of Commando operations to that of any other Australian Army Commando Squadron of the era.

There are several reasons for this uniqueness. Alone amongst the Commando squadrons 2/8th Commando Squadron was not posted to the Atherton Tablelands, and thus did not undergo the training regime designed to redefine and retrain the Australian Army's Commandos. It was also not attached to any Cavalry Commando Regiment which allowed the squadron to remain an autonomous unit. As 2/8th Independent Company, the squadron had been formed in July 1942, and was the last company to have been trained under the original Independent Company regime at Wilson's Promontory. Following that training it was posted to Yandina in Queensland and then the Northern Territory of Australia, originally to reinforce the Commandos on Timor, and when this proved impracticable it was tasked to patrol between Darwin and Adelaide River a rural area 113 kilometres to the south of Darwin. This duty was monotonous and occupied the Squadron from the last months of 1942 until the first half of 1944.[1] This changed in July 1944, when the company, now redesignated a Commando Squadron, was moved to Townsville in Queensland, and then sent directly to Lae in New Guinea.[2] While in Lae an element of the Squadron took part in a clandestine landing on New Britain during which it provided beach security for an advanced party of officers from 5th Division which was preparing to land on

---

1 AWM, AWM 3 DRL 2529 Item 78, Lt. General Savige, Stanley George; Papers: Bougainville 2 Corps Report on Operations 2/8 Commando Sqn Nov 1944–August 1945, p. 3.
2 Ibid.

New Britain. The Squadron thus bypassed the Atherton Tablelands training experience, subsequently avoiding the army's intention to retrain its Commandos away from the Independent Company standard. The consequence of this was that the squadron retained its Independent Company character. Reinforcing the maintenance of the Independent Company spirit were the personnel who made up the Squadron. The Squadron Commander was Major Norman Winning. Winning, a Scot who was known as the 'Red Steer' due to his red hair and bold, energetic, confident manner of command, had an impeccable Independent Company pedigree.[3] He was formerly a member of and then commander of 2/5th Independent Company, and had commanded of the 1942 Salamaua raid. As soon as he assumed command of 2/8th Commando Squadron in June 1944 Winning set to building up the numbers in the squadron which was under strength, due in no small measure to the squadron's establishment being reduced when 80 of its fittest men were transferred to the nascent Australian parachute battalion in October 1943.[4] Winning knew the type of men he wanted for his Squadron and set about deliberately seeding his squadron with Independent Company veterans. He openly canvassed for and recruited veterans from 2/3rd, 2/5th and 2/6th Commando Squadrons and succeeded in attracting 70 men from those Squadrons who joined him in Lae. Winning set about attracting independently minded individuals, veterans of the Independent Company style of warfare. Two examples of this were Peter Pinney and Claude Dunshea.[5] Pinney was a character who embodied all the attributes of the Independent Company soldier. After a wild teenage life in which he had once hung upside down from the Sydney Harbour Bridge, he had joined the army in July 1941 'craving adventure'. After serving time in the Middle East he returned to Australia and joined George Warfe's 2/3rd Independent Company to take part in the Wau Salamaua Campaign.[6] During that campaign Pinney made a reputation for himself as something of a daredevil reconnaissance specialist. Such a personality did not settle comfortably into the routine demanded of Commandos when they returned to Australia and the Atherton Tableland training regime. Pinney, who was a prolific and articulate letter writer, wrote that during this time of enforced inertia he suffered what he described as 'violent claustrophobia'. Luckily for Pinney he had discovered 2/8th Commando Squadron. He summed up the attraction the squadron had for him, writing that 'The 8th is what our turnout used to be – an

---

3   Pirie, 'Commando Double Black', p. 67.
4   AWM, AWM 3 DRL 2529 Item 78, Lt. General Savige, Stanley George; Papers: Bougainville 2 Corps Report on Operations 2/8 Commando Sqn Nov 1944–August 1945, p.3.
5   AWM, AWM52 2/2/60, 2/8 Commando Squadron War Diary, January to July 1944; AWM, AWM 3 DRL 2529 Item 78, Lt. General Savige, Stanley George; Papers: Bougainville 2 Corps Report on Operations 2/8 Commando Sqn Nov 1944–August 1945; Pirie, *Commando Double Black*, p.354.
6   Australian Dictionary of Biography <http://adb.anu.edu.au/biography/pinney-peter-patrick-18951> (consulted 18 May 2017).

independent unit, nobody's baby, liable to go anyplace + do anything'.[7] Pinney saw the Squadron as his opportunity to get back into action and operate in the autonomous independent manner which he thrived upon. Subsequently he set about making himself a nuisance within 2/3rd Commando Squadron and eventually managed to cause enough trouble that his superiors were happy to rid themselves of him. Even then Pinney sat for several weeks waiting for his transfer to happen. Rebelling against the sluggish bureaucracy Pinney exercised his initiative and hitched a ride on an airplane to Bougainville where 2/8th Commando Squadron had been posted in October 1944. True to form the Army posted him as Absent Without Leave as he was missing from his billet back in Australia. Undeterred he arrived in Bougainville and reported to Norman Winning. Winning, who knew of Pinney and his reputation, accepted him without query and Pinney joined the Squadron.[8] Claude Joseph Patrick Dunshea had served with 2/7th Independent Company during the Wau Salamaua campaign and later in the Ramu Valley. He was awarded the Military Cross and Bar for his service during these campaigns. During this time Dunshea when operating as a Scout had alone attacked a Japanese outflanking force killing six of them and forcing the rest to flee. He also conducted a long range reconnaissance patrol to the Bogadjim Road in the Japanese occupied Ramu Valley. During this he, accompanied by only one other soldier and an indigenous Constable, moved without being detected the 80 kilometres to Bogadjim and back, and observed and recorded the Japanese work on the Bogadjim Road.[9] The inclusion of such personalities as these and numerous other Independent Company veterans combined with the avoidance of the army's Commando training regime ensured that throughout the war the Squadron maintained its identity as an Independent Company and never saw itself as a Commando Squadron.[10]

Every aspect of what became the squadron's operational style reflected this. The willingness to strike at the Japanese at any time and any place, the avoidance of costly set piece battles, multi day long range patrols, extraordinary prowess at stealth and stalking in the jungle environment, intimate understanding and relationship with the indigenous population, and operational independence and self-reliance, all marked it as a unique force within the Australian Army in 1945. Further to its military character its voluminous articulate and frequently witty, irreverent and sarcastic correspondence including its war diary reflected a very different spirit to that pertaining in other Commando squadrons.

Bougainville is part of the Solomon Islands, not part of New Guinea, and was administered by Australia under a League of Nations mandate.[11] Australia thus had

---

7   UQFL, UQFL288, Papers of Peter Pinney Box 13, Pinney to Mother 13 October 1944.
8   UQFL, UQFL288, Papers of Peter Pinney Box 13, Pinney to Family 25 October 1944.
9   NAA, B883 QX16381, Claude Joseph Patrick Dunshea, Service Record, Page 27 and 30.
10 AWM, AWM52 2/2/60 Box 58, 2/8 Commando Squadron War Diary, 18 Sept 1945.
11 Papua, New Guinea and Bougainville were all under Australian authority. Papua was administered separately as a Territory under the Papua Act of 1902. New Guinea and Bougainville were managed under a post-First World War League of Nations Mandate.

a dominant pre-war presence on Bougainville, and knew and understood both the physical and human environment there. This would prove to be advantageous in the forthcoming campaign. Australian troops arrived at Torokina Bougainville on 15 October 1944, to relieve US troops who had been there since November 1943. When 2/8th Commando Squadron disembarked they found their stores had been pilfered at some stage during their journey with boxes and cases opened and locks sawn off sealed containers. The pilfering of Army stores by dock workers in Australia and corrupt Army personnel en-route was a perennial problem throughout the war. Luckily for the Squadron US forces at Torokina stepped in to supply rations.[12] On 18 October Winning and Dunshea, keen to get a feel for the country they would patrol, flew in a reconnaissance aircraft over the Squadron's area of operations.[13] At the same time Winning established contact with ANGAU and the local representatives of the AIB, both of who managed the indigenous population.[14] Not wanting to announce its presence prematurely to the enemy the first Commando patrol went out on 24 October accompanying US troops, with the Commandos dressed and equipped as US troops.[15] Despite these preparations the squadron received no instructions from 3rd Division to whom it was attached. The lack of instruction caused frustration for the Commandos.[16] It was not until 30 October that the squadron received any instruction from the Division, which when it came was a rather undemanding task to conduct a topographical survey, with patrols beginning on 6 November. Unlike Aitape-Wewak where commandos began their reconnaissance and clearance tasks as soon as they landed the commando experience in Bougainville certainly did not begin with a flying start.[17]

November for the Squadron was a month of patrolling to Kuraio Mission, the Reini-Tekessi Sector and Cape Motlke, areas where there was little chance of encountering Japanese. Instructions for the patrols were to destroy or capture any enemy, obtain information from indigenous people, and record all relevant track information.[18] These were, as it eventuated, somewhat optimistic instructions. There were no Japanese present and although some Japanese equipment was found at Cape Moltke the month passed quietly. Things were, however, about to change. On 27 November

12   AWM, AWM52 2/2/60, 2/8 Commando Squadron War Diary, 15–17 Oct 45.
13   AWM, AWM52 2/2/60, 2/8 Commando Squadron War Diary, 18 Oct 45.
14   AWM, AWM52 2/2/60, 2/8 Commando Squadron War Diary, 20 Oct 45.
15   AWM, AWM52 2/2/60, 2/8 Commando Squadron War Diary, 24 Oct 45.
16   UQFL, UQFL288, Papers of Peter Pinney, Box 16, Pinney personal diary, 29 September 1944.
17   Major General Bridgeford the commander of 3 Div admitted that there were 'teething troubles' at the beginning of his Divisions relationship with 8 Commando, but never elaborated in what those troubles were, see: AWM, AWM52 2/2/60 Box 58, 2/8 Commando Squadron War Diary September to November 1945.
18   AWM, AWM52 2/2/60, Report on Operations Patrols: Cape Moltke-Kuaraio Mission Area by 2/8 Commando Squadron from 7 Nov 45 to 10 Dec 45, 2/8 Commando Squadron War Diary January 1945.

the commander of 3rd Division Major General William Bridgeford visited the Squadron. There is no record of what transpired during the visit but on 11 December the unproductive areas being patrolled by the Squadron were handed over to infantry formations.[19] This freed up the Squadron to range out to conduct reconnaissance and search for the enemy. As a consequence in December the squadron killed its first Japanese, when two unarmed Japanese stragglers were encountered in an unnamed village approximately two kilometres from the mouth of the Toru River. The two Japanese refused to surrender and were shot – a precursor to the uncompromising attitude the Squadron was to bring to its operations in Bougainville.[20]

In January the Squadron redeployed to the Jaba River area, in which Japanese activity was much more pronounced. The squadron relieved 42nd Infantry Battalion and began to patrol. They did this despite 42nd Battalion leaving them very little useful information about the tracks in the country over which they were to patrol.[21] This was a major annoyance for the Squadron as, in accordance with its Independent Company protocols, the very first task for Commandos when arriving in a new area of operations was to locate and map tracks. It was imperative that all tracks in the area be known. Not doing so could result in an enemy appearing unexpectedly or slipping past undetected. Knowing the tracks also assisted in planning the movement of patrols, and knowing the limitations and possibilities of such movement. Reporting on terrain for higher formations was also important. It was essential for planning purposes to know such things as the condition of tracks, roads, river crossings, gradients, and vegetation. The creation, correction and collection of maps and reports to determine such things became second nature to the Commando squadrons. As we have seen the first two months of the commandos experience at Aitape was consumed with reconnaissance aimed at mapping the area into which 6th Division would move. On Bougainville 2/8th Commando Squadron devoted a great deal of its time over nine months to conducting terrain surveys. The 42nd Battalion had not done this, or if it had had not passed what it knew onto the Squadron. Consequently Winning was keen for those infantry battalions nearby to understand and coordinate their activities with his Commandos. To facilitate this he met with the commanding officer and Intelligence officer of the nearby 61st Battalion, the Commanding Officer of Division Signals and the General Staff Officer of 3rd Division.[22]

On 25 January, the Squadron established its base camp at Sovele Mission, which was far out to the left flank of 7th Brigade. This gave the squadron a secure, remote and autonomous base from which it could patrol and dominate the adjacent country.[23] Australian commanders on Bougainville were very keen on taking the fight to the

---

19   AWM, AWM52 2/2/60, 2/8 Commando Squadron War Diary, 27 Nov 45, 11 Dec 45.
20   AWM, AWM52 2/2/60, 2/8 Commando Squadron War Diary, 9 Dec 45.
21   AWM, AWM52 2/2/60, 2/8 Commando Squadron War Diary, 9 Jan 45.
22   AWM, AWM52 2/2/60, 2/8 Commando Squadron War Diary, 13 Jan 45.
23   AWM, AWM52 2/2/60, 2/8 Commando Squadron War Diary January 1945, 25 Jan 45.

Japanese; it was only natural that the Commandos would mirror this desire.[24] The means the squadron chose to do this reflect how its concept of operations was notably different to that of its commando comrades elsewhere. Rather than being kept on a leash by high command as were other Commandos, 2/8th Commando Squadron was permitted to range out to strike at the enemy. This they did. One such incident occurred on 27 January when a reconnaissance patrol consisting of Troopers Don Fitzgerald, Peter Pinney and indigenous guides discovered a Japanese bivouac situated in an indigenous village. This was reported and a patrol commanded by Dunshea and ANGAU Captain Ray Watson followed up and observed the village for several hours, counting 25 Japanese. The patrol then split into two parts one commanded by Dunshea the other by Watson. At 6.50 p.m. the two patrols attacked concentrating their automatic fire onto the completely surprised Japanese, eight of whom were killed and ten wounded, with the rest fleeing into the surrounding jungle. The following day Dunshea, who had remained behind killed three more Japanese. A considerable amount of Japanese equipment, weapons, and a case containing documents and maps were found. A welcome bonus was the discovery of a large number of American cigarettes in their cartons. There were no commando casualties.[25] On 30 January, eight Japanese were killed as they slept in a well cultivated garden they had been tending.[26] On 21 March a party of Japanese were followed from a garden and ambushed when they went for a swim in a river. Four were killed and the remainder fled.[27] On 3 June 18 Japanese were killed as they slept beside huge stack of garden produce.[28] The willingness to hunt down the Japanese, and strike at them in their supposedly safe areas, was a cardinal feature of the Squadron's operational style.[29]

Winning's patrol orders reflected this aggressive spirit. In Winning's words the enemy were to be hunted down and 'annihilated'.[30] On 8 March in response to a group of Japanese crossing the Puritata River, and moving to threaten the Squadrons line of communication, Winning ordered his patrols to, 'Destroy all enemy at all cost', reinforcing this later with, 'This party must be DESTROYED', the capitals being Winnings.[31] In March in response to a young officers failure to pursue the enemy

24 Horner, *High Command Australia and Allied Strategy 1939–1945*, p. 400.
25 AWM, AWM52 2/2/60, 2/8 Commando Squadron War Diary, 27–28 Jan 45.
26 AWM, AWM52 2/2/60, 2/8 Commando Squadron War Diary, 30 Jan 45; AWM, AWM52 2/2/60, Box 58, 2/8 Commando Squadron Narrative and list of Events.
27 AWM, AWM52 2/2/60 Box 55, 2/8 Commando Squadron War Diary, 21 Mar 45.
28 AWM, AWM52 2/2/60 Box 57, 2/8 Commando Squadron War Diary, 3 June 45; UQFL, UQFL 288, Papers of Peter Pinney, Box 6.
29 Numerous reports of such ambushes can be found throughout 2/8 Commandos War Diary, see: AWM, AWM52, 2/2/60.
30 AWM, AWM52 2/2/60 Box 55, 2/8 Commando Squadron War Diary, 18–19 Feb 45, 22 Feb 45; AWM, AWM52 2/2/60 Box 55, 2/8 Commando Squadron War Diary February 1945, Appendices, Winning to Lt. Col. Farger 3 Div Sigs 12 Feb 45.
31 AWM, AWM52 2/2/60 Box 55, 2/8 Commando Squadron War Diary, 8 Mar 45, AWM52, 2/2/60, Box 55; 2/8 Commando Squadron War Diary, 8 Mar 45, SAINT to TIGER.

with sufficient zeal he wrote, 'On such a pursuit ones camping sites must go hang.... At such time better had he had taken rations off the 'whingers' and weaklings and travelled hot foot with patrol reduced in size but better integrity.[32] The intention to carrying out these sanguine tasks was often expressed informally. One such case, for example, was an exchange between Squadron headquarters and 7 Section when 7 Section requested permission to 'do' a group of enemy. Squadron headquarters replied with, 'O.K. – have a smack'.[33] At another time the order to one patrol was simply, 'find and kill them'.[34]

Winning was in no doubt what the role of his Squadron should be. In February he prepared a provisional time table of Squadron operations in which one of his objectives was to inflict as many casualties as possible.[35] During the same month he also wanted Infantry battalions to assume responsibility for the areas which had been allocated to the squadron, so that his troops would be free to extend their ability to hunt and harass the Japanese more effectively.[36] In March he wrote to Captain MacMichael, the General Staff Officer III Intelligence 3rd Division, asking that his squadron be allowed to, 'spread our gospel and throw him [the Japanese] into confusion'.[37] The squadron's officers were of the same opinion with Dunshea instructing one patrol after an ambush in February to continue to 'institute further bastardry' on the Japanese.[38]

Ambushing was a brutal business. Peter Pinney recalled ambushing two Japanese. He had been out on patrol with Dunshea and eight others, five of who were indigenous guides. Pinney had hidden, a camouflage net over his face, and screened by light foliage. Two Japanese came walking slowly down a grassy path. The first Japanese was wearing a khaki uniform with a dark blue waistcoat. The Japanese stopped and raised his rifle, about to shoot one of the guides when Pinney shot him, the bullet passing through his breast and exiting out to smash his left arm at the elbow. Pinney, who was next to Dunshea, turned and said, 'got the bastard' and with that drew an X with spittle on a sapling. The other Japanese turned and ran but was shot in the legs by an Owen Gun blast and dropped to the ground. The wounded Japanese soldier lay there groaning as the commandos came over to him. He was a small man, his uniform ragged, but he himself was in generally fair condition. Dunshea attempted

32   AWM, AWM 52 2/2/60 Box 55, 2/8 Commando Squadron War Diary, Appendices, Patrol Report 9–12 March, Winnings hand written comments on the report dated 18 March.
33   AWM, AWM52 2/2/60 Box 57, 2/8 Commando Squadron War Diary, 8 Jun 45.
34   AWM, AWM52 2/2/60 Box 57, 2/8 Commando Squadron War Diary, 10 Jun 45.
35   AWM, AWM52 2/2/60 Box 55, 2/8 Commando Squadron War Diary February 1945, Appendix G to WD Provisional Time Table Feb 45.
36   AWM, 2/8 Commando Squadron War Diary February 1945 Appendices, 12–13 Feb, AWM52, 2/2/60.
37   AWM, AWM52 2/2/60 Box 55, 3 Aust Div 23 March 1945, 2/8 Commando Squadron War Diary March 1945, Adv HQ 2/8 Aust Cdo Sqn to Capt. MacMichael.
38   AWM, AWM52 2/2/60, 2/8 Commando Squadron War Diary February 1945 Appendices, Dunshea to Winning 18 Feb.

to get information out of him, but to no avail. There was a suggestion to take the wounded Japanese soldier prisoner, but he was near death and moving him would have been pointless. Pinney, without remorse, 'put a bullet in his brain'. Such was the merciless nature of the war in the jungle.[39] In a reprise of the attitude to killing the enemy exhibited by earlier Independent Companies the killing of Japanese was undertaken without any hint of sentimentality. It was seen as 'claiming scalps' and something to be celebrated.[40] In response to a patrol ambushing and killing eighteen Japanese, Winning wrote, 'Good show yesterday. That bumps up A Tp and puts Sqn well over the century. Keep it up'.[41] It was not just the Commandos who celebrated the Commandos killing of enemy troops. On 8 June Lieutenant Colonel Francis Hassett, the General Staff Officer Grade I of 3rd Division wrote to Winning, 'Your recent bag of 44 in one day was quite a highlight. We are looking forward to similar successes in the future'.[42]

A significant factor in the operational style of 2/8th Commando Squadron was the teaming of its aggressive spirit with an astute understanding of the physical environment in which it was operating. As has been pointed out, within the ranks of the squadron there were many Independent Company veterans. These brought with them the physical toughness, experience and jungle skills from their former service. It was the influence of these veteran Independent Company members which fundamentally characterised the manner in which the Squadron embarked on its war against the Japanese. In February a special scout group was formed within the squadron.[43] This group was made up of members who could speak pidgin fluently, who understood and could manage indigenous people, and who were expert Bushmen. The scout group answered directly to Winning, and came under the immediate command of Dunshea. The task of the scouts was to go out ahead of patrols in pairs, reconnoitre the terrain, find the enemy and report their position and number to the patrols. The patrols would then close in for the kill. Scouts were considered to be invaluable for finding tracks and providing information about topography as well as finding enemy positions.[44] The scout group also provided a direct link to the indigenous population which offered a source of information that was otherwise difficult to obtain or simply unavailable.[45]

39 UQFL, UQFL288, Papers of Peter Pinney Box 13, Diary entry 24 December 1944.
40 AWM, AWM52, 2/2/60 Box 55, 2/8 Commando Squadron War Diary, 23–25 Feb 45. The actual quote for 23 Feb mentions hunting Japanese and 'claiming scalps' and for 25 Feb states, 'moved out in hope of claiming 2 further scalps'.
41 AWM, AWM52 2/2/60 Box 55, Patrol Report 9–12 March, 2/8 Commando Squadron War Diary April 1945 Appendices.
42 AWM, AWM52 2/2/60 Box 57, 2/8 Commando Squadron War Diary June 1945, Appendices (2), F.G. Hassett to Maj. N. Winning OC Raffles Force 8 Jun 45.
43 AWM, AWM52, 2/2/60, 2/8 Commando Squadron War Diary, 9 Feb 45.
44 AWM, AWM52 2/2/60 Box 55, 2/8 Commando Squadron War Diary March 1945, Appendices.
45 AWM, AWM52, 2/2/60, 2/8 Commando Squadron War Diary, 17 Feb 45.

The technique used by 2/8th Squadron to find and destroy the enemy was both innovative and effective. It was recognised that stealth was just as important as offensive action. A 10 day reconnaissance patrol sent out 23 June – 2 July 1945 was given special instructions that it was to 'NOT' [the capitals were in the order] to allow the enemy to be aware of their presence in the area.[46] In April, following an ambush when four Japanese were killed, the bodies were buried and all traces of the ambush removed, the object being for the patrol to 'remain invisible in the jungle'.[47] So attuned to the need for silence were the commandos that even the muffled sound of a signaller generator in its deep dugout caused concern.[48] Searching silently for the enemy was a fundamental technique. Main tracks were not used, instead 'kanaka' (indigenous) tracks were used, or troops would break bush, which was to move through virgin jungle.[49] So as to leave no recognisable prints the scout group, often wearing only socks or greenhide sneakers made from soft raw leather excelled at stealthy movement through the jungle.[50] Demonstrating this ability was one incident when the Japanese came within two metres of Trooper Jack Guerin without seeing him.[51] Any confirmed report of enemy movement including from indigenous people would be responded to by despatching a fighting patrol. For example a 6 April a report from indigenous people that 10 Japanese carrying bags of garden produce had been spotted resulted in the immediate despatch of fighting patrol to intercept them.[52] Such tactics reflected the ability of the Commandos on Bougainville to adapt intelligently, quickly, and effectively to the challenges they faced.

It is worthwhile to compare the Bougainville Commandos with the Commandos at Aitape-Wewak. Unlike any of the other Australian Commando Squadrons during 1944–1945 both groups saw nine months of active service against the Japanese. The manner in which each group of Commandos did so helps to illustrate the radical difference between the two operating styles. Unlike the Aitape-Wewak Commandos who spent a significant amount of time in camp and subsequently out of action

---

46   AWM, AWM52 2/2/60 Box 57, 2/8 Commando Squadron War Diary June 1945, Appendices (2), 2/8 Aust Cdo Sqn Patrol Instr No.11, 2 June 45; RAFFLES FORCE Patrol Instr No.2, 3 Jun 45.
47   AWM, AWM52 2/2/60, 2/8 Commando Squadron War Diary April 1945, Appendix K, Contact Report Panakai Area 23 April 45.
48   Astill, *Commando White Diamond*, p. 87.
49   AWM, AWM 3 DRL 2529 Item 78, Savige, Stanley George, Papers: Bougainville 2 Corps Report on Operations 2/8 Commando Sqn Nov 1944–August 1945, p. 30.
50   AWM, AWM52 2/2/60 Box 55, 2/8 Commando Squadron War Diary, 29 Apr 45; AWM, AWM52 2/2/60 Box 55, 2/8 Commando Squadron War Diary, April 1945, Patrol Report FALCON 30 Apr 45; AWM, AWM 3 DRL 2529 Item 78, Savige, Stanley George, Papers: Bougainville 2 Corps Report on Operations 2/8 Commando Sqn Nov 1944–August 1945, p. 30.
51   AWM, AWM52 2/2/60 Box 58, 2/8 Commando Squadron War Diary August 1945 Appendices, *Sydney Sun* and *Guardian* 24 June 1945.
52   AWM, AWM52 2/2/60 Box 55, 2/8 Commando Squadron War Diary, 6 Apr 45.

"Spreading our Gospel" – The Commandos on Bougainville 233

2/8th Commando Squadron were operationally active throughout their nine month campaign on Bougainville. Constant pressure was maintained on the Japanese by regularly raiding their rear 'safe' areas. The impact of these tactics resulted in Japanese troops concentrating their numbers so as to frustrate ambush tactics, shifting their bivouacs every two or three days, and halting vehicles often to scout ahead. They also began using streams rather than tracks so as not to leave tracks, frequently opening fire for no apparent reason and shooting indiscriminately into the surrounding area. In a further mark of their apprehension they cleared back the jungle from important communication routes, and ceased to use one of the major tracks completely.[53] In a somewhat amusing cameo the Japanese acknowledged that they were fully aware of the impact the tactics of 2/8th Commando Squadron was having on them. Later in the campaign a Japanese force managed to insert itself along 3rd Division's line of communication and conduct ambushes. The Japanese Colonel in command of the force took the trouble to write a note to Winning, in which he thanked Winning for the lesson in how to conduct guerrilla raids Winning had given him when Winning's troops were successfully raiding the Japanese line of communication.[54]

The relationship between the commandos on Bougainville and their higher formations was another element of divergence between them and the Aitape-Wewak commandos. The crucial difference related to the organisational placement of the commandos within the administrative framework of their relative forces. The three commando Squadrons under 6th Division's command at Aitape-Wewak were managed as a group entity, under the command of 2/6th Cavalry Commando Regiment. As such their individual actions were dictated by the requirements of the Regiment, which itself was responding to instructions it had received from Division. The method of management of 2/8th Commando Squadron was notably different. There was no regimental organisation controlling the squadron and although it was still responsible to complying with operational instruction from a higher authority it was autonomous in every other regard, entirely responsible for maintaining and administering itself. As an individual unit it was responsible for communicating directly with higher formations be it Brigade, Division and at times Corps. Winning frequently wrote or spoke directly with each. For example in two letters he wrote to 3rd Division, one of which was 19 pages long, he offered his detailed advice on future deployment of the Division.[55] That a mere Squadron commander presumed he could

---

53 AWM, AWM52 2/2/60 Box 58, 2/8 Commando Squadron 1945 Raffles Force Messages, Stuart to Raffles 25 July 45, Raffles Force to 3 Div 29 July 45; AWM, AWM52 2/2/60 Box 55, 2/8 Commando Squadron War Diary, 4 Apr 45; AWM, AWM52 2/2/60 Box 56, 2/8 Commando Squadron War Diary, 7 May 45; Astill, *Commando White Diamond*, p. 67.
54 UQFL, UQFL288, Papers of Peter Pinney Box 8, 'A week has passed', 6 September 1945.
55 AWM, AWM52, BOX 55, 2/2/60, 2/8 Commando Squadron War Diary February 1945, Winning to G.O.C 3 AUST DIV 1 Feb 1945; AWM, AWM52, BOX 55, 2/2/60, 2/8 Commando Squadron War Diary March 1945, Adv HQ 2/8 Aust Cdo Sqn to Capt. MacMichael 3 Aust Div 23 March 1945.

advise a Division on how it should deploy indicates remarkable self-assurance, as well as the existence of a special relationship between Winning and those he corresponded with. No doubt his communications irritated some staff officers, but he nonetheless continued to write and was well received by those he addressed his correspondence to. Indeed the amount of communication generated by 2/8th Commando Squadron was extraordinary. In the month of May 1945 71,000 radio messages were passed between the Squadron Head Quarters and other formations, including to and from its own patrols. During the week ending 3 June 1945 19,369 radio groups were passed.[56]

Independent operations were sometimes forced onto the Squadron because higher authority chose to ignore the Squadron, and failed to issue it clear directions. Such was the case on 3 April 1945 when the squadron complained that it had not been visited by a liaison officer from the Brigade to which it was technically attached at that time since 21 March. Because of this the squadron's operational activities had been left entirely up to Winning. It was also noted that when a Brigade liaison officer did appear, after three weeks, that officer was ill informed and unable to tell the Squadron anything useful.[57] In such circumstances all operational and tactical decisions were made by Winning with no reference to any other formation. In this respect the Squadron's Independent Company heritage put it in good stead.

It was in fact the intention of 3rd Division and 2nd Corps, which had overall authority on Bougainville, to allow the Squadron considerable independence and autonomy. Instrumental in this recognition of the value of autonomous unconventional operations was that the Commander of 2nd Corps was Lieutenant General Stanley Savige. As we have seen previously Savige's appreciation of the unconventional attributes of his Commandos, which he described as special and peculiar, was finely honed.[58] This was confirmed on 23 May 1945 when 3rd Division established 'Raffles Force'. Raffles Force consisted of 2/8th Commando Squadron, elements of ANGAU, and one company of the Papuan Infantry Battalion, all under the command of 2/8th Commando Squadron. It was the task of Raffles Force to obtain information on enemy movements, strengths dispositions and topographical material. Importantly and reflective of the intention to use unconventional forces aggressively, it was also to harass the enemy constantly by raids and ambushes.[59] The autonomy given to Raffles Force was absolute, provided it operated within the geographic boundaries set for it and complied with operational instructions issued by the Division. To assist Raffles Force range out further to strike at the enemy it was informed that it no longer

---

56 AWM, AWM52 2/2/60, Box 57, 2/8 Commando Squadron War Diary, 10 Jun 45.
57 AWM, AWM52 2/2/60 Box 55, 2/8 Commando Squadron War Diary, 3 Apr 45.
58 AWM, AWM54 613/4/15, 2 Australian Corps Operations Instructions Nos 1 to 20 – Bougainville 1944 to 1945.
59 AWM, AWM52 2/2/60 Box 56, 2/8 Commando Squadron War Diary May 1945 Appendices, 3 Aust Div OP Instr No.36, 23 May 45.

had to operate within the range of supporting artillery.[60] It was exactly the form of warfare favoured by the Squadron and characterised by Winning when he wrote 'We're Monkeys. We shin up and down lengths of Kunda, swing on the ends by our tails and scream derision, we're good'.[61] Such a regime was entirely different to the restrictions imposed on the Aitape-Wewak commandos. This autonomy would not, however, come without causing some aggravation to regular units. The range over which Raffles Force patrols were permitted to operate caused some concern for 3rd Division, which found its freedom to deliver artillery in support of Infantry Brigades curtailed because commando patrols would frequently be found to be in the target areas. The problem was solved by direct negotiation between 3rd Division and Raffles Force, which in itself underscored the autonomy of Raffles Force.[62] Winning managed Raffles Force until the end of July when it was wound up. Both the access to higher formations enjoyed by Raffles Force and hence 2/8th Commando Squadron, and the broad operational autonomy granted it was a unique feature and never replicated by any other Australian Army Commando formation during the period 1944–1945.

It was certainly easier for commandos to strike out at the enemy than for the regular formations encumbered by logistics, motor transport and all the multifarious ephemera of conventional war. Commandos were supplied by air, and their logistical needs were much less than a regular formation. Poor weather did however adversely affect the ability of the commandos to carry out their tasks, but only indirectly. Active operations of the squadron were delayed when poor weather prevented regular formations to position themselves within supporting range of the Squadron. Torrential rain, which fell throughout July 1945 made it impossible for the Army's supply train of three ton trucks to negotiate the unsealed roads which constituted its main line of communication.[63] This slowed the rate of advance of the regular battalions. The Squadron operated out on the flank of these regular battalions and it was important that communication was maintained with those battalions. Any delay in the ability of those battalions to push forward forced the Squadron to comply with the battalion's movement and thus retarded its ability to continually push forward against the Japanese. This was particularly the case with the 61st Battalion which was posted to the immediate flank of the Squadron. The Battalion's slowness to move, caused by a

60 AWM, AWM52 2/2/60, Box 56, 2/8 Commando Squadron War Diary, 2 May 45, 25 May 45.
61 AWM, AWM52 2/2/60, Box 58, 2/8 Commando Squadron War Diary August 1945 Appendices Box 58, Winning to Stephens, 5 July 1945.
62 AWM, AWM52 2/2/60 Box 58, 2/8 Commando War Diary June 1945 Appendices; AWM, AWM52 2/2/60 Box 57, 2/8 Commando War Diary August 1945; AWM, AWM52 2/2/60 Box 57, 2/8 Commando War Diary August 1945, includes Messages with entries related the issue of commando patrols and artillery support for infantry formations.
63 AWM, AWM52 2/2/60, 2/8 Commando Squadron War Diary, 24 July 45; Gailey, Harry, *Bougainville 1943–1945 – The Forgotten Campaign* (University of Kentucky Press: Lexington, 1991), pp. 202 and 209.

multitude of factors mentioned later in this chapter, delayed the Squadrons plans to advance by ten days in January-February 1945. If the squadron had advanced it would have opened up a gap between it and its flank Battalion and created an open area on the flank of 3rd Division.

Despite this the Commandos continued to range out independently to seek and harass their enemy. This was acknowledged by the Division which congratulated Winning on the Squadron's 'splendid' patrolling in the enemy rear acknowledging that the Squadrons actions had materially assisted the Division's operations.[64] On 8 April Winning discussed the Squadrons future with Divisional Staff, the consequences of which were that the Division acknowledged the Squadron's primary role was one of reconnaissance and harassment of the enemy.[65] This demonstrated that 3rd Division had arrived at an astute appreciation of how to exploit the unconventional attributes of the Squadron and that by employing it in such a way could add value to its overall operations.

As with all Commandos a major role for 2/8th Commando Squadron was topographical surveys and reports. Many such reports were voluminous and covered every aspect of the terrain examined. Division appreciated the reconnaissance asset they had in the commandos, and how information so gleaned could support operations. For example on 8 June 1945 the Squadron was instructed to send out patrols to do a topographical survey of a specific area, so as to determine the feasibility of conducting local outflanking moves against the enemy.[66] The attention to detail in the reports reflects the care and skill with which the Squadron undertook this task. An extract from one such report from June 1945 included items related to river banks, river bottoms, track quality, vegetation, and possible vehicular access.[67] Topographical reports had priority, even over fighting patrols. For example, an instruction was issued to Dunshea that he was not allowed to attack the enemy until after his reconnaissance mission had been completed.[68] Such patrols in fact had a direct influence on the planning made at Divisional level. The Operation Order issued by 3rd Division on 15 May 1945 included topographical information which those in the Squadron noted was 'almost a reproduction' of the information supplied to the Division by the Squadron.[69] In April 3rd Division complimented the Squadron for the 'most valuable' patrol work it

64 AWM, AWM52 2/2/60 Box 57, 3 Div to RAFFLES, 30 June 1945, 2/8 Commando Squadron Diary June 1945 Appendices.
65 AWM, AWM 3 DRL 2529 Item 78, Savige, Stanley George, Papers: Bougainville 2 Corps Report on Operations 2/8 Commando Sqn Nov 1944–August 1945, p.17.
66 AWM, AWM52 2/2/60 Box 57, 2/8 Commando Squadron War Diary June 1945, Appendices (2), F.G. Hassett to Maj. N. Winning OC Raffles Force, 8 Jun 45.
67 AWM, AWM52 2/2/60 Box 57, 2/8 Commando Squadron War Diary June 1945, Appendices, Raffles Force to 3 Div, 29 Jun 45.
68 AWM, AWM52 2/2/60 2/8 Commando Squadron War Diary April 1945 Appendices, Patrol instructions issued by 2/8 Sqn to Captain C.J.P. Dunshea OC EAGLE, 20 April 45.
69 AWM, AWM52 2/2/60, Box 56, 2/8 Commando Squadron War Diary May 1945, 15 May 45.

had been doing.[70] Such patrols continued throughout the whole nine months of the Bougainville campaign.

In nine months of operations on Bougainville 2/8th Commando Squadron killed 282 Japanese with a possible 30 more.[71] The peak month was June 1945 in which sixty four were killed including on one day, 3 June, when in three separate engagements forty six were killed.[72] In almost every case these enemy casualties were as a result of guerrilla raid or ambush, unlike the experience of the Commandos at Aitape-Wewak whose aggregate enemy casualties scores were similar to those of 2/8th Commando Squadron, but where many of their enemy were killed in conventional battle.

One common feature for both the Aitape-Wewak and Bougainville Commando campaigns was the firepower that could be generated by Commando patrols. Commandos had always made use of automatic weapons. During 1942 and the first half of 1943 the Thompson sub-machinegun, the Tommy gun, was the favoured weapon. These weapons feature in many accounts of actions, for example in accounts of the Salamaua Raid.[73] Ron Garland's broadsides of automatic fire at Ambush Knoll, was another example of the Commandos employment of the Tommy gun to deliver concentrated firepower. The weight of such firepower can be gleaned from the extraordinary expenditure of ammunition during the battle of Ambush Knoll. During this three day period some 16,050 sub-machine gun rounds were fired. In comparison for the seven days following the battle 4764 sub-machinegun rounds were fired.[74] Automatic weapons being used by Australian commandos are mentioned in Japanese accounts. Japanese soldiers were warned not to move individually and to move in columns when on roads to avoid guerrilla attack and taking heavy casualties to enemy automatic fire.[75] The Japanese were reluctant to engage the commandos because of their firepower, with one Japanese soldier admitting that the, 'men in the long gaiters and green berets' had been allowed to walk through Japanese ambushes because the Japanese had been afraid to open fire due to the 'terrific' fire power the commandos possessed.[76] For the Commandos in 1944–1945 the average strength

---

70   AWM, AWM52 2/2/60, 3 Div to 2/8 Cdo Sqn, 26 April 45, 2/8 Commando Squadron War Diary April 1945.
71   AWM, AWM52 2/2/60 Box 58, 2/8 Commando Squadron War Diary August 1945 Appendices.
72   AWM, AWM52 2/2/60 Box 57, 2/8 Commando Squadron War Diary June 1945, Message Raffles Force to 3 Division, 3 June 1945.
73   Mal Bishop, interviewed by Dr. Peter Williams, 26 June 2004.
74   AWM, AWM 54 587/7/12 Part 2, Report on Operations of 3 Australian Division in Salamaua Area from 22 April 1943 to 23 August 1943.
75   AWM, AMW55 1/1, Allied Translator and Interpreter Section, South West Pacific Area Bulletins 1942–1943, Bulletin 2915, Item 13, 2915; AWM, AMW55 1/4, Allied Translator and Interpreter Section, South West Pacific Area Bulletins 8 August – 14 September 1943, Bulletin 288 17 Aug 43 Item 1, 3098.
76   UQFL, UQFL288, Papers of Peter Pinney Box 8, 'Letters to Mother, 3 June 1945' and 'Well it looks as if I have made a blue'.

for a fighting patrol was one Section armed with two Bren guns, no more than two rifles and the balance being Owen guns.[77] This gave Commando patrols a significant weight of automatic fire. In the Wewak Sauri village operation of the 160 commandos of 2/7th Commando Squadron there were only eight rifles, all of which were fitted with grenade launchers. All other weapons were either Owen or Bren guns.[78] It was acknowledged that the Owen gun gave the Commandos an advantage over the Japanese who lacked such weapons.[79] The Owen gun at close range was devastating. Pinney recalled one ambush when, 'in about 2 seconds at least a dozen nips were shot to pieces in a withering blast of fire'. It may also have been that dum-dum bullets were used, as Pinney Mentions using these during this engagement.[80] David Dexter's ambush on the Ramu River related at the beginning of this history is another example of the devastating impact of the Owen gun. Overwhelming firepower was a consistent feature of commando operations during all their campaigns of 1944–1945.

A fundamental feature of Commando operations was the relationship Commandos established with their operational environment, both physical and human. An intimate knowledge of the terrain was a prerequisite for the management of commando operations. Equally the management of the human environment, both within units, and among the indigenous population ensured both productivity and efficiency.

Of great importance to the Squadron was its ability to understand and manage the human environment it operated within. The human environment had two aspects, Squadron personnel and the indigenous population. Maintaining a stable working relationship within the Squadron was essential to ensure that the Squadron would function efficiently and effectively. Maintaining a working relationship with the indigenous population ensured the safety of the Squadron, the ability to collect valuable and timely intelligence, and the availability of carriers and labour when necessary, which was essential to maintaining a force in the field.

There was never at any time any concern for the morale or resilience of commandos during 1944–1945. Commandos were not immune to the onset of poor morale. Lack of food, poor management and frustration at not being employed effectively had all contributed to damaging the morale of Independent Companies and Commandos at one time or the other. Commandos, however, possessed a buffer against poor morale having any lasting effect on their capacity to engage in operations. This was the mystique, if one can use the word, of the 'Commando' persona. The self-esteem of being a Commando provided a buffer against the vagaries and fluctuations of morale. A survey of the various Commando unit histories reveals

---

77   AWM, AWM 3 DRL 2529 Item 78, Savige, Stanley George, Papers: Bougainville 2 Corps Report on Operations 2/8 Commando Sqn Nov 1944–August 1945, p. 31.
78   Bottrell, *Cameos of Commandos*, p. 257.
79   AWM, AWM52 2/2/60 Box 58, 2/8 Commando War Diary August 1945 Appendices, *Sydney Sun and Guardian* 24 June 1945.
80   UQFL, UQFL288, Papers of Peter Pinney Box 11, 'With the 2/8th Independent Company Bougainville November 44–November 45, 27-5-45.

numerous references to the special qualities inherent amongst those who made up the Squadrons. Chaplain to the Commandos Arthur Bottrell explained the relationship between personnel with the squadrons, describing it as reciprocal with each man intimately associated with his peers. It was a tight community in which each man was prepared and ready to fight both for himself and to support his peers.[81] A fundamental attribute of the Commandos was an intimate knowledge and understanding between members of the unit. An example of this was when Winning sent a message to Jaguar Patrol, under the command of Lieutenant Keith Stephens. It was written in such a way that if it fell into enemy hands they would have been unable to make sense out of it, but Stephens knowing the way Winning's mind worked would have had no trouble. Winning called this his 'Secret Sensible Nonsense' and it went like this,

> Message Saint to Steve Jaguar 8 May 45 0587 Secret sensible nonsense. Hunch and ops haywire. Have your GG --- Young. Waste not want not return your fodder by line. All JB till noon. Bash highway anytime. Collect spoils and come home to mum. JB bully beef may vamoose by hungry Xing. Balls to his Winklestein. If Kanda and MUDA would call to accept my hospitality they are cordially welcome. Don't go south darling.[82]

That such a message could be sent, with the expectation that the receiver would be able to understand the hidden meaning within what was essentially a litany of gibberish indicates just how well both the sender and the receiver understood each other. Any unit in which the bond between its commander and those he commanded was so strong was fortunate indeed. A further example of the affinity that existed between the members of 2/8th Commando Squadron can be found in a war dairy entry of 1 April, which given the date explains it to a degree. Writing as if it is an instruction from Winning, who spoke with a pronounced Scottish accent, the entry went, 'Gie ye ma forrw'd dispositions?!! Ah'm --- if a will!' That the writer could have fun at the officer in command's expense, and that the entry which had to be read and signed off by Winning, would be allowed to remain in the dairy indicates the depth of good natured mutual respect and understanding that existed. No such frivolity appears in any of the official documentation connected with any other Commando Squadron.

One factor, which set the commandos apart from the infantry of some of the battalions, was their resilience. From the evidence it appears that the combat effectiveness of some infantry units in the jungle environment wore down quickly. Gavin Keating in his book *A Tale of Three Battalions* argues that this was certainly the case on

---

81   Bottrell, *Cameos of Commandos*, p. 251.
82   AWM, AWM52 2/2/60 Box 56, 2/8 Commando Squadron War Diary May 1945, Appendices (5).

Bougainville.[83] He identified a number of factors which contributed to these failings, these being a lack of experienced Non Commissioned Officers, the difficult terrain encountered, the nature of the warfare faced with unseen enemy firing from only a few metres away and extended periods spent without relief. Of the battalions with which 2/8th Commando Squadron had close contact, 61st Battalion in particular exhibited behaviour which seriously affected its combat ability. Within 61st Battalion, there were incidences of combat refusal by individuals and whole sub-sections of the battalion. Officers failed to provide leadership, with many pleading for transfer back to Australia. The situation in combat for the battalion was no better with troops retreating in disorder from engagements with the enemy. Patrols avoided their duties by sitting in the jungle and not moving. The battalion's tactical preparation was also poor. In February a patrol of 2/8th Commando Squadron entered the perimeter of 61st Battalion using an unguarded track. When the local 61st Battalion Company commander was informed of the track he 'cheerfully' replied that another nearby track was covered. The patrol simply shrugged and decided 'Who are we to argue'.[84] Such was the state of the battalion that its own commanding officer wrote that it was, 'incapable of moving forward'.[85] All this indicated a serious collapse of morale, fighting spirit and lack of command competence within the Battalion. The 61st Battalion was a militia battalion which had fought efficiently at Milne Bay in August 1942, but had seen no further action until Bougainville more than two years later. On Bougainville a combination of losses from disease, casualties, combat fatigue, and poor leadership led to a state of poor morale. While the case of 61st Battalion was certainly not indicative of all the infantry battalions on Bougainville, some of who were very good battalions indeed, it was the battalion with which the Squadron was expected to work with.

The Commandos on Bougainville, nor in any other theatre of operations during 1944–1945, did not suffer this reduction in effectiveness. This was despite their facing exactly the same physical conditions as the infantry, the same combat environment and in the case of the Bougainville Commandos seldom being granted leave. Whilst individual Commandos no doubt enjoyed being relieved from front line duty, too much leave was considered by the 2/8th Commando Squadron to hamper its ability to conduct operations. When 3rd Division instituted a compulsory period of two weeks leave for shifts of 20 personnel from the Squadron to go to Torokina and rest the squadron resisted the move considering that the reduction in numbers would hamper its ability to give 'the Nip some curry'.[86] There is no record of any pressure from within the Squadron to take the leave Division was insisting on, indeed much the opposite,

---

83 Gavin Keating, 'A Tale of Three Battalions Combat morale and battle fatigue in the 7th Australian Infantry Brigade', Bougainville, 1944–1945, *Warfare Studies Centre*, Canberra, 2007, p. 28.
84 AWM, AWM52 2/2/60, 2/8 Commando Squadron War Diary February 1945, 26 Feb 45.
85 Keating, 'A Tale of Three Battalions', p. 28.
86 AWM, AWM52 2/2/60 Box 57, 2/8 Commando War Diary June 1945, 8 Jun 45.

"Spreading our Gospel" – The Commandos on Bougainville 241

with one Commando writing proudly how commandos remained at the front without a break while infantry worked in forty two day shifts.[87]

It is apparent that in the case of Bougainville Commandos were certainly more resilient than some standard infantry in the same jungle environment. There were several reasons for this. The first was the quality of the leadership, which especially in 2/8th Commando Squadron at officer and Non Commissioned Officer level was in most cases highly experienced, capable, empathetic and stable; an important factor in small unit warfare. Battalions did not always have this advantage. The second reason was the nature of the tasks carried out by the commandos. These consisted of independent reconnaissance, raids and ambushes planned and conducted by the unit, the success or failure of which ascribed to the unit collective and no outside force. Such independent operations, especially when successful as they often were, could only build confidence and resilience in those conducting them and add to the self-esteem of the unit as a whole. It was thought that the Commandos in fact had an easier job than the regular infantry because of the Commandos mobility and ability to conceal themselves from the enemy.[88] Battalion infantry could not hope to achieve such a degree of independence or self-reliance. A third reason was the personal character of a significant number of those 2/8th Commando Squadron's ranks. These were veterans of the Independent Companies, long experienced in small unit jungle warfare and inured to the isolation, hardships, frustration, brutality and very individual nature of such warfare. They were men who had originally volunteered because they were attracted to the opportunity to operate in an independent and self-reliant manner and subsequently possessed an inherent sense of self assurance and resilience. Very few members of the infantry Battalions would have enjoyed such a legacy. A forth reason, was the strength of personal relationships, easy to achieve in small units. Max Luff in his diary gives some indication of the bond which existed between the commandos of 2/10th Squadron when towards the end of the war he wrote:

> One never realises the attachments or rather the strength of Comrade attachments until it is time to sever one; as you (crossed out – indecipherable) look back over all you've been through together it seems as though you've been sharing; eating, sleeping, fighting, dying, fear & laughter with these people for 6,000 years just as if there has been nothing else to do in this big wide world, but just that. Then as suddenly as it all began; it terminates! (indecipherable – crossed out) leaving one with the feeling of having a limb or other very important part of the body severed & as you walk away from them, all the time a voice seems to be screaming at you to stop & go back to them.[89]

87 UQFL, UQFL288, Papers of Peter Pinney Box 8, 'Letter to Mother, 29 August 1945', 'A week has passed'.
88 Ibid.
89 George MacAfie Diary, 10 August 1945.

Throughout 1944–45 the morale and resilience of the Australian Commandos Squadrons was never in question. This was not unsurprising considering the character of the Squadrons, the relative material and logistical superiority enjoyed by Australian troops at the time, and that the enemy despite incongruously persisting in their resistance, was known to have been well and truly defeated.

The role played by indigenous people and the relationship established between them and Australian Forces during the campaigns in New Guinea and Bougainville was of fundamental importance. A cooperative indigenous population made the conduct of operations vastly more efficient and effective, while an uncooperative indigenous population would result in the opposite effect. The Commandos at Aitape-Wewak and Bougainville both inevitably had contact with the indigenous populations of those places, yet their capacity to work effectively with indigenous people was not at all the same.

The first item on the 1st Army Operation Instruction of 17 October 1944 to 2/6th Cavalry Commando Regiment, as it embarked for Aitape, was to support and assist ANGAU patrols. This was a direct order to work with ANGAU and thus the indigenous population.[90] Despite this the war diaries of 2/7th, 2/9th and 2/10th Commando Squadrons mention indigenous contact infrequently. The war diary of 2/7th Commando Squadron mentions 'indigenous reports' in December 1944, and 'indigenous patrols' in July 1945, but there is no other reference to indigenous people. The war diary of 2/9th Commando Squadron makes no mention of indigenous people until July 1945, when 'indigenous patrols' are referred to.[91] The War Diary of 2/10th squadron is more forthcoming, noting in February 1945 that 'Indigenous support and information on enemy movements and providing guides invaluable'.[92] In March 1945 the Squadron comments on the antipathy felt by indigenous people towards ANGAU. Later in the month the squadron pays a compliment to the indigenous guides on the reliability of their information and warnings to patrols of enemy ambushes.[93] The squadron indirectly acknowledges indigenous people when it mentions that ANGAU took over patrolling in their area in July.[94] The war diary of 2/6th Cavalry Commando Regiment mentions ANGAU's Cole Force in October 1944.[95] 'Cole Force' was an ANGUA patrol, named after its commander Captain Robert Cole, and came under

---

90   AWM, AWM 52/2/51 Box 41, 2/6 Cavalry Commando Regiment War Diary Appendices, October to December 1944, First Aust Army Operation Instruction No.48 to CO 2/6 Aust Cav (Commando) Regt 17 Oct 44.
91   AWM, AWM52, 2/2/61, 2/9 Commando Squadron War Diary, November 1944 to August 1945.
92   AWM, AWM52, 2/2/62, 2/10 Commando Squadron War Diary, February 1945.
93   AWM, AWM52, 2/2/62, 2/10 Commando Squadron War Diary, March 1945.
94   AWM, AWM52 2/2/62, 2/10 Commando Squadron War Diary, July 1945.
95   AWM, AWM 52/2/51 Box 41, 2/6 Cavalry Commando Regiment War Diary Appendices, October to December 1944, First Aust Army Operation Instruction No.48 to CO 2/6 Aust Cav (Commando) Regt 17 Oct 44.

"Spreading our Gospel" – The Commandos on Bougainville 243

the command of 2/10th Commando Squadron. Cole Force consisted of two officers, one soldier, two US Signallers, 18 indigenous police and 60 indigenous carriers. The association of the Squadron with Cole Force did comply with the instructions for the Commandos to establish a direct link between the Commandos and ANGAU.[96] Just what the association did achieve, is however questionable, as the war diary of the Squadron makes very little mention of Cole Force and apart from one patrol by Cole Force in which some members of the Squadron participated there seems to have been very little interaction.

The lack of interaction between the Aitape-Wewak Commandos and indigenous people did cause some concern. Chaplain Bottrell recalls that the lack of indigenous guides accompanying Commando patrols made it difficult to 'smell out' Japanese, with the result that enemy ambushes were often not detected.[97] It appears that the relationship between the Commandos of 2/6th Cavalry Commando Regiment and indigenous people was restricted at best. The situation with 2/8th Commando Squadron was vastly different.

On 12 February 1945, 2/8th Commando Squadron formed an indigenous scout group to operate as part of the squadron.[98] Armed with Japanese weapons these scouts would perform the same tasks as the Commando scouts. That such a group would be formed indicates the trust and rapport the squadron had established with the local indigenous people. A main player in the establishment of a working relationship with the indigenous population was Captain Ray Watson of ANGAU, who worked side by side with Winning. That Watson an ANGAU officer held equal prominence within the Squadron with Winning, at least in relation to the administration of indigenous people, says much for the squadron's appreciation of the human environment in which they were operating. Watson's task was to ensure that the indigenous people who came into contact with the squadron were managed in a manner which both ensured their wellbeing and maintained their contribution to the Australian war effort. Watson was directly responsible for the establishment of a network of indigenous agents throughout Japanese occupied territory. While such a policy was not entirely unique to Bougainville, with ANGAU doing much the same at Aitape, the difference was, however, that while at Aitape ANGAU managed such agents in isolation, on Bougainville the agents became an integral part of 2/8th Commandos operational repertoire.[99] These agents operated clandestinely and openly. They kept

---

96 AWM, AWM 52/2/51 Box 41, 2/6 Cavalry Commando Regiment War Diary Appendices, November 1944, "A" Aust FS Det at Baibiang GIII (i) 6th Aust Div, 21 Nov 44, Copy to 2/6th Aust Cav (Commando) Regt; AWM, AWM 52/2/51 Box 41, 2/6 Cavalry Commando Regiment War Diary Appendices, October to December 1944, First Aust Army Operation Instruction No.48 to CO 2/6 Aust Cav (Commando) Regt 17 Oct 44.
97 Bottrell, *Cameos of Commandos*, p. 251.
98 AWM, AWM52, 2/2/60, 2/8 Commando Squadron War Diary, 12 Feb 45.
99 AWM, AWM54 603/7/27, Sixth Australian Division Report on Operations – Aitape-Wewak Campaign ANGAU Cooperation, 26 Oct 1944 – 13 Sep 1945.

the Squadron informed of Japanese dispositions, movements, and numbers. They ambushed and killed isolated Japanese and marked targets for air strikes, the latter at considerable risk to themselves. They even provided the names of 48 Japanese soldiers who were inclined to surrender if the right offer could be made to them.[100] The case, for example, of Japanese Sergeant Tanaka illustrates the value of the agent network in this regard. Tanaka had been the indigenous liaison officer with his unit. In that role he had become friendly with two indigenous men and confessed to them that he had no desire to die in Bougainville, and would like to surrender if it could be arranged. The indigenous men arranged Tanaka's 'capture' and he was handed over to 2/8th Commando Squadron who sent him on to 3rd Division. Tanaka proved to be most cooperative and did not hold back in telling his captors everything he knew about Japanese plans. These plans involved the dispatch of the seven raiding parties, known as Tais, to attack Torokina. One of these parties had been tasked with finding and killing the Corps Commander Lieutenant General Stanley Savage.[101] Because of the warning none of the raiding parties succeeded in penetrating the Torokina perimeter, and as it transpired a clash between a 2/8th Commando Squadron patrol and a group of Japanese, which killed nine of them and captured one, discovered on the bodies detailed maps and aerial photographs of Torokina indicating that the group killed may well have been one of the raiding Tais.[102]

Maintaining faith with the indigenous agents was an ongoing concern. One example of just how careful the management of the indigenous people had to be occurred in March, when the Squadron was told that no aircraft were available for an air strike which had been planned. Indigenous agents had at great risk to themselves placed white lap laps on trees to mark the target. The Squadron did not hesitate to inform 2nd Corps that it was imperative that faith be kept with the agents, and that an airstrike occur as soon as possible.[103] If this did not happen the Japanese would discover the signs the agents had planted to guide the airstrike, and the repercussions for the agents and the local indigenous people would be grim. The Squadron was not impressed that it seemed hard to convince senior officers of this.[104] Ensuring the operation of the network of agents was of paramount importance and anything which might threaten this always caused alarm. In April Watson expressed his concerns at a program to drop propaganda leaflets over the area where the Siwai people lived. His apprehension was that dropping leaflets would incite the Japanese to extra watchfulness and that

---

100 AWM, AWM52 2/2/60 Box 56, 2/8 Aust Commando Sqn to Lt. Col. Hassett 3 Aust Div, 11 May 45, 2/8 Commando Squadron War Diary May 1945, Appendices (5).
101 AWM, AWM52 2/2/60 Box 55, 2/8 Commando Squadron War Diary, 11 Mar 45, AWM52, 2/2/60, 2/8 Box 55; 7 Bde to 2/8 Cdo Sqn; HQ 3 Aust Div Language Detachment 16 April 45, Draft Preliminary Interrogation Report No 30 3ADP035 Second Lieutenant Masaru Sannomiya, 2/8 Commando Squadron War Diary, 13 Mar 45.
102 AWM, AWM52 2/2/60 Box 55, 2/8 Commando Squadron War Diary April 1945.
103 AWM, AWM52 2/2/60, 2/8 Commando Squadron War Diary, 18 Mar 45.
104 Ibid.

this would place his agents in danger. He thought it was best to lull the Japanese into a false sense of security so his agents could operate unimpeded.[105] In a related case in July Winning decided not to send 'European' patrols into one area for a time. This was to avoid exciting Japanese vigilance in that area and thus allowing ANGAU's agents to work more effectively among the local indigenous population in the hope of persuading them to come across to the Allied cause.[106]

It must be noted, however, that the relationship between Commandos and indigenous people was not that of equals. It was a relationship born from an era of colonial administration and reflected colonial attitudes of race and the relative position in society of the indigenous people and their 'white masters'. ANGAU's manner was very much a colonial one.[107] Winning, whose civilian career had been as a planter, also possessed a colonial attitude. He was of the opinion that the only way to impress indigenous people was to immediately lay down the law. Appropriate punishments should be imposed so as to reinforce the 'voice of the government'.[108] Nevertheless even though steeped as it was in the colonial attitudes of the time, the relationship was also a very pragmatic one with attitudes and responses modified according to the situation of the moment. When indigenous people proved loyal and cooperative they were treated well, if paternalistically, and their contributions to the cause acknowledged. When faced with a situation in which the indigenous people were not demonstrating sufficient loyalty, or enthusiasm for the Australian cause, the response was harsh. Winning thought nothing of describing those considered to be disloyal as 'a rotten untrustworthy crowd', 'miserable B-S' and 'crazy coons'.[109] Some indigenous people were in fact supporting and aiding the Japanese, and this exacerbated such attitudes. Such aid to the enemy was seen as a serious threat to Commando operations. Those who were identified as doing so were marked as prime targets for elimination. Watson observed that any Siwai person who actively consorted with the enemy would suffer the fate of 'E buggerup pinish' which translated as being exterminated by his peers.[110] Removing indigenous people from Japanese control was an ongoing quest and exercised a great deal of the energy of ANGAU and the Commandos. One such case was

---

105 AWM, AWM52 2/2/60 Box 56, 2/8 Commando Squadron War Diary April 1945 Appendix E, ANGUA ADO 2/8 Cdo Sqn Subject Native TAI TAI area middle SIWAI.
106 AWM, AWM52 2/2/60 Box 57, 2/8 Commando Squadron War Diary, 21 Jul 45.
107 UQFL, UQFL288, Papers of Peter Pinney Box 8, Letters to Mother, 'Hiya' 29-8-45.
108 AWM, AWM52 2/2/60 Box 58, 2/8 Commando Squadron War Diary August 1945, Winning to Stephens 5 July 45.
109 AWM, AWM52 2/2/60 Box 58, 2/8 Commando Squadron War Diary August 1945, Winning to Hassett, 7 July 45; AWM, AWM52 2/2/60 Box 58, 2/8 Commando Squadron War Diary August 1945 Appendices; Winning to Stephens 5 July 1945, Winning to Pimpernel; AWM, AWM52 2/2/60 Box 58, 2/8 Commando Squadron War Diary August 1945 Appendices, 'Jottings Disconnected' 25 July 1945.
110 AWM, AWM52, 2/2/60 Box 56, 2/8 Commando Squadron War Diary April 1945 Appendices, Appendix E, ANGAU ADO 2/8 Cdo Sqn Subject native TAI TAI area middle Siwai; Bottrell, *Cameos of Commandos*, p. 102.

in July 1945 when Winning considered the sexual activity of the Japanese in relation to the indigenous population. In a letter to Hassett he wrote:

> Many moons ago when the native and the Nip in this area were friendly the native below catered to the Nips sexual lust and supplied him with concubines. Now by virtue of these concubines, the Nip holds a certain proportion of the native population in thrall. As long as the Marys are there the Nip is loath to leave.
>
> Therefore by hook and mainly by crook I'll have to remove the concubines and the natives....Have lightly sounded those who the Nip holds in bondage and I think it can be done by guile.[111]

Winning wanted the Japanese to leave the area and was willing to use any gambit to make that happen. That he would consider manipulating the sexual relationship between the indigenous population and the Japanese, so as to interrupt Japanese proclivity is indicative of his decidedly unconventional approach to operations.

This extraordinary network of agents, and the intimate interaction between the indigenous population and 2/8th Commando Squadron, was not replicated by any other Commando squadrons during 1944–1945.[112]

One aspect of 2/8th Commando Squadron's relationship with indigenous people, albeit not local indigenous people, was its association with the troops of the Papuan Infantry Battalion (PIB) who were attached to Raffles Force. The relationship was never a comfortable one. Winning only cautiously accepted the attachment of PIB to his squadron. He considered PIB to be unreliable with their reports on enemy strength, disposition and the results of engagements with the enemy to be untrustworthy. He considered that such reports were only verifiable when confirmed by Commando patrols.[113] Pinney who accompanied PIB patrols considered the PIB to be 'just a ruddy nuisance'.[114] Contributing significantly to this uneasy association was the poor relationship the PIB had with the local indigenous people. As Papuans the PIB shared no affinity to the people of Bougainville, and the association between the two was a troubled one with the result that local guides would not cooperate with PIB.[115] The practical result of this was that without local guides, PIB could not patrol out into

---

111 AWM, AWM52, 2/2/60 Box 58, 2/8 Commando Squadron War Diary August 1945, Appendices.
112 Whereas 2/10 Commando Squadron did have ANGAU's Cole Force attached to it for a time there is no record of any close relationship developing between Cole Force and the Squadron.
113 AWM, AWM52 2/2/60 Box 57, 2/8 Commando Squadron War Diary June 1945 Appendices (1), Message 15 Bde for info Adv 2/8 Cdo Sqn 17 Jun 45.
114 UQFL, UQFL288, Papers of Peter Pinney Box 8, Letter to Mother 29 August 1945, 'Hiya'.
115 AWM, AWM52 2/2/60, Box 57, 2/8 Commando Squadron War Diary, 12 Jul 45.

unknown territory, which severely limited their operational versatility. In response to this Winning allotted the PIB Company to guarding the Raffles Force line of communication, a role in which they did valuable work.[116]

The management of the indigenous peoples by 2/8th Commando Squadron was not immune from interference from friendly sources, over which the Squadron had little influence. This was no better illustrated than by the ongoing tension between the squadron and the local AIB representative Pilot Officer Robert Stuart. AIB operations contributed to the war effort by organising indigenous people in areas outside of Army control.[117] On Bougainville Stuart managed a camp far forward of the main Australian lines. From this camp he recruited local indigenous people, some of who he formed into a spy network to operate in Japanese occupied areas, and some of who he used for occasional guerrilla attacks on the Japanese. Stuart was an experienced operator, having been with AIB since June 1943, and having operated independently in the jungle with US Forces on Guadalcanal and well as Bougainville. Australian authorities thought well of him awarding him the Military Cross for his work with AIB on Bougainville, his citation emphasising his effectiveness working with indigenous people and organising reconnaissance to guide air strikes.[118] Being isolated and left very much to his own devices Stuart managed his affairs in a decidedly idiosyncratic manner. This proved to be a bone of contention with the Squadron. According to Dunshea who visited Stuart's camp Stuart 'has never moved beyond his latrine. He lives like a King swathed in parachute silk clothing'. This uncomplimentary assessment may have been because Stuart had refused Dunshea entry to his camp, after Dunshea and his patrol has made a particularly arduous trek to the camp.[119] As Winning saw it Stuart, because he was forced to work alone without the capacity to draw upon any military authority, was forced to 'soft soap' the indigenous people, and appease them. He did this, for example, by giving them lap laps made from parachute material.[120] ANGAU or the Squadron could not equal this largesse which made it difficult to attract the support of some indigenous people. Security was another issue, with Winning accusing Stuart of not being careful enough about allowing those with Japanese sympathies

---

116 AWM, AWM52 2/2/60 Box 57, 2/8 Commando Squadron War Diary June 1945 Appendices (2), RAFFLES FORCE Patrol Instr No.15, 9 Jul 45.
117 See: David Horner, 'Australia and Allied Intelligence in the Pacific during the Second World War', Canberra October 1980, Working Paper, *Australian National University*, Strategic and Defence Studies Centre.
118 AWM, AWM119 248/14 Part 14, Military Cross citation for Pilot Officer Robert Stuart, 7th and 9th Division Periodicals.
119 AWM, AWM52 Box 2/2/60 Box 55, 2/8 Commando Squadron War Diary March 1945, Appendices.
120 AWM, AWM52 2/2/60 Box 58, 2/8 Commando Squadron War Diary August 1945, Winning to Hassett, 7 July 45; AWM, AWM52 2/2/60 Box 58, 2/8 Commando Squadron War Diary August 1945, 2/8 Commando Sqn to Hassett, 6 July 45.

to infiltrate his group.[121] This was despite Stuart referring to disloyal indigenous people as 'swine' and expressing his support for shooting them.[122] Winning was adamant that the influence of the AIB 'spoiled' the indigenous people and that AIB was a liability in the Squadrons efforts to establish a consistent relationship with them. As Winning was concerned when it came down to it 'We can't have two bosses'.[123] Stuart, however, painted a different picture of his operations. He was convinced that he alone had been responsible for the Siwai people changing their allegiance to the Australians, and that he had succeeded in disrupting Japanese outposts and capturing prisoners.[124] He was aware that when Winning's Squadron moved into an area he was currently operating in the Squadron 'will want control of the coons', and that subsequently there would not be room for both AIB and the Commandos.[125] The tension between 2/8th Commando Squadron and Stuart's AIB operation was unfortunate but in the context of the human environment in which operations were occurring understandable. The root cause was the contest to control the important resource represented by the indigenous population. Added to this was a fundamental clash of style in dealing with the indigenous people, with Winning and ANGAU representing more traditional attitudes and Stuart a more *laissez-faire* style. The consistent complaints of 2/8th Commando Squadron regarding Stuart need to be viewed in this context.

The great difference in style between Commando operations on Bougainville and during the Aitape-Wewak campaign, and on later campaigns in Borneo, which will be dealt with in the following chapter, is a mark of the inconsistency of the Army's management of its commandos at that stage of the War. In all the campaigns except Bougainville the Army maintained a standard system in the manner in which Commandos were employed. This was essentially according to the guidelines established for Commandos in late 1943 and early 1944. Such a system did not apply, however, to the operations of 2/8th Commando Squadron on Bougainville. This was solely due to the influence of the local senior commander on how Commandos were to be employed. The inconsistency in that such commanders essentially ignored Army Commando guidelines remained the key failing of the Army's Commando management system during the period 1944–1945. Essentially, despite its promulgation of Commando guidelines, the Army had not progressed in its management of Commandos from 1942–1943 when Independent Companies operated very

---

121 AWM, AWM52 Box 58 2/2/60, 2/8 Commando Squadron War Diary August 1945, 2/8 Commando Sqn to Hassett 6 July 45.
122 NAA, B3476, 83, Report by Pilot officer R Stuart RAAF (AIB) on coverage of Siwai-Buin Areas from 17th Feb 1944 to 12th Sept 1944.
123 AWM, AWM52 2/2/60 Box 58, 2/8 Commando Squadron War Diary August 1945Winning to Hassett, 7 July 45.
124 NAA, B3476, 83, Report by Pilot officer R Stuart RAAF (AIB) on coverage of Siwai-Buin Areas from 17th Feb 1944 to 12th Sept 1944.
125 Ibid.

"Spreading our Gospel" – The Commandos on Bougainville 249

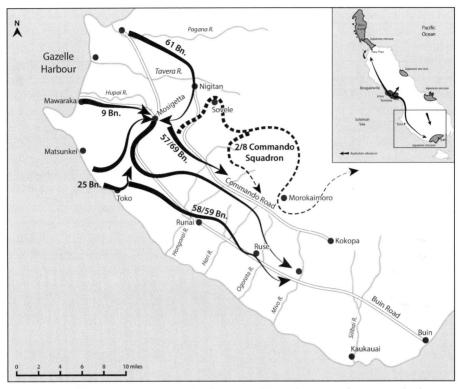

Map 10 The southern Bougainville Campaign November 1944–August 1945. 2/8 Commando Squadron operated as an autonomous force out on the flank of 3rd Division.

much in whatever manner the local senior commander deemed that they should. Individual commanders could still simply ignore the guidelines. This is what occurred on Bougainville with the influence of Lieutenant General Stanley Savige who as commander of 2nd Australian Corps was in overall command. Allowing his Commandos to act in this way suited the requirements of the campaign. On Bougainville the main component of the campaign on the Southern portion of the island was conducted with one flank resting on the coast and one open to the rugged hinterland. In such circumstances using a highly mobile autonomous commando squadron to operate on the inland flank of the main advance, to act as a tripwire and to disrupt any Japanese moves from that direction, was an effective economical use of force. Due to a lack of shipping, the main supply line for 3rd Division on Bougainville was entirely overland creating a long and vulnerable line of communication, another reason to employ Commandos as a mobile flank guard. The fact that the weather caused innumerable delays of the advance of the main force, sometimes for weeks at a time, resulted in long periods when significant pressure could not be put on the enemy. In such circumstances guerrilla harassment was a viable means to ensure the discomfit of the enemy. For a commander possessing tactical imagination such as Savige, the aggressive employment of Commandos provided an asset which added value to the operational requirements of the campaign he was waging.

In the final analysis, however, the primary cause of the inconsistency in Commando operations was both the fundamental difference in character between the Commandos on Bougainville and Commandos elsewhere and Savige's allowance for them to operate in the manner that they wished to. Winning was a constant advocate of guerrilla warfare, his reasons for this being entirely pragmatic. He considered the Bougainville campaign to be an exercise in futility and reasoned that the best way to minimise the chance of his men becoming casualties would be for them to operate as guerrillas where they could minimise their exposure to the enemy.[126] Thus Winning continually promoted the idea of autonomous guerrilla activity for his Squadron. Decisions taken by the Division in relation to the employment of the Squadron indicate that he was listened to. The character of the Squadron, its leadership and the consent of Divisional and Corps commanders allowed the Squadron to engage in autonomous guerrilla operations and in so doing created a unit which was unique in the Australian Army in the last year of the war.

---

126 UQFL, UQFL288, Papers of Peter Pinney, Box 11, Extract.

12

"We Blew the Hell out of the Place" – Borneo 1945

The campaigns conducted by the Australian Army in 1944 and 1945 remain controversial. There was at the time and in hindsight a perception that the campaigns fought were futile exercises which caused unnecessary Australian casualties. By late 1944 the war was winding down in the South West Pacific and South East Asia. The Japanese in the region were strategically isolated and tactically impotent. Australia found itself in a strategic situation where because its enemy had been in effect neutralised its own ability to contribute to the war had been bypassed. From late 1943 and through most of 1944 the Australian Army, found itself confined to the Atherton Tableland in northern Queensland training, and had done very little significant fighting. If this continued it would weaken the political influence of Australia's on the post war settlement. Australia thus had to find a way for itself to get back into the war.

The conquest of Borneo provided one such opportunity. MacArthur had conceived of a two pronged push against Japanese forces in the South West Pacific and South East Asia area. The first of these would be against the Philippines, which for political reasons, was to be an entirely American affair. The second arm of this offensive was to be against Borneo to secure the oil reserves there for future use in the invasion of Japan, and to act as spring board from which an invasion of the Dutch East Indies including Java could be launched. The place of Australian forces in this venture was at first uncertain. The Australian Government had informed the US Joint Chiefs that Australian forces would be available for operations on 2 June 1944. The Joint Chiefs, uncertain what to do with those forces asked MacArthur where they should be sent with the caveat that it was the Australians who should ultimately decide where they wished to be deployed. On 26 June MacArthur met with the Australian Prime Minister John Curtin. Illustrative of the immense influence MacArthur enjoyed over the Prime Minister, Curtin did not invite Blamey to the meeting. During this discussion MacArthur suggested that Australian forces be used to invade Borneo and eventually the Netherlands East Indies. Curtin accepted MacArthur's recommendation and by 31 October 1944 this idea had metamorphosed into the Princeton Plan from which Operation Montclair, which involved the return to the Philippines and occupation of Borneo, emerged. To ensure that his US forces would not be drawn into any conflict in Borneo or the Netherlands East Indies MacArthur on 14 December 1944 informed General George Marshall the Chief of the US General Staff that Australians did not want to serve anywhere except the South West Pacific and that their forces were adequate for the task. Following MacArthur's advice the Joint Chiefs resolved on 7 February 1945 that no US troops would be used in the Netherlands East Indies which would be left to Australian forces. With this established on 26 February 1945 a time line for the Australian invasion of Balikpapan was established.[1] It is to be remembered that there was in developing these plans no knowledge of the imminent forthcoming end of the war due to the atomic bombs. The campaign as envisaged was simply a continuation of the progressive elimination of Japanese forces within the South West Pacific and South East Asian regions and establishing a secure rear area for the invasion of Japan. Even so, there was resistance to the concept. Blamey as Commander in Chief of the Australian Army was opposed to the Balikpapan landings in Borneo, which he saw as a diversion of resources. MacArthur's hold over Curtin, however, ensured that Blamey was overruled and that the campaign proceeded.

Elsewhere by 1944 New Britain had been bypassed and neutralised, yet it remained occupied by a large Japanese force. New Britain, and Rabaul, its main town and Port was occupied by the Japanese in January 1942. It was quickly developed into a major air and naval base and headquarters of the Eight Area Army and became the centre of operations for the Japanese South West Pacific area. It was planned during 1942 to assault and recapture Rabaul, but it soon became apparent that the resources needed to undertake such a task did not exist. In addition the Japanese offensive in Papua and fighting in the Solomon Islands distracted Allied resources from any move against Rabaul throughout all of 1942. By mid-1943 it had been decided that Rabaul could be bypassed and neutralised, this was successfully achieved. By the end of 1943 direct communications between Rabaul and Japan were severed, not to be re-established until after the war had finished. Instead the town was subjected to repeated bombing raids which continued on a regular basis until the end of the war. US Forces landed on New Britain in September 1943 and engaged the Japanese in several land battles. Eventually the fighting died down and both sides settled into a mutual stand-off. In the second half of 1944 it was decided to replace US Forces with Australian troops and to this end the 5th Australian Division, which included 2/2nd Commando Squadron was despatched to New Britain in October 1944.

Despite being isolated the Japanese garrison of Rabaul was considerable, some 53,000 Army troops and 16,000 Navy troops. When the Australians arrived there was some heavy fighting around the Waitavalo–Tol area with Japanese forces that were already there, but once this was concluded Australian forces were not challenged by the Japanese again. The Japanese indeed were content to retain their forces in Rabaul.

1 Details of the communication between the US War Department, MacArthur and the Australian Government over the planning for the invasion of Borneo can be found in MAA, RG4 B17F1, RG4 B8F4, RG3B158, RG4B17F3.

The primary reason for the Japanese reluctance to launch an offensive against the Australians was the nature of the terrain on the island. The country between Rabaul and the Australian line was very rough and utterly undeveloped, dotted with volcanic mountains and covered in thick tropical rain forest. This made the movement of any significant number of troops virtually impossible, and thus nothing occurred. The same situation faced the Australians who established a containment line and made no attempt to move on Rabaul. The 2/2nd Commando Squadron were tasked with patrolling the fringes of the Australian line. The Japanese sent out small reconnaissance patrols but made no attempt to contact the Australians. It was very much what the Squadron came to call a 'more leisurely war'.[2] With little else to do the Squadron sent out a patrol to penetrate the jungle up to the outskirts of Rabaul. This twenty four day patrol was noted for the extreme weather conditions it encountered with rain falling torrentially every day and night. The patrol determined that the terrain between Rabaul and the Australian lines was so bad that no Japanese force of any size could cross it. On 6 August a radio message announced the atomic bombing of Hiroshima and on 9 August the atomic bombing of Nagasaki. Five days later Japan Surrendered. The war for 2/2nd Commando Company was over.

Allied planning to invade Japanese occupied Borneo came under the collective Operation title of Oboe. The invasion of Tarakan island was designated Oboe 1, Oboe 2 was the landing and occupation of Balikpapan, Oboe 3 the assault on Bandjermasin, Oboe 4 the capture of Surabaya. Oboes 5 and 6 would be to clear the remainder of the Netherlands East Indies including the British protectorates of Labaun Island and Brunei. As it was only Oboes 1, 2 and being specifically Labaun island, 6 were carried out.

Oboe 1, the capture of Tarakan Island, was the first of the assaults on Borneo to occur. Tarakan is an island off the North West coast of Borneo. The island is twenty four kilometres long and 18 kilometres wide. Its shores are muddy and tangled with Mangroves. Inland the island was a wild jumble of hills and small steep gullies, all covered in a dense rain forest.[3] The island as with all of Borneo was part of the Netherlands East Indies and had since early 1942 been occupied by Japan. Tarakan was a source of oil, producing some 500,000 tons per annum is peacetime. Despite damage caused by the Dutch to the oil facilities the Japanese by 1945 had restored the island's oil production to almost pre-war levels. Strategically Tarakan was of uncertain merit. It was suggested that it could be a base for the British Pacific fleet, despite Britain expressing no interest in it being so. The airfield on Tarakan could be used to support planned operations elsewhere in Borneo as well as Brunei, even though there were other airfields available. The island's oil production while useful was also considered to not be any significant gain. On 21 March MacArthur instructed Lieutenant General Leslie Morsehead, the commander of the 1st Australian Corps, to use 26 Brigade Group, commanded by Brigadier David Whitehead, to capture the island.

2   Ayris, *All the Bull's Men*, p. 467.
3   Long, *The Final Campaigns*, p. 407.

The primary object of the operation was to capture the Tarakan airfield for use by the First Tactical Air Force.[4]

Whitehead's 26 Brigade Group was approximately 12,000 men strong, almost as strong as an Australian Army Jungle Division which numbered 13,115. The Brigade Group included three infantry battalions 2/23rd, 2/24th and 2/48th. All of these were battle hardened formations having served since 1939. In addition were artillery, engineers and the 2/4th Commando Squadron. Intelligence gathered from aerial reconnaissance, signals intelligence, and Dutch colonial sources, had determined the strength of the Japanese garrison on the island to be roughly 1,800. These included 860 men of the 455th Battalion and 900 men of the 2nd Naval Garrison Force within included a company of the Kure Special Naval Landing Force. Some concrete bunkers had been built by the Dutch, and there was evidence of tunnels dug into hills and fieldworks constructed by the Japanese. There were five artillery guns covering the channel which ships had to use to dock at Tarakan. In addition there were 24 Anti-Aircraft guns and a wide anti-tank ditch which had been dug across the road from the beach into Tarakan town which was some 2,000 metres from the beach. The beach itself was protected by parallel rows of poles and rails driven into the mud out to 120 metres from the shoreline. It was also thought that oil tanks near the beach could be discharged and ignited on the beach.[5]

Australian forces assaulted Tarakan on 1 May 1945. Prior to the landing the island had been intensively bombed from 12 to 29 April. Primary targets were the oil tanks which overlooked the landing sites as it was feared the Japanese might ignite the oil and use it against the landing force. Attempting to surprise the Japanese was not part of the equation and the landing was conducted as an exercise of sheer brute force. Sea mines laid by the Japanese and the considerable beach obstacles needed to be cleared by the navy and Army combat engineers. The landing was preceded by a heavy naval and air bombardment and infantry were carried ashore in American Landing Vehicle Tracked (LVT). The beach itself was found to be mostly mud and this caused great congestion of vehicles and hampered efforts to move quickly inland. The tides which rose and fell some 2.7 metres also caused problems with landing vessels being marooned on mud. Japanese resistance to the landing was, however, negligible and by the end of the first day the beachhead was secure and the main force moved inland. As they did Japanese resistance increased considerably most notably as the Australians approached the town of Tarakan itself.

Tarakan Hill was a thickly timbered feature which dominated Tarakan town and the lower country around it for a distance of some one thousand metres in all directions. Tarakan Hill blocked the approaches to numerous important features on the right flank of Tarakan town as well as the entrance to an important track that led inland. Continued Japanese occupation of it would compromise any move by

4   Ibid, p. 406.
5   Long, *The Final Campaigns*, p. 409.

Australian forces out of the town and in the direction of the airfield. The Japanese, realising its tactical significance, had fortified the hill with system of tunnels, dugouts and pill boxes, all expertly camouflaged. Australian troops had without success been struggling to neutralise Tarakan Hill since 2 May when 2/23 Battalion made two fierce, but unsuccessful assaults on the hill. Attempting to overcome Tarakan Hill was proving to be a major distraction from achieving this primary objective of advancing to capture the airfield, which according to the plan had to be occupied by D+6, the day on which a squadron of fighter aircraft were planned to land and operate from the strip. Australian troops had reached the airfield, but not in sufficient strength to overcome Japanese forces who were stubbornly defending it. With the deadline for seizing the airfield approaching it became imperative that steps needed to be taken to ensure that the airfield was captured on time. To achieve this more Australian force would have to be applied, and this meant more troops. To this end Brigadier Whitehead shifted the 2/23rd Battalion which had been hammering itself against Tarakan Hill out to assist in the fight for the airfield. This left Tarakan Hill still in Japanese hands. With no other regular infantry available Whitehead substituted 2/4th Commando Squadron as the force to deal with Tarakan Hill. To give a Commando squadron, which lacked any support weapons, the task of capturing a heavily fortified enemy position that a battalion had failed to capture was an extraordinary decision. It was, however, in the circumstances an understandable one. The task to do so therefore fell to 2/4th Commando Squadron which according to the Army's guidelines could be expected to take their place in the line of battle as regular infantry whenever called upon to do so. Even so, it was a case of Commandos being dragooned into an infantry task, not because they were eminently suited for the task, but because the circumstances of the moment dictated that it be so.

The Squadron arrived at Tarakan Hill at 4.00 p.m. on 3 May and relieved D Company of 2/23rd Battalion that had been occupying a position on the right hand of Horseshoe Ridge overlooking the hill. The plan was to assault the hill the next morning, and during the night a patrol from 1 Section 'A' Troop of the Squadron scouted the hill for targets for a planned air bombardment to take place the next morning. The patrol found nothing though, having lost half the Section in the dark and reporting that all they heard was Japanese voices.[6] At 8.00 a.m. the next morning nine B-25 Mitchells bombed the hill which was followed by naval bombardment, the whole directed by the Squadron's second in command Captain Patrick Haigh. At 10.15 a.m. the Squadron began its assault. The plan for the assault was for two Troops of the Squadron to advance. 'C' Troop would conduct the initial assault and 'A' Troop would then move through them and occupy the hill. 'B' Troop would remain in reserve. Mortars and Vickers guns firing from Horseshoe Ridge would support the attack. Taking advantage of destroyed buildings for cover 'C' Troop advanced

6   Patrick Share (ed.), *Mud and Blood "Albury's Own" Second Twenty-Third Australian Infantry Battalion Ninth Australian Division*, Heritage Books Publications, Frankston, 1991, p.374.

to about 150 metres from the hill. Once there 8 Section commanded by Lieutenant Jack Eley moved ahead, hugging the cover of a burned out bank and ablution block. On the base of the hill opposite the bridge was a concrete entrance to a tunnel, about which were concealed Japanese pill boxes.[7] The only way to get at them was to cross a seven metre wide creek and ditch that was spanned by a narrow footbridge. The creek was full of a mangled tangle of barbed wire and electrical wire that had been thrown into it by the bombardment. With no other course left to them the Section sprinted forward and immediately encountered a hail of fire from the pill boxes. Eley was hit immediately and fell to the ground. Crawling behind a discarded filing cabinet he signalled that he was done for and died. Trooper Billy Eaton was shot by a sniper and killed. Troopers Mick Townrow and Charles Schwartz were wounded. Bullets splintered the wood of the bridge as the men raced across. Three men, Lance Corporal Ken Moss, Troopers Frank Beatty and Kevin O'Regan got across. They managed to knock out a machinegun with a grenade and moved on another one that was firing from a concrete pill box when Beatty was hit in the stomach. He rose to throw a grenade when another bullet slammed into his elbow and he tumbled to the ground. Seeking shelter in a bomb crater he was joined there by Moss, O'Regan and Trooper Anthony Buntman. Buntman used his first aid kit to bandage Beatty's elbow and stomach wounds. Under fire from machineguns, snipers in the trees and grenades being rolled down the slope from the pillboxes, the three Commandos returned what fire they could. As they were doing so Buntman was hit in the head by a machinegun and killed instantly. O'Regan was cut across the head by a sniper's bullet and stunned. Undeterred, with blood coming from his scalp and blinding him in one eye, he struggled to his feet determined to get the sniper who has shot him. One grenade tumbled into the crater and was thrown out, but as it was it exploded showering the Commandos with fragments. Moss was blinded and had his thumb almost severed. Almost out of ammunition and in no condition to continue the fight the three remaining defenders of the bomb crater decided to withdraw while they could. Just then a fifth Commando, Colin Webster, appeared. He had been in the scrub picking off snipers. He was told to go back. There were some men sheltering in the creek bank and these gave the withdrawing Commandos covering fire. Using the creek bank as cover Beatty with O'Regan assisting Moss made their escape and got to cover in the wrecked factory buildings at the base of the hill. As they made their way to the Aide Post to get their wounds treated Beatty encountered Brigadier Whitehead. Without hesitating he told Whitehead that '.303s were no match for concrete pill boxes and that the boys could do with some tanks on the hill'.[8] Major Kevin Garvey the squadron commander had been on the radio attempting to get tanks to support 8 Section, but nothing eventuated for several hours, a delay which is difficult to explain given that the tanks were not too far distant and only partially engaged elsewhere

7   Lambert, *Tidal River to Tarakan*, p. 352.
8   Lambert, *Tidal River to Tarakan*, pp. 352–56.

at the time. Eventually though the Matilda tanks of 13 Troop, C Squadron, 2/9th Armoured Regiment came forward to add their firepower. The Australian Army in 1945 made extensive use of Matilda II tanks. While these had long since become obsolete on the European battlefields they were perfectly suited for the war against the Japanese, whose own tanks, when they were present, were of limited capability, and whose anti-tank weaponry was equally limited. The Matilda's thick armour made them impervious to everything the Japanese could throw against them except mines, and on the rare occasion when such were available, heavy calibre coastal artillery.[9] The Matilda was armed with the 2-pdr gun; this in itself was of limited usefulness on the well-established Japanese fortified tunnels, pillboxes and bunkers on Tarakan Hill. It was fortunate though that within each tank Troop there was one tank armed with a 3 inch howitzer. These fired delayed action 231 fused ammunition, which penetrated the bunkers before exploding. Engaging from 50 metres range and using such rounds, two bunkers and one tunnel were destroyed.[10] This allowed the commandos to get close to the pillboxes and bunkers and exploit the damage done by the tanks.

While 8 Section were undergoing their ordeal 7 Section commanded by Lieutenant Ken Wightman had gone out to the left in an attempt to outflank the Japanese defenders, but got pinned down by heavy fire and could not assist 8 Section. The Japanese had constructed a system of cleverly concealed, interlaced dugouts and tunnels that enabled an enfilading cross fire to dominate all approaches. It also allowed the Japanese, moving through their network of tunnels, to reoccupy destroyed or abandoned bunkers and from these fire into the rear and flanks of 'C' Troop wounding two commandos.[11]

With 'C' Troop locked in its brutal fight 'B' troop moved out to the right flank hoping to find a way up onto the hill that was not swept by Japanese fire. The Troop managed to advance to the crest of the hill only encountering scattered fire from snipers. Once at the crest, however, two concrete pill boxes blocked any further progress and Japanese light machineguns and mortars began to play upon the Troop. Repeated attempts were made to evict the Japanese from the pillboxes and eventually this was achieved, with one pillbox being destroyed by a hit from a PIAT anti-tank projectile.[12] Even though the pillboxes had been taken Japanese sniper fire was contin-

---

9   On Balikpapan in July 1945 the Japanese employed 120mm naval coastal artillery against Matildas and knocked out four of them in one engagement.
10   AWM, AWM54 617/7/3, "C" Squadron 2/9 Aust Armoured Regt Operational Reports – Tank – Army Fighting Vehicles and activity reports, Oboe One Tarakan.
11   AWM, AWM 617/7/2, 2/4 Aust Cdo Sqn, Tarakan Interviews by NX108622 Lieut W.N. Prior.
12   PIATs were present on the table of equipment of Australian infantry in 1945, but were seldom if ever employed, the example on Tarakan Hill being a rare case. Given the difficulty of carrying a heavy piece of kit, such as the PIAT, for which there was virtually no use, in a jungle environment when every gram of weight was an issue, it is unsurprising that PIATs were left behind in stores. All the official literature of the Australian Army from the period 1944–1945 refers to the PIAT as a 'PITA' gun. Other than a clerical error

uous and made it impossible to advance any further. Two sections were withdrawn into cover.

When dusk came the Commandos were in control of all but about one quarter of the surface of the hill. The Japanese were still well ensconced in their labyrinth of underground tunnels and bunkers. Throughout the night Japanese armed with grenades, fused 75mm shells which they used as grenades or suicide bombs, and spears which they used to probe for booby traps, attempted to infiltrate the Commando's positions on the slopes of the hill. The method the Japanese used was to crawl on their bellies as silently as possible, probing forward with their spears.[13] Four Japanese were killed doing so but not before they wounded Trooper John Brandis of 'B' Troop. There was nothing for the Commandos to do that night but lay still; taking turns of one hour to sleep and one hour to watch. Trooper Bob Phillips remembered that night well. He and two other Commandos were occupying a forward post in the remains of a steel derrick, sheltering behind a girder. A Japanese soldier came up with no regard for hiding and threw a grenade at his position. Luckily the flash as the Japanese soldier struck the base of his grenade against his helmet to arm the grenade was spotted. By chance the grenade landed in front of a steel beam and its blast was deflected. Thinking that their luck had run its distance the three Commandos withdrew from their exposed post.[14] Trooper Bill McMicking recalled lying on his back attempting to sleep. He had been posted last in line down a track. As he lay there he felt something at his feet. He knew he was last in line, so it had to be a Japanese soldier. Carefully he pulled his rifle out and swinging like a club struck the intruder on the head. The next thing he knew he was grabbed from behind and struck in the chest. He shouted out, 'look out they've got me!' As it turned out he had struck a Commando named Jack Gates and had been grabbed by Keith Dale another Commando. Both had thought he was a Japanese soldier trying to sneak up on them in the dark. In fact the hill was getting too crowded and to prevent incidents such as the one McMicking had fortuitously survived some men were pulled off the hill.[15] During the night 'B' Troop was relieved by 'A' Troop.

The next day Japanese sniper fire was so persistent and coming from so many hidden locations that it took until late afternoon before the whole hill was occupied by the Commandos. Occupation was indeed all they could achieve, as there were still an unknown number of Japanese who had not surrendered inside the tunnels on the hill. To deal with this the sappers of 2/3rd Pioneer Regiment worked from tunnel to tunnel sealing each one with explosives, and trapping within those Japanese who were there. The Commandos lost five killed and thirteen wounded taking Tarakan Hill.

       in the original transcription of the term PIAT, which was then perpetuated throughout the system, no reason for this idiosyncratic spelling of PIAT can be found.
13 Share, *Mud and Blood*, p. 374.
14 Lambert, *Tidal River to Tarakan*, p. 362.
15 Ibid, pp. 360–61.

The number of Japanese who died on the hill will never be known. Three weeks later on 24 May the tunnels were opened by engineers but it was impossible to go very far in due to the stench. There was no doubt that many Japanese were sealed forever in their tunnels.

The losses suffered in the assault on Tarakan Hill had a profound effect on Major Kevin Garvey the commanding officer of 2/4th Commando Squadron. Garvey was a compassionate soldier who deeply cared for his men. To have them killed in what seemed a senseless frontal assault against a heavily fortified enemy position in an action for which his Commandos were utterly unsuited, was too much for him. This was especially so as many of those killed had been with Garvey since the formation of the squadron as an Independent Company in 1941. The official records have Garvey being relieved of command the evening following the capture of Tarakan Hill due to Medical reasons.[16] Those who were present were more forthcoming recalling that with the impact of the deaths of his men Garvey broke down emotionally, crying unashamedly on at least one occasion when the death of soldier was reported to him.[17] Captain Patrick Haigh took over command.

Following the capture of Tarakan Hill the squadron moved on to working its way along a track that was known as Snag's Track. The track was laced with booby traps and one man was killed after he stepped on a fused 75mm Shell.[18] Progress was consequently slow and cautious. Sniper fire dogged the advance as well as Japanese light machineguns which opened fire killing two men on 9 May. That same day allied aircraft bombed 'C' Troop mistaking the smoke from mortars the Troop had called in as an enemy target. That night 'C' Troop established its perimeter on a hill feature overlooking the track. Japanese troops armed with 3.6 metre spears and throwing fused 75mm shells attempted to infiltrate the Troops position.[19] On 13 May as the squadron probed forward Japanese light machineguns opened fire. The enemy were on either flank which made the standard Commando procedure of outflanking the enemy impractical. Eventually 'C' Troop, which had three men wounded, negotiated a path out wide to the right flank and the Japanese withdrew, but not before losing seven killed. The squadron pushed on but only to walk into Australian booby traps which had been set by 2/48th Battalion across the line of their advance. Clearing these 'A' Troop occupied an inverted V-shaped feature which had been given the name Agnes.[20] The Agnes feature dominated the immediate country. Despite its obvious importance the Japanese had neglected to place any men on it. The assumption from the Commandos later was that the Japanese figured that the Australians would be more interested in clearing Snag's Track than occupying Agnes. The Japanese soon

16 AWM, AWM52 2/2/56, 2/4 Commando Squadron War Diary, 20 May 1945.
17 Lambert, *Tidal River to Tarakan*, p. 367.
18 AWM, AWM52 2/2/56, 2/4 Commando Squadron War Diary, 7 May 1945.
19 AWM, AWM52 2/2/56, 2/4 Commando Squadron War Diary, 9 May 1945.
20 Stanley, *Tarakan an Australian Tragedy*, p. 122.

realised their mistake and attacked the feature, being repulsed and losing 16 soldiers. Clashes with small numbers of Japanese scouts followed. In one two Japanese soldiers were killed with two shots, enthusing one Commando to exclaim, 'two men – two shots – two dead Japs – two swords – two good souvenirs'.[21] On 15 May 'B' Troop relieved 'A' troop, one section digging in on the Snag's track junction adjacent to Agnes. It was not long before that section could hear Japanese voices in the gully below. From their sound they guessed that there were a large number of them. This would prove to be so. In the early afternoon the Japanese attacked. The Japanese, about 50 in number, lunged out of the thick brush only 40 metres distant. Supported by machinegun fire and shouting loudly, with an officer screaming 'Banzai Banzai', they rushed up the slope at the Commandos.[22] Heavy fire tore into the Japanese ranks, but on they came. Australian mortar fire supported the Commandos, with bombs landing only three metres to their front. The fight went on for an hour before the Japanese withdrew even though their machineguns and mortars continued to work over Agnes. The defending section was isolated. Its phone lines had been cut, there was no radio communication, and ammunition was low. Trooper 'Horse' Collins stood up in his pit dropping his empty weapon and pulling out a machete challenged the Japanese to come again.[23] Men went out to the forward pits to collect what ammunition they could. The Japanese machineguns and mortars ceased firing by 4.30 p.m. Night came. A patrol probed out from the section and found 22 dead Japanese. The squadron had suffered three wounded in action.[24] One Japanese soldier had managed to penetrate the section's defensive perimeter. He had been shot down by a burst from an Owen gun fired at a range of one metre. Later when a commando crawled out to check the body for documents the 'dead' Japanese sprang to his feet, threw a grenade, and fled. No one who saw the incident could believe it, the only explanation they could find being that the Japanese must have been wearing a bullet proof vest.[25]

Following the fight for Anges the three Troops of the Squadron were given different tasks. 'A' Troop was to patrol out to the Macks feature, 'B' Troop was to patrol to the Susie feature and 'C' Troop was sent to the Djoeta oilfield to patrol the area from the oilfield to the north and north east. There had been an intention to use the Commandos to assault a number of features, but thankfully the strength of the squadron was assessed to not be strong enough to do so and 2/48th Infantry Battalion was given the task instead. Despite their reprieve it did seem that Commandos were to continue in the role of assault troops, indicating the general consensus amongst the high command to use its commando asset as an infantry force. This combined with the

---

21 AWM, AWM 617/7/2, 2/4 Aust Cdo Sqn, Tarakan Interviews by NX108622 Lieut W.N. Prior.
22 Long, *The Final Campaigns*, p. 434.
23 Lambert, *Tidal River to Tarakan*, p. 375.
24 Stanley, *Tarakan an Australian Tragedy*, p.122.
25 AWM, AWM 617/7/2, 2/4 Aust Cdo Sqn, Tarakan Interviews by NX108622 Lieut W.N. Prior.

failure to relieve the Commandos from front line duty, while infantry companies were regularly relieved, led one commando officer to observe that there was 'nil' cooperation between other units and the Squadron. He also observed that infantry commanders, reacting to the perception common amongst some of them that Commandos were 'supermen', and deliberately gave the commandos tasks which they were unsuited for so as to prove that they were not. This bred a degree of ill feeling between the Commandos and the infantry.[26]

On 23 May, 10 Japanese armed with fused 75mm shells, spears and Dutch grenades and rifles attacked. They were repulsed with one being killed. While 'A' and 'C' Troops patrolled to features in the immediate area, 'B' Troop remained at Agnes. Prominent in the area was a knoll which had been given the name of Freda. The 2/48th Infantry Battalion had been fighting to control Freda for several days without success. A large Japanese bunker sat on the crest of the Freda knoll with an uninterrupted field of fire for approximately one hundred metres all around. There was very little cover as all the foliage including trees had been flattened by the incessant bombardment. The Japanese in their bunker hung on tenaciously withstanding repeated air, artillery and mortar bombardments and infantry assaults. 'B' Troop was ordered to move from the Anges feature to reinforce 2/48th Battalion at Freda. Two Sections began moving through the jungle at night to do so. These became involved in repulsing a determined Japanese assault just before dawn the next morning in which two Commandos were mortally wounded. Unable to take Freda the infantry and Commandos were withdrawn to a safe distance so that yet another airstrike could be made.

Following Freda 'B' Troop occupied the Susie feature unopposed and patrolled without encountering any Japanese. 'A' Troop and the Squadron Headquarters moved to the Djoeata oilfield. At the Djoeata oilfield the three Troops of the Commandos concentrated and began to patrol in self-supporting independent sections. This was the type of work they had been trained for. They discovered a network of pillboxes and communication trenches. The Japanese had a number of Formerly Dutch 75mm guns positioned at Cape Djoeata to guard against invasion and one section from 'C' Troop was given the task of neutralising those guns. When the section arrived at the gun positions they found them abandoned, along with several bunkers and concrete buildings used as magazines. The guns were disabled by removing the sights and recoil systems. A large amount of food and personal items were found in the concrete buildings. The Commandos were thinking about destroying these but could not think of just how that could be done, when a Dayak paddled his canoe up to the beach. He was delighted at the chance to secure a supply of food and paddled away soon returning with a great number of other Dayaks and their canoes. The Japanese food was soon loaded on the canoes and paddled away. Having secured the guns the section began patrolling and clashed with a Japanese machinegun on 28 May when Trooper Tony

26 AWM, AWM 617/7/2, 2/4 Aust Cdo Sqn, Tarakan Interviews by NX108622 Lieut W.N. Prior.

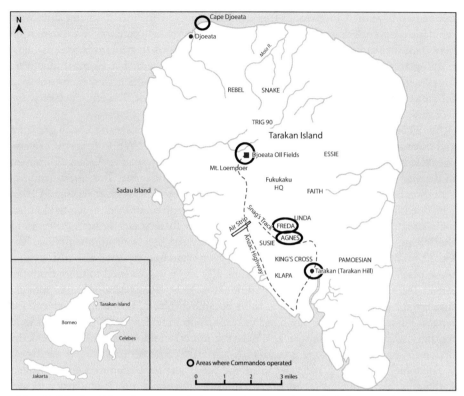

Map 11 Tarakan May–August 1945, showing the areas where 2/4th Commando Squadron operated.

Kayes was killed. Despite this, contact with the Japanese during the day was very rare, but night was another matter. Japanese movement could be constantly heard in the jungle nearby. The Commandos realised that this was a ploy by the Japanese to get the Commandos to fire on them and thus reveal their locations and did not respond. Nevertheless having to be forever on guard was very wearying and as one Commando put it they 'slept with one eye open'.[27] Booby traps were placed, including one trap made from Japanese 75mm shells which had their nose caps removed and electric detonators inserted. The traps proved effective and killed and wounded several Japanese.

The experience of 2/4th Commando Squadron on Tarakan was a classic case of a Commando unit being included in a force as something of an afterthought. Because the Squadron was part of 2/9th Cavalry Commando Regiment which was a component of 9th Division it was attached by default to 2/6 Brigade Group which was

27 Lambert, *Tidal River to Tarakan*, p. 391.

created from elements of 9th Division. Nothing in the planning for the assault on Tarakan addressed employing a Commando Squadron, in any Commando related role. Indeed the limited physical dimensions of the island of Tarakan did not provide anything like the range of territory over which a Commando Squadron could be expected to operate. Illustrative of the lack of any clear goal for the Commandos was the first task given. This was to land on the unoccupied Sadua Island and act as security for a battery of 25pdr guns. Any unit could have done this, but given that the Commandos were in effect supernumerary, and effectively with nothing else to do, they got the job. Due the exigencies of events in Tarakan the Squadron, as the only infantry unit available was taken from Sadau island and deployed immediately to Horseshoe Ridge for an assault on Tarakan Hill. Following Tarakan Hill the move up Snag's Track and defence of the Anges feature was conducted purely as infantry. The same occurred in the fighting for the Freda feature. The scouting that was carried out was of a limited and purely tactical nature. Throughout all of this the Squadron was given no relief, unlike companies in infantry battalions which could be given a spell from action. Commandos were given task after task, all infantry work, until they were exhausted. Due to the requirements of the campaign, limitations imposed by terrain, requirement to overcome enemy resistance within a limited timeframe, and limited manpower available to achieve this, the Commandos of 2/4th Commando Squadron found themselves unable to employ their unique resume of skills. In purely technical terms the roles to which the commandos were put on Tarakan were within the guidelines for commandos established by the Army. Thus it could be argued that they were not misused in the tasks they were given, although the manner in which they were used certainly did not make use of any of the unique attributes the Squadron did have to offer.

The experience of the other two Commando Squadrons of 9th Division during the Oboe 6 phase of the Borneo campaign, to capture Labaun Island and Brunei, was another example of commandos being supernumerary to the main force. As with 2/4th Commando Squadron both 2/11th and 2/12th Commando Squadrons as components of 2/9th Cavalry Commando Regiment belonged to 9th Division. It was 9th Division's task to not only provide 26 Brigade group to assault Tarakan but to also assault and capture Labuan Island and Brunei. As such 2/11th and 2/12th Commando Squadrons would participate in the campaign to do so. The forward planning to employ the Commandos during this campaign was uninspiring. While 2/11th Commando Squadron was given a relatively active role, it saw very limited contact with the enemy. Reflecting the lack of any desire to employ the Commandos in anything like an effective manner 2/12th Commando Squadron spent the bulk of the campaign sitting aboard ship as the Divisional reserve. Eventually 2/12th Commando Squadron would be sent ashore, to conduct a topographical survey of the island. The intention by the Division to utilise its Commandos for anything more challenging was conspicuously absent.

The Oboe 2 phase of the Borneo Campaign would see 7th Division land at the oil port town of Balikpapan and push inland to secure the region. This campaign was opposed by Blamey who considered it a waste of resources and lives, yet under MacArthur's direction and fully supported by the Australian Government it would occur. The landing at Balikpapan was to be conducted as a full scale amphibious assault. The 2/7th Cavalry Commando Regiment, attached to 7th Division, was composed of 2/3rd, 2/5th and 2/6th Commando Squadrons, with Lieutenant Colonel Norman Fleay in command. Its role was to support regular infantry formations.

Air and naval bombardment preceded the assault troops. The amount of firepower employed was formidable and in the words of one soldier who witnessed it 'We had everything backing us up going into Balikpapan. Ships firing rockets and aeroplanes going over dropping bombs, everything was weighted our way ... we blew the hell out of the place'.[28] Following the naval bombardment American and Australian bombers reduced the 100 or so large fuel tanks on shore to flaming cauldrons.[29] The landing then went ahead with the troops being carried in a mix of landing craft and LVTs.

The role of the Commandos was to land after the first wave of infantry and move through them. They were then to operate as an advance guard and scout ahead for the enemy. This was classic light infantry work, very much in line with the Army's conception of how Commandos were to be employed. Despite apprehensions that it might not be so the Japanese offered negligible resistance to the landing. This disrupted somewhat the timetable which had been establish for the landing of the Commandos with 2/6th Commando Squadron, which was to land on D+2 being landed instead on the first day. This was to be somewhat anti-climactic as the Squadron was not assigned to any active duty and allocated instead to guarding the Divisional Head Quarters. Following a day spent on that task the Squadron was detailed to conduct patrols. During these five Japanese were captured and three dead Japanese were discovered. Numerous unexploded bombs and electrically detonated mines were found in the area. Enemy bunkers and pill boxes were discovered, but all had been abandoned. The squadron reported that the Japanese had withdrawn. The Japanese had, however, not entirely disappeared and that evening one Japanese soldier infiltrated the squadron perimeter and killed Corporal P. Danne emphasising the dangers the night entailed. The next task the squadron was given was to assist 2/25th Battalion to clear the Baroe Peninsula. This they did by moving through the battalion and scouting ahead, discovering as they did a Japanese training ground. One Japanese soldier was killed, but otherwise the peninsula was cleared without opposition.

In the same manner 2/5th Commando Squadron which was to land on the second day discovered that it was now to land on the first day. Then, however, in what would seem to be a classic example of the military art of delay and obfuscation the squadron was told to clean up the officers camping area aboard their landing ship. The men were angry considering that this was the way the army was going to employ its Commandos for the landing at Balikpapan. Later that day, after their cleaning chore

---

28   Dean, *1944–1945 Victory in the Pacific*, p. 55.
29   Garland, *Nothing is Forever*, p. 336.

was completed, the squadron was landed on the beach and moved out. It was during this time that the Squadron encountered a distinguished visitor. General Douglas MacArthur had come ashore with the Commander of the Australian First Corps Lieutenant General Leslie Morsehead to witness the progress of the landing and he had come to the Squadron's location. Trooper Andy Pirie recalled seeing MacArthur standing there carrying a cane, and sporting his gold braided cap. With MacArthur were 15 to 20 other officers as well as a body guard of Marines. MacArthur stood there regarding the scene around him when suddenly a Japanese machinegun opened fire, its bullets striking the ground not far from him. All of MacArthur's entourage leaped for cover, but MacArthur remained still, not moving. He stood there alone looking in the direction from where the fire had come. Pirie, who was impressed by MacArthur's demeanour, could not believe what he was seeing.[30]

In stark contrast to how its day had begun by cleaning up after the officers 2/5th Commando Squadron would find itself engaged in serious action later on the first day. The Squadron had been briefed on Morotai from aerial photographs which pointed out the exact routes the Squadron would use when they landed. The plan was for the Squadron to move through the infantry to establish a forward screen in an area where the ground began to rise and there were gullies and scattered trees. The ultimate objective was, in support of the infantry moving up from the coast, to seize an airstrip by surprise. The squadron was to be well supported with a 25pdr battery and naval gunfire in support. A B 24 would be above them to provide a lookout as well as machinegun support if needed. As the Squadron moved forward through the 2/14th Battalion, they encountered the enemy. A Section of the Squadron had just crested a ridgeline when they ran into the concentrated fire of six Japanese light machineguns and one heavy machinegun from pillboxes hidden in the thickly forested area ahead of them. Four Commandos were killed and Lieutenant Frederick Pearson the officer commanding the Section and six men fell wounded. The Squadron Medical Officer Captain Raymond Allsopp oblivious of his own safety rushed forward and dressed the wounds of Pearson and Private Steve Usher. He sent Pearson, who was able to move, back and lifted Usher onto his shoulders and carried him. He had gone only thirty metres or so when he was wounded in the left thigh and Usher was hit again, this time mortally. Laying Usher down Allsopp moved over to assist another wounded soldier and dressed his wounds, he then returned to Usher and gave him some water. Caring nothing for his own wound Allsopp then went to Private Frank McKeown who was unable to move, dressed his wounds and carried him to safety. He then went out again and lifting up another badly wounded man carried him back. Allsopp then tended to the dead and wounded and when he went forward again was hit in the temple by a fragment from either a mortar bomb or grenade.[31] Allsopp fell clutching

---

30   Pirie, 'Commando Double Black', p. 417.
31   Two versions of Allsopp's mortal wounding exist. The first is that of Lieutenant George McLeod who states that Allsopp was hit by a fragment of a mortar bomb, the second by

his temple and moaning loudly. Lieutenant George McLeod and a soldier carried him to the rear but he died shortly after. Allsopp's selfless courage in circumstances where at no time was he not exposed to enemy fire was outstanding. He had for one hour tended the wounded and dying with absolutely no regard for his own safety. Allsopp's courage was attested to by six witnesses and Major Ian Kerr his squadron Commander recommended Allsopp for a posthumous Victoria Cross. The recommendation was forwarded on to the Regimental Commander Fleay who endorsed it. There is no record of what happened to the recommendation documentation once Fleay had endorsed it and Allsopp was not awarded the Victoria Cross or any other award. It was only in March 1947 that Allsopp was awarded a posthumous Mentioned in Dispatches. In a postscript to this in 2016 following an appeal from Doctor Patrick Allsopp to review the failure to award a Victoria Cross to Raymond Allsopp, an award of the modern Australian Military Star of Gallantry was made for Allsopp's actions on 1 July 1945. [32]

The timing of 2/3rd Commando Squadron ran more to schedule with the Squadron waiting until the infantry had landed at 8.00 a.m. and then going ashore at 11.00 a.m. On landing the Squadron was presented with a scene of devastation with smashed trees, bomb and shell craters, fires raging and burning oil pouring from ruptured fuel tanks.[33] Japanese snipers and concealed machineguns made their presence felt and Private Robert 'Curley' Villaume was shot and killed and three men were wounded. Lieutenant Bob McRae and Private Burnie Bailey were wounded by machine gun fire around the same time. That evening the Squadron halted behind 2/5th Commando Squadron.[34]

It was during the advance and contact with the enemy that Fleay, obviously imagining himself to be an operational commander, which was not the prescribed role for Commando Regiment Headquarters staff, came forward. Lieutenant Lloyd Jelbart, of 2/5th Commando Squadron, who was acting Troop commander, lay in the long grass in a hollow on top of a small knoll, and Fleay settled next to him. Jelbart had previously sent a message back to Squadron Headquarters for Major Ian Kerr the Squadron commander to come forward and assess the situation, but Fleay arrived in Kerr'a place. Parting the grass provided a reasonable view. A heavy Japanese machinegun was firing intermittent but dangerous bursts from about 2,000 metres, the rounds striking the ground to the left of the knoll on which Jelbart and Fleay lay. Japanese snipers were also playing on the Commandos having killed one man already. Without consulting

---

    several members of the Squadron who state that Allsopp was hit by a grenade thrown by a Japanese, see: Australian Department of Defence file: Allsopp and the Department of Defence Re: Allsopp [2016] DHAAT 31 (25 August 2016) File Number(s) 2015/029, and Pirie, 'Commando Double Black', pp. 422–3.

32 Australian Department of Defence file, Allsopp and the Department of Defence Re: Allsopp [2016] DHAAT 31 (25 August 2016) File Number(s) 2015/029.
33 Garland, *Nothing is Forever*, p. 337.
34 Ibid, p. 338.

him Fleay ordered Jelbart to assault a hill which he had determined dominated the area. In a mark of the spirit of independence which still harboured itself within the Commandos Jelbart refused to comply and told Fleay that he 'dare' not give such and order. Shocked by the defiance Fleay angrily retorted 'Don't you dare speak to your CO like that!' Jelbart shot back, 'I'll do more than speak! Your last orders to us were to avoid casualties. I have four dead and four wounded already. If you try to take that hill – we will have 40 dead and 40 wounded'. Fleay, stumped by such defiance, backed down. Jelbart suggested using naval gunfire on the hill and Fleay acquiesced, arranging for a naval forward observer to join the squadron. After a delay the naval gunfire arrived.[35] In another incident Fleay was held responsible for the death of Lieutenant Frank Redhead. Redhead was one of the Intelligence Officers for 2/5th Commando Squadron and he reported to Fleay that he felt sure based on the reports of scouts that the Japanese were still entrenched at a position known as the Gate. Fleay angrily snapped at Redhead telling him that he needed to know for certain if the Japanese were there and that it was Redhead's responsibility as Intelligence Officer to know that. Infuriated Redhead snatched up a Bren gun and made off in the direction of the enemy. He pushed past men who were on the track in front of him and turning a corner disappeared from view. A moment later a machinegun burst sounded. As the men following crept forward Redhead could be seen lying still. He did not respond to calls. Lieutenant Bob Halliday managed to extricate his body and bring it back. Fleay demanded to know what had happened and Halliday replied angrily 'I'll tell you what bloody well happened. You've just killed Lieutenant Redhead. That's what!'[36]

As the campaign progressed and the men acclimatised to conditions the Squadrons, all of who were veteran Independent Companies and still retained personnel from that era, began to recall the operational style they had earlier practised. The Japanese had begun conducting a series of ambushes and infiltration along the Australian line of communication. To counter this, 2/6th squadron began to range out to hunt the enemy and conduct aggressive patrols. These were effective and over a short period forty eight Japanese were ambushed and killed. Not everything went the way of the Squadron, however, and enemy booby traps were a major problem. The Japanese had constructed traps using 250lb aerial bombs electrically fused or detonated by trip wire. In one incident on 13 July an ambush in which the Japanese detonated bombs killed three members of the Squadron outright and wounded three, two of who would later die from their wounds.[37] Not to be outdone and to give as good as they got the Squadron also made use of booby traps. They did so to such an extent that eventually the large number of traps sewn by both sides made it dangerous for all. Nevertheless 25 Brigade, whose task it was for 2/6th Commando Squadron to protect its flanks and scout ahead continued its advance.

---

35   Pirie, 'Commando Double Black', p. 420.
36   Ibid, pp. 433–34.
37   Trigellis-Smith, *The Purple Devils*, pp. 244–5.

268   Jungle Cavalry

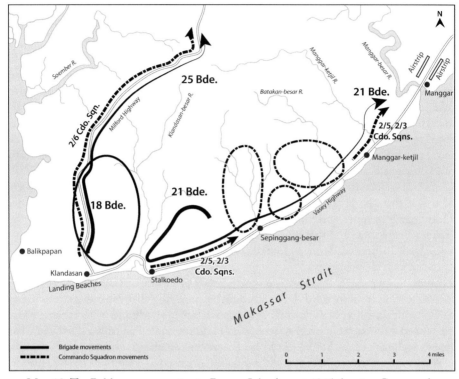

Map 12 The Balikpapan campaign in Borneo July–August 1945 showing Commando movements in support of 7th Division.

Towards the end of July 25 Brigade established semi-permanent camps and the 2/6th Commando Squadron was sent out to protect the forward limits of the brigade's advance. No Japanese were found. Not content with this passive role the Squadron mounted a series of aggressive patrols behind enemy lines. The objective of these patrols was to keep the enemy off balance and to gain as much information as possible of Japanese movements. Any Japanese encountered were killed such as on 2 August when a fighting patrol conducted an ambush that killed 10 Japanese. It can be seen here that the Independent Company ethos had not entirely disappeared from the Commandos of 1945.

It was apparent, however, to all that the campaign was coming to a close, and that the war with Japan, at least in their part of the world, would soon be over. Not wanting to become a casualty at such a time weighed on the minds of many Commandos. The last Commando casualties occurred on 30 July when a jeep carrying a wounded Commando was ambushed and a Commando was wounded. On the same day a security patrol contacted the enemy and one Commando was killed in action. On 10

August orders came through to cease all aggressive actions and on 15 August the end of the war with Japan was announced.

The campaign on Balikpapan lasted for only seven weeks before the war with Japan ended. During this time the Commandos were used as light infantry. They provided flank guards and acted as forward scouts. They performed their role competently and successfully. It was apparent that from the point of view of Divisional command there was no intention to allow the Commandos any form of unconventional or irregular operations even though in the later stages of the campaign the Commandos, under their own initiative, began to exhibit traits of unconventional warfare. Perhaps if the campaign had gone on longer this regression to an Independent Company operational style by the Commandos would have become more pronounced. This was, however, not to be.

13

Australian Commandos in the International Context

Specialist formations concerned with irregular warfare, as a special type of military unit first emerged during the Second World War.[1] This narrative has focussed on the Australian Army's experience of those specialist forces. Australia was not of course alone amongst the Allied nations in raising specialist unconventional forces during the Second World War, with both Britain, who led the way, and the United States raising significant numbers of specialist unconventional units during the war. Given the priority of Britain and the United States to focussing their energies on defeating Germany, the level of specialist forces allocated to the Pacific theatre by those powers was significantly less than to the war in Europe. Nevertheless such forces were deployed to the Pacific and Burma. It is the purpose of this chapter to compare and contrast some of the Allied specialist unconventional forces that were deployed to fight the Japanese, with those raised by the Australian Army. By so doing the characteristics which were shared and those which were distinctly Australian can be examined.

Because of the vast theatre of operations represented by the Pacific, South East Asia and Burma and subsequently the number of allied specialist formations involved this chapter will focus only on those with a direct relevance to Australia. Of these there are two specific groups which are of special interest. The first of these are the British Commandos, because it was from these that the inspiration and ethos to raise the Australian Independent Companies came. The second group to be studied are the United States Marine Corps Raiders, which operated in the South West Pacific area during 1942 and 1943, the main area of operations for Australia during the Pacific War. Examining these two case studies of Allied special service units allows a relevant contextual comparison with the Australian Army's Commandos. A note needs to be made here of the reason why units such as Australian Z and M Force special service units, the US Army's 6th Ranger Battalion, and the US 6th Army's 6th Special Reconnaissance Unit 'The Alamo Scouts' have not been included in this comparison.

---

1   Hargreaves, *Special Operations in World War II*, p. 269.

While possessing all of the required specialist characteristics of Commandos Z and M Forces operated not as part of the Australian Army and thus provide no basis for assessment against Australian Army Commandos. The US 6th Rangers which were raised and trained in Port Moresby and the 'Alamo Scouts' who were raised on Ferguson Island New Guinea both began their service later in the war and operated outside the area of Australian Army operations.

Andrew Hargreaves in *Special Operations in World War II: British and American Irregular Warfare* provides a useful set of broad criteria to help us examine specialist forces. Among these criteria are: Inception, Command and Control, Employment, and Cost Effectiveness. Supplementary to these are five criteria identified by David Thomas in 'The Importance of Commando Operations in Modern Warfare 1939–1882'. These are: The existence of a formal military command structure authorised to conduct Commando operations; the inclusion of Commandos in war planning and strategy and doctrine; the acceptance of Commando operations as an important form of warfare; the presence of a coherent doctrine for Commando forces; and the recognition of the value of integrating Commando operations with the mission of regular forces.[2]

Both Hargreaves and Thomas's criteria provide a comprehensive template to enable an evaluation of the Australian Army's experience with its Independent Companies and Commandos and the British Commandos and United States Marine Corps Raiders. For the purposes of this Chapter, to assist the flow of the narrative, the term 'Commando' will frequently be used when referring to the personnel of the Australian, British and United States specialist formations examined, even when it is Independent Companies or Raiders that are being referred to.

There is a common thread present in the inception phase of British, Australian and United States Commando units; this is the influence of national emergency and crisis on the formation of specialist forces. For Britain this was following the defeat of British forces on mainland Europe, their evacuation back to Britain and the looming threat of German invasion in June 1940. For Australia it was the seemingly unstoppable Japanese offensive down through South East Asia and the South West Pacific which directly threatened the Australian mainland. For the United States it was the desire to strike back at the Japanese after their attack on Pearl Harbor, at a time when the United States military resources were scanty and disorganised. These were responses driven by the exigencies of the moment. They were, understandably, responses that were somewhat tainted by the shade of desperation, and consequently somewhat emotional rather than coldly rational. Prior to these events the thought of Commando style units, while not entirely ignored, was certainly not seriously

---

2   David Thomas, 'The Importance of Commando Operations in Modern Warfare 1939–1982', *Journal of Contemporary History*, Vol. 18, No.4, Military History, October 1983, p. 690.

considered by any allied military establishment. The circumstances faced by each nation at different times during the War changed this.

The British, energised by their perilous situation in June 1940, started the ball rolling by the establishing the Commandos during that month. The manner in which this was done was typical of the unconventional nature of the proposed force. The initial idea for Commandos came essentially from the fertile imagination of Prime Minister Churchill and what was euphemistically termed a number of gifted officers.[3] Churchill wanted troops of what he called the 'hunter class' who, as he succinctly put it, could inflict a reign of terror along the enemy occupied coast and leave 'a trail of German corpses behind'.[4] At first the idea was to form a 5000 strong 'Barrage Force' with no clear explanation of just what this meant. When this idea foundered, 'striking companies' were considered, which soon gave way to 'raiding companies'.[5] Raiding companies, not to be confused with the Commando raiding companies which eventually appeared, were intended to provide a well-armed, highly mobile reserve with which to strike at any German invaders on British soil. When the threat of invasion receded, the ideas for the use of raiding companies evolved into one of 'special parties' more closely resembling Churchill's original intent of raiding the German occupied coast. At first there was confusion and muddle in just exactly what role the Commandos were to play in this revised concept, with no clear idea just what the term 'special parties' meant or what role they were to play apart from that they were to participate in 'smash and grab' missions.[6] There was an idea that the aggressive activities of such parties could be used to boost civilian morale at home, and possibly regain some degree of tactical initiative from the enemy.[7] Still, fanciful proposals continued, one being the landing by Commandos in Brittany, to incite a revolt against the Germans.[8] Despite the tangle of proposals and ideas there was, however, at the highest levels a definite intention to formalise the coordination and employment of the Commandos. By the beginning of July 1940 a raiding policy had been drafted and agreed to by Churchill. On 17 July Churchill appointed Admiral Sir John Keyes as head of the Combined Operations Organisation (COO).[9] The COO's function was to coordinate Commando operations and to plan for any means by which the enemy could be attacked using such formations. A Memorandum for a combined operations plan from the Chiefs of Staff was sent to

---

3   Thomas, 'The Importance of Commando Operations', p. 694.
4   John Wukovits, *American Commando – Evans Carlson. His WWII Raiders, and America's First Special Forces Mission* (Caliber: New York, 2009), p. 22.
5   Charles Messenger, *The Commandos 1940–1946* (William Kimber & Co. Ltd: London, 1985), p. 26.
6   TNA, WO 193/384, Note from D.M.O. & P, 20 June 1940; TNA, WO 33/1668, Commando Training Instruction 15 August 1940.
7   Thomas, 'The Importance of Commando Operations', p. 694.
8   Messenger, *The Commandos 1940–1946*, p. 35.
9   Ibid.

Churchill on 22 July.[10] The formation of COO and the planning that accompanied it established a formal military command structure whose focus was unconventional warfare and how to most effectively employ Commandos in such operations. Even so, initial Commando operations were modest, 'pin pricks' in the dismissive opinion of Churchill, and in reality achieved very little of military value.[11] Despite this they provided 'a good tonic for the general public' and were presented as successes by an Army desperately seeking positive appraisal.[12] In October 1941 Keyes, who had never had a good relationship with the Chiefs of Staff was removed and replaced by Lord Louis Mountbatten.[13] Under Mountbatten's patronage the Commandos increased in number.

The Australian Army's experience of forming its Commandos came some eighteen months after the British. As we have seen in Chapter 1 the initial formation of the Independent Companies in Australia was fraught with difficulties. These difficulties stemmed from the initial idea to establish the companies being the consequence of a decision made without Australian Army oversight or approval. Very much as had been in Britain with Churchill the inspiration for Australia's Commandos came from one individual, in this case Lieutenant General Brudenell White, who did not consult with the army. Thus, caught off guard, the Australian Army during 1940 and 1941 was not prepared to assimilate anything as radically unconventional as the Independent Companies. With the Japanese threat in December 1941 this antagonism evaporated and the Commando training program was hastily revitalised. Provoked in response to a direct threat to national security, this reaction to raise Commandos in Australia directly echoes the British reasons for establishing its Commandos. It was, however, at this point that the Australian and British experiences diverged. They did so in the level of direct support the Australian military establishment would grant its Commandos. Indicative of this was that there never was any attempt by the Australian military to develop a formal command structure to coordinate Commando operations as had occurred in Britain. No COO was ever established in Australia. There were no Commando planning directives or memoranda generated by the Australian Chiefs of the General Staff. There was never any thought of employing other services such as the navy and air force to assist deploy the Commandos. Australian Commandos would remain autonomous sub-units managed solely by the Army.

The inception of specialist unconventional units within the United States followed both the British and Australian patterns. Following the Japanese attack on Pearl Harbour in December 1941 the United States sought to strike back at the Japanese. In late January 1942 Admiral Chester Nimitz requested Commando units for 'speedy

10 Ibid.
11 Christopher Mann, 'Combined Operations, the Commandos and Norway 1941–1944', *The Journal of Military History*, April 2009, p.4 74.
12 Messenger, *The Commandos 1940–1946*, p. 34.
13 Mann, 'Combined Operations', p. 474.

and surprise' demolition raids against isolated lightly defended Japanese island bases.[14] President Franklin Roosevelt had been influenced by Churchill's advocacy of Commando type operations and, encouraged by those, such as his son a serving Marine Corps officer and keen promoter of Commando operations, resolved that the United States should possess a similar capability with which it could attack the Japanese.[15] To this end Roosevelt ordered the United States Marine Corps to establish two 'Commando' battalions. Despite resistance from within the Marine Corps High Command to the establishment of such units, the Marine Corps, presented with the fait accompli of a Presidential directive, had no option but to comply.[16] Subsequently two 'Commando' battalions titled 'Raider Battalions' came into existence in January and February 1942. Just as in Australia, however, there was no attempt by the United States to establish any formal organisation to manage its Commando operations. The Raiders were to be the sole preserve of the Marines.

Any examination of the recruitment and training regimes of the British, Australian and United States Marine Corps Commandos must consider that over time these changed. There is however, especially in the period 1940–1942, significant similarities as well as some distinctive differences, between the manner in which the three services recruited and trained it Commandos.

During the period 1940–1942 the common feature of each service was the preference for the independence of its Commandos, organisationally and operationally and as a character trait of those who served. For the British the emphasis on an independent personality was a fundamental requirement for the volunteers who applied for Commando service. Such individuals were to be aware that from the moment they were accepted they were irregular soldiers, and that they were required to be self-reliant and expect no 'nursing'. Their officers were to be imbued with personality, tactical ability and imagination.[17] This insistence on an independent spirit was also a fundamental tenet of the training of Australian Commandos. Australian Commandos needed to possess the independent resilience to enable them to operate in small groups autonomously for extended periods of time and achieve success.

One difference of the Australian to the British Commando training programme was that British Commandos were required to comply with the formal governors of military decorum such as drill and strict adherence to personal turnout.[18] This was not

---

14   Joseph H. Alexander, *Edson's Raiders* (Naval Institute Press: Annapolis, 2001), p. 29.
15   USMCA, Oral History Transcript, Major General Omar T. Pfeiffer US Marine Corps (Retired), Mr. Benis M. Frank, Interviewer, History and Museums Division, Headquarters US Marine Corps Washington D.C. 1974, p. 198.
16   David J. Ulbrich, *Preparing for Victory – Thomas Holcomb and the Making of the Modern Marine Corps, 1936–1943* (Naval Institute Press: Annapolis, 2011), pp. 124–25.
17   LHMA, Laycock 1/3, The Papers of Major General Robert Laycock, The personal characteristics of recruits for Commando training.
18   LHMA, KC Laycock 2/8, The Papers of Major General Robert Laycock, Commando Training From Lt. Col. R.E. Laycock 10 Jan 42.

the case with the Australian Commandos who were not required to practice drill or achieve a spick and span turnout. This attitude was very much a product of the radical independent philosophy of the original Australian Independent Company British training team. With the conversion of the Australian Independent Companies into Commandos from late 1943 this did change however, and a more formal military culture was instituted for Australian Commandos.

The importance and understanding of 'independence' within the Marine Raiders depended very much on which of the two battalions is considered. While self-reliance and personal initiative were required in both battalions, the concept of independence was far more important in the 2nd Battalion than in the 1st Battalion. Lieutenant Colonel Evans Carlson commanded the 2nd Battalion was an officer whose ideas were decidedly contrary to the main stream. This had come about because of a career that had been anything but standard. He had served two years with Chinese Communist guerrillas fighting the Japanese during the late 1930s and assimilated much of their military procedure and philosophy. Central to Carlson's philosophy of command was what he called the 'Gung Ho' spirit. Taken from the Chinese words for 'working together', 'Gung Ho' underlined every aspect of how Carlson commanded his battalion.[19] Carlson insisted that a soldier's individual independence be subordinated to the 'Gung Ho' spirit. Carlson admitted that such a philosophy ran counter to the American culture in which 'greed and rugged individualism predominated'.[20] Nevertheless he persisted. In Carlson's battalion the idea of independence was that of collective independence where members of a unit would naturally cooperate, and by doing so foster solutions to challenges unhampered by what Carlson dismissively referred to as 'chicken shit authority'.[21] This idea was not entirely different to what the Australian Independent Companies strove for, other than Carlson practiced and inculcated it in a distinctly idiosyncratic manner. It was also an idea which generated significant scepticism and opposition from within the mainstream Marine Corps, just as did the independent ethos within the Australian Army.

One common feature shared by all the Commando services of each nation was the importance of voluntary enlistment for those who wished to join the Commandos. In each of the services applicants were taken only from volunteers, at least in the first few years. We have seen that in some instances this did not always occur in the Australian experience, but nevertheless the ideal of the volunteer was a quality that was valued

---

19   Another meaning for 'Gung Ho' may have been that it was a corruption of 'Gongye Hezhoushe' or 'Industrial Cooperative' with the emphasis on the first syllabus of the first and last words. It is, however, generally accepted that Carlson's interpretation of Gung Ho as working together is how the term should be understood, see: Gordon Rottman, *Carlson's Marine Raiders Makin Island 1942* (Osprey: Oxford, 2014), p.9 fn 2.
20   USMCHD, PC56/COLL3146 Box 2, Carlson Evans F, BFEN, Address of the Commanding Officer Marine Raider Battalion Lieutenant Colonel Evans F. Carlson on the Occasion of the First Anniversary of the Organization of the Battalion, p. 2.
21   USMCHD, Folder Raiders: 2nd Marine Raider Battalion – Carlson.

highly and striven for. For the British voluntary enlistment was considered to be what made the fundamental difference between the standard regular soldier and the Commando. It was considered a principle to which Commandos must adhere.[22] At least in theory the same applied in Australia. For British Commandos and Australian Independent Companies volunteers could come from any units within the army. Raider volunteers could come only from within the Marines. The manner in which these volunteers were processed was another feature each of the three services had in common, albeit with individual variations to the theme. In the British and Australian models a personal interview for each applicant was an important feature. In the period 1940–1942 British Commando leaders would personally select their Troop leaders, Troop leaders would then personally select the members of their Troop.[23] During 1941–1942 Australian volunteers were individually interviewed by selection boards or Independent Company recruitment officers, unless of course they were 'detailed' as related in Chapter 1. The Raiders differed due to the nature of how each of the two battalions was formed. There are no records of the procedure for how volunteers for Lieutenant Colonel Merrit Edson's 1st Battalion were processed. Edson was a straight down the line Marine officer and it is assumed that this was done in an orderly and organised manner. The 2nd Battalion had been raised less formally and Carlson its commander was obsessive about the personnel who wished to join his battalion. His attitude was that:

> I won't take a man who does not give a damn about anything – But if he has a deep feeling about wanting to fight, even for the wrong reasons, take him. I know I can shape him into wanting to fight for the right reasons.[24]

Carlson made it a point to personally interview every applicant. He would ask a series of provocative questions such as, 'Can you cut a Jap's throat without flinching?', and, 'Can you choke him to death without puking?' He concluded each interview with 'I promise you nothing but hardship and danger. When we get into battle, we ask no mercy, we give no mercy'.[25]

All three services faced the issue of unsuitable personnel finding their way to the Commandos. In Britain this manifested itself in men 'volunteering' when they had no idea what they were volunteering for, and many being unfit both physically and mentally for the role. A request was made that British army units not hinder Commando

---

22 TNA, WO 32/10417, Maj. Gen. Charles Haydon to Maj. Gen, J.S. Steele Director of Staff Duties, The War Office, 13 October 1943.
23 TNA, WO 193/384, Memorandum by the D.M.O. & P. on the employment of Irregular Commandos Now being raised in the United Kingdom, 13 June 1940.
24 Shultz, *Evans Carlson, Marine Raider, The Man Who Commanded America's First Special Forces* (Westholme: Yardley Pennsylvania, 2014), p. 41.
25 Ibid.

recruitment and release suitable personnel.[26] We have seen how in Australia Army units and the recruiting process both were resistant and uncooperative in recruiting volunteers for the Independent Companies. The United States Marine Raiders fared no better with the 1st Battalion complaining at one time that the replacements were apathetic, indifferent and disinterested. The Battalion made the point that it was regrettable no system had been established to procure volunteers when their enthusiasm was at its peak.[27] As for the 2nd Battalion, Carlson's personal grilling of every recruit would most likely have weeded out any types considered by him, at least, to be unsuitable. In Britain and Australia where unlike the Raiders which were disbanded at the beginning of 1944, Commandos remained in existence throughout the war, the adherence to voluntary enlistment faded with time and eventually disappeared as the war progressed, but at the inception of each Nations Commando experience it was an ideal that was highly valued.

The training of the British, Australian and United States Commandos shared a common expectation of physical hardship, individual challenge and psychological resilience. The details of the training varied from nation to nation although the objective of each was to produce a hardened individual capable of operating effectively in all conditions. British Commando training involved extreme physical demands as well as the requirement to master weapons and a variety of skills ranging from motorcycle riding to swimming.[28] Commandos were required to self-motivate, act alone and use initiative, very different requirements to a regular infantryman.[29] It was considered that an outstanding feature of British Commando training was the individual's ability to maintain an offensive spirit.[30] Courses such as 'The Death Ride' a toggle rope crossing of the Arkaig river at the Achnacarry training camp in Scotland, with live rounds being fired and live grenades thrown at the participants, characterised what was asked of British Commando Trainees.[31] In a variation to what would occur in Australia British Commandos did not receive any more than cursory training in demolitions. Each Commando Troop had a trained demolitions section and it was thought that training those not belonging to that section in demolitions was a waste of time and resources. It was in fact thought by some that with demolitions, 'a little learning is a dangerous thing'.[32] In another variation to the Australian model the atti-

26 TNA, WO 33/1668, Colonel E.R. Herbert Director of Organisation to the War Office Cheltenham, 23 April 1941.
27 USMCHD, Folder – Raiders: 1st Marine Raider Battalion – Edson, Griffith to Cmd Gen First Marine Amphibious Corps, First Marine Battalion in the Field – 26 February, 1943,
28 *British Commandos*, Military Intelligence Service, War Department, Washington, 1942, pp. 12–13.
29 LHMA, Laycock 2/3, Papers of Major General Robert Laycock, Papers of Major General Robert Laycock, Training December 1940.
30 LHMA, Laycock 2/8, Papers of Major General Robert Laycock, Commando Training From Lt. Col. R.E. Laycock, 10 Jan 42.
31 Donald Gilchrist, *Castle Commando* (Oliver and Boyd: Edinburgh, 1960), p. 78.
32 LHMA, Laycock 2/8, Papers of Major General Robert Laycock, Commando Training From Lt. Col. R.E. Laycock 10 Jan 42, LHCMA.

tude of British Commandos, or at least their senior staff, towards automatic weapons was ambivalent at best. While individual soldiers of any rank were keen to get hold of such weapons, the official policy was that for officers and senior Non Commissioned Officers to use such weapons encouraged them to get 'carried away with gangster ideas' and to forget their duties as leaders.[33] Robert Laycock, who as a Major General would come to command COO and thus all Commandos, was of the opinion that no one senior in rank to a Corporal should be allowed to touch a 'Tommy Gun'.[34]

Australian Independent Company volunteers experienced similar physical demands to the British trainees. There was nothing equivalent to the 'Death Ride' but nevertheless the physical strain on volunteers was relentless. Australians were expected to master weapons and other skills which emphasised field-craft, self-reliance, and stamina. Exercises such as the 'Akbar' which involved three days humping heavy packs over mountains, rivers and swamps, moving constantly and living on iron rations with only 10 minutes rest each hour were representative of the demands put on the volunteers.[35] The focus of Australian physical training was to ensure that the troops develop the stamina, both physical and mental, that would keep them in the field for extended periods of time. The idea that Independent Company soldiers had to be all-rounders, capable of multiple tasks was a feature of Australian training, unlike the British where the official attitude was that training men to be all-rounders was a 'grave error'.[36] In Australia demolitions was given intense individual attention, with all ranks being given extensive opportunities to practice with explosives. The official attitude to automatic weapons was also manifestly different to the British. Automatic weapons such as the Thompson Sub Machinegun and Bren gun were given full attention by all ranks, indeed officers relished firing such weapons and no restrictions were placed in their way to do so. There was also a notable competitive aspect to the training, especially when that training was conducted by the original British training team in 1941. Racing Spencer Chapman to the summit of Mount Latrobe illustrated the competitive ingredient injected into the training programme. When the change to 'Commandos' occurred in 1944–1945 the training regime remained physically demanding, albeit not as demanding as it had been during the earlier training of the Independent Companies. It also de-emphasised the small unit aspects of Commando work and focussed on operational aspects designed to create sub units that could work as integrated components of a larger more formal military structure.

The training received by the United States Marine Raiders cannot be simply characterised, as the two battalions were trained in radically different ways. It is worth a digression to examine just how this came about. The 1st Battalion which was stationed

33   Ibid.
34   Ibid.
35   Lambert, *Commando – From Tidal River to Tarakan*, p. 9.
36   LHMA, Laycock 2/8, Papers of Major General Robert Laycock, Commando Training From Lt. Col. R.E. Laycock, 10 Jan 42.

at Quantico Virginia, under the eyes of the Marine Corps high command, and commanded by Edson, a conventional officer, received standard Marine rifle battalion training with elements of raiding attached. The 2nd Battalion stationed at Fort Ellis on the west coast of California, thus remote from official scrutiny, was commanded by Carlson. When Roosevelt ordered the raising of the Raider battalions he appointed Carlson as the commander of one of the battalions with approval to command it as he saw fit.[37] Carlson set to his task with characteristically manic enthusiasm. Drawing on his Chinese guerrilla experience he created a unique battalion. There were no ranks, private soldiers were encouraged to speak their mind, and Non Commissioned Officers and officers while acknowledged as leaders were given no special privileges or deference. Training was strenuous but conducted on a purely individual basis. Individual Physical conditioning, hand to hand combat, judo, knife throwing, crouch shooting, and marksmanship were practiced. Very little time was devoted to tactical small unit training or working in teams.[38] The 'Gung Ho' philosophy dominated every aspect of training. Every day all ranks of Carlson's battalion would gather for a 'Gung Ho' session. These were forums for anyone to speak their mind regardless of status or rank, and for a group consensus to be arrived at. Carlson considered that such sessions developed a 'deep spiritual conviction' and 'righteousness' in his soldiers and justified for them why they endured and fought.[39] As can be imagined Carlson's methods did not find favour with traditional Marines.[40]

Organisationally British Commandos were structured as; battalions, squadrons, troops and sections. While these mirrored the basic structure of an infantry battalion, the relationship between the component parts of a Commando battalion was different to that of a standard infantry battalion. Within the standard infantry battalion each company and platoon was a component part of the whole, designed and intended to operate as such. Within the Commando battalion each component was an independent entity designed to operate autonomously if required to, as well as trained to support each other if needed to do so. The Australian Independent Companies only every operated as individual companies, and more often than not this was only as elements of these, in small groups. When the companies were transformed into Commandos and absorbed into Commando Regiments, they remained operationally organised as distinct Squadrons and continued to operate in small groups drawn from within the Squadrons. In 1945 there was only one occasion when more than one Australian Commando Squadron was tasked to the same mission; 2/6th Cavalry Commando Regiment's defence of the Jikkoku Pass. The continuance of this Commando model differed markedly to the British where from 1943 on Commandos would be deployed in battalion and brigade groups. The Marine Corps model varied

37 Shultz, *Evans Carlson, Marine Raider*, pp. 19–30.
38 USMCA, COLL/1 378, Land Charles T, 17–18 August 1942, Makin Raid.
39 Wukovits, *American Commando – Evans Carlson*, pp. 265–6.
40 USMCA, COLL/1 378, Land Charles T, 17–18 August 1942, Makin Raid.

from both the British and the Australian. The Raiders were organised as battalions with each battalion operating in distinctly different styles. The 1st Battalion with only one exception always operated as a full conventional battalion, while the 2nd Battalion only every operated in groups of companies.

The operational employment of British, Australian and United States Commandos once again exhibit similarities and marked differences. British Commandos began their career in small teams raiding the German occupied European coast. Many of these raids achieved very little of military consequence, although those such as Operation Claymore against the Lofoten Islands in Norway 4 March 1941, and Operation Chariot, the St. Nazaire Raid, 28 March 1942 achieved lasting results. A standard Commando mission during 1940–1942 would be to land, from boat, ship or submarine, proceed to the objective, carry out whatever function had been decreed for the mission, and return to their transport and depart. A raid was normally planned to not last longer than 24 hours before the raiding party was withdrawn.[41] This role began to transform at the beginning of 1943 with the changing strategic situation, resulting in the need for raiding the enemy diminishing. Around this time British Commandos were reorganised, with the addition of 3-inch mortars and Vickers machineguns to their formations, indicating a move away from the lightly equipped raiding modus operandi.[42] During the 1943 Italian campaign Commandos were used to spearhead landings and advances, capture coastal objectives and seize strategic features. Small unit raiding was not entirely ignored and during the December 1943 Operation Hardtack a series of reconnaissance raids along the French coast was conducted.[43] Operation Overlord, 6 June 1944, saw two brigades of Commandos act as spearheads for the Normandy landings. Commandos undertook a similar role for Operation Dragoon in southern France, 15 August 1944. Through the remainder of 1944 and 1945 Commandos undertook a number of roles all of which were essentially conventional in nature. There was a brief interlude in the closing days of the war in Europe in which the old spirit of the Commando raid returned, when Commandos were detailed to Operation Plunder, in which they had to escort teams of technical experts ahead of the main Allied forces, and raid German sites to secure documentation and equipment before they could be destroyed or removed by the retreating Germans.[44] The role the Commandos undertook in the Far East during 1944 and 1945 involved some amphibious spearhead work, but was essentially conventional in nature supporting larger formations and relying on heavy weapon and tank support.[45]

The Australian Commando experience was an evolutionary one, moving from capricious deployments, to well-conceived independent operations, and on to a final role

---

41 TNA, WO199/1849, Formation of Irregular Commandos 1940 June to 1942 Sept.
42 Messenger, *The Commandos 1940–1946*, p. 191.
43 Ibid, pp. 251–255.
44 Ibid, pp. 316–19.
45 Ibid, pp. 383–406.

of close tactical support for higher formations. This involved the two distinct phases of the Independent Companies 1941–1943 and Commandos 1944–1945. During the Independent Company phase the basic combat technique was, in the vernacular of those who conducted it, to 'Punch 'em and piss off'.[46] Just what 'piss off' meant though was very different to the British model where raiders would withdraw entirely. In the Australian case it meant to pull back to a location which was still within operational and tactical reach of the enemy. The length of time Independent Companies remained in operational areas was a characteristic of the companies that distinguished them markedly from their British or US peers. The 2/2nd Independent Company remained in the field for eleven months as did 2/5th Independent Company. The 2/6th Independent Company for six months in Papua, and a further six months from Kaiapit and into the Ramu Valley. During the Salamaua campaign 2/3rd Independent company was in the field for eight months, and the Bena Force companies for eight months with one of those companies, 2/7th Independent Company, which was at Wau-Salamaua and Bena Force being in the field for an extraordinary 14 months. Both the Commandos of 2/6th Cavalry Commando Regiment and 2/8th Commando Squadron were in the field for nine months during 1944–1945. Such extended periods of unconventional operations were unique to Australian Commandos and markedly different to that practiced by British Commandos or Marine Raiders. The tasks allocated to Australian Commandos also varied from those allocated to British and Marine Commandos. Rather than quick raids as with British and 2nd Battalion of the Marine Raiders, Australian Commandos during 1942–1943 acted as autonomous units conducting ongoing detailed reconnaissance and harassing enemy rear areas. This was a distinctively Australia characteristic of Commando warfare at this stage of the war. During the Commando phase of the Australian Commando experience during 1944–1945 this all changed with Commandos losing their autonomy and operating in the role of light infantry in direct support of larger formations. This was much more akin to how the British Commandos were operating at the same time although not in the larger formations the British were employing. Only one of the eleven Commando squadrons, 2/8th Commando Squadron did not follow this pattern and continued to operate in the Independent Company style.

The employment of the Marine Raiders was both similar to and very different to that of the British and Australian experience. As we have seen there were two distinct models operating within the Raiders. The 1st Battalion was trained as a standard rifle battalion with raider attributes, the 2nd Battalion as a radically organised and managed guerrilla force. The experiences of each reflected these different characteristics. The first employment of the 1st Battalion was to land on Tulagi Island on 7–9 August 1942. Together with two other rifle battalions the Raider battalion cleared the island of Japanese. The 1st Battalion then went on to Guadalcanal where it played a decisive role in the battle for Edson's Ridge on 12–14 September, and the crossing

46 Pinney, *The Barbarians*, p. 108.

of the Matanikau River 7–10 October 1942. In all these actions the 1st Battalion operated in a conventional manner. There was one moment when the 1st Battalion broke the conventional mould and did conduct a raid, when two companies landed on the north coast of Guadalcanal at Tasimboko on 8 September 1942. There they captured and destroyed a radio station as well as a major Japanese supply dump. Documents were also captured which revealed plans for a forthcoming offensive by the Japanese. The battalion was withdrawn from combat in December 1942 and after an eleven month hiatus returned to active service on 1 November 1943, at Cape Torokina Bougainville, in which it assaulted Japanese beach defences. In January 1944 it was withdrawn from combat once again and did not return to service as a Raider battalion. The 2nd Raider battalion's experiences were markedly different. Having sent two companies to Midway Island as a garrison in May, a decidedly non-Raider task, two other companies of the battalion landed from submarines to raid Makin Island, the northern most of the Gilbert Islands, on 17 August 1942. Rough seas, faulty motors on their rubber boats, and contradictory and confusing orders issued by Carlson at the last moment, resulted in the raid becoming confused. Despite killing numerous Japanese on the island the withdrawal was mismanaged and nine Raiders were left behind.[47] This first sortie of the Carlson's Raiders was officially described as a raid with 'mixed results', but in reality it achieved very little.[48] None of the objectives of the raid; to capture prisoners, documents, destroy facilities and equipment, distract Japanese resources from Guadalcanal and disrupt Japanese plans to strike further south were achieved.[49] Historian Gordon Rottman in *Carlson's Marine Raiders Main Island 1942* delivers a harsh tactical analysis of the Makin raid pointing out the basic tactical and operational errors committed by Carlson and his raiding party during the raid.[50] Nevertheless, as one of the first strikes back by US land forces at the Japanese since Pearl Harbor, the Makin Island raid provided the fodder for a propaganda bonanza, with the raid being presented in newspapers, magazines and even a Hollywood movie as a great victory.[51] If there was one practical positive outcome of the Makin Island raid it was to validate Carlson's organisation of his rifle squads into three fire teams. This organisation was adopted by the entire Marine

47 The nine Raiders left behind attempted to escape but were captured on Kwajalein Island and executed there by the Japanese, see: Rottman, *Carlson's Marine Raiders Main Island 1942*, pp. 72–3.
48 USMCHD, Folder Raiders: 2nd Marine Raider Battalion – Carlson.
49 Rottman, *Carlson's Marine Raiders Makin Island Raid 1942*, pp. 56–7.
50 Ibid, pp. 75–7.
51 A search of Newspapers.com <https://www.newspapers.com/search/#query=makin+island+raid&offset=15> (consulted 20 June 2017), for Makin Island raid reveals 39,682 hits. While not all of these will be contemporary newspapers it does indicate the extent to which the press played up the raid for propaganda purposes. The movie portraying the Main Island raid was 'Gung Ho' Walter Wagner Productions, Universal Studios released 20 December 1943 and starring Randolph Scott. The movie was a box office success, see: <https://en.wikipedia.org/wiki/Gung_Ho!_(1943_film)#Plot> (consulted 1 August 2017).

Corps in 1944, and remains the organisation of Marine rifle squads to this day. The next foray for the 2nd Battalion was when it embarked on a trek across Guadalcanal Island, 6 November to 4 December 1942. Ostensibly intended to cut off any Japanese retreating from combat with the main Marine force, Carlson's mission resulted in his force operating in a jungle environment for some 29 days. When the trek finished Carlson claimed to have killed 488 Japanese. The cost however was debilitating. From a total force of 316 only 57 of Carlson's Raiders remained fit for duty when the mission ended, 16 had been killed and 18 wounded by the enemy, but there had been 225 non battle casualties from illness.[52] In an environment in which Australian Independent Companies operated efficiently for months on end Carlson's Raiders were essentially destroyed in only 29 days. The Makin and Guadalcanal expeditions marked the only significant actions of the 2nd Raider Battalion. Two more Raider battalions were added during 1943, with the 3rd Battalion seeing service on Bougainville. By January 1944 the Marine's war had become one of 'amphibious blitzkrieg' against increasingly fortified enemy islands. The time had come to bulldoze the Japanese from their island outposts by brute force.[53] The number of specialised landing ships had increased allowing amphibious assaults by any number of units. Marine Battalions had become multi mission forces with sub-units trained in raider tactics and skills. The scope of amphibious warfare had outgrown the Raiders.[54] Under this new reality there was simply no reason to maintain the Raiders. With this the axe fell and the Marine High command, which had never approved of the Raiders, especially Carlson's Raiders, disbanded the Raider Battalions.

One common feature of all three Commando services was the resistance and opposition they confronted from their regular mainstream military establishments. This was not uncommon and reflected the reluctance of regular troops to accept what was for them the unnecessary exceptional character of the Commandos. Commandos did not conform to any standard of operational behaviour with which regular commanders had been familiar. In Britain during 1940 the opposition came as a normal consequence of Commandos taking the best troops from units at a time of national emergency. This manifested itself by units being reluctant to release troops for Commando service and unloading unsuitable personnel to the Commandos. An example of this was a July 1940 response to an instruction to release personnel for Commando service received from the commanding officer of the 1st Battalion Scots Guards, who informed the Army that his Battalion would not send any more officers and was 'not in a position'

---

52 USMCHD, Folder Raiders: 2nd Marine Raider Battalion– Carlson; USMCHD, Headquarters, Second Marine Raider Battalion First Marine Amphibious Corps, Subject: Report of the operations of this battalion on Guadalcanal between 4 November and 4 December, 1942 – December 20, 1942, Folder Raiders: 2nd Marine Raider Battalion – Carlson.
53 Hargreaves, *Special Operations in World War II*, p. 308.
54 Alexander, *Edson's Raiders*, p. 303.

to send any other ranks.⁵⁵ Commandos also challenged entrenched social conventions within the Army. In December 1940 Dill issued an instruction to units which stated that the Commandos needed officers. The only prerequisite for a commission in the Commandos was to show promise and ability, and that men from the ranks who displayed such attributes could be recommend for officer training. This struck at the time honoured prerequisite for an officer to be a gentleman. In a direct refutation of this Dill made the point that it did not matter what school you came from when officer candidature was concerned.⁵⁶ The reluctance to support Commandos from within the British Army was exacerbated by the feeling amongst many soldiers that given the infrequency of Commando operations Commandos were not 'earning their keep'.⁵⁷ There was also some resentment at the Commandos being portrayed as the harbinger of Britain's offensive spirit, rather than to disseminate that spirit more broadly amongst the army.⁵⁸ In such a climate having to surrender troops to the Commandos was considered an imposition. This prejudice against Commandos remained entrenched. As late as January 1942, Commandos were described by one senior officer as, 'undisciplined rabble'.⁵⁹ The very top of the Allied command hierarchy was not immune from underplaying Commandos. Both Generals Dwight D. Eisenhower and Lieutenant General Harold Alexander were accused by Lord Louis Mountbatten, who was then head of COO, of ignoring advice on the best way to manage Commandos and subsequently making decisions that would disadvantage Commando units.⁶⁰ There was a sense amongst senior Commando officers that the General Staff had little knowledge or understanding of Commando characteristics and capabilities.⁶¹ Laycock would complain that the 'powers to be', as he called them, showed a 'dismal obstinacy' at understanding how best to employ Commandos.⁶² It could be argued that such complaints were the result of the Commandos expressing their anger at not being held in the high regard and priority they assumed was theirs. Senior commanders no doubt had a great many more things to consider that placating Commandos, but nonetheless there was indeed a distance between Commando expectations and the realities of operations on the grand scale, and this was often interpreted by Commandos as opposition to Commandos.

55 LHMA, Laycock 1/3, Papers of Major General Robert Laycock, From Lt. Col. Commanding 1 Battalion Scots Guards, 18 July 1940.
56 LHMA, Dill 3/1/10, Papers of Sir John Dill, June 40–Mar 41.
57 Messenger, *The Commandos 1940–1946*, p. 407
58 Ibid, p. 408
59 LHMA, Laycock 2/8, Papers of Major General Robert Laycock, Commando Training From Lt. Col. R.E. Laycock, 10 Jan 42, LHCMA.
60 LHMA, Laycock 5/25, Papers of Major General Robert Laycock, Mountbatten to Col. A.H. Head 11 March 43.
61 LHMA, Laycock 5/27, C Papers of Major General Robert Laycock, Colonel Will Glendining to Laycock 9 Jan 1943.
62 LHMA, Laycock 6/16, Papers of Major General Robert Laycock, Laycock to 'Tom' 11 March 1943.

Opposition to Commandos within the Australian army depended very much on the stage of the war in which it occurred. From the very first moments the Independent Company training team set foot in Australia they met with opposition. Calvert's experience of being accused of being a Nazi agent, and the suspicion the team came under as a consequence was the first manifestation of the distrust of the Independent Company concept by the Australian Army. Once these initial false impressions had been resolved, opposition dissipated to the degree that an Independent Company training program was allowed. This tolerance, however, evaporated in November 1941 when the Commando training programme was terminated. When the programme was reinstated in December 1941 opposition continued but in a fragmented manner. A characteristic feature of the Army's relationship with its Commandos up until late 1943 was that tolerance of Commandos was entirely dependent upon individual perceptions and prejudice. As an institution the Army expressed no interest in Commandos, which in its own way illustrates its opposition to the concept. When the Army finally in late 1943 early 1944 devised a collective set of guidelines for Commandos it chose to define its Commandos as conventional light infantry, thus emphasising that there was no place within the Army's perception of military operations for autonomous unconventional units. The Australian Army did in fact increase the number of Commando Squadrons from seven to eleven during 1944–1945. It did so, however, entirely on conventional terms and with no intention of allowing unconventional Commando operational methods, even if 2/8th Commando Squadron broke the mould intended by the Army.

Opposition to the United States Marine Raiders occurred from the very beginning, and from the very top of the Marines command hierarchy. Establishing Commandos as part of the Marine Corps was seen as danger to the integrity of the Marine Corps.[63] None other than Major General Thomas Holcomb the Commandant of the Marine Corps expressed his opinion that Commandos as a separate entity within the Marine Corps would be inappropriate and would be bitterly resented by Marine personnel.[64] In Holcomb's opinion Carlson's Raiders achieved very little and the unit was consequently of little use.[65] It was considered that there was no reason to establish

---

63 USMCA, Thomas Holcomb Series 1.1 Correspondence December 1941–January 1942, Major General Chas F.B. Price to Maj. Gen. Thomas Holcomb, 16 January 1942.
64 USMCA, Thomas Holcomb Series 1.1 Correspondence December 1941–January 1942, Holcomb to Samuel W. Meek 19 January 1942.
65 D.J. Ulbrich, *Preparing for Victory*, p.125. An argument put to this author by one historian at the United States Marine Corps History Division was that the Raiders achieved very little because the Marine high command did not want them to. The high command had no interest in seeing the Raiders succeed, and by not utilising the Raiders as much as they could have they were able to use this as evidence that there was no use for them: conversation with Annette Amerman, Historian United States Marine Corps History Division, 17 May 2016.

an elite force within an organisation that saw itself as elite.⁶⁶ The consensus was that any well trained Marine unit could perform Raider type tasks, and that it served no useful purpose to create such a unit.⁶⁷ Unable to halt the creation of the Raiders due to Presidential patronage the Marines were compelled to raise two Raider battalions. When Carlson embarked on his radical training program with the 2nd Raider Battalion it challenged every traditional value of the Marine Corps. In such circumstances entrenched opposition was guaranteed. The opinion of Charles Land, a senior Non Commissioned Officer who found himself in Carlson's battalion due to a transfer and no choice of his own, epitomized this attitude. Land considered Carlson was indulging in double talk and ridicule of the Marine Corps with his ideas. He was further of the opinion that Carlson ran his battalion as a 'selfish concern not part of the Marine Corps' and that 'Gung Ho' rather than 'Working Together' really meant 'Hooray for me I've got mine'. He considered Carlson's Raiders to be an over-publicised rabble.⁶⁸ There was a fundamental conflict of culture and values between the concept of Raiders and the Marine Corps. This influenced every aspect of the relationship and would eventually lead to the disbandment of the Raiders.

Did war planning play any part in Commando operations in Britain, Australia and the United States? War planning in this context is defined as either strategic or grand tactical planning, and is not related to day to day tactical planning. It is certain that British strategic war planners considered Commandos during 1940–1942, if for no other reason than to lift national morale and attempt to win back some strategic initiative from the enemy. From 1943 onwards Commandos receded in importance in relation to strategic war planning, although they played an important role in grand tactical war planning being used in a variety of roles such as specific reconnaissance, spearhead, storming of enemy strong points, and flank guards for Divisional and Corps sized formations. In the Australian context, Commando operations feature at both the strategic and grand tactical levels of war planning. There are three examples of Commandos being used as strategic assets; the deployment of an Independent Company to Wau in May 1942, the employment of 2/6th Independent Company to scout 7 Division's left flank on the Kokoda Track and the deployment of Independent Companies to the Bena Bena plateau in May 1943. With two of these deployments, Wau and Bena Bena, the intention was to 'hold the line' in strategically important areas and deny the enemy unimpeded access to those areas. With the

---

66   USMCHD, Study 11988, 17 Dec 43. This antipathy was expressed as late as 2011 when the Commandant of the Marine Corps Gen. Jim Amos refused to rename the modern USMC MARSOC (Marine Corps Forces Special Operations Command) 'Raiders' after the WW2 Raiders. Justifying his decision Amos said, 'your allegiance, your loyalty…is to the Marine Corps…we're Marines first.' See: *Marine Corps Times*, February 28, 2011. It seems, however, that due to ongoing pressure from MARSOC to adopt the title 'Raiders' that the title was granted to MARSOC on 6 August 2014.
67   USMCHD, Document 30906: 24 December 1943. Memo for Assistant Chief of Staff.
68   USMCA, COLL/1 378, Land Charles T, 17–18 August 1942, Makin Raid, pp.12 and 16.

actions of 2/6th Independent Company on the Kokoda Track it was to provide 7th Division with strategic intelligence to determine if the enemy were threatening the left flank of the main Australian force along the Kokoda Track. The role played by 2/3rd Independent Company during the Wau-Salamaua campaign fell between strategic and grand tactical. In the strategic sense the Company provided reliable security for the left flank of 3rd Division allowing it to conduct its primary operations. It also provided invaluable intelligence on terrain, topography and enemy strengths, positions and movements which provided the commander of the Division with the information he required to plan his operations. For the Marine Raiders the only example of war planning involving a Commando operation was the Makin Island Raid. The intention of the raid was to capture prisoners and by revealing to the Japanese the vulnerability of their island outposts hopefully get them to redeploy troops away from the Solomon Islands to reinforce those outposts. That the raid failed on both counts does not diminish the plan.

Whether or not Commandos were seen as an important form of warfare depends very much by what is meant by important. If important is defined as offering something unique and of value to operations which provided some advantage to the overall war effort, then it is certainly the case in the early stages of the War that British and the United States Commandos were important elements in bolstering public morale. In the Australian experience this aspect of Commando service was not so pronounced, although the raid on Salamaua and the Independent Company on Timor did receive a great deal of attention from the press and helped with public morale. In the context of a unique contribution to war fighting capacity British Commandos, with the exception of the Lofoten and St Nazaire raids, achieved little of military significance, while the Marine Raiders, when acting as Commandos achieved little of any real significance at all. As British Commandos moved to take their place in the line alongside regular troops they tended to lose the unique character they enjoyed earlier in the war. With this any special acknowledgment of their unique importance ceased. Acknowledgement of the importance of Commando warfare by the Australian Army was inconsistent at best during the Second World War. During 1940 and 1941 there was no support for the idea of Commandos from the Army at all with the consequence that they were employed on a number of ill-considered missions. In 1942 this changed slightly, with recognition that Commandos were capable of fulfilling an economy of force function as well as providing specialist reconnaissance assistance to the main force. By 1943 Commandos had come to be recognised, at least by some senior commanders as important assets, with them playing significant roles during the Salamaua campaign, Bena Force and at Kaiapit. However, as we have seen, the Australian Army as an institution had no intention of continuing its unconventional Commando experience. When in 1944–1945 it did develop Commando guidelines it was to transform Commandos into a more conventional character. Thus the importance of Commandos for the Australian Army is determined by the stage of the war and which level of the army is considered with a fundamental difference between individuals and the institution as a whole.

Were the manpower and resources devoted to Commandos well spent? Lieutenant General William Slim dismissed special service units as a waste of manpower and resources and questioned the place of Special Forces in an ongoing conventional campaign.[69] For Slim, wars were not won by 'super soldiers', but by the average quality of standard units.[70] Slim's observations came from a commander who had to balance the availability of resources to maintain his forces in a harsh tropical environment against the demands of Major General Orde Wingate to divert those resources from the main effort to special operations. Slim's concerns do, however, resonate when one considers the relative ineffectiveness of British Commando operations when placed alongside the resources allocated to them. Commando raids required the use of sea and land assets. For this expenditure Commandos only achieved two notable successes; the Lofoten Islands and St Nazaire. It could be argued that the propaganda value of Commando actions justified the resources expended, but this would be difficult to justify to military commanders grasping for every crumb to support their formations. The cost effectiveness of the Marine Raiders is questionable. Resources allocated to the Raiders do not appear to have delivered commensurate returns. The 1st Raider Battalion, with only one exception, operated as a standard infantry battalion, negating any meaningful assessment of its cost effectiveness as a Commando unit. The 2nd Raider Battalion, did act as Commandos, and was supplied with special equipment in the form of boats, outboard motors, and special weapons. The battalion also required the use of naval transport in the form of troop carrying submarines to deploy for one mission, and transport to Guadalcanal for another. In both cases the battalion achieved very little of any military consequence and were essentially in military terms a waste of resources. They were not, however, an unmitigated waste. The Raiders provided a valuable propaganda panacea for the US public at a time when public morale was in great need of a boost.[71] Only in this non-operational context can it be argued that the Marine Raiders were cost effective. In contrast Australian Independent Companies and Commandos would prove to be eminently cost effective. The Australian military was never overwhelmingly supplied with resources and had to make the best use of what it had at any time. The fact that Australian Army Commandos operated at Company or Squadron in size limited the resources allocated to them. In addition Australian Army Commandos were never provided with extensive inventories of equipment, nor were they provided with any special transport facilities. During 1941 and 1942 the Army maintained its Independent Companies on a shoestring budget, indeed with 2/3rd Independent Company on New Caledonia it did not maintain the Company at all. The practical result was that at this time the Independent Companies caused no strain on Army resources. The operations of

---

69 William Slim, *Defeat into Victory* (The Reprint Society London: London, 1957), pp. 529–31
70 Ibid, p. 529
71 Alexander, *Edson's Raiders*, p. 307.

2/6th Independent Company in Papua during 1942 also posed no strain on Army resources, indeed the Americans provided some of the resources necessary to maintain the Company. During 1943 Independent Companies were maintained through normal army supply channels. The cost of maintaining Bena Force was only a fraction of what it would have been to maintain a battalion sized mainstream unit. In the same way maintaining 2/3rd Independent Company during the Salamaua campaign was eminently cost effective considering the contribution made by the Company to the campaign. During 1944–1945 the Army's logistical base had developed to a point where it was easily able to maintain its Commandos and they posed no drain on resources. It can therefore be argued that Australian Commandos proved themselves to be eminently cost effective.

Determining the value added to operations by Commandos is problematic. The claim has been made that no Commando operation in any theatre of war can be said to have made an indispensable contribution to the tactical and strategic success of the regular army in any battle'.[72] This is essentially true as in every case victory was ultimately achieved with or without the contribution of Commandos. What this assertion does not take into account, however, is the value Commandos offered to regular army operations which assisted to make the outcomes of those operations more effective. Examples of such contributions amongst the early British Commandos and Marine Raiders, other than the Lofoten Islands and St Nazaire, are difficult to find. Later British Commando contributions did assist in mainstream operations but by that time, Commandos were generally operating very much as conventional infantry. The Marine Raiders did contribute significantly to mainstream operations on Guadalcanal but as conventional infantry. Marine Raiders operating as Commandos contributed only once, when 1st Marine Raiders destroyed the Japanese supply base at Tasimboko, to the tactical and strategic success of regular formations and then only indirectly. Other than that Marine Raiders contributed nothing to the success of any mainstream forces. The same cannot be said for Australian Commandos who contributed profoundly to the tactical and strategic success of the regular army on more than one occasion. The scouting activities of 2/6th Independent Company, the operations of 2/3rd Independent Company and Bena Force all contributed significantly to mainstream operations. The capture of Kaiapit by Commandos was another example of a crucial contribution by Commandos to the wider war effort. While it is true that in every case the absence of Commandos in Australia's battles with the Japanese would not have changed the ultimate outcome of those battles, the achievement of objectives occurred more smoothly than it would have without the contribution of Commandos. In this way while not technically indispensable Australian Commands certainly proved themselves to be valuable components of the success for Australian forces.

Longevity for Commando units provides a further comparison between the way in which such units were managed by Britain, the United States and Australia. The

---

72 Thomas, 'The Importance of Commando Operations', p. 698.

British maintained their Commandos until the end of the war, even though some Commando units were disbanded and the nature of Commando service changed and adapted as the war continued. In contrast the United States Marines disbanded and disposed of the Raiders in November 1943, converting the Raider battalions into infantry battalions. The Australian Commando experience was something of an amalgam of the British and United States experience. In an echo of the attitude of the Marine High Command the Australian Army never fully accepted the idea of Independent Companies and tolerated its unconventional Commandos until 1943 but then, as the nature of the war evolved into one of big formations and overwhelming firepower, that tolerance disappeared. Rather, however, than take the line of the Marines when faced with similar circumstances, and completely dispose of its Commando units the Australian Army chose to retain and adapt those units to the new circumstances. In this way the Australian Commando experience was more akin to the British experience.

The 'misuse' of Commandos or claims that Commandos have been misused is a common feature of Commandos in any army and occurred in the management of the British, United States Marine and Australian Commandos. In many ways the perception of misuse is entirely subjective and determined very much by the perceived role the Commandos saw for themselves, as opposed to the role that the Army envisaged for them. These roles were not always the same, and the role often changed depending on circumstance and the necessity of whatever current priorities existed. British Commandos were convinced that they were being misused in North Africa during 1943. In January 1943 Colonel Will Glendining, who was at the time commanding Commandos in Tunisia, bemoaned the fact that his Commandos were given all sorts of odd jobs, none of which were related to the Commando or combined operations role.[73] British high command was suffering a shortage of manpower at the time and Commandos were being used as conventional infantry as a matter of necessity. Commandos of course, did not see it this way. British higher command was not always oblivious to the failure to employ Commandos in a manner appropriate to their training. In July 1944 during the battle for Normandy, Montgomery acknowledged that he had kept Commandos far too long in the line as regular infantry and wanted to withdraw them, but was unable to due to manpower shortages on the front line. There were, however, times when Commandos were blatantly misused. Perhaps the most extreme example of the British misuse of Commandos was the employment of the Long Range Desert Group (LRDG) to assault the Aegean Island of Levitha in October 1943. The LRDG was not trained or equipped for the task, nor had any part of its previous experience prepared it for such a mission. Those who planned the mission ignored protests from the LRDG pointing these facts out. No prior reconnaissance was conducted for the assault before 50 LRDG raiders were sent in against

---

73 LHMA, Laycock 5/27, Papers of Major General Robert Laycock, Colonel Will Glendining to Laycock 9 Jan 1943.

the German garrison which enjoyed complete control of the air. The raid was a disaster with 41 of the raiders being lost. In an equally incongruous follow up to this disaster the LRDG was used to garrison the island of Leros which fell to the Germans, killing 10 LRDG and capturing 100.[74] Australia had its fair share of examples of misuse of Commandos. The deployment of the 2/1st Independent Company in penny packets to the Island Barrier in June 1941 was a foolish exercise which doomed the company. The failure to maintain 2/3rd Independent Company on New Caledonia was an abrogation of the basic responsibilities towards the welfare of a unit. Other misuse was relatively trivial with local middle level commanders imposing their concept of how Commandos should behave, which often led to them having to perform tasks they were unsuited for. Moten's cry that Commandos were not 'proper infantry' is one case in point. The assault of 2/4th Commando Squadron on Tarakan Hill in May 1945 appears to be misuse but as explained earlier was brought about by the pressures of the circumstances of the moment. Interestingly the Marine Raiders were never misused as Commandos. Their one Commando raid was conceived as a mission entirely appropriate for the Raiders, in that it did not succeed was the consequence of mismanagement during the raid rather than faulty conception beforehand. The failure to employ Commandos at all is one example of how Armies mismanaged their Commandos. This was a feature of the British, United States Marines and Australian Commando experience. In May 1941 Laycock wrote to Major General Arthur Smith, the Chief of the General Staff in the Middle East, complaining that his Commandos had been sitting idle, and that the patience of the men was almost exhausted. He went further to warn that the men were beginning to feel that they had been recruited under false pretences.[75] So frustrating did this become for the Commandos that one Commando scrawled on the troop deck of his ship, 'Never in the whole history of human endeavour have so few been buggered about by so many'.[76] This was no doubt not an unusual reflection by a soldier on his superiors, but nonetheless reflected a sense of frustration. The Marine Raiders only conducted two Commando style raids in their brief history. It is tempting to speculate that the reluctance of the Marine Corps to employ its Commandos as Commandos may well have been due to a deliberate reluctance to employ them so as to build a case to argue for their elimination on the grounds of their lack of utility. In the Australian context keeping 2/8th Commando Squadron on essentially meaningless patrol duty in the remote Northern Territory of Australia from 1942 until 1944 was an example of the refusal of the army to deploy to active service a trained Commando unit. It could equally be argued that the Atherton Tableland experience was an abject waste of valuable Commando assets, although the army would have argued this was not so as it transformed what it saw as the now

74 Hargreaves, *Special Operations in World War II*, p. 191.
75 LHMA, Laycock 6/3, Papers of Major General Robert Laycock, Laycock to Maj. Gen. Arthur Smith C.G.S. G.H.Q. Middle East 6 May 41.
76 Messenger, *The Commandos 1940–1946*, p. 95.

useless Independent Companies into useful Commando Squadrons. It is certainly the case that 2/12th Commando Squadron at Labaun Island in July 1945 was not employed as Commandos and that 2/11th Commando Squadron was underemployed as Commandos. Accusations of disuse can be countered by referring to the available lack of opportunities to employ Commandos as Commandos, especially later in the war. It is, however, hard to distance oneself from the belief that with a little imagination such opportunities could have been found.

This chapter has, by comparing and contrasting the Australian Army's Commando experience with that of its allies, provided an insight into the strengths and weaknesses of the Australian management of Commandos during the Second World War. It has shown that despite common features Australian Commandos evolved a very distinctive character and operational style especially so during the period 1942–1943. This distinctiveness was generated very much by the unique physical nature of their theatre of operations. The primitive tropical wilderness found in New Guinea, Bougainville and New Britain represented virgin territory of the most extreme kind. Within this environment Australian Commandos, acting autonomously in small highly mobile groups, and without fixed lines of communication or supply, operated in a manner which effectively adapted to their unique circumstances. They were, in this unique operational environment, able to practice their skills and attributes of boldness, self-reliance, improvisation, and aggression. It is debateable if they would have been able to adopt similar tactics in surroundings where the terrain was not so underdeveloped, or where the enemy were emplaced in fixed defences with limited access to their flanks or rear areas. It was notable though that they did so within the context of the environment in which they served. Australian Army Commandos were, at least in the mid war period, more consistently active and directly effective in the impact they had upon the enemy than either British Commandos or United States Marine Raiders. This was a great achievement and one that needs to be acknowledged.

Conclusion

This book has presented a history of the Australian Independent Companies and Commandos from their inception in July 1940 until the end of the Second World War in August 1945. This history has followed the evolution of the Australian Army's management of its Commandos from initial rejection and disinterest, to astute appreciation of how to employ their unique unconventional attributes, and finally to a restrained conventional utilisation of them. Throughout this history the conflict between the conservative and unconventional perceptions of warfare resonates. The Institutional culture of the Australian Army during the 1930s and 1940s was deeply conservative befitting an organisation that was complacent with its own capabilities and one that did not consider that anything outside of its experience had anything of value to add. The radically unconventional Independent ethos of the original Independent Companies could only be opposed in such a cultural milieu. Even so some elements within the Army, represented by localised senior commanders, did not share this conservatism and this led to an inconsistency in the management of Commandos by the Army which persisted throughout the War. When in late 1943 the Army finally made the effort to develop an overall set of guidelines for its Commandos it was still unable to impose its concept of Commando warfare as it wished on the Army as a whole.

Throughout this history the theme of initiative features prominently. This initiative reveals itself in a number of ways. The first being by individual Commandos who took the step to volunteer for service in formations of which initially virtually nothing was known. The second, being the evolution of tactics both at an individual level and as units, where adaptation to the physical environment and the tactical circumstances were essential. The third being the initiative demonstrated by individual senior commanders who operating on their own recognisance permitted Commandos to operate in a manner which extracted maximum value from their distinct qualities.

In the same way the theme of resilience cannot be discounted. One distinctive feature of Australian Commandos was that they remained on active service as Commandos for extraordinarily long periods of time. Be it the isolated guerrilla force on Timor, the 'Ragged Arsed 5th'; the long range patrols along the fringes of the Kokoda Track; the brutal fighting at Buna; the long arduous campaign to reclaim Salamaua; the lengthy denial operation of Bena Force; the mobile campaign of ambush and harassment on

Bougainville; or the fighting in New Guinea or on Borneo in the closing days of the War, all proved the stamina and resilience of the Australian Commandos.

While Australia's war would still have been won without the Commandos they undeniably added value to military operations when they were employed appropriately. The achievements of the Australian Army's Commandos, when they were allowed to operate in a manner suited to their temperament and training, indicate that any army which possesses such troops and uses them in an intelligent, assertive and aggressive manner will add value to the operational capabilities of the main force. This was a lesson which remained unlearned by the Australian Army. Australia's Commandos were quickly disbanded following the War's end and the Army discarded that experience from its collective memory. It would not be until 1957, with the formation of one company of Special Air Service troops that the Army began to take tentative steps back along the path of unconventional warfare. The value added to main force operations by Commandos should not be underestimated. Armies that ignore this do so to their disadvantage.

One important lesson which this history does impart is how not to introduce and subsequently manage Special Forces units. Failure to consult at the stage of inception, failure to develop an agency dedicated to the coordination of those forces, failure to develop any clearly identified strategic or tactical role for those forces were all characteristics of the Australian Army's initial management of its Commandos. As the war progressed the army as an institution made little headway in its understanding and management of its Commandos, even though individual commanders did employ them effectively. Even when the Army devised guidelines for its Commandos, these were not universally adopted. There was never at any time during the war any general consensus within the army on just how its Commandos were to be managed. In general terms Australia's management of its Commandos during the Second World War was not how Special Forces should be administered.

The Independent Companies – Commandos are acknowledged today within the Australian Defence Force as setting the example and as the foundation for Australia's modern Special Forces.[1] In reality this presumed lineage and association is more emotional than actual, given that the Commandos were all disbanded by the beginning of February 1946 and the concept of unconventional warfare forgotten by the Australian Army until the formation of a Special Air Service company in 1957 and the Special Air Service Regiment in 1964. Even then the attitude of the army as a whole to its Special Forces was lacklustre at best and remained so for most of the remainder of the 20th century. In a conversation with Brigadier Christopher Roberts former commanding officer of the Special Air Service Regiment (SAS) and later Commander Special Forces he recalled that the attitude of the army towards Special Forces during most of the post-war period fluctuated between ambivalent to hostile.

---

1   Major General Jeff Sengelman Special Operations Commander Australian Army, BAE Theatre Australian War Memorial, 2 August 2016.

The main resistance came from elements within the army, most notably the Infantry which considered there was no need for Special Forces as an infantry battalion could do whatever Special Forces could do, even if as Roberts pointed out they never did. As Roberts saw it there was not much imaginative thinking beyond the old conventional and jungle warfare mindset. When there was support from high level individuals it was a mixed blessing as despite their best intentions they did not know how to use Special Forces. This was reflected in the lack of direction received by Special Forces. Roberts mentioned that during his time as commanding officer of the SAS he never received any direction on what was expected of the Regiment, and that the Regiment was left to its own devices to determine how it should be used. When the Army did intervene it was very much in the old conservative refrain to direct the Regiment to disband its unconventional warfare capabilities. The Commando companies which were part of the Australian Army Reserve were left pretty much to themselves. This did change when Roberts, fighting against resistance from within the Army, established a headquarters for Special Forces and the Special Forces Group which consisted of the SAS and 1st Commando Regiment. This has subsequently evolved into the modern Special Operations Command (SOCOM). The profile of Special Forces did improve with the advent of counter terrorism but this was driven by political factors and even while Special Forces did receive extra funding and support from high level command there was still resistance from elements in the Army. The situation is very different now, with Special Forces being very high profile and the force of choice for politicians. SOCOM has a Major General in command and Special Forces are being used in a wide range of operations.[2] Thus to claim a direct lineage between the Australian Army's Commandos of the Second World War and today's Special Forces is stretching the lineage a tad too far. There is, however, certainly an important and undeniable inspirational debt owed by the special warfare ethos of the modern Australian Army to those practitioners of the art during 1941–1945.

Australian Independent Companies were unique formations. The tactics they employed, time spent as Commandos on active operations and autonomy they were at time granted were distinctive. The history of Australia's Second World War Independent Companies and Commandos, as presented in this history is the first time their story as a collective component of the Australian Army during the Second World War has been attempted. This history fills a gap in the story of the Australian Army's Commandos that has remained empty for far too long. It is the author's hope that this history in some small way has contributed to a more nuanced understanding of what were remarkable military sub-units and the equally remarkable individuals who formed them.

---

2   Conversation with Brigadier Christopher Roberts AM, CSC. 6 November 2018.

Bibliography

Unpublished sources

Australia
Australian Defence Force Academy Library
>D767.7 R46 1945 B/C 438011 Report on Operation Oboe 1 Tarakan Borneo May 1945.
>MS 341 Keating, G., Research papers.

National Archives of Australia
>Series:
>A571 Correspondence files.
>A1241 Diaries of Sir Cyril Brundenell White as (1) Chief of the General Staff and (2) Chairman of the Public Service Board.
>A12383, Royal Commission on Intelligence and Security, correspondence files.
>A1608, Correspondence files.
>A2670, Reference set of War Cabinet agenda with minutes.
>A2680, Advisory War Council Agenda files.
>A2684, Advisory War Council Minute files.
>A5954, The Shedden Collection – Records of Sir Frederick Shedden.
>A6390, Registration and Movement cards, correspondence files.
>A7665, Master set of Army Training Films.
>B883, Second Australian Imperial Force Personnel Dossiers, 1939–1947.
>B3476, Coast-watching files.
>B6390, Routine Orders Part 2.
>MP385/5, Security classified (Secret) correspondence.
>MP508, General Correspondence files.
>MP729/7, Secret Correspondence files.
>MP742, General and civil staff correspondence files and Army personnel files.
>MP917/2, Casualty registers of Australian servicemen in the war 1939–45.
>SP300, ABC Talk Scripts.

Australian War Memorial
>Series:
>52, 2AIF Unit War Diaries.
>54, Written Records, 1939–1945 War.
>55, Allied Translator and Interpreter Section (ATS) publications.
>63, 2nd 2AIF Headquarters (Middle East), registry records.
>67, Official History, 1939–45, Records of Gavin Long, General Editor.

93, Australian War Memorial files – First Series.
113, Records of the Military Section (Army)
124, Naval Historical Collection.
172, Official History, 1939–45 War, Series 1 (Army) Volume VI, Records of David Dexter.
193, Eastern Command 'G' Branch registry files.
243, Inter-service Demobilisation Committee Records.
315, Australian War Memorial registry files – second series.
361,Official Records Microfilm Collection.
DRL, Private Records, Donated Records List.
Manuscripts: MSS1960 Geoffrey Thomas Fraser., *Highly Irregular;* 063813 T. Yoshihara, *Southern Cross: account of the Eastern new Guinea Campaign.*
SO4152, Neil MacDonald recorded interviews with members of the Independent Companies.
University of Queensland Freyer Library
UQFL288, Papers of Peter Pinney.

United Kingdom
National Archives Kew, London
Series:
WO199, War Office: Home Forces Military Headquarters Papers, Second World War.
WO208, War Office Directorate of Military Intelligence and Directorate of Military Intelligence, Ministry of Defence Intelligence Staff. Files.
HS8, Records of Special Operations Executive (SOE), Headquarters Records.
Imperial War Museum Research Centre, London.
Series: 9942 audio recorded interview Michael Calvert
Liddell Hart Military Archive – King's College, London
Series:
Papers of Field Marshal Sir John Dill.
Papers of Major General Sir Robert Laycock.

United States
Archives Branch Historical Division U.S. Marine Corps, Quantico, Virginia
Oral History Transcripts.
Dwight D. Eisenhower Library, Abilene, Kansas
Journal of 1st Bn 128th Infantry, September – November 1942 (incomplete), Series II Library Reference Publications.
MacArthur Memorial, Norfolk, Virginia
Historical Index Cards (Actual) Record Group 3.
'Studies in the History of General Douglas MacArthur's Commands in the Pacific "Establishment of the Southwest Pacific Area and the Papuan Campaign 7 December 1941–22 January 1943"'
National Archives and Records Administration, Washington, D.C.
Series:
RG 319, Records of the Army Staff.
RG407, Records of the Adjutant General's Office.

RG496, Records of General Headquarters, Southwest Pacific Area and United States Army Forces, Pacific (World War II)
Records of the Army Staff Center of Military History – Victory in Papua.
U.S. Marine Corps History Division, Quantico, Virginia
Series: PC56, Folder – Raiders: 1st and 2nd Marine Raider Battalions.

Printed books

Alexander, J.H., *Edson's Raiders*, Naval Institute Press, Annapolis, 2001.
Alexander, L., *Shadows in the Jungle – The Alamo Scouts Behind Japanese Lines in World War II*, New American Library, New York, 2009.
Ambon and Timor Invasion Operations, Military History Section Headquarters Army Forces Far East, Office of the Chief of the Military History Department of the Army, 1953.
Anders, L., *Gentle Knight the Life and Times of Major General Edwin Forrest Harding*, Kent State University Press, Kent State, Ohio, 1981.
Anderson, N., *To Kokoda*, Australian Army Campaigns Series, Australian Army History Unit, Big Sky Publishing, Sydney, 2014.
As You Were 1948, Australian War Memorial, Canberra, 1948.
Astill, D., *Commando White Diamond: Memoir of Service of the 2/8 Australian Commando Squadron, Australia and the South-West Pacific 1942–1945*, Loftus, Sydney, 1996.
Astley, J.B., *The Inner Circle: A View of War at the Top*, The Memoir Club, Stanhope, 2007.
Australian Army at War – The Battle of Wau, Brochure Number One, Department of the Army, 1943.
Australian Army at War – Jungle Trail, Brochure Number Two, Alfred Henry Pettifer Acting Government Printer, 1944.
Australian Army at War – Battle of the Ridges, Brochure Number Three, Alfred Henry Pettifer Acting Government Printer, 1944.
Ayris, C., *All the Bull's Men: No.2 Australian Independent Company (2/2 Commando Squadron)*, published by 2/2 Commando Association, Hamilton Hill, Western Australia, 2006.
Ball, R., *Torres Strait Force 1942–1945: The Defence of Cape York – Torres Strait and Merauke Dutch New Guinea*, Australian Military History Publications, Sydney, 1996.
Barker, R., *One Man's Jungle: A Biography of F. Spencer Chapman*, Chatto & Windus, London, 1975.
Bidwell, S., *The Chindit War: Stillwell, Wingate and the Campaign in Burma: 1944*, Macmillan, New York, 1979.
Bottrell, A.E.E., *Cameos of commandos: Memories of Eight Australian Commando Squadrons in New Guinea and Queensland*, A.E.E. Bottrell, Daw Park, S.A. 1971.
Boxall, J., *Story of the 2/5 Australian Commando Squadron 2AIF*, Metropolitan Printers, Lakemba, NSW, 1961.
Bullard, S., *Japanese Army Operations in the South West Pacific Area – New Britain and the Papua Campaign*, Australian War Memorial, Canberra, 2007.
Brown. C.A (ed.), *The Official History of Special Operations – Australia*, 3 Vols, Organisation, SOA Books, Lexington Kentucky, 2011.
Butlin, S.J., *Australia in the War of 1939–194*, Series Four CIVIL, Volume III, War Economy 1939–1942, Australian War Memorial, Canberra, 1955.

British Commandos, Military Intelligence Service, War Department, Washington, 1942.

Bradley, P., *Hell's Battlefield – The Australians in New Guinea in World War II*, Allen and Unwin, Sydney, 2012.

—— *To Salamau*, Cambridge University Press, Melbourne, 2010.

—— *The Battle for Wau*, Cambridge University Press, Melbourne, 2008.

P. Brune; *The Spell Broken: exploding the myth of Japanese invincibility: Milne Bay to Buna-Sanananda 1942–43*, Allen and Unwin, St Leonards, 1998.

—— *Those Ragged Bloody Heroes: from the Kokoda Trail to Gona Beach 1942*, Allen and Unwin, St Leonards, 1991.

Callinan, B., *Independent Company: The Australian Army in Portuguese Timor 1941–43*, Heinemann, Richmond, Vic, 1984.

Calvert, M., *Prisoners of Hope*, Cooper, London, 1971.

Campbell, A., *The Double Reds of Timor*, John Burridge Military Antiques, Swanbourne, 1995.

Charters, D. and Tugwell M. [ed.], *Armies in Low-Intensity Conflict*, Brassey's Defence Publishers, London, 1989.

Churchill, W.S., *The Second World War Vol.2 Their Finest Hour*, Cassell & Co Ltd, London, 1949.

Cleary, P., *The Men who Came Out of the Ground – a gripping account of Australia's first Commando campaign*, Hachette, Sydney, 2016.

Collins, L., *New Guinea Narrative – The Round trip 1942–1943*, self published, Blairgowie Victoria, 2001.

Collins, P., *Strike Swiftly: The Australian Commando Story*, Watermark Press, Sydney, 2005.

Coyne, R., *The First Commandos: Ralph Coyne's Wartime Experiences 1942–1945*, Petraus Press, Belconnen, 2009.

Dean, P (ed.)., *Australia 1942 – In the Shadow of War*, Cambridge University Press, Melbourne, 2013.

—— *Australia 1943 The Liberation of New Guinea*, Cambridge University Press, Melbourne, 2014.

—— *Australia 1944–45 Victory in the Pacific*, Cambridge University Press, Melbourne, 2016.

Dennis, P. and Grey, J (eds.)., *The Foundations of Victory: The Pacific War 1943–1944*, Australian Army History Conference, 2004.

Derham, R., *The Silence Ruse: Escape from Gallipoli – A Record and Memories of the Life of General Sir Brudenell White KCB KCMG KCVO DSO*, Cliffe Books, Armadale, 1998.

Dexter, D., *The New Guinea Offensives*, Australia in the War of 1939–1945, Series One Army, Volume VI, Australian War Memorial, Canberra, 1961.

Doig, C.D., *The History of the Second Independent Company*, C.D. Doig, Perth, 1986.

Downs, I., *The New Guinea Volunteer Rifles NGVR 1939–1945: A History*, Pacific Press, Broadbeach Waters, 1999.

Duffy, J.P., *War at the End of the World – Douglas MacArthur and the Forgotten Fight for New Guinea*, New American Library, New York, 2016.

Elting, E.M., *Men, Machines, and Modern Times*, M.I.T Press, Cambridge Massachusetts, 1966.

Feuer, A.B. (ed.), *Coast watching in the Solomon Islands – The Bougainville Reports, December 1941–July 1943*, Praeger, New York, 1992.

Fitzsimons, P., *Kokoda*, Hachette, Sydney, 2008.

Foot, M.R., *SOE – The Special Operations Executive 1940–1946*, British Broadcasting Corporation, London, 1984.
Fraser, G., *Highly Irregular*, self-published, Sunshine Coast, 2003.
Gailey, H.A., *MacArthur Strikes Back – Decision at Buna, New Guinea 1942–1943*, Presidio Press, Novato, 2000.
—— *Bougainville 1943–1945 – The Forgotten Campaign*, University of Kentucky Press, Lexington, 1991.
Gamble, B., *Darkest Hour: the True Story of Lark Force at Rabaul, Australia's Worst Military Disaster of World War II*, Zenith Press, St. Paul Minnesota, 2006.
Garland, R., *Nothing is Forever: The History of 2/3rd Commandos*, self published, Malabar Heights, NSW, 1997.
Gates, D., *The British Light Infantry Army c.1790–1815 — Its creation, and Operational role*, B.T. Batsford Ltd., London, 1987.
Gilchrist, D., *Castle Commando*, Oliver and Boyd, Edinburgh, 1960.
Gray C.S., *Explorations in Strategy*, Greenwood Press, Westport, 1996.
—— *Modern Strategy*, Oxford University Press, Oxford, 1999.
—— *The Strategy Bridge*, Oxford University Press, Oxford, 2010.
P. Ham., *Kokoda*, ABC Books, Pymble, 2004.
Hargreaves, A., *Special Operations in World War II: British and American Irregular Warfare*, University of Oklahoma Press, Norman, 2013.
Hogan, D.W., *U.S. Army Special Operations on World War II*, Center of Military History Department of the Army, Washington, D.C., 1992.
Hoffman, J.T., *From Makin to Bougainville: Marine Raiders in the Pacific War*, Marines in World War II Commemorative Series, Director of Marine Corps History and Museums, Marine Corps Historical Center, Washington, 1995.
Hollege, J., *Deeds that Made the AIF*, Hortwitz Publications, Sydney, 1961.
Horner, D., *High Command Australia and Allied Strategy 1939–1945*, Allen and Unwin, Sydney, 1982.
—— *SAS : Phantoms of the jungle : a history of the Australian Special Air Service*, Allen and Unwin, Sydney, 1989.
Inglis, K.S (ed.)., *The History of Melanesia – 2nd Waigan Seminar*, The University of Papua New Guinea-The Research School of Pacific Studies The Australian National University, 1968.
Japanese Army – Notes on Characteristics Organisation Training etc., General Staff Army Headquarters Melbourne, Arbuckel Waddell Pty Ltd, Melbourne, 1942.
James, C., *ANGAU One Man Law*, Self published, Riverwood, 2005.
James, K., *The Hard Slog – Australians in the Bougainville Campaign 1944–45*, Cambridge University Press, Port Melbourne, 2012.
—— *Double Diamond: Australian Commandos in the Pacific War*, Australian War Memorial, Canberra, 2016.
Johnston, G., *War Diary 1942*, Collins, Sydney,1984.
Johnston, M., *Fighting the Enemy – Australian Soldiers and their Adversaries in World War II*, Cambridge University Press, Cambridge, 2000.
—— *The Silent 7th – An Illustrated History of the 7th Australian Division 1940–1946*, Allen & Unwin, Crow's Nest, 2005.
Jungle Warfare – With the Australian Army in the South West Pacific, Australian War Memorial, Canberra, *1944.*

Keating, G., *A Tale of Three Battalions: Combat Morale and Battle Fatigue in the 7th Australian Infantry Brigade, Bougainville, 1944–1945*, Warfare Studies Centre, Canberra, 2007.

Keogh, E.G., *South West Pacific 1941–1945*, Grayflower Productions, 1965.

Khaki and Green – With the Australian Army at Home and Overseas, Australian War Memorial, Canberra, 1943.

King, M.J., *Rangers: Selected Combat Operations in World War II*, Leavenworth Papers, Combat Studies Institute, U.S. Army Command and Staff College, Fort Leavenworth, Kansas, 1985.

Laffin, J., *Raiders: Great Exploits of the Second World War*, History Press, Stroud, 1999.

Ladd, J., *Commandos and Rangers of World War II*, St. Martin's Press, New York, 1978.

Lambert, G.E., *Commando, From Tidal River to Tarakan: The Story of the No. 4 Australian Independent Company 2AIF Later Known as 2/4th Australian Commando Squadron 2AIF, 1941–45*, 2nd/4th Commando Association, Melbourne, 1994.

Lampe, D., *The Last Ditch*, Cassell, London, 1968.

Larsen, C.R., *Pacific Commandos – New Zealanders and Fijians in Action – A History of Southern Independent Commando and First Commando Fiji Guerrillas*, A.H. and A.W. Reed, Wellington, 1946.

Liddell Hart, B., *The Future of Infantry*, Faber and Faber Ltd, London, 1933.

Linderman, A.R.B., *Rediscovering Irregular Warfare: Colin Gubbins and the Origin of Britain's Special Operations Executive*, University of Oklahoma Press, Norman, 2016.

Long, G., *The Final Campaigns, Australia in the War of 1939–1945*, Series One Army, Volume VII, Australian War Memorial, Canberra, 1963.

Macksey, K., *Commando: Hit-and-Run Combat in World War II*, Jove Books, New York, 1991.

Medcalf, P., *War in the Shadows*, University of Queensland Press, St Lucia, 2000.

Messenger, C., *The Commandos 1940–1946*, William Kimber & Co. Ltd, London, 1985.

Meyers, B.F., *Swift Silent and Deadly – Marine Amphibious Reconnaissance in the Pacific 1942–1945*, Naval Institute Press, Annapolis, Maryland, 2004.

Miller, R., *Commandos*, Time-Life Books, Alexandria, 1981.

Milner, S., *United States Army in World War II – Victory in Papua*, Office of the Chief of Military History Department of the Army, Washington, DC, 1957.

McCarthy, D., *First Year: Kokoda to Wau, Australia in the War of 1939–1945*, Series One Army, Volume V, South West Pacific Area, Australian War Memorial, Canberra, 1959.

McDonald, N. and Brune, P., *Kokoda Front Line*, Allen & Unwin, Sydney, 1994.

McNab, A., *We Were the First: The Unit History of No.1 Independent Company*, Military History Publications, Sydney, 1996.

Mathews, R., *Militia Battalion at War – The History of the 58/59th Australian Infantry Battalion in the Second World War*, 58/59th Battalion Association, Sydney, 1951.

Moynahan, B., *Jungle Soldier: The True Story of Freddy Spencer Chapman*, Quercus, London, 2009.

Murray, M., *Escape a Thousand Miles to Freedom*, Rigby, Adelaide, 1965.

Noonan, W., *The Surprising Battalion: Australian Commandos in China*, Bookstall Co, Sydney, 1945.

O'Leary, S., *To The Green Fields Beyond: The Story of 6th Australian Division Cavalry Commandos*, Sydney: Sixth Division Cavalry, Unit Historical Committee, 1975.

Pirie, A.A., *Commando Double Black: An Historical Narrative of the 2/5th Australian Independent Company, Later the 2/5th Cavalry Commando Squadron, 1942–1945*, Australian Military History Publications, Sydney, 1996.

Pinney, P., *The Barbarians*, University of Queensland Press, St. Lucia, 1988.

—— *The Glass Cannon*, University of Queensland Press, St. Lucia, 1990.

—— *The Devil's Garden*, University of Queensland Press, St. Lucia, 1992.

Powell, A., *The Third Force: ANGAU's New Guinea War*, Oxford University Press, Melbourne, 2003.

Prados, J., *Islands of Destiny: The Solomons Campaign and the Eclipse of the Rising Sun*, New American Library, New York, 2012.

H. Purcell., *The Last English Revolutionary: Tom Wintringham 1898–1949*, Sutton Publishing Ltd, Thrupp, Gloucestershire, 2004.

Robertson, J., and McCarthy, J., *Australian War Strategy 1939–1945*, University of Queensland Press, St. Lucia, 1985.

Reconquest – New Guinea 1943–1944, The Australian Army at War, The Director General of Public Relations, Arbuckle Waddell Pty Ltd, Melbourne, no date.

Rems, A., *South Pacific Cauldron: World War II's Great Forgotten Battlegrounds*, Naval Institute Press, Annapolis, Maryland, 2014.

Robins, D., *Proud To the Third: Personal Recollections, Photographs and a Biographical Roll of the 2/3rd Australian Independent Company/Commando Squadron in World War Two*, self published, 2007.

Rottman, G., *Carlson's Marine Raiders Makin Island Raid 1942*, Osprey, Oxford, 2014.

Russell, B., *The History of the Second Fourteenth Battalion*, Angus and Robertson, Sydney 1949.

Russell, W.B., *There Goes a Man: The Biography of Sir Stanley Savige*, Longmans, Melbourne, 1959.

Ryan, P., *Fear Drive My Feet*, Angus and Robertson, Sydney, 1959.

Savige, S., *Tactical and Administrative doctrine for jungle warfare applicable to all formations under command 2 Aust. Corps (2AIF)*, HQ 2 Aust. Corps (2AIF) (New Guinea): N.G. Press Unit, 1945.

Schultz, D., *Evans Carlson, Marine Raider: The Man Who Commanded America's First Special Forces*, Westholme, Yardley Pennsylvania, 2014.

Share, P. (ed.), *Mud and Blood: "Albury's Own" Second Twenty Third Australian Infantry Battalion Ninth Australian Division*, Heritage Books Publications, Frankston, 1991.

Slim, W., *Defeat into Victory*, Reprint Society, London, 1957.

Smailes, J., *The Independents*, Kewdale Printing Co., Perth, 1994.

Special Forces in the Desert War, Public Records Office, Kew, 2001.

Spencer-Chapman, F., *The Jungle is Neutral*, Chatto and Windus, London, 1949.

Stanley, P., *Tarakan: an Australian Tragedy*, Allen and Unwin, St Leonards, 1997.

Sublet, F., *Whatever Man Dares: The Second World War Memoirs of Lieutenant Colonel Frank Sublet DSO MC*, Kokoda Press, 2013.

—— *Kokoda to the Sea – A History of the 1942 Campaign in Papua*, Slouch Hat Publications, McCrae, 2000.

Tanaka, K., *Operations of the Imperial Japanese Armed Forces in the Papua New Guinea Theatre During World War II*, Japan Papua New Guinea Goodwill Society, Tokyo, 1980.

Threlfall, A., *Jungle Warriors*, Allen and Unwin, Crow's Nest, 2014.

Thompson, J., *War Behind Enemy Lines*, Imperial War Museum, Sidgwick & Jackson, London, 1998.
Thorne, C., *Allies of a Kind: The United States, Britain and the War against Japan, 1941–1945*, Hamish Hamilton, London, 1978.
Treichel, H.F., *Commando Army Service 1941–1946*, Privately published, Wahpunga, 1994.
Trigellis-Smith, S., *The Purple Devils: A History of the 2/6 Australian Commando Squadron, Formerly the 2/6 Australian Independent Company, 1942–1946*, published by 2/6 Commando Squadron, Melbourne,1992.
Ulbrich, D. J., *Preparing for Victory: Thomas Holcomb and the Making of the Modern Marine Corps 1936–1943*, Naval Institute Press, Annapolis, Maryland, 2011.
Updegraph, C.L., *U.S. Marine Corps Special Units of World War II*, History and Museums Division Headquarters U.S. Marine Corps, Washington, D.C. 1972/1977.
Uren, M., *A Thousand Men at War: A History of the 2/16th Australian Infantry Battalion 2AIF*, Australian Military History Publications, Sydney, 2009.
Walker, A., *Middle East and Far East, Australia in the War of 1939–1945*, Series Five Medical, Volume II, Australian War Memorial, Canberra, 1953.
—— *The Island Campaigns, Australia in the War of 1939–1945*, Series Five Medical, Volume III, Australian War Memorial, Canberra, 1957.
Walker, F., *Commandos: Heroic and Deadly ANZAC raids in World War II*, Hachette, Sydney, 2015.
Walker, R. and Walker, H., *Curtin's Cowboys: Australia's Secret Bush Commandos*, Allen and Unwin, Sydney, 1986.
Warby, J., *The 25 Pounders' Campaigns in Syria, Kumusi River, Salamaua, Lae, Finschafen and Balikpapan*, 2/6 Field Regiment Association, Pymble, 1995.
Wartime Translations of Seized Japanese Documents – Allied Translator and Interpreter Section reports 1942–1946, Bibliography, Congressional Information Service Inc, Bethesda, Maryland, 1988.
Wartime Translations of Seized Japanese Documents – Allied Translator and Interpreter Section reports 1942–1946, Indexes, Congressional Information Service Inc, Bethesda, Maryland, 1988.
Wigmore, L., *The Japanese Thrust, Australia in the War of 1939–1945*, Series One Army, Volume IV, Australian War Memorial, Canberra, 1957.
Wigzell, F.A., *New Zealand Army Involvement, Special Operations Australia – South West Pacific World War II,* The Pentland Press, Edinburgh, 2001.
Wiles, T., *Forgotten Raiders of 42: The Fate of the Marines Left Behind on Makin*, Potomac Books Inc., Washington, D.C., 2007.
Wintringham, T., *New Ways of War*, Penguin Books, London, 1940.
Wray, C.H., *Timor 1942: Australian Commandos at War with the Japanese*, Hutchison Australia, Hawthorn, 1987.
Wukovits, J., *American Commando Evans Carlson, His WWII Marine Raiders, and America's First Special Forces Mission*, New American Library, London, 2009.
Wynter, H.W., *The History of the Long Range Desert Group June 1940 to March 1943*, Public Records Office, Kew, Surrey, 2001.
Zedric, L., *Silent Warriors of World War II – The Alamo Scouts Behind Enemy Lines*, Pathfinder Publishing of California, Ventura, 1995.

Journals and Papers

Andrews, E.M., 'Mission 204 Australian Commandos in China, 1942', *Journal of the Australian War Memorial*, No.10 (1987), pp.11–19.
Bradley, P., 'The "Jap Track": The Japanese Route to Wau', January 1943, *Sabretache* Vol XLIX No.2 – June 2008, pp.25–29.
Cavalry News, Official organ of 6th Div. Cav. Commando. Regt. Association. [NSW].
CDO NEW BRITAIN, Vol 1:1, 11 July '45.
Despatch, Monthly Journal of the New South Wales Military Historical Society, Vol. XII No.12, June 1977.
Digest of Digests, September 1943.
Dobbie, E.V.K., 'The Word Commando', *American Speech*, Volume XIX, April, 1944, Number 2, pp.81–90.
Edmonds-Wilson, J., 'No. 1 Independent Company A.I.F at Kavieng', *Australian Army Journal*, No. 197, October 1965, pp. 33–1.
Garland, R., 'Ambush Knoll: A Classic Defence', *Australian Army Journal*, No.195, August, 1965, pp.5–16.
James, K., 'Double Diamonds', *Wartime*, Issue 76, Spring 2016, pp.58–60.
—— 'Uncle Stan and the Staff Corps', *Sabretache*, Vol XLV No.2, June 2004, pp.5–9.
Mann, C., 'Combined Operations, the Commandos and Norway 1941–1944', *Journal of Military History*, April 2009, pp.471–495.
Marine Corps Times, February 28, 2011.
Parkin. R., 'The Sources of the Australian tradition in irregular warfare, 1942–1974', *Small Wars & Insurgencies*, 20:1, Canberra Directing Staff, 08 April 2009, pp.118–40.
Richmond, K., 'Some Logistical Challenges for the Japanese in the New Guinea Campaign', *Sabretache*, Vol XLVI No.2, June 2005, pp. 31–42.
Rogerson, E., 'The "Fuzzy Wuzzy Angels": looking beyond the myth', Australian War Memorial, SVSS paper, 2012.
The 2/4-THER, published by the 2/4th Australian Commando Association.
Thomas, D., 'The Importance of Commando Operations in Modern Warfare 1939–1882', *Journal of Contemporary History*, Vol. 18, No.4, October 1983, pp. 689–717.
'Salamaua Siege', *The Australian Army at War*, Brochure Number Four, Alfred Henry Pettifer Acting Government Printer, 1944.
Walker, E., 'History of No.7 Infantry Training Centre and the formation of the Independent Companies 1941–1942', *Despatch*, Vol. XII No.12, June 1977, p.334–39.
Williams, Peter D., and Nakagawa, N., 'The Japanese 18th Army in New Guinea', *Wartime*, Australian War Memorial, Canberra, October 2006, pp.58–63.

Theses

Bentley, J., 'Champion of ANZAC: General Sir Brudenell White, the First Australian Imperial Force and the emergence of the Australian Military Culture 1914–1918', PhD thesis, School of History and Politics, University of Wollongong, 2003.
Glover, C.L., 'Storm in a Teacup – An analysis of four Australian Behind the Lines Guerrilla Operations Against the Japanese during World War II', B.A. (Honours) thesis,

Department of History University College The University of New South Wales Australian Defence Force Academy, 1994.

Howard, J.T., 'Raiding the Continent – The Origins of the British Special Service Forces', M.A. thesis, Faculty of the U.S. Army Command and General Staff College, Fort Leavenworth, Kansas 1980.

Mallet, R. A., 'Australian Army Logistics 1943–1945', PhD thesis, School of Humanities and Social Science, University of New South Wales, Australian Defence Force Academy, 2007.

Moreman, J.C., 'A Triumph Of Improvisation – Australian Army Operational Logistics and the Campaign in Papua, July 1942 to January 1943', PhD thesis, School of History, University of New South Wales, Australian Defence Force Academy, 2000.

Nixon, J.C. 'Combined Special Operations in World War II', M.A. thesis, Faculty of the U.S. Army Command and Staff College, Fort Leavenworth, Kansas, 1993.

Stevenson, R.C., 'The Anatomy of a Division: The 1st Australian Division in the Great War, 1914–1919', PhD thesis, School of Humanities and Social Sciences, University of New South Wales, 2010.

Threlfall, A., 'The Development of Australian Army Jungle Warfare Doctrine and Training, 1941–1945', PhD thesis, School of Social Sciences, Faculty of Arts, Education and Human Development, Victoria University, June 2008

Unpublished Manuscripts

George MacAfie 'Max' Luff Diary: service with 7 Section 2/10 Commando Squadron, 2/6 Cavalry Commando Regiment, 6 Australian Division 1 February – 5 October 1945.

AWM063813, Yoshihara, T., translated Heath, D., *Southern Cross: account of the Eastern new Guinea Campaign*, loose leaf manuscript.

Hocstrasser, L., *They Were the First – The Story of the Alamo Scouts*, MacArthur Memorial Record Group 15, Box 90.

Interviews

Bishop, Mal, 2/5 Independent Company, interviewed by Dr. Peter. D. Williams, 26 June 2004.

Dexter, David., interviewed by Mel Pratt for the Mel Pratt collection, 1976, <http://nla.gov.au/nla.oh-vn719109>, consulted 10 August 2015.

Murray-Smith, Stephen, interviewed by Hazel de Berg in the Hazel de Berg collection, 1961, <http://nla.gov.au/nla.oh-vn237365>, accessed 9 August 2015, 23 July 2016.

Major Masao Horie, staff officer of 51st Division and later staff officer, 18th Army Headquarters, 1943–45. Interviewed by Dr. Peter. D. Williams and Naoko Nakagawa, March 2006.

Major Takahisa Okamoto, staff officer in 41st Division, 1943–45. Interviewed by Dr. Peter. D. Williams and Naoko Nakagawa, March 2006.

Lt. Colonel Masuo Shinoda, battalion commander, 66th Infantry Regiment, 41st Division, from 1943 to 1945. Interviewed by Dr. Peter. D. Williams and Naoko Nakagawa, March 2006.

Captain Kokichi Nakamura. Platoon then company commander, 66th Infantry Regiment, 41st Division. 1943–1945. Interviewed by Dr. Peter. D. Williams and Naoko Nakagawa, March 2006.

AWMSO4158 – John Lewin, officer 2/3rd Independent Company. Interviewed by Neil Macdonald, no date.

AWMS04164 – Ron Garland, officer 2/3 Independent Company. Interviewed by Neil Macdonald, no date.

AWMS04156 – John Winterflood, officer 2/3rd Independent Company. Interviewed by Neil Macdonald, no date.

AWMSO4160 – Neil Macdonald interview with 2/3rd Commando Squadron member, no name, no date.

AWMSO4161 – Neil MacDonald interview with 2/5th Independent Company member, no name, no date.

IWM 9942 Michael 'Mad Mike' Calvert reels 3–5, consulted 8 September 2016.

Conferences

Australian Army Amphibious Operations in the South West Pacific 1942–1945, Australian Army History Conference 15th November 1994, Army Doctrine Centre, 1995.

Newspapers

Australian
Adelaide News
Bowen Independent
Cairns Post
Kalgoorlie Miner
Lithgow Mercury
Maryborough Chronicle, Wide Bay and Burnett Advertiser
Mercury
National Advocate
Newcastle Morning Herald and Miners' Advocate
Sunday Mail
Warwick Daily News
Tweed Daily
The Advertiser
The Age
The Argus
The Armidale Express and New England General Advertiser
The Australasian
The Courier Mail
The Daily News
The Macleay Chronicle
The Newcastle Sun

The Sun
The Sydney Morning Herald
The Weekly Times
The West Australian

United States
New York Times

Websites

1st Independent Company <https://www.awm.gov.au/unit/U56146/>, accessed 14 March 2016.
2/2 Commando Association of Australia 'Trainer and long term friend of the Double Reds' <https://doublereds.org.au/forums/topic/85-brigadier-michael-calvert-1913%E2%80%931998-%E2%80%93-trainer-and-long-term-friend-of-the-doublereds/>, accessed 10 July 2017.
2/2 Commando Courier Vol.20. No. 188. November 1965, p.12, <https://doublereds.org.au/couriers/1965-11%20-%20Courier%20November%201965.pdf>, accessed 12 October 2016.
2/2 Commando Courier, Vol.6 No.68, December 1952, p.5. <https://doublereds.org.au/couriers/1952-12%20-%20Courier%20December%201952.pdf>, accessed 16 August 2016.
Australian Dictionary of Biography <http://adb.anu.edu.au/biography/pinney-peter-patrick-18951>, accessed 18 May 2017.
Australian War Memorial image 027400 <https://www.awm.gov.au/collection/027400/>, accessed 14 June 2016.
C 47 Aircraft, <https://www.britannica.com/technology/C-47>, accessed 9 March 2018.
Dexter, David. and Pratt, Mel. *David Dexter interviewed by Mel Pratt for the Mel Pratt collection [sound recording]* 1976 <http://nla.gov.au/nla.obj-221579220>, accessed 26 November 2015
Gung Ho! (1943 film), https://en.wikipedia.org/wiki/Gung_Ho!(1943_film)#Plot, accessed 1 August 2017.
L.H.Q. TRAINING CENTRE (JUNGLE WARFARE) CANUNGRA, QLD DURING WW2<http://www.ozatwar.com/locations/canungracamp.htm>, accessed 13 January 2017.
Special Operations Australia <http://www.specialoperationsaustralia.com/>, accessed 14 July 2016.
'Remembering Australia' Wars: Hangings of Papua New Guineans by Australian Soldiers in WWII Complicate our National Narratives', <http://aph.org.au/remembering-asutralia%e2%80%99s-wars-hangings-of-papua-new-guineans-by-australian-soldiers-in-wwii-complicate-our-national-narratives>, accessed 12 August 2016.
Scott, William John (1888–1956) Australian Dictionary of Biography <http://adb.anu.edu.au/biography/scott-william-john-8373>, accessed 12 October 2016.
The history of SS. Rimutaka: <https://en.wikipedia.org/wiki/SS_Mongolia_(1922)#Rimutaka.2C_1938.E2.80.9350>, accessed 3 March 2017.

Index

Index of People

Alexander, Lieutenant General Harold 65, 274, 283-284, 288
Allen, Major General Arthur xi, 47, 50, 86, 113, 133, 153, 180, 202, 208

Blamey, Lieutenant General Sir Thomas 23, 44, 75, 86-88, 93, 102, 125, 177, 181, 188, 196, 198, 202, 204, 251-252, 264
Bottrell, Chapain Arthur xi, 23, 87, 96, 129, 174, 179, 192, 196, 200-201, 216-217, 220, 238-239, 243, 245
Boxall, Jack 31, 34, 180, 197
Bridgeford, Brigadier William 18, 227-228

Callinan, Captain Bernard 67-68, 70-72, 74, 76-78, 81, 83, 299
Calvert, Captain Michael xiii, 20-21, 23, 25-27, 33, 40-41, 285
Carlson, Lieutenant Colonel Evans xiv, 272, 275-277, 279, 282-283, 285-286
Chapman, Captain Freddy Spencer 19-21, 25-27, 33, 38-40, 278
Cole, Captain Robert 242-243, 246
Coyne, Ralph 34-35, 41, 44

Dawson, B 89, 97, 99, 109, 150, 196
Dexter, Captain David ix-x, xii, xiv-xv, 26, 32-33, 39-40, 45, 63-64, 136, 139, 155, 159-160, 163, 165-167, 170, 172, 176-178, 182-183, 238
Dill, Field Marshal Sir John Dill xiii, 17-18, 284
Dunshea, Lieutenant Claude 166, 225-227, 229-231, 236, 247

Edmunds-Wilson, Major James 49-51, 53-56
Edson, Lieutenant Colonel Merrit 274, 276-277, 279, 281, 283, 288

Fleay Major Norman 87, 90, 96, 103-104, 109, 195-202, 264, 266-267
Fraser, Geoffrey 32-34, 36, 42-43

Garland, Lieutenant Ron vii, xiv, 59-60, 131, 133-135, 139-147, 149-150, 178, 186, 189, 192-193, 200, 237, 264, 266
Goode, Captain Allen 50, 208, 211

Hancock, Robert 41, 131, 153, 198
Harcourt, Major Harry vi, 116-122, 124-125, 202
Harding, Major General Edwin 115, 119-120, 124
Hargreaves, Andrew 32, 270-271, 283, 291
Hassett, Lieutenant Colonel Francis 231, 236, 244-248
Herring, Lieutenant General Edmund 125, 136, 139, 169-170, 179

Keating, Gavin 239-240, 296, 301
Kerr, Lieutenant John 100, 195-196, 266
King, Captain Gordon xiii, 18, 171, 247, 297, 301
Kneen, Captain Paul 56-57, 95-96

Laycock, Robert 32, 274, 277-278, 284, 290-291
Lewin, Lieutenant John vii, xiv, 58-60, 129-130, 133-135, 142-143, 147, 149-150, 153-154
Luff, Max 210, 213-215, 221, 241

MacAdie, Lieutenant Colonel Thomas 166-167, 183-184
MacArthur, General Douglas 75, 86-88, 93, 102, 115, 175, 193, 251-253, 264-265
Mawhood, Lieutenant Colonel John 19-24, 26-28, 44-45
McAdam, James 86, 90, 97
McCarthy, Major Dudley xii, 22, 52, 87-89, 92, 95-97, 99-103, 105-107, 112, 116, 122, 124, 136, 204
McNider, US Brigadier General Hanford vi, 115-116, 118, 120-121, 124
Morris, Major General Basil 28, 87, 100-102, 196-197
Morsehead, Brigadier Leslie 18, 253, 265

Moten, Brigadier Murray 130-136, 141, 156, 159, 207, 210

Northcott, Major General John 18, 24, 48

Parer, Damien 81, 153-154
Pinney, Peter vii, xiii, 139, 153, 176, 178, 198, 225-227, 229-231, 233, 237-238, 241, 245-246, 250, 281
Pirie, Andy 31-32, 34-35, 40, 42-43, 91, 93, 95, 98-101, 103-104, 106, 179-180, 188, 193-194, 196-197, 202, 225, 265, 267
Powell, Bill 103, 112, 192, 197

Roosevelt, President Franklin D. xiv, 274, 279
Rowell, Lieutenant General Sydney 48, 105-106, 109

Savige, General Stanley 119, 131, 136-140, 142, 149, 152, 154-155, 179, 185, 214, 224-225, 232, 234, 236, 238, 244, 249-250
Scott, Major William John 24-25, 282
Sheehan, Michael 41, 87-88, 90-93, 100-101
Smith, Ross 69, 111, 114, 116, 171-172, 187-193, 199, 201, 267

Spence, Major Alan 64, 71, 81
Stephens, Lieutenant Keith 35, 235, 239, 245
Stuart, Pilot Officer Robert 25, 34, 233, 247-248
Sturdee, Major General Vernon 21, 24, 48

Tanaka Sergeant 92, 154, 156, 244
Thompson, Alan 33, 43, 117, 237, 278

Vasey, Major General George 86-88, 105-106, 155, 164-165, 170, 173, 179, 183, 201

Walker, Major 'Mac' 20, 28-29, 39, 79, 97, 99-100, 132, 217
Walpole, Private Brian 132-134, 138, 140, 153, 185
Warfe, Major George vii, 129-131, 133-136, 138-140v, 143-144, 148, 153-154, 156-157, 201, 225
Watson, Captain Ray 229, 243-245
Winning, Captain Norman Winning vii, 90-92, 103-104, 195, 198-199, 225-231, 233-236, 239, 243, 245-248, 250
Winterflood, Lieutenant John xiv, 33, 41, 59-60, 129-130, 134, 145-146, 148

Index of Places

Aitape v, viii, 191, 204-205, 208, 214, 219, 222-223, 227-228, 232-233, 235, 237, 242-243, 248
Ambush Knoll 143-145, 147-149, 152, 156, 237
Atherton Tableland 175, 178, 188, 192, 195, 200, 202-203, 225, 251, 291

Balikpapan viii, 252-253, 257, 263-264, 268-269, 303
Bena Bena plateau vii, 128, 136, 159-160, 165, 167, 169, 171, 174, 286
Bobdubi Ridge 134, 136, 139-142, 156
Bogadjim viii, 161, 163-164, 166, 226
Borneo v, viii, 132, 248, 251-253, 263, 268
Bougainville v, vii-viii, 55, 60, 174, 183, 204, 224-228, 232-238, 240-244, 246-250, 282-283, 292, 294
Brisbane 32, 35, 55, 60, 194
Buka 48, 50, 55
Bulolo Valley 86, 88, 103-104, 107, 159
Buna v-vi, viii, xiv, 89, 93, 98, 103, 109-110, 115-119, 121-126, 128, 157, 169, 293, 299-300
Burma 27, 105, 270

Canberra x, xii-xiii, 18, 22, 97, 212, 240, 247
Canungra 45, 139, 158, 185, 187, 307
China 26, 52, 67, 275, 279

Darwin 58, 63, 224
Dili 63-70, 74-80, 82, 163, 194
Dutch Timor 64, 67, 72, 78-79, 83

East Indies 52, 68-69, 83, 251-253
Eastern New Guinea 93, 128, 297, 305

Finschafen 158, 169, 303
France 50, 55-60, 129, 131, 280
Germany 17, 49, 134, 169, 271-272, 280, 291
Gona 98, 103, 110, 118, 125, 299
Guadalcanal 60, 93, 247, 281-283, 288-289

Heath's Plantation 85-86, 89-90, 93, 96-98, 106
Huon Peninsula 85, 87, 158

Japan xv, 37, 47-48, 50-51, 57, 60, 69, 77, 91, 127, 143, 154, 166, 210, 212, 221, 251-253, 268-269, 302-303
Jikkoku Pass 220, 222, 279

Kaiapit v, viii, 128, 158, 169-174, 179, 281, 287, 289
Kavieng viii, 48, 50-56, 61, 93
Kokoda v, viii, xii, 22, 76, 87-89, 92, 95-103, 105, 107-116, 118, 122, 124, 126, 136, 153-154, 157, 173, 198, 286-287, 293

Kokoda Track viii, 98, 101-102, 107, 110-115, 118, 126, 157, 286-287, 293
Komiatum Track vi, 139-141

Labaun Island 253, 263, 292
Lae 85-90, 92-93, 95-98, 103-108, 110, 127-129, 142, 158-159, 163, 165, 167-168, 174, 197-198, 224-225
Lofoten Islands 280, 287-289
Lorengau 48, 50, 52

Makin Island 275, 279, 282-283, 286-287, 300, 302-303
Malaya 22, 29, 107
Mandi Creek 216-217, 219
Manus 48, 50, 55
Markham 85, 88-89, 96, 103, 105, 127, 138, 141, 168-169, 178, 182
Melbourne ii, xii-xiii, 23, 32, 35, 48-49, 69, 81, 84, 103-104, 127, 131, 138, 299-303
Middle East xi, 29, 47, 51, 81, 129, 131, 138, 200, 225, 291, 296, 303
Milne Bay 53, 55, 85, 87, 93, 107, 115, 129, 240, 299
Mount Hagen 159, 163, 165-166
Mubo 90, 93, 97, 103-106, 129, 134, 136, 138-144, 149, 153, 156, 169, 198

Nadzab 85, 97, 104, 167-169, 171
Netherlands East Indies 52, 69, 251-253
New Britain 20, 48, 90, 127, 183, 204, 224-225, 252
New Caledonia v-vi, viii, 47, 56-62, 69, 91-92, 95, 126, 129, 140, 288, 291
New Guinea x-xii, 22, 45, 48, 85-89, 93-94, 96-109, 111, 115, 119, 121, 124-130, 132-133, 136-137, 139, 141, 152-157, 159-161, 163, 165-170, 172, 176-179, 182-183, 185, 188, 191, 193, 196-197, 202, 204-205, 216, 224, 226, 242, 271, 292, 294, 297-300, 302, 304-305
New Hebrides viii, 48-51, 61
New Ireland v, viii, 47-48, 51, 53-55, 61, 86
New South Wales xiii, 18, 20, 23, 33, 147, 304-305
New Zealand 20-21, 24, 27-28, 56,
North Africa 29, 47, 51, 80, 290
Northern Territory 22, 48, 58, 62, 66, 81-83, 112, 195, 209, 224, 291
Norway 17, 41, 273, 280, 304

Pacific Region xii, 20, 22-23, 36, 54-55, 75, 83-84, 86-89, 93, 98, 103, 106-107, 115-116, 119, 124, 127, 138, 140-142, 163, 167, 174, 181, 209, 237, 247, 251-253, 264, 270-271, 297-303, 306
Pearl Harbor 29, 271, 282
Philippines 29, 86, 175, 204, 251
Port Moresby 54, 86-87, 98, 100-101, 106-111, 115, 117, 126, 128, 132, 160, 170, 271
Portugal 63-67, 71-72, 74, 77-79, 82-84
Portuguese East Timor 63, 83

Queensland xiii, 45, 52, 113, 139, 153, 158, 175, 177, 204, 224, 251, 297-298, 301-302

Rabaul 48, 51-52, 85, 127, 142, 252-253
Ramu River ix, 127, 160, 162, 164-166, 168-169, 238
Ramu Valley 163, 165-166, 168-169, 178, 182, 226, 281

Salamaua vi-viii, xii, 85-92, 94-95, 97-99, 101-108, 127-129, 134, 136-142, 144, 151, 153-159, 165, 176, 179, 195-200, 210, 222, 225-226, 237, 281, 287, 289, 293
Singapore 27, 48, 98
Solomon Islands 48, 55, 60, 127, 204, 226, 252, 287
South East Asia 251, 270-271
South Pacific Region 20, 54, 302
South West Pacific Region 22, 55, 75, 83-84, 86-87, 98, 103, 124, 127, 138, 140-142, 174, 237, 251-252, 270-271

Tarakan vii-viii, 29, 32-34, 37, 40, 44, 80-81, 158, 180, 253-263, 278, 291, 296, 301-302
Tarakan Hill vii, 254-255, 257-259, 263, 291
Timbered Knoll vii, 149-150, 152
Timor v-vi, viii, 22, 61-64, 66-67, 70-73, 75-79, 81-84, 98, 107, 128, 157-158, 176, 194, 224, 287, 293, 298-299, 303
Torokina 35, 227, 240, 244, 282
Tulagai 48, 50, 55

Victoria 23, 32, 35, 48-49, 266, 299, 305
Vila viii, 48, 50-51, 55-56, 61, 67-68

Wau viii, xii, 22, 76, 85-90, 92, 95-107, 109, 112, 116, 122, 124, 126-132, 134, 136-137, 142, 153-154, 156-160, 163, 165, 169, 179, 195-198, 200, 210, 225-226, 281, 286-287, 298-299, 301, 304
Wewak v, viii, 204-205, 208, 215-217, 219-220, 222-223, 227, 232-233, 235, 237-238, 242-243, 248
Wilson's Promontory vi, 23, 28, 33, 37, 39, 41, 185, 187, 224

Index of Military Formations & Units

Australian Army
2/2nd Commando Squadron 164, 183, 190, 194, 252-253
2/3rd Commando Squadron 178, 186, 192-194, 200-201, 226, 266
2/4th Commando Squadron vii, 186, 254-255, 259, 262-263, 291
2/5th Commando Squadron 180, 186, 193, 195, 197-198, 264-267
2/6th Commando Squadron 155, 168, 188, 190-191, 195, 264, 267-268
2/8th Commando squadron vii, xiii, 174, 183, 195, 224-229, 231, 233-237, 239-241, 243-244, 246-248, 281, 285, 291
2/9th Commando squadron 183, 185-188, 191, 201, 203, 205-207, 209, 211, 214-216, 219, 221, 242, 257, 262-263
2/10th Commando Squadron 188, 191-192, 206, 208-209, 211-212, 214-216, 218-219, 221, 243
2/11th Commando Squadron 186, 203, 263, 292
2/12th Commando Squadron 186, 189, 203, 263, 292

2/1st Independent Company 28, 44, 48-56, 60-62, 64, 86-87, 291
2/2nd Independent Company 28, 32, 34, 48, 58, 61-66, 69-70, 75, 81-82, 98, 128, 157, 159-160, 163-164, 176-177, 183, 190, 194, 209, 252-253, 281
2/3rd Independent Company 28, 33, 35, 41, 56, 58-62, 126, 128-131, 133-138, 140-142, 144, 148-149, 151-158, 174, 178, 185-186, 192-194, 197-201, 209, 211, 214, 225-226, 258, 264, 266, 281, 287-289, 291
2/4th Independent Company 28-29, 33, 57, 79, 81-83, 98, 157-158, 179, 186, 254-255, 259, 262-263, 291
2/5th Independent Company 31, 34, 86-90, 92-98, 101, 103-105, 108-109, 126, 128-129, 132-133, 136, 157, 179-180, 186, 193, 195-199, 201, 209, 225, 264-267, 281
2/6th Independent Company 45, 108-118, 120, 122-126, 128-129, 148, 155, 157, 168-170, 173-174, 179, 183, 187-188, 190-192, 195-196, 199, 201-202, 205-210, 215, 220-222, 225, 233, 242-243, 264, 267-268, 279, 281, 286-287, 289
2/7th Independent Company viii, 45, 104, 112, 128-129, 132-133, 136, 154, 157, 159-160, 162-163, 183-185, 189-191, 195-197, 199-202, 205, 207, 209, 211, 213-216, 218, 221, 226, 238, 242, 264, 281
2/8th Independent Company 34, 112, 224, 238

2/7th Battalion 133, 154, 157, 159-160
24th Battalion 138-139, 142, 157
58/59th Battalion 138, 142, 156-157
New Guinea Volunteer Rifles (NGVR) 85-90, 92, 94-98, 100, 106, 110, 197
Papuan Infantry Battalion (PIB) 170, 234, 246-247

6th Cavalry Commando Regiment 187, 191-192, 196, 206-210, 215, 220-221, 233, 242-243, 279, 281
2/6 Cavalry Commando Regiment 180, 188, 191-192, 205-206, 213, 217-218, 242-243
2/7th Cavalry Commando Regiment 183-184, 189-191, 195-197, 199-202, 264
2/9th Cavalry Commando Regiment 186, 188, 191, 201, 262-263

Bena Force v, vii-viii, 110, 136, 158-169, 174, 179, 183, 194, 281, 287, 289, 293
Cole Force 242-243, 246
Kanga Force v, 85-90, 96-109, 111, 113, 132, 136, 160, 169, 196-197
Raffles Force 231-237, 246-247
Sparrow Force 62-64, 70-72, 77-81

15 Brigade 138, 152, 156
17 Brigade 104, 115, 128-132, 134-135, 138, 141, 144, 148-149, 207, 210, 222
19 Brigade 205, 208-209, 215-217
25 Brigade 112, 267-268

3rd Division viii, 128, 136, 138, 140-141, 144, 149, 151, 154-155, 160, 183, 227-228, 230-231, 233-236, 240, 244, 249, 287
6th Division 196, 205-209, 214, 218, 220, 222-223, 228, 233
7th Division viii, 110, 112-114, 125-126, 128, 164, 167-170, 173-174, 183, 186, 196, 263-264, 268, 286-287
9th Division 158, 247, 262-263
32nd Division 115, 119, 121, 124-125

American Army
United States Marine Corps xiv, 270-271, 274-275, 277-279, 282, 285-286, 290-292
United States Marine Raider Battalions 270-271, 274, 279, 282-283, 286, 288, 290

Index of General & Miscellaneous Terms

104 Military Mission xiii, 19-22, 24-27, 57
25pdr Field Gun 51, 263, 265

Air Forces xi, 28-29, 33, 51, 57, 86, 93, 115, 155, 174, 211, 254, 273
Aitape-Wewak campaign v, 204-205, 222-223, 243, 248
Army Intelligence Bureau AIB 103, 227, 247-248
Australian Army i-ii, x-xiii, xv, 17-19, 21-24, 27, 29-30, 44-45, 59, 67, 69, 71, 86-87, 101, 107, 109, 115, 117, 130, 140, 167, 174-178, 180, 183, 202, 205, 217, 222, 224, 226, 235, 250-252, 254, 257, 270-271, 273, 275, 285, 287-288, 290, 292-295
Australian Imperial Force AIF 18, 29, 31, 33, 35-37, 42, 49-51, 60, 62, 107, 115, 128-130, 137-138, 174, 176
Australian Independent Companies i, iii, xii-xiii, 17, 28, 30, 32, 88, 178, 270, 275-276, 279, 283, 288, 293, 295
Australian New Guinea Administrative Unit (ANGAU) 103, 159, 164, 166, 169, 205-206, 221, 227, 229, 234, 242-243, 245-248

Bren Machin Gun x, 43, 65, 117, 145-146, 186-187, 190, 238, 267, 278
British Army 17, 178, 276, 284
Bully Beef 64, 99, 116, 167, 239

Combined Operations Organization COO 272-273, 278, 284

Distinguished Service Order DSO 25, 131, 173, 196, 198-199, 202

Fieldworks 42, 118, 254
First World War 18-19, 24-25, 136, 202, 226, 305
Forward Observers and Observation Posts 86, 154, 166, 218

Gelignite 40-41, 68, 186
Guerrilla Warfare 26, 28, 32, 36-38, 40, 42-45, 56, 60, 73-77, 80, 82-84, 88, 176, 250, 275, 301
Guerrilla Warfare School 40, 42-43, 45

Independent Company Training Centre 23-25, 29, 45

Jungle Cavalry iii, v, xi, 127, 137, 142, 152, 154, 156-157, 168

Jungle Warfare Centre 45, 185

Malaria 54, 64, 81, 88, 99, 132, 192
Marine Raiders xiv, 275, 277-278, 281-282, 285, 287-289, 291-292
Military Cross 202, 226, 247
Military Intelligence xiii, 19, 277, 297, 299
Military Intelligence – Research MI(R) xiii-xiv, 19-20, 24
Military Missions xiii, 18-22, 24-27, 57
Militia 25, 29, 33, 37, 51, 58, 132, 138, 186, 240, 301
Morse Code 36, 42, 70
Mountain Gun 113, 146, 148

Navies xi, 29, 51, 57, 93, 177, 252, 254, 273
No.7 Infantry Training Centre vi, 20, 28-29, 37-40, 45, 62, 304

Owen Gun 230, 238, 260

Papuan Campaign 101-102, 105, 109, 113, 115, 119, 126
Porters 66, 68, 211
Prisoners of War 25, 55, 76, 125, 207, 211, 222

Recruitment 31-33, 35-37, 44, 46, 181-182, 274, 276-277
Royal Australian Air Force RAAF 28, 48-49, 159, 191, 207, 248

Salamaua Campaign vi-viii, xii, 137, 151, 153-154, 156-157, 165, 179, 200, 210, 222, 225-226, 281, 287, 289
Snipers 122, 130, 256-257, 266
Special Forces 222, 272, 276, 288, 294-295
Special Operations Executive (SOE) xi, 17, 21-24, 26-27, 44-45, 297, 300-301
Swamps 23, 40, 118, 122, 125, 278

Unconventional Warfare 18, 27, 107, 196, 269, 273, 294-295
United States Armed Forces 59-60, 116, 118, 125-126, 175, 227, 247, 251-252

Vickers Machinegun 79, 139-140, 142-144, 146, 148-149, 255, 280

War Office 21, 24, 276-277